SPACE WARFARE
AND DEFENSE

SPACE WARFARE AND DEFENSE

A Historical Encyclopedia
and Research Guide

BERT CHAPMAN

A B C ⬬ C L I O

Santa Barbara, California   Denver, Colorado   Oxford, England

Cataloging-in-Publication Data is on file with the Library of Congress

12   11   10   09   08   1   2   3   4   5   6   7   8   9   10

This book is also available on the World Wide Web as an ebook. Visit www.abc-clio.com for details.

ABC-CLIO, Inc.
130 Cremona Drive, P.O. Box 1911
Santa Barbara, California 93116–1911

Production Editor: Alisha Martinez
Production Manager: Don Schmidt
Media Manager: Caroline Price
Media Editor: Julie Dunbar
File Management Coordinator: Paula Gerard

This book is printed on acid-free paper. ∞
Manufactured in the United States of America

To Becky, who personifies Proverbs 31:10.

CONTENTS

ACKNOWLEDGEMENTS

Numerous factors are required to make book production successful. Steve Danver, Craig Hunt, Julie Dunbar, Alisha Martinez, and Alex Mikaberidze of ABC-CLIO have been consummate professionals in guiding me through company publishing practices and procedures. I received valuable research assistance from various research individuals in this process including Sharon Kelly of the John F. Kennedy Presidential Library, Barbara Risser of the Pentagon Library, and the presidential Office of Science and Technology Policy.

I am particularly fortunate to work at Purdue University Libraries, which encourages its library faculty to achieve scholarly excellence, and I am grateful to God for the professional and personal opportunities He has given me.

Finally, I am grateful to my wife Becky who encourages me to reach for the heavens while keeping me firmly grounded.

Introduction

The authorities essential to the common defense are these: to raise armies; to build and equip fleets; to prescribe rules for the government of both; to direct their operations; to provide for their support. These powers ought to exist without limitation, *because it is impossible to foresee or define the extent and variety of national exigencies, or the correspondent extent and variety of the means which may be necessary to satisfy them.* The circumstances that endanger the safety of nations are infinite, and for this reason no constitutional shackles can wisely be imposed on the power to which the care of it is committed (Hamilton 1787).

... while some might view that space can be kept a weapons-free sanctuary free of military systems, *history tells us that each time new technological opportunities present themselves, nations invariably employ them to avoid being placed in an inferior defense position.* (Orr 1984).

The key factor in early 21st-century American national security policy has justifiably been the U.S. Government's responses to the September 11, 2001 terrorist attacks. This has been demonstrated by controversial wars in Iraq and Afghanistan; acrimony over the USA Patriot Act; contentious debate over the treatment and legal status of terrorist detainees; disputes over the legal and constitutional propriety of the National Security Agency's wireless surveillance program; and other affiliated topics such as homeland security, the complexities of counterinsurgency warfare, and U.S. relations with Islamic countries. As these words are being written, public attention is riveted on the release of the Iraq Study Group's 2006 report containing possible suggestions for dealing with what has become an increasingly frustrating situation in that country, and which has claimed significant U.S. military casualties and financial resources.

This work urges that increased public attention be focused on the growing importance of space as a U.S. and international security priority and highlights the extensive historical documentation of how this growth evolved. It is likely that most individuals do not realize how important space has become to their personal lives and to domestic and international economics and security. If you use a cell phone, it contains a Global Positioning System (GPS) that uses space assets to track your location. When you make an Internet e-commerce purchase, satellites may be used. Every time you use an ATM at a bank, satellites are involved, and they are also involved when international currency or stock market transactions occur.

Space plays a critical role in telecommunications. When you watch coverage of news or sporting events from other domestic or international locales, satellite technology is being used. GPS systems are used to guide commercial airlines and container ships to their destinations. Police, fire departments, and ambulances also rely on GPS satellites. Tracking the development and evolution of storms such as hurricanes also requires satellites. This technology can be used to monitor the locations of convicted sex offenders, lost children, or relatives with Alzheimer's disease. Computer networks such as the Internet also make extensive use of space-based assets.

The U.S. intelligence community uses satellites to detect troop and ship movements, watch and listen in on the conversations of hostile government national leaders and terrorists, monitor and verify compliance with international arms control agreements, and other tasks. U.S. and other military forces use satellite technology to locate friendly and hostile ships at sea, provide weapons targeting information to friendly forces, give troops information on the physical terrain and environment they are operating in, provide meteorological and other environmental information about areas of operations, detect and track the flight path of incoming ballistic missiles while attempting to destroy these missiles, provide navigational information to friendly forces in unfamiliar environments, and numerous other activities.

All of these factors highlight the crucial need for unimpeded domestic and international access to space resources. Our way of life would be significantly changed if we did not have access to space. We would not be able to use the Internet, a cell phone, or other electronic communication devices. We would live in a world without near real-time access to information from all corners of the globe, such as meteorological information on an incoming storm. Such scenarios could happen if there were attacks on U.S. or other international civilian or military space assets by terrorists, electronic sabotage such as electromagnetic pulse, or attacks against these assets by nations or organizations opposed to market economics and international political pluralism.

Space has been a center of civilian and military activity since it became technologically possible to reach it and work there. A significant body of international political, diplomatic, and legal work has sought to promote an image of space as an idyllic venue of international cooperation and harmony. The United Nations and that organization's Office for Outer Space Affairs (OOSA) have sought to present this image, and some success has been achieved in convincing many sectors of international political opinion of the laudability of this utopian vision.

However, space has also been an arena of historical, contemporary, and future interest to world militaries as a venue for military intelligence and potential operations. The former Soviet Union made extensive efforts to achieve a military presence in space, and its successor, the Russian Federation, still retains significant military space assets. The United States is currently the nation with the largest military presence in space, has produced significant military space doctrinal and operational documentation, and has the greatest dependence on space assets for its national security. China is developing an increasing interest in military space that may prove antithetical to U.S. national security interests. The European Union is also showing greater interest in space's military potential, and countries such as India, Israel, and Japan are also interested in using space as a means of defending their national interests.

Space Warfare and Defense chronicles the historical development and evolution of military space policy of the United States and other countries with particular emphasis on the Soviet Union/Russian Federation, China, and the European Union through early 2007. This work demonstrates that while significant information on this subject is classified, significant amounts of substantive information on military space programs are available in U.S. Government and military documents, the documentation of some foreign governments, in scholarly books and journal articles, and in analyses produced by U.S. and international research institutions or think tanks. Many of these resources are freely available on the Internet.

Specific chapters in this work address U.S. Department of Defense (DOD) resources on this topic; U.S. Government resources produced by other executive branch agencies, Congress, independent agencies, and commissions; individual U.S. military space programs such as Defense Support Program (DSP) satellites; the development of U.S. space weapon and defense systems such as the Airborne Laser and Space-Based Radar; the work of U.S. and foreign research centers; U.S. laws and international agreements on military uses of space; relevant scholarly journals; and searchable databases, scholarly books, documentary collections, and other library research strategies. A chronology and glossary are also provided.

Space warfare and defense is a very interdisciplinary topic covering subjects in the physical and social sciences. Relevant physical science research venues include cutting-edge scientific and technology research in fields such as astronautics, electronics, nanotechnology, physics, radar, reconnaissance, surveillance, and weapons-systems development. Social science fields covered by this topic include accounting, aerospace industry studies, economics, government procurement and contracting, history, military strategy, political science, and U.S. and international law.

My hope is that this work will stimulate serious and substantive research on this topic. It is a subject that deserves sober scrutiny from all individuals interested in U.S. and international security and cannot be dismissed as "Buck Rogers" fantasies or with a superficial epithet such as "Star Wars." Irrespective of personal political belief or opinion, space has become a vitally important arena of military activity. This importance will increase in subsequent years. Having reliable access to space is critical for U.S. domestic and international economic development, growth, and national and international security. It would seem to be a misguided vision to believe that an international government organization such as the United Nations could serve as the sole governing authority for national and international space activities. Surrendering space access to nations or terrorist organizations opposed to market economics and political pluralism would have horrific consequences for the United States and international economics and security and should be avoided at all costs.

References and Further Reading

Hamilton, A. 1787. *Federalist No. 23: The Necessity of a Government as Energetic as the One Proposed to the Preservation of the Union*, 1. [Online article or information; retrieved 12/6/06.] http://thomas.loc.gov/home/histdox/fed_23.html.

Orr, V. 1984. In U.S. Congress, House Committee on Appropriations. Subcommittee on the Department of Defense. *Department of Defense Appropriations for 1984: Part 2*. Washington, D.C.: U.S. Government Printing Office.

CHRONOLOGY OF KEY EVENTS IN SPACE WARFARE AND DEFENSE HISTORY

1903

Russian schoolteacher Konstantin Tsiolkovsky writes *Beyond the Earth,* which describes orbiting space stations where humans will live in space.

1941–1945

The work of Tsiolkovsky, Friedrich Zander, Helmut Grottrup, Wernher von Braun, and others is used to develop German military rockets during World War II and influences later American and Soviet space rocket programs.

1946

May: The Air Force-supported Project Rand, later known as the Rand Corporation, publishes *Preliminary Design of an Experimental World-Circling Spaceship,* which speculated on the engineering feasibility of a space vehicle.

1947

October 14: U.S. test pilot Chuck Yeager breaks the speed barrier flying an Air Force X-1 plane.

1953

October 30: National Security Council completes report 162/2 announcing Eisenhower administration's New Look Policy, which emphasized nuclear air power as a key instrument of national military strategy.

1955

May 20: Eisenhower administration National Security Council issues NSC 5520 document *United States Interest in the Scientific Exploration of Outer Space.*

July 18–23: Eisenhower introduces Open Skies proposal at Geneva Conference of "Big Four" leaders of United States, United Kingdom, France, and the Soviet Union.

Open Skies would allow for unhindered aerial surveillance of other countries' military capabilities. Proposal rejected by the Soviet Union.

July 29: United States announces its intention to launch a satellite as part of the International Geophysical Year (IGY).

July 30: Soviet Union announces its intention to launch a satellite for the IGY.

1957

January 10: Eisenhower proposes mutual international control of space missile and satellite development in his State of the Union address.

August 8: U.S. Army Ballistic Missile Agency (ABMA) launches a Jupiter-C rocket and its nose cone as the first man-made object successfully recovered from space.

August 27: Soviet Union announces it has successfully tested an Intercontinental Ballistic Missile (ICBM).

October 4: Soviet Union launches Sputnik as the first artificial satellite.

November 3: Soviet Union launches Sputnik 2 carrying a dog into space.

November 7: The U.S. Government's Gaither Report recommends rapid expansion of missile programs research and development and a fallout shelter program.

November 14: United Nations adopts Resolution 1148 (XII) in an effort to ensure space is used exclusively for "peaceful and scientific purposes."

December 6: U.S. Vanguard TV-3 rocket launch failure.

1958

January 31: U.S. launches ABMA Explorer 1 for the United States' first orbital satellite. Explorer discovers Van Allen radiation belts.

March 17: United States launches Vanguard 1. Its mission provides the first space measurements of the earth's shape and included a Geiger counter and magnetometer.

July 29: National Aeronautics and Space Act of 1958 enacted creating the National Aeronautics and Space Administration (NASA). Statute specifies that military space activities are to be conducted by the Defense Department.

August 6: Defense Department reorganized and the President's Science Advisory Committee and the position "Special Assistant to the President for Science and Technology" are created.

August 18: National Security Council Document 5814/1 *Preliminary U.S. Policy on Outer Space* finished.

December 18: United States launches Score, the first active communications satellite.

1959

January 2: Soviet Union launches Luna 1, the first spacecraft to escape Earth's gravity and to transmit data to and from space.

February 17: United States launches Vanguard 2, which takes the first space photograph of the earth.

March 14: United States submits first substantive proposal for international space co-operation at the Committee on Space Research (COSPAR) meeting in the Hague.

August 7: United States launches Explorer 6, which broadcasts the first television pictures from space.

September 14: The Soviets Luna 2 aircraft is the first spacecraft to land on the moon.

October 7: Luna 3 takes first photos of moon's far side.

December 12: United Nations Resolution 1472 (XIV), establishes a permanent Committee on the Peaceful Uses of Outer Space (COPUOS).

1960

January 2: Eisenhower approves National Security Council Document 5918 "U.S. Policy on Outer Space."

April 1: United States launches TIROS 1, the first weather satellite.

April 13: United States launches Transit 1B, the first successful navigation satellite.

May 24: United States launches MIDAS 2 (Missile Defense Alarm System) making it the first early-warning missile detection satellite.

August 18: The Central Intelligence Agency (CIA) recovers first satellite photographs of the Soviet Union from the Discoverer 14 satellite.

October 4: United States launches Courier 1B, which becomes the first delayed repeater satellite.

1961

January: Outgoing Eisenhower administration issues NSC 6108 *Certain Aspects of Missile and Space Programs.*

January 10: Report to the president elect of the Ad-Hoc Committee on Space (Wiesner Report) advises incoming Kennedy administration of space's increasing military significance.

February 21: Soviet Union launches Sputnik 5 as the first orbital platform launch.

April 12: Soviet Union launches Vostok 1 with Yuri Gagarin as the first man to reach space.

May 5: United States launches Freedom 7, with Alan Shepard into a suborbital flight.

May 12: Kennedy administration issues National Security Action Memorandum (NSAM) 50 on official announcements on launching nuclear power systems into space.

July 21: United States launches Liberty Bell 7, with Virgil Grissom into a suborbital flight.

September 25: Kennedy addresses United Nations General Assembly advocating international cooperation in space.

December 20: United Nations Resolution 1721 (XVI) applies international law to space exploration and expands COPUOS membership.

1962

February 20: United States launches Friendship 7 with John Glenn orbiting the earth three times.

February 23: NSAM 129 issued covering U.S.–Soviet cooperation in space exploration.

March: Expanded COPUOS meets for the first time.

March 16: Soviet Union launches Cosmos 1 military satellite from Kapustin Yar site.

May 26: NSAM 156 issued covering disarmament, the peaceful uses of outer space, and whether satellite reconnaissance is politically legitimate under international law.

June 7: Soviet Union proposes to COPUOS that reconnaissance satellites be prohibited by international law.

July 9: NSAM 172 issued covering bilateral talks on U.S.–Soviet cooperation in outer space activities.

July 28: Soviet Union launches Cosmos 7 as its second military intelligence satellite.

August 27: NSAM 183 *Space Program of the United States* issued.

August 31: United States enacts Communications Satellite Act (COMSAT) Public Law 87-624.

October 1: NSAM 191 covering Project Defender issued, which documents military ballistic missile defense programs in the Advanced Research Projects Agency.

October 24: NSAM 198 covering Project Kingfish issued regarding the effects high altitude nuclear explosions might have on satellites.

December 14: United Nations Resolution 1892 (XVII) calling for international cooperation and the peaceful use of outer space passed.

1963

May 3: NSAM 237 covering Project Mercury manned spaceflight issued.

June 20: United States and Soviet Union conclude the "hotline" agreement establishing direct telegraphic links between their national leaderships.

August 5: The Limited or Partial Test Ban Treaty banning nuclear weapons tests in the atmosphere, outer space, and underwater signed by the United States, Great Britain, and the Soviet Union.

October 17: United Nations Resolution 1884 (XVIII) seeks to ban nuclear weapons from space.

November 12: NSAM 271 issued covering cooperation with the Soviet Union on outer space issues.

December 13: United Nations Resolutions 1962 and 1963 (XVIII) establish the beginnings of space law.

1964

February 11: Johnson administration issues NSAM 285 concerning cooperation with the Soviet Union on outer space issues.

May 19: White House issues NSAM 300 *Review of Alternative Communications, Navigation, Missile and Space Tracking, and Data Acquisition Facilities.*

July 28: The United States' Ranger 7 takes the first close-up pictures of the moon.

August 20: United States and 18 other nations form the International Telecommunications Satellite Organization (INTELSAT) as a satellite communications consortium. Consists of 68 national members by 1969.

October 12: Soviet Union launches Voshkod 1 featuring three crew members.

1965

March 18: Soviet cosmonaut Alexei Leonov becomes first human to walk in space outside Voshkod 2 spacecraft.

April 6: United States launches Early Bird as the first geosynchronous commercial communications satellite over the Atlantic Ocean.

June 3: United States launches Gemini 4, and astronaut Ed White becomes the first American to walk in space.

December 21: United Nations Resolution 2130 (XVIII) adopted and calls for expanding international space law.

1966

Soviet Union founds Interkosmos to coordinate space collaboration with other communist nations.

February 3: Soviet Luna 9 lands on moon and transmits photos from its surface.

March 4: NSAM 342 issued covering establishing communications satellites for less-developed nations.

March 31: Soviet Union launches Luna 10, which becomes the first satellite to orbit the moon.

July 29: NSAM 354 issued covering U.S. cooperation with the European Launcher Development Organization an organization seeking to develop Western European space launch capabilities.

December 19: United Nations Resolution 2222 (XXI) adopted and includes the first draft space law treaty.

1967

January 25: Soviet Union launches Cosmos 139, which is the first test of its Fractional Orbital Bombardment System (FOBS) to launch ICBMs over the South Pole to avoid the United States' Ballistic Missile Early Warning System (BMEWS).

January 27: United Nations approves Treaty on the Use of Outer Space.

April 25: United States, Soviet Union, Great Britain, and 57 other nations sign the Outer Space Treaty.

June 8: United States uses superpower hotline for the first time informing the Soviet Union of aircraft use near Israel.

July 1: United States launches DODGE, which takes the first complete color picture of Earth.

July 12: National Security Council issues NSAM 338-R *Policy Concerning U.S. Assistance in the Development of Foreign Communications Satellite Capabilities.*

December 19: United Nations Resolution 2345 (XXI) covering the rescue and return of astronauts and space objects is adopted.

1968

March 29: NSAM 369 covering the Sentinel Antiballistic Missile program issued.

April 22: United States and Soviet Union sign Agreement on Rescue and Return of Astronauts and Space Objects.

October 20: Soviet Union tests the first co-orbital antisatellite (ASAT) device.

1969

January 15: Soviet Union launches Soyuz 5 whose three-member crew docks with Soyuz 4 resulting in the first docking between piloted spacecraft and the first crew transfer in space.

July 16: United States launches Apollo 11 and Neil Armstrong sets foot on the moon on July 20.

September 4: National Security Study Memorandum (NSSM) 72 issued covering the International Space Cooperation Committee.

1970

Soviet Union begins developing new Antiballistic Missile defense system around Moscow.

July 10: National Security Decision Memorandum (NSDM) 70 issued on U.S.–Soviet activities concerning international space cooperation.

1971

April 19: Soviet Union launches Salyut 1 as its first space station, which stays active until October 11.

1972

January 5: President Nixon approves development of the space shuttle.

May 22: United States and Soviet Union sign agreement on cooperation and using outer space for peaceful purposes and preparing for Apollo–Soyuz joint mission.

May 26: Nixon and Brezhnev sign ABM Treaty and Strategic Arms Limitation Treaty (SALT).

July 23: United States launches LANDSAT 1, the first earth resources technology satellite to map earth.

August 30: NSDM 172 issued covering U.S. technology and launch assistance in international space cooperation.

1973

May 14: United States launches Skylab 1; three piloted spacecraft dock with this space station.

1974

May 17: United States launches SMS-1, its first geostationary weather satellite.

June 24: Soviet Union launches Salyut 3 military space station; one piloted spacecraft docks with it.

1975

May 31: European Union creates European Space Agency consolidating Western European space initiatives into a single agency.

July 15–21: Apollo-Soyuz test mission; U.S. and Soviet craft dock in space, and U.S. and Soviet astronauts board each other's spacecraft.

September 24: Ford administration issues NSDM 306 on U.S.–Japan space cooperation.

1976

February 19: United States launches Marisat 1, the first commercial maritime communications satellite.

June 22: Soviet Union launches military space station Salyut 5, and two piloted spacecraft dock with it.

July 7: Ford administration issues NSDM 333 dealing with the enhanced survivability of U.S. military and intelligent space systems.

1977

January 18: Ford administration issues NSDM 345 dealing with U.S. ASAT capabilities.

March 23: Carter administration issues Presidential Review Memorandum (PRM) 23 urging the formulation of a "coherent space policy." Results in PD 37 issued May 11, 1978.

May 11: United States and Soviet Union sign agreement on manned space flight cooperation.

May 14: NSC issues PRM 26 calling for ABM Treaty review.

November 22: United States launches Meteosat 1, its first European Space Agency satellite.

1978

Carter initiates U.S.–Soviet talks to ban space weapons, which fail in 1979.

May 11: Presidential Directive (PD) 37 on National Space Policy issued.

June 15: Soviet Union launches Soyuz 29 whose crew spends a record 140 days on Salyut 6 space station.

October 10: PD 42 *Civil and Further National Space Policy* issued by Carter administration.

1979

June 18: Carter and Brezhnev sign SALT II Treaty.

1980

    December 6: United States launches the first fifth generation INTELSAT V communications satellite.

1981

    April 12: United States launches the space shuttle Columbia as the first reusable spacecraft.

    November 13: Reagan administration issues National Security Decision Directive (NSDD) 8 on Space Transportation System.

1982

    July 4: NSDD 42 *National Space Policy* issued by Reagan administration.

    August 6: NSDD 50 *Space Assistance and Cooperation Policy* issued by National Security Council.

    November 11: United States launches shuttle Columbia with a four-person crew and launches two communication satellites.

1983

    March 23: Reagan calls for ballistic missile defense system in a nationally televised address; Strategic Defense Initiative (SDI) inaugurated.

    March 25: NSDD 85 *Eliminating the Threat from Ballistic Missiles* issued by National Security Council.

    April 11: NSDD 5-83 study on the feasibility of a permanently based and manned space station is authorized.

    June 13: NSDD 97 *National Security Telecommunications Policy* issued by National Security Council.

1984

    January 6: National Security Council issues NSDD 119 on SDI.

    January 25: Reagan urges NASA to build a permanently manned space station within 10 years.

    February 3: Shuttle Challenger launched and tests a Manned Maneuvering Unit for space walks.

    April 7: Shuttle Challenger launched and crew conducts first in-space satellite repair.

    July 17: LANDSAT satellites privatized by Public Law 98-365, the Land Remote Sensing Commercialization Act.

    August: NSDD 144 on National Space Strategy issued by Reagan administration.

    October 11: Congress approves $254.1 million for new F-15 fighter plan ASAT weapon research and development.

1985

January 24: Shuttle Discovery launched on a dedicated Defense Department mission.

February 25: NSDD 164 National Security Launch Strategy issued.

June 1: NSDD 172 on presenting SDI released by National Security Council.

October 30: NSDD 195 covering U.S. positions on nuclear and space arms reduction talks released.

November 11: NSDD 192 covering SDI and U.S. interpretation of the ABM Treaty issued.

November 21: United States and Soviet Union sign agreement on cooperation in various scientific and technical fields.

1986

Soviet Mir space station begins operation.

January 28: U.S. space shuttle Challenger explodes on liftoff killing seven astronauts and temporarily grounds manned U.S. space program.

September 5: United States launches SDI payload on a Delta rocket.

October 11–12: Reagan and Gorbachev meet in Reykjavik; proposed arms reductions fail because of disagreement over SDI.

December 27: NSDD 254 *U.S. Space Launch Strategy* issued.

1987

Soviet crew spends more than a year in space on Mir claiming record for longest continuous human presence in space. United States begins developing ground-based laser ASAT systems as part of SDI.

January 14: NSDD 256 released, which features instructions for U.S. negotiators at the 7th U.S.–Soviet nuclear and space negotiations.

February 3: NSDD 257 issued featuring negotiating instructions for the U.S. delegation on space station negotiations with Canada, Japan, and Western Europe.

February 6: NSDD 258 issued describing the United States' ASAT Weapons program.

February 18: NSDD 261 issued describing consultations on SDI with Congress and U.S. allies.

May 7: NSDD 271 released featuring instructions for U.S. negotiators at the 8th U.S.–Soviet nuclear and space negotiations.

December 8: Reagan and Gorbachev sign treaty banning intermediate range nuclear forces.

1988

January 14: NSDD 295 released featuring instructions for U.S. negotiators at the 9th U.S.–Soviet nuclear and space negotiations.

February 11: NSDD 293 on national space policy released.

July 18: NSDD 310 released featuring instructions for U.S. negotiators at the 10th U.S.–Soviet nuclear and space negotiations.

August 8: NSDD 312 released containing negotiating instructions for the third five-year review of the ABM Treaty.

August 15: NSDD 313 released containing revised U.S. delegation negotiating instructions for the ABM Treaty review.

October 24: NSDD 318 issued covering additional information about U.S. positions at the nuclear and space talks.

December 2: United States launches shuttle Atlantis on dedicated Defense Department mission.

1989

February 14: United States launches GPS-1 to begin its Global Positioning System satellite program.

June 14: Bush administration issues National Security Directive (NSD) 14 on ICBM modernization and the Strategic Defense Initiative.

August 8: Shuttle Columbia launched on dedicated Defense Department mission.

November 2: Bush administration issues National Space Policy Directive (NSPD-1) on National Space Policy.

November 21: United States enacts Public Law 101-162, which prohibits the export of U.S.-built satellites to China unless the president informs Congress that China achieves certain political and human rights reforms or that such satellite sales are in the U.S. national interest. This law was reinforced by provisions in the 1990–1991 Foreign Relations Authorization Act (Public Law 101-246) on February 16, 1990.

November 23: Shuttle Discovery launched on dedicated Defense Department mission.

1990

February 28: Shuttle Atlantis launched on dedicated Defense Department mission.

September 5: NSPD 2 on commercial space launch policy issued by Bush administration.

September 7: NSD 46 covering commercial participation in the Cape York, Australia launch site.

November 15: Shuttle Atlantis launched on dedicated Defense Department mission.

1991

February 11: NSPD 3 issued covering U.S. commercial space launch policy guidelines.

April 28: Shuttle Discovery launched on dedicated Defense Department mission.

July 10: NSPD 4 National Space Launch Strategy issued.

July 31: Bush and Gorbachev sign Strategic Arms Reduction Treaty (START), making it the first treaty to reduce long-range nuclear weapons.

November 24: Shuttle Atlantis launches Defense Support Program satellite.

1992

February 13: NSPD 5 on LANDSAT remote-sensing strategy issued.

March 24: United States, Russia, Byelorussia, Ukraine, Georgia, and other NATO and Warsaw Pact countries sign Open Skies Agreement allowing approved overflights of national territory.

June 17: Bush and Yeltsin sign agreements expanding space cooperation between the United States and Russia.

September 18: Defense Department confirms the existence of the National Reconnaissance Office (NRO) established in 1960.

October 28: Land Remote Sensing Policy Act of 1992 (Public Law 102-555) returns LANDSAT to government control and seeks to promote private sector development of new satellite systems. Stipulates that the government can require satellite operators to stop obtaining or distributing imagery for national security reasons.

December: A Post Cold War Assessment of U.S. Space Policy report released by National Space Council.

1993

January 3: Bush and Yeltsin sign START II treaty proposing additional cuts in nuclear warhead arsenals.

September 2: United States and Russia sign agreement on international space station and permitting U.S. satellite exports to Russia if Russia is in compliance with the Missile Technology Control Regime.

September 12: United States launches shuttle Discovery, which deploys the first Advanced Communications Technology Satellite.

October 26: Russia launches Cosmos 2265, a military calibration satellite.

December 22: Russia launches Molniya 1, a primarily military communications satellite.

1994

February 4: Japan launches its first rocket that is capable of putting satellites in orbit.

February 5: Russia launches military communications satellite Raduga 1.

February 18: Russia launches military communications satellite Raduga 31.

April 11: Executive Order (EO) 12906 *Coordinating Geographic Data Acquisition and Access: The National Spatial Data Infrastructure* issued by the Clinton administration.

April 28: Russia launches Cosmos 2280, a photoreconnaissance satellite.

May 3: United States launches $1 billion NRO payload on Delta rocket.

May 10: White House issues Presidential Decision Directive (PDD) 2 on the convergence of U.S. polar-orbiting operational environmental satellite systems and PDD 3 LANDSAT Remote Sensing Strategy.

August 5: Russia launches Cosmos 2286 launch detection satellite. White House issues PDD 4 National Space Transportation Policy.

August 26: Russia launches Cosmos 2290 advanced photoreconnaissance satellite.

October 24: India enters space by launching its first polar satellite launch vehicle.

1995

February 24: Clinton issues EO 12951 *Release of Imagery Acquired by Space-Based National Intelligence Reconnaissance Systems.*

March 2: Russia launches radar calibration satellite Cosmos 2306 for possible anti-ballistic missile use.

May 15: Clinton administration's National Science and Technology Council issues Presidential Review Directive (PRD-2) on U.S. space policy.

May 18: Clinton administration announces review (PRD-3) of U.S. Global Positioning System (GPS) satellite policy.

May 24: Russia launches early warning satellite Cosmos 2312.

1996

February 6: Clinton waives sanctions from Public Law 101-246 permitting various satellites to be exported to China for launch.

March 14: Clinton administration transfers commercial communications satellites export jurisdiction from State Department to Commerce Department facilitating their export to China.

March 29: White House issues PDD 6 on U.S. Global Positioning System policy.

September 19: White House issues PDD 8 on National Space Policy.

September 23: Public Law 104-201, the 1997 Defense Authorization Act, prohibits the collection, release, and U.S. Government declassification of satellite imagery of Israel unless this imagery is no more detailed or precise than commercially available imagery.

1997

March: Air Force's National Air Intelligence Center apparently concludes in a classified report that Loral and Hughes corporations provided expertise to China to help it improve its ballistic missiles guidance systems and that U.S. national security was damaged because of this.

1998

Loral Space and Communications signs agreement with China's Great Wall Industry Corporation to launch five Loral communication satellites between March 1998–March 2002 using Long March 3B rockets.

April 4: New York Times reports that a classified 1997 Defense Department report claims Loral Space and Communications provided technical information to China that increased the reliability of Chinese nuclear missiles.

June 18: U.S. House of Representatives votes to create "Select Committee on U.S. National Security and Military/Commercial Concerns with the People's Republic of China" (the Cox Committee) chaired by California representative Christopher Cox.

August 31: North Korea launches medium range Taepo-dong 1 ballistic missile, which overflies the Japanese island Honshu before plunging into the Pacific Ocean.

December 30: Classified version of Cox Committee report concludes that China's technology applications, including those associated with satellite launches, damaged U.S. national security.

1999

January 16: Taiwan's first satellite Rocsat-1 launched at Vandenberg Air Force Base.

May 3: Cox Committee releases the declassified version of its report.

November 20: A Long March 2F rocket launches the Shenzou spacecraft in China's first successful flight test of an unmanned spacecraft.

2000

January 25: China launches a communications satellite, which the *Washington Times* believes is the first military satellite for a battle management system.

October 12: Raytheon announces its ground-based prototype radar successfully acquired, tracked, and discriminated two targets of operational test missions of Minuteman III ICBMs launched from Vandenberg Air Force Base toward the South Pacific Kwajalein Missile Range.

November 1: National Commission on the National Reconnaissance Office releases its report on future directions for this office.

November 22: China issues "White Paper on Space Activities" stressing that it places high importance on space activities in advancing national security, economic development, and scientific and technological growth.

December: Report of the Independent Commission on the National Imagery and Mapping Agency (NIMA) released.

2001

January 10: China launches and successfully tests its second unmanned spacecraft.

January 11: Rumsfeld Commission report on U.S. national security space management and organization released, which proposes drastic changes in the management of Defense Department and intelligence community space programs.

July: U.S. senators Jesse Helms, Fred Thompson, Richard Shelby, and Jon Kyl write President George W. Bush to ask him not to grant waivers for exporting satellites to China.

September 7: Senate Armed Service Committee approves a defense spending bill that cuts $1.3 billion in missile defense spending requested by the Bush administration.

November 8: National Security Advisor Condoleezza Rice announces that effective missile defense is a high priority for U.S. national security.

2002

May 15: China launches weather and ocean survey satellites and claims this is its 25th straight successful launch since October 1996.

July 28: President Bush directs National Security Council to review national space policy in National Security Presidential Directive (NSPD) 15.

October 9: U.S. Army Space Command opens new building at Peterson Air Force Base, Colorado.

October 27: China launches a satellite used for military photoreconnaissance.

November: Commission on the Future of the U.S. Aerospace Industry releases its report.

December 17: British Ministry of Defence announces that it will seriously consider a U.S. request to upgrade the early warning radar Royal Air Force base Flyingdales for missile defense purposes.

December 26: The State Department's Office of Defense Trade Controls issues a letter charging Hughes Electronics Corporation and Boeing Satellite Systems (the owners of Loral) with 123 Arms Export Control Act and International Traffic in Arms Regulations violations in connection to technology transfers to China after failed Chinese satellite launches in January 1995 and February 1996.

2003

January 6: White House releases new U.S. Space Transportation Policy which authorizes use of foreign commerce if such use is consistent with U.S. foreign policy and national security objectives.

April 25: NSPD 27, the new U.S. policy on commercial remote sensing, signed and directs U.S. Government to use commercial remote sensing space capabilities to maximum extent.

May: Defense Science Board and Air Force Scientific Advisory Board release report on acquisition cost increases in Defense Department space program.

October 6: India's Chief of Air Staff announces that a new aerospace command has begun working to develop weapons platforms for space.

November 11: European Commission adopts space action plan with the acceptance of the policy paper *Space: A New European Frontier for an Expanding Union.*

December 11: The Missile Defense Agency and Navy announce the successful test of an Aegis ballistic missile defense flight test at the Pacific Missile Test Range in Kauai, Hawaii.

2004

January 1: A report by Taiwan's National Space Program Office urges that country's Ministry of National Defense to strengthen its capabilities to deal with what it sees as the threats posed by Chinese military satellites.

January 9: A Missile Defense Agency successfully conducted a test launch of a Ground-Based Midcourse Defense system designed to intercept and destroy long-range ballistic missiles.

January 13: U.S. and Australian officials begin talks on possible Australian participation in U.S. missile defense programs.

February 18: Russian president Vladimir Putin says Russia may begin building its own missile defense system and that its military will possess "new strategic weapons."

May 6: Secretary of the Army announces that a Patriot Missile battery will be deployed in South Korea in September for missile defense purposes.

July 7: U.S. defense secretary Donald Rumsfeld and Australian defense minister Robert Hill sign agreement on Australian participation in U.S. missile defense activities.

August 5: Canadian defense minister Bill Graham and foreign minister Pierre Pettigrew announce that Canada is amending the North American Aerospace Defense Command (NORAD) agreement with the United States. This amendment enables NORAD to make its missile warning function available to U.S. commands conducting ballistic missile defense.

September 15: Air Force secretary James Roche announces that during 2003 insurgent forces in Iraq unsuccessfully used jammers to thwart coalition global positioning system precision-guided munitions, which he described as the first time hostile forces tried to impede U.S. forces to use space as they wish.

September 16: Air Force Space Command commander general Lance Lord warns space power is essential to winning wars in a speech to the Air Force Association's Air and Space Conference and Technology Exposition.

December 13: Edwards Air Force Base announces that an airborne laser aircraft flew for 2 hours and 31 minutes during a December 9 test.

December 21: NSPD 40 *U.S. Space Transportation Policy* released.

2005

January 31: Russia and Iran reach agreement with Russia to design and launch the first Iranian communications satellite Zohre.

February 24: Canadian prime minister Paul Martin announces that Canada will not participate in U.S. ballistic missile defense programs.

March 24: Participants in the International Conference on Safeguarding Space Security in Geneva acknowledge that existing international standards do not guarantee space will be weapons free according to a Russian Foreign Ministry statement.

March 27: Pakistan president Pervez Musharraf announces his country will attempt to manufacture and launch its own satellite.

April 12: Russian defense minister Sergei Ivanov says his country will continue participating in U.S.–Russian theater ballistic missile defense exercises.

May 5: Armed Forces Press Service news story details how geospatial intelligence has saved the lives of U.S. forces in Afghanistan and Iraq.

July 22: Japan's Parliament passes law enabling the defense minister to order missile interceptions in emergencies without consulting the prime minister or Cabinet.

October 17: China successfully completes its second human spaceflight mission, which lasted five days and involved two astronauts.

November 17: U.S. Missile Defense Agency successfully shoots down a warhead launched over Hawaiian waters in the first test of shooting down a warhead that left its booster rocket.

December 28: Galileo satellite launched from Kazakhstan. This satellite is part of a partnership between the European Space Agency and European Commission and gives Europe GPS capability, which is interoperable with American and Russian GPS systems.

2006

U.S. Army issues *United States Army Space Master Plan* outlining areas of service military space policy interest.

May 2006: Edition of Defense Department report *Military Power of the People's Republic of China* maintains that China is pursuing an offensive ASAT system and that it can destroy satellites by launching ballistic missile of a space-launched missile armed with nuclear weapons.

August 31: Bush administration issues National Space Policy document stressing critical importance of space to U.S. national security policy.

September: News reports maintain China fires lasers at orbiting U.S. satellites in simulated attacks.

2007

January 11: China destroys a polar-orbiting weather satellite at altitude of 865 kilometers (537 miles) using ASAT system launched from China.

2008

February 20: USS *Lake Erie*, an Aegis-class missile cruiser, fires a missile to destroy an errant US spy satellite. The satellite, that had been completely out of communication since launch in December, 2006, carried a thruster fuel of Hydrazine, a toxic substance that would have been lethal in aerosol or liquid form if the thruster fuel cell had not completely burned up on re-entry.

PART 1

1

Development of
U.S. Military Space Policy

THE HISTORICAL ORIGINS of U.S. military space policy date back to World War II, and a variety of accomplishments, setbacks, trends, and developments have been experienced during its six decades of existence. This chapter examines this historical development and places great emphasis on the military and political documents that have contributed to U.S. military space policy during this period. The first part of this chapter emphasizes military and military-related documents on U.S. space policy, while the second part of the chapter examines presidential space policy documents, which are generally produced by the National Security Council (NSC).

Background information on these documents and developments are provided, along with excerpts from these documents so readers can gain an understanding of the policies or programs that document writings were trying to communicate and advocate at the time of their creation. The documents should also provide illumination of the political and military environments prompting their creation. Many of these documents are compiled from two superlative documentary collections: *Orbital Futures: Selected Documents in Air Force Space History,* edited by David Spires (2004) and *National Security Space Project Presidential Documents: NSC Documents,* compiled by Stephanie Feycock. A particularly useful Web resource for some of these documents is the Federation of American Scientists Presidential Directives and Executive Orders Web site (www.fas.org/irp/offdocs/direct.htm).

This documentary enumeration is chronological and exhaustive but not comprehensive. It strives to list many of the major U.S. military space policy documents produced during the past six decades. Historians of the United States' civilian and military space programs will have divergent views on the significance of these documents and programs. This work hopes to give readers a substantive overview of these documents and the policy developments behind them.

Recognition that World War II's technological advances such as the German V-2 rockets made space a potential future forum for military activity began appearing in scientific literature as the war concluded in 1945. Writer Arthur C. Clarke (1917–), best known for science fiction novels such as *2001: A Space Odyssey* wrote an article in the October 1945 issue of the British technical journal *Wireless World Radio and Electronics* in which he asserted the feasibility of putting communication satellites in geosynchronous orbit around the earth (Clarke 1945, 305–308). Clarke's proposals on the growing possibility of space be-coming an arena for human military activity and potential conflict was soon reflected in various documents produced by the U.S. military or for the military by civilian contractors.

Military Documents—Karman Report Toward New Horizons (1945)

One of the earliest U.S. military reports examining potential military applications of space was produced through a collaborative effort between Army Air Forces commander general Henry (Hap) Arnold (1886–1950) and California Institute of Technology (Cal Tech) aeronautics professor Theodore von Karman (1881–1963) (Daso 2000; Gorn 1992). Arnold, a key leader in the development of U.S. military aviation, had met von Karman through a mutual acquaintance at Cal Tech in 1935, and the two developed a rapport with Arnold making regular visits to the university to watch wind tunnel experiments and discuss uni-versity aeronautical and rocket propulsion matters with von Karman. This collaboration continued throughout World War II and eventually resulted in a research project involv-ing civilian and military researchers to examine future trends in military aeronautics (Spires 1998, 1–2, 7–10).

The cumulative result of this collaboration was the monumental series of reports entitled *Toward New Horizons* consisting of 34 monographs in 12 volumes, which Arnold received in December 1945. An exemplar of then cutting-edge scientific and technological forecasting, *Toward New Horizons* identified trends and potential opportunities in high-speed aerodynamics; aircraft materials and structures; designing and developing solid and liquid fuel rockets; guided missiles; unmanned aerial vehicles; guided and radar homing missiles; explosives and terminal ballistics; and aviation medicine. Von Karman authored two of the monographs "Science, the Key to Air Supremacy" and "Where We Stand" and used these works to advocate an enhanced research program for the emerging Air Force, predict that Intercontinental Ballistic Missiles (ICBMs) would achieve eventual opera-tional success, and determine that earth-orbiting artificial satellites were feasible (U.S. Air Force Aeronautical Systems History Office 2002, 2; Spires 1998, 10–11).

Excerpts from *Toward New Horizons* emphasize the targeting options provided by emerging aeronautical technology; timely and accurate warning and response to attack; the importance of aerial reconnaissance for surveying enemy territory; transportation infrastructure and military installations; the need to integrate warning networks with fighter and missile squadron control to defeat enemy attack; and the need to have strong offensive forces to defeat enemy attacks as demonstrated by recent World War II experi-ences involving Britain and Japan (Gorn 1994, 128, 165, 168).

Toward New Horizons had significance in postwar Air Force development, because it ensured the importance of science and long-range forecasting within the Air Force. It rec-ognized that ICBMs and other missile systems would become increasingly important in the years to come. Von Karman and his collaborators also proposed various organizational

Theodore von Karman, aeronautical theoretician and co-founder of the Jet Propulsion Laboratory (JPL) in Pasadena, California. Photo taken around 1950. *(NASA)*

reforms to military aviation including establishing separate facilities for supersonic and unpiloted aircraft and proposing a facility where aerodynamics, propulsion, control, and electronics could be studied in an integrated manner. These influences and subsequent developments and reports eventually moved U.S. military aviation to see itself as an armed service whose operational orientation and mission would encompass both aeronautical and astronautic responsibilities, which would go under the combined term aerospace (Spires 1998, 11; Gorn 1994, 14–16).

Earth Circling Spaceship (Project Rand) (1946)

A second early document produced with military and civilian collaboration that helped sculpt postwar U.S. military aerospace thought was the 1946 Project Rand report *Preliminary Design of an Experimental World-Circling Spaceship.* Project Rand was a military sponsored think tank based in Santa Monica, California, which later became known as the Rand Corporation. Examining existing technological capabilities and anticipated future engineering trends, this prescient document contended that technology and operational

art had reached the ability to design and build vehicles capable of penetrating the atmosphere and achieving enough speed to become satellites orbiting the earth.

Report predictions contended that the United States could launch a 500-pound satellite into a 300-mile orbit within five years for $150 million. Additional factors covered
in this report include technical feasibility studies examining matters such as craft propulsion options, the potential dangers of meteor strikes, trajectory analyses, the challenges
involved in getting these vessels to reenter the earth through atmospheric heat, and the
possibility of using a three-stage liquid hydrogen rocket booster instead of an existing
single-stage Navy rocket. Report writers believed none of these technical challenges to be
insurmountable.

Another section of this report examined potential military satellite uses in the chapter
"The Significance of a Satellite Vehicle." This section asserted that satellites were nearly im-
pregnable observation platforms capable of providing weather and bomb assessment data.

Additional assessments of this section maintained that a satellite could serve as a communications relay station positioned approximately 25,000 miles above the earth's surface
so their rotational period would be the same as that of the earth. In this location, satellites
could stay in geosynchronous orbit and provide effective global communications (Collins
2002, 74–75; Spires 1998, 14–15).

Regarding a satellite's military applications, this work also discussed the possibility of
using satellites as offensive weapons, maintaining that satellites could provide accurate
guidance for missiles and serve as missiles themselves (Spires 1998, 15). An example of this
report's observations stressing compatibility between missile and satellite technology plus
launch velocity requirements is reflected in the following passage:

> There is little difference in design and performance between an intercontinental
> rocket missile and a satellite. Thus a rocket missile with a free space trajectory of
> 6,000 miles requires a minimum energy of launching which corresponds to an
> initial velocity of 4.4 miles per second, while a satellite requires 5.4. Consequently,
> the development of a satellite will be directly applicable to the development of an
> intercontinental missile (Project Rand 1946, 10).

Another report prognostication, although somewhat overstated, presented a visionary
future for the role satellite technology would play in subsequent decades, contending that
a satellite could be an extremely powerful scientific tool and that the United States could
inflame mankind's imagination by producing satellite craft (Project Rand 1946, 1–2).

This report clearly established the technical possibility of orbiting a satellite while
ruling out its use as an offensive weapon, because existing propulsion systems were unable to launch heavy atomic weapons into Earth's orbit. This caveat and the high cost of
developing weaponized satellites precluded further research in this area, and there would
be greater military emphasis on developing missiles (Spires 1998, 16). Despite these short-
comings, this 1946 Rand report must be seen as the first authoritative recognition of the

military potential of satellites and how space could become an arena for gathering military intelligence, if not conducting military operations. Subsequent years saw U.S. civilian and military policymakers make the first tentative steps toward incorporating space into overall national security priorities.

Operational Requirements for Satellite Operational System (1955)

Rand's emphasis on the feasibility and desirability of orbiting a reconnaissance satellite to monitor Soviet military activities eventually received greater receptivity from U.S. military planners despite initial skepticism.

During April 1951, Rand investigators produced two reports, "Utility of a Satellite Vehicle for Reconnaissance" and "Inquiring into the Feasibility of Weather Reconnaissance Vehicle," which asserted that improvements in television resolution technology would make satellite reconnaissance possible (Spires 1998, 28).

The March 1, 1954 Rand report "Project Feedback" provided further clarification on these 1951 reports by describing how an electro-optical television system could transmit data directly from satellites to ground receiving stations and a camera scanning technique that could be used to record satellite data. Project Feedback went on to assert that a satellite reconnaissance capability could be built with existing guidance, propulsion, and television technology within seven years for $165 million (Spires 2004, 1:200).

Subsequent technological and political developments led the Air Force to issue *General Operational Requirement #80 For a Strategic Reconnaissance Satellite Weapon System* on March 15, 1955. This document called for producing a visual reconnaissance capability of providing continuous coverage of airfields and missile sites at a resolution of 20 feet per side by 1965 (Spires 2004, 2:978).

Document content, which can be considered as an official U.S. commitment to developing a satellite reconnaissance surveillance system, covers a multifaceted variety of operational and technical topics including stressing support for developing a satellite weapon system capable of providing continuous reconnaissance of the earth to determine potential enemies war-making capabilities, that this satellite be launched from the continental United States and have Western Hemisphere monitoring stations, that system launch facilities be fixed, and that monitoring facilities be capable of continuous data and image handling, not susceptible to hostile interference, and be able to transmit this data to pertinent agencies (Spires 2004, 2:978–979).

Army Space Programs (1950s)

The Air Force was not the only U.S. military branch to express interest in developing the military potential of space. The U.S. Army also expressed interest in space as an emerging forum for conducting military operations during the 1950s. This interest had been

Wernher von Braun developed the V-2 rocket for Germany during World War II. After the war, von Braun emigrated to the United States and worked for the U.S. Army developing more advanced rockets. His work was integral to the development of the U.S. space program. *(Library of Congress)*

influenced by the German Wehrmacht's role in developing Germany's V-1 and V-2 rockets during World War II (Neufeld 1996).

Wernher von Braun (1912–1977), one of the leaders of Germany's rocket program, engineered the surrender of his top rocket scientists, plans, and test vehicles to the United States as World War II concluded in Europe. Von Braun and his colleagues were extricated from Germany by the U.S. Army in Operation Paperclip and installed at Fort Bliss, Texas. These individuals worked with the U.S. Army to develop ballistic missiles for the Army launching them at White Sands Proving Ground, New Mexico before moving to Redstone Arsenal near Huntsville, Alabama in 1950 where they began working on the Jupiter ballistic missile. This work achieved significant success for the United States in rocket guidance, solid-fuel technology, and warhead design and would likely have given the United States the first entry into space if the Eisenhower administration had not chosen to emphasize the importance of civilian astronautic research for political reasons. Consequently, the October 4, 1957 Soviet Sputnik launch became the first artificial satellite in space (Lambakis 2001, 11–12; U.S. National Aeronautics and Space Administration, Marshall Space Flight Center History Office, n.d. 1–2).

During February 1955, the Army Ballistic Missile Agency (ABMA) in Huntsville contracted with Western Electric Company and Bell Telephone Laboratories to study ways of countering emerging air defense threats such as ballistic missiles. In December 1955, Bell presented their findings to Redstone Arsenal's chief of army ordnance concluding that developing and deploying a missile defense system was feasible. The Bell study based this assessment on a series of 50,000 analog computer computations simulating the interception of ballistic missile targets, which concluded that intercepting an ICBM was possible and that a ballistic missile defense system could be deployed by late 1962 (Walker, Bernstein, Lang 2003, 25–26).

A subsequent Bell proposal in October 1956 involved the use of existing Nike missiles and an interchangeable variety of missile nose cones to handle the complete variety of potential ICBM threats. This proposal would have involved the Nike carrying 400-pound nuclear warheads and be capable of executing 10-G maneuvers at 100,000 feet to track and intercept hostile incoming missiles. A Nike intercepted a high-altitude supersonic target missile in November 1958 and in 1960 shot down two ballistic missiles during tests at White Sands, marking the first time a ballistic missile was destroyed by another missile (Walker, Bernstein, Lang 2003, 26).

In November 1956, Secretary of Defense Charles Wilson (1890–1961) gave the Army responsibility for developing, procuring, and manning land-based surface-to-air missile systems for point defense. The Army was given responsibility for developing missiles whose range was less than 200 miles while Air Force responsibilities covered missiles whose ranges exceeded 200 miles. Such defense was responsible for focusing on designated geographic areas, cities, crucial military and industrial installations, and covered air targets at altitudes out to a broad range of 100 nautical miles. On January 16, 1958 new secretary of Defense Neil McElroy (1904–1972) assigned the Army primary responsibility for ballistic missile defense missions involving missile, launch site, radar, and computer components (Walker, Bernstein, Lang 2003, 27, 30).

Prior to the National Aeronautics and Space Administration's (NASA) 1958 creation, the Army had launched the United States' first ballistic missile, and the first U.S. astronauts were sent into orbit by modified Army Redstone-designed rockets. During the summer of 1958, ABMA made the audacious proposal to plant a military colony on the moon. Designated Project Horizon, the Army wanted to land on the moon in 1965 and establish a 12-man outpost there by 1966.

Army estimates posited that this moon base would require logistics support from 64 Saturn rocket launches per year with each rocket carrying more than 266,000 pounds of cargo at a cost of $6 billion. Project Horizon plans called for constructing an underground lunar base that would include living quarters, storage areas, nuclear reactors, laboratories, a hospital, communications center, and dining and recreation rooms. Horizon never got off ground due to the Eisenhower administration's impending creation of NASA, which terminated the program and inherited most Army space programs (Walker, Bernstein, Lang 2003, 30–31; Springer 1999, 34–38; Neufeld M. J. 2005, 737–757).

Nevertheless, this project initiated the U.S. Army's interaction with space, which continues to the present as demonstrated by the presence of agencies such as the U.S. Army

Space and Missile Defense Command—an important part of current U.S. military space activities.

1958 Space Act

An important development affecting the future of U.S. military space programs was the 1958 Space Act creating NASA as the principal civilian U.S. Government space policy agency. The October 4, 1957 Sputnik satellite launch by the Soviet Union was an important factor propelling U.S. Government interest in developing an agency to coordinate U.S. space policy efforts. Another was the desire of many congressional leaders, led by Senate majority leader Lyndon Johnson (Democrat from Texas) (1908–1973), to make sure Congress was directly involved in directing U.S. space agency policy making. On February 6, 1958, the Senate created the Special Committee on Science and Astronautics with Johnson as its chair (McDougall 1997, 169–170). The House established a Select Committee on Astronautics and Space Exploration on March 5, 1958, which was chaired by House majority leader John McCormack (Democrat from Massachusetts) (1891–1980) (Portree 1998, 5).

The next several weeks saw a series of legislative maneuvers between Congress and the Eisenhower administration. Addressing a joint session of Congress on April 2, 1958, President Dwight D. Eisenhower (1890–1969) called for the creation of what became known as NASA to replace the existing National Advisory Committee on Aeronautics (NACA). Since NASA was intended to be a primarily civilian department, Eisenhower issued a directive ordering NACA and the Defense Department (DOD) to prepare to transfer non-military DOD space capabilities to NASA (Portree 1998, 5; Anderson 1981, 14–17).

Johnson and Senator Henry Styles Bridge (Republican from New Hampshire) (1898–1961) introduced the Senate version of this legislation, S. 3609, on April 14, and McCormack introduced the House version, H.R. 11991, on the same day with hearings beginning the next day (Portree 1998, 5). Subsequent weeks saw considerable legislative haggling over the military role of NASA and its relationship with DOD. The House version of this legislation gave DOD freedom to conduct space-related research and development and directed NASA to cooperate with DOD, which was at variance with Eisenhower administration sentiment that NASA *may* cooperate with DOD. The House sought to ensure that NASA remain free from military dominance without obstructing civilian or military activities by this agency (Erickson 2005, 73).

The Senate version of this legislation went beyond the House's and firmly established DOD's ability to have control over space program aspects that were uniquely associated with defense, and the Senate was more concerned that NASA would restrict DOD's space role. The Senate version won out in the end creating a National Aeronautics and Space Policy Board to coordinate civilian and military space policy operations and that NASA would remain a civilian agency except for "activities peculiar to or primarily associated with the development of weapons systems or military operations, [which] shall be directed

President Dwight Eisenhower speaks with Wernher von Braun at the dedication of the George C. Marshall Space Flight Center on September 8, 1960. *(Dwight D. Eisenhower Presidential Library)*

and controlled by the Department of Defense" (Erickson 2005, 73–75; U.S. Congress. Senate Special Committee on Space and Astronautics 1958, 1, 6, 12).

Further legislative maneuvering and a July 7 White House meeting between Johnson and Eisenhower saw the president agree with Johnson's suggestion that the president become the National Aeronautics and Space Policy Board chair and the group, which became known as the Space Council, would function like the NSC. On July 15, a House–Senate conference committee worked out the final version of this legislation, which unanimously passed both houses by voice votes the following day (Erickson 2005, 75).

Eisenhower signed the National Aeronautics and Space Act of 1958 on July 29. It called for the creation of NASA in October 1958 and made the following declaration of this new agency's institutional mandate:

The Congress believes that the general welfare and security of the United States require that adequate provision be made for aeronautical and space activities. The Congress further declares that such activities shall be the responsibility of, and shall be directed by, a civilian agency exercising control over aeronautical and space activities by the United States, except that activities peculiar to or primarily associated with the development of weapons systems, military operations, or the defense of the United States (including the research and development necessary to make effective provision for the defense of the United States) shall be the responsibility of, and shall be directed by, the Department of Defense; and that determination as to which agency has responsibility for and direction of any such activity shall be made by the President.... (Erickson 2005; National Aeronautics and Space Act of 1958, 85–568).

Besides creating an organization that would have a significant impact in facilitating U.S. space science and exploration (Logsdon 1992; Launius 1994; Boone 1970; Portree 1998), this statute created two organizations to facilitate DOD–NASA coordination. The Space Council was charged with advising the president concerning duties prescribed in the Space Act. The Civilian-Military Liaison Committee (CMLC) was responsible for giving DOD and NASA the ability to advise and consult with each other on matters concerning aeronautical and space activities and keeping each organization informed on such activities their organizations engaged in. Subsequent years saw the Space Council periodically used as a forum for upper level administration officials to discuss space policy while CMLC proved ineffective because appointed members were powerless in DOD and NASA, and their perspectives could be ignored without consequence (Erickson 2005, 76–77).

Air Force Space Program Memo to Secretary of Defense (1958)

Creation of NASA, coupled with the February 1958 creation of the Advanced Research Projects Agency (ARPA) within DOD, resulted in the Air Force having to reluctantly relinquish management of its manned space programs to ARPA. In mid-August 1958, Eisenhower transferred overall responsibility for human spaceflight to NASA, which prompted Air Force undersecretary Malcolm MacIntyre (1908–1992) to write Secretary of Defense McElroy on September 17, 1958 urging him to clarify civil–military space roles and advocating ongoing Air Force–DOD participation in manned space activity. MacIntyre's argument also emphasized the Air Force's space booster monopoly and stressed avoiding program duplication with NASA (Spires 2004, 2:762).

MacIntyre's letter contents emphasize that space vehicles used for military reconnaissance or atmospheric or space weapons be DOD's responsibility, that space vehicles for nonmilitary space and exploration be NASA's responsibility, and that testing human reactions and capabilities in space be DOD and NASA responsibilities, while using existing expertise within the Air Force and its contractors (Spires 2004, 2:762–763).

Program duplication and coordination problems between NASA and DOD remained unresolved. The Air Force remained particularly concerned with NASA contractual, procurement, and technical support involvement with civilian contractors serving the Air Force and DOD. An August 15, 1959 Air Force–NASA agreement sought to encourage single-manager program responsibility and NASA use of Air Force facilities and procurement procedures. Delineating Air Force–NASA responsibilities became increasingly difficult under the Eisenhower and Kennedy administrations (Spires 2004, 2:762; Erickson 2005, 112–114; 296–314).

Special Panel on Satellite Reconnaissance (Killian Report) (1960)

The need for accurate intelligence reconnaissance of Soviet military capabilities was becoming increasingly important to U.S. policymakers in the late 1950s and prompted the development and programs of the U-2 spy plane and an increasing interest in satellite surveillance of the Soviet Union (Pedlow and Welzenbach 1998; Arnold 2005). Existing satellite surveillance programs such as Corona under Central Intelligence Agency (CIA) auspices (Day, Logsdon, and Latell 1998) and the Air Force's independent reconnaissance satellite Samos (Erickson 2005, 120, 182–183) were at various stages of development during the Eisenhower administration's final year.

Eisenhower had expressed concern to the U.S. intelligence community about specific technical requirements that reconnaissance satellites should possess to carry out their responsibilities. On July 5, 1960, the United States Intelligence Board (USIB), an interagency information exchange entity within the U.S. intelligence community at this time, issued the report "Intelligence Requirements for Satellite Reconnaissance," which was chaired by presidential science advisor and former Massachusetts Institute of Technology (MIT) president James Killian (1904–1988).

Killian's USIB panel recommendations asserted that the highest priority of U.S. satellite reconnaissance efforts should be developing a system capable of general search coverage emphasizing the Soviet rail network and ICBM sites, with coverage repeated monthly. The panel went on to recommend that the photographic resolution needed to accomplish such searches needed to approach 20 feet on a side, that surveillance of suspect ICBM

James R. Killian, president of the Massachusetts Institute of Technology (1948–1959), and special assistant for science and technology to President Dwight D. Eisenhower (1957–1959). Killian was an important early presidential science advisor on military space matters. *(Library of Congress)*

sites required a resolution capable of identifying ground objects five feet on a side, and that a system resolution exceeding five feet on a side would be essential before the end of 1962 to garner technical information on the highest priority targets (Spires 2:969).

Subsequent sections of Killian's report addressed management problems within the Samos program, criticized program duplication within other Air Force and DOD component organizations, advocated the need for developing a recoverable capsule high-resolution stereo-quality satellite photography capability, and supported the development of a centralized national film processing and evaluation center, which resulted in the January 18, 1961 creation of the National Photographic and Interpretation Center (NPIC) (Spires 2:970–71).

Representative conclusions from the Killian Report include the need for the United States to develop and maintain an operational satellite reconnaissance system with multi-faceted capabilities and the recommendations that information acquired by photographic reconnaissance is now and will be of greater value than that obtained by electronic reconnaissance systems, that satellite reconnaissance information is most crucial in providing strategic intelligence information and should provide supplemental information on Soviet intentions, that satellite reconnaissance's most crucial assignment is locating suspect ICBM launch sites, and that when an ICBM site is located then a satellite reconnaissance system with satisfactory ground resolution should maintain surveillance of that site and report changes in its status (Spires 2004, 2:1050–1053).

Wiesner Committee Report (1961)

The victorious 1960 presidential campaign of John Kennedy (1917–1963) saw him place considerable emphasis on space policy and criticize what he regarded as deficiencies in the Eisenhower administration's response to Soviet space accomplishments. Following his narrow election triumph, Kennedy and his presidential transition organization appointed a committee to review the U.S. space program.

Chaired by MIT electrical engineering professor and later president Jerome Wiesner (1915–1994), the committee issued its report on January 10, 1961, which was highly critical of NASA organization and management and a "fractionated military space program." This report proceeded to recommend that one agency or military service assume responsibility for all military space development and asserted that the Air Force was the logical inheritor of this responsibility. Additional Wiesner report recommendations included the United States placing greater emphasis on booster development, manned space activities, and military applications in space, which convinced the Kennedy administration to adopt a more unified national space program with the Air Force receiving military space leadership preeminence (Spires 1998, 86–87; Spires 2004, 1:254).

Wiesner report content stressed both military and civilian benefits of an active role in space policy and concomitant scientific and economic enhancements. These included developing ballistic missiles for military security, emphasizing the importance of national prestige by stressing how space exploration had captured the imagination of international public opinion, that some space developments besides missiles can enhance national security through arms control inspections, and the importance of space in civilian applications such as satellites communications, broadcasting, navigation, geodesy, mapping, and meteorology (Spires 2004, 1:255).

Significant portions of the Wiesner report address critical emerging military benefits of an active U.S. role in space including land mass surveillance of Soviet–Sino bloc nations, the U.S. Air Force providing at least 90% of the resources and physical support required by other agencies and being the United States' principal source for future space system development and operations except for scientific research legally assigned to NASA. Additional Wiesner report content stressed the need for military research and development of large rocket boosters, the potential presence of large orbital bombs and 100–200 megaton ICBMs, communications blackouts resulting from space nuclear explosions, and crash programs to destroy or neutralize satellites, all of which could become part of future space security environments (Spires 2004, 1:260–261).

DOD Directive 5160.32 DOD Support of NASA (1961)

Concern over duplication between DOD and NASA military space programs as emphasized in the Wiesner report led Kennedy's Secretary of Defense Robert McNamara (1916–) to issue *DOD Directive 5160.32 Development of Space Systems* on March 6, 1961.

Secretary of Defense Robert McNamara works at his desk in the Pentagon in 1961. Originally focused on reorganizing the Pentagon's budgetary and bureaucratic processes, McNamara is most remembered for his role in major foreign policy decisions such as the Vietnam War. *(U.S. Department of Defense)*

Upon taking office in January 1961, McNamara assigned DOD's Office of Organization and Management Planning Studies to review military space program fractionation described in the Wiesner report. The resulting directive consolidated the Air Force's preeminence in military space matters. The directive mentioned that individual military services could conduct "preliminary research to develop new ways of using space technology to perform its assigned function" then went on to stress that subsequent technology proposals beyond this had to undergo review by DOD's deputy director of research and engineering (DDR&E) and had to receive ultimate approval from the secretary of Defense (Erickson 2005, 274–275; Wolf 1987, 363–64).

DOD Directive 5160.32 terminated interservice competition for space with the only remaining non-Air Force space programs being the Navy's Transit navigation satellite and the Army's Advent communication satellite. An additional result of this directive was its provisions granting DDR&E and the secretary of Defense final approval for all military space projects. This drastically restricted the Air Force's ability to do space development work without explicit DDR&E authorization. Furthermore, it reduced the Air Force ability in multiple efforts to place humans in space and extend U.S. nuclear deterrence capabilities into orbit, resulted in McNamara and his advisors insisting that Air Force space proposals produce clear identifiable enhancements to U.S. security, and insured that Air Force proposals not duplicate NASA research and development (Erickson 2005, 276).

Management of National Reconnaissance Program (1961)

The growing success of the Corona satellite reconnaissance program by fall 1961 provided a measurable contrast with the failings of the Samos program. Corona's success increased pressure to incorporate the Army's mapping satellite project within Corona. The failed April 1961 Bay of Pigs mission in Cuba temporarily diminished the CIA's influence within U.S. national security policymaking and increased the desire of McNamara and other DOD officials to consolidate reconnaissance programs under DOD direction.

These developments bore fruit with a September 6, 1961 agreement between DOD and the CIA creating the National Reconnaissance Office (NRO) (Spires 2004, 2:973, 1081).

This agreement established a National Reconnaissance Program (NRP) for NRO to run all overt and covert satellite and overflight reconnaissance projects. Covert projects were to be run jointly by the CIA's deputy director for Plans and the under secretary of the Air Force, who was also appointed special assistant for Reconnaissance to the secretary of Defense and who reported directly to McNamara. The Air Force was given operational responsibility for managing and conducting NRP (Spires 2004, 2:973, 1081).

Examples of NRP's wide-ranging responsibilities and the secretive requirements of its institutional mandate include NRP comprising all overt and covert satellite and overflight reconnaissance projects encompassing photographic projects for intelligence, geodesy, mapping, electronic signals intelligence, and communications intelligence; establishing a

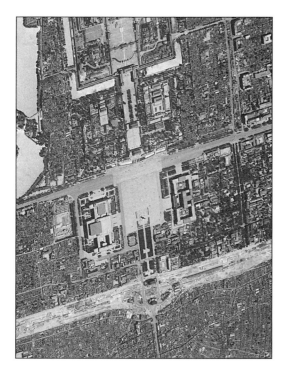

Satellite image of Beijing, China taken by the KH-7 satellite, developed by the National Reconnaissance Office, on May 27, 1967. This image is an example of Corona satellite imagery which was crucial for U.S. monitoring of foreign military developments. *(USGS)*

covert NRO to manage this program; developing a uniform security system to ensure only users designated by the U.S. Intelligence Board receive its products; and developing requisite cover and public information plans with the assistant secretary of Defense, Public Affairs, to lessen the potential political vulnerability of these programs (Spires 2004, 2:1081–1082).

This document ensured that NRO's existence would remain secret until it was publicly acknowledged for the first time in September 1992 (Day, Logsdon, and Latell 1998, 13).

Air Force Space Plan (September 1961)

Policy developments such as *DOD Directive 5160.32* and ongoing contentiousness between civilian and military policymakers over whether the U.S. military should play a role in space policy illustrated continuing controversy within the U.S. Government. The Air Force was determined that it should play a military role in space and that there should not be an artificial distinction between peaceful and military space activities.

An example of this growing Air Force realization's of space's military importance was expressed by retiring Air Force chief of staff general Thomas White (1902–1965) who asserted "I make this prediction, in the future, the people who control space will control the world" (Futrell 1989, 2:215). Concern over this perceived arbitrary space policy mission orientation between DOD and NASA was expressed by a number of Air Force leaders

including General Bernard Schriever (1910–2005), the head of the Air Research and Development Command (Air Force Systems Command after April 1, 1961) and widely regarded as the architect of the Air Force's space and missile programs (U.S. Air Force 2005, 1;
Lonnquest 1996; Neufeld J. 2005).

Schriever went on to argue that military space programs had not been supported
properly, that there was little technical distinction between DOD and NASA space programs, and that the same sense of urgency existing around U.S. civilian space programs
at that time should be applied to U.S. military space programs. Such sentiments proved
to be critical drivers for the Air Force in developing the first Air Force Space Plan unveiled
in September 1961. This plan saw the Air Force describe what it wanted to do in space, the
programs it believed were required in areas such as a space station, weapons in space, and
a major applied research effort distinct from NASA research, and the projected costs that
would result in a nearly $1 billion increase in military space programs over the next two
years (Erickson 2005, 277–278; Spires 2004, 1:324).

Specific plan details called for this applied research program to be conducted in fields
such as guidance, propulsion, and sensors to insure that properly developed military
potentials be quickly identified and decisively pursued. Plan writers maintained that this
initiative would be supportive of an integrated national space program where Air Force
capabilities and infrastructure would support the United States' national space program.
Space plan proponents also contended that space capabilities would only be used when
determined to be the best available or most cost-effective options to support existing
mission areas such as reconnaissance and surveillance, defense, offense, command control,
and support (Spires 2004, 1:148).

Document contents, including the review of Soviet military astronautic developments,
stress the need to develop space technology for improving and maintaining national defense and assuring access to space for peaceful purposes; to develop an applied research
program to insure national security, recognizing Soviet interest in militarily exploiting
space; and the importance of the United States assessing the military potential of men in
space (Spires 2004, 1:325–326).

A subsequent portion of this document expressed the then prevalent belief that manned
systems could be more effective than unmanned systems in conducting certain military
space activities. It concluded by stressing that the speed of human response is critical for
effective military counteractions such as employing electronic countermeasures and that
human adaptability to rapidly changing situations could be the only practical way of
achieving successful performance in military space functions (Spires 2004, 1:327).

Air Force Space White Paper (1962)

The 1961 Air Force Space plan underwent revision that occurred during 1962, with
an updated document being issued in July that placed particular emphasis on manned
spaceflight even though there was no consensus on the role military personnel should

play in space. This revised plan reiterated the 1961 plans' emphasis on the Air Force's two reasons for being in space as enhancing the United States' military posture and having military patrol ability in space. It went on to stress the need to protect U.S. scientific activities in space and advocated enhanced space boosters; space weapons; developing reliable rendezvous, docking, and transfer procedures; and developing maneuverable reentry and precision recovery of spacecraft. These proposals did not gain Kennedy administration approval but provided insight into then existing institutional military space policy thinking and reappeared in modified form in future policy documents (Erickson 2005, 280–283; Spires 2004, 1:336).

The document's thinking demonstrated a more focused approach to incorporating military space policy into prevailing administration political priorities, which placed greater emphasis on supporting NASA programs. It also incorporates information learned from manned space missions such as John Glenn's (1921–) February 20, 1962 earth-orbiting mission and recognition of the technological challenges of operating in space. Applicable conclusions include strong Air Force advocacy of an aggressive military space program while acknowledging the undesirability of artificial separation between military and non-military space responsibilities; recognizing the technological and operational challenges of space systems due to the absence of gravity and atmosphere and the presence of radiation; and the emerging importance of space systems in warning of ballistic missile attack, detecting nuclear explosions, geodetic measuring, providing surface navigation assistance, and meteorological surveillance (Spires 2004, 1:339–340).

Manned Orbiting Laboratory (1963)

The Manned Orbiting Laboratory (MOL) originated as a 1961 Air Force proposal to establish an ongoing military presence in space with piloted craft, manned surveillance, and a space station. Both the Air Force and Navy participated in MOL, whose program objectives included understanding what individuals could do in space, possible defense purposes of this capability, developing the technology and equipment to improve manned and unmanned spaceflight, and relevant technology and equipment experiments. MOL was designed to support two men in orbit for 30 days and its personnel were 17 astronauts selected by DOD who were test pilots and graduates of the Aerospace Research Pilot School at Edwards Air Force Base, California (Posey 1998, 75; U.S. Congress, House Committee on Science and Technology 1985, 208).

MOL formally began with a December 10, 1963 DOD announcement giving the Air Force program responsibility if the military could define and justify a military space mission NASA was unable to perform. The laboratory was intended to be launched to a 150-mile-high orbit and astronauts would leave their Gemini capsule to move to their work area. Cape Kennedy, Florida was the initial launch site, but this was then shifted to Vandenberg Air Force Base, California to achieve enhanced coverage of the Soviet Union. These astronauts were to stay in orbit for one to two weeks with a 30-day maximum

Concept image of the Manned Orbiting Laboratory, 1960. *(NASA)*

before returning to Earth. Astronaut responsibilities aboard MOL were to photograph Soviet bloc activity and inspect and destroy hostile satellites if necessary. MOL experiments
were planned in areas such as tracking earth and space targets, electromagnetic intelligence
surveys, multispectral photography, and poststrike target assessment. Air Force objectives
were to launch an unmanned MOL in 1968 and have manned crews follow (Posey 1998,
75–76; Spires 1998, 129–130).

MOL experienced success in 1966 when the Air Force conducted a series of successful
tests, including nine on-board experiments using a Gemini capsule, and the following
year saw MOL planners complete design configuration work with a Gemini module and
Titan rocket (Spires 1998, 131). Unfortunately for MOL, these accomplishments could not
overcome congressional concern that MOL duplicated an ongoing NASA Apollo Applications Program involving lunar exploration and growing public displeasure over defense
spending due to the Vietnam War. MOL was the most expensive Air Force research and
development program that was not related to the Vietnam War. All of these factors and
DOD's growing belief that national security space missions could be accomplished with
unmanned spacecraft resulted in the program's cancellation on June 10, 1969 (U.S. Congress, House Committee on Government Operations 1966, 46; Spires 1998, 133). A more
complete analysis of MOL is provided in the next chapter.

Outer Space Treaty (1967)

The Outer Space Treaty (OST), also known as the International Agreement on Peaceful Uses of Outer Space, is officially called "Treaty on Principles Governing the Activities of States in the Exploration and Use of Outer Space, Including the Moon and Other Celestial Bodies" was signed in Washington, London, and Moscow on January 27, 1967. The intent of this agreement was to prevent participating countries from putting nuclear weapons or other weapons of mass destruction in orbit around the earth or on the moon, planets, or artificial satellites, and that human uses of the moon and other celestial bodies would be for peaceful purposes and not be used for establishing military bases, installations, or fortifications; from testing weapons; or from conducting military exercises (U.S. Department of State Bureau of Verification, Compliance, and Implementation, n.d, 1–2; U.S. Congress Senate Committee on Aeronautics and Space Sciences 1967; U.S. Congress Senate Committee on Foreign Relations 1967).

OST has served as the principal international legal mechanism and source of international political sentiment for keeping space demilitarized. It has been the subject of a variety of assessments, and since its enforcement provisions are nonexistent, the treaty has been unable to prevent states or even transnational organizations like terrorist groups from using space as a real or potential arena for military conflict (Martinez 1998; Berry 2001; Sparling 2003). More detailed information on this treaty and textual excerpts are found in chapter 5.

Transitional Developments (1960s–1970s)

Technological and strategic developments were gradually increasing military uses of space as the 1960s wore on and this was reflected in fields such as meteorology and communications. During a nationally televised interview in May 1967, the Seventh Air Force Commander general William Momyer (1916–) discussed how space assets drastically enhanced military commanders battlefield knowledge and provided data for mission planning and implementation:

> As far as I am concerned, this weather picture is probably the greatest innovation of the war. I depend on it in conjunction with the traditional forecast as a basic means of making my decisions as to whether to launch or not launch the strike. And it gives me a little better feel for what the actual weather conditions are. The satellite is something no commander has ever before had in war (Spires 1998, 169–170).

U.S. military operations in Vietnam were also assisted by imagery derived from NASA's Nimbus satellites and by images produced by the Defense Meteorological Satellite Program (DMSP), which had been providing imagery for military planners since 1962. Such timely and accurate imagery enabled U.S. military commanders to know when weather would clear over targeted areas and made it possible to use night sensor imagery to forewarn pilots of enemy camouflage such as burning rice paddies that would produce smoke intended to obscure targets. Satellite meteorological information was particularly helpful in assisting Navy efforts to destroy the strategically important Thanh Hoa Bridge in North Vietnam, and assisted planners of the 1970 raid to rescue American prisoners of war at Son Tay by allowing the raid's schedule to coincide with a break in two tropical storms moving across the South China Sea onto the Vietnamese mainland (Spires 1998, 170; U.S. Air Force 2006; 1–2).

Notable communication satellite technology enhancements at this time benefiting military operations include the then unprecedented ability to provide real-time communications from operational theaters to U.S. military commanders as far away as Washington, D.C. This made it possible for military analysts to provide almost real-time battlefield intelligence far from the battlefield, which raised questions as to who would be responsible for commanding and controlling operational forces. It also posed the problem of creating a dispersed communications system connecting several remote terminals with a single central terminus that could be vulnerable to hostile interference or attack (Spires 1998, 170–171).

Military space policy developments at this time were also affected by the growing domestic and international opposition to the Vietnam War. This opposition was reflected in displeasure at U.S. attempts to build the Safeguard and Sentinel Antiballistic Missile (ABM) systems by both the Johnson and Nixon administrations by domestic and international critics of U.S. military policies. Critics of proposed U.S. ABM weapon systems believed they were of questionable technical reliability and doubted the Soviet missile arsenal warranted deploying an ABM system (U.S. Congress 1969, 22478–22749).

ABM system proponents, however, pointed to the need to counter ongoing growth in Soviet nuclear missile development and deployment, the need for having a dispersed domestic ABM capability to decrease the possibility of a third country or crazed military commander provoking a U.S.–Soviet nuclear exchange by decapitating U.S. military command and control authorities in Washington, increasing Soviet deployments of ABM facilities in dispersed regions of that country, and the belief that deploying an ABM system could be used as a bargaining chip in U.S.–Soviet arms control negotiations (U.S. Congress 1969, 22483; U.S. National Security Council 1970, 1–4; U.S. Central Intelligence Agency 1970, 20; Schneider 1971, 33).

Both domestic and international sentiment for superpower arms control agreements proved more politically and diplomatically potent than taking prudent defensive measures against a growing Soviet nuclear arsenal. This resulted in President Richard Nixon (1913–1994) and Soviet general secretary Leonid Brezhnev (1906–1982) signing the ABM Treaty on May 26, 1972. Terms of this pact saw both nations agree to a limit of two ABM sites each with one of these sites being near the national capital and the other near an ICBM complex. Treaty provisions stated each ABM site could have 100 missiles, 100 launchers, and 15 additional launchers at test sites while regulating the types of radars at

President Richard Nixon and a Soviet official sign the Anti-Ballistic Missile (ABM) treaty on May 26, 1972. Soviet president Leonid Brezhnev stands in the background. The ABM treaty was the first significant arms limitation treaty between the United States and the Soviet Union and represented a major, if temporary, thaw in the Cold War. *(National Archives)*

each site. The ABM Treaty ultimately prevented each of these countries from defending their entire territory, which effectively negated its deterrent effect (Walker, Bernstein, and Lang 2003, B-17).

The absence of congressional support for even this minimal U.S. ABM capability caused the House of Representatives to vote to deactivate the Safeguard ABM system on October 2, 1975 and the Joint Chiefs of Staff (JCS) ordered the program terminated on February 10, 1976 (Bowen 2005, 50).

Ongoing concern over military space program duplication led Secretary of Defense Melvin Laird (1922–) to issue an updated version of *DOD Directive 5160.32* on September 8, 1970. This edict declared that space systems would be acquired and assigned according to guidelines used by other weapon systems. Existing programs were not affected by this policy, which meant that the Air Force would retain responsibility for developing and deploying space systems responsible for conducting warning and surveillance of enemy nuclear delivery capabilities and launch and orbital vehicle support operations. In addition, the other armed services could now compete on an equitable playing field for future military space programs in areas such as communications, navigation, mapping, charting, and geodesy. An ultimate result of this order was that it caused uncertainty in deciding

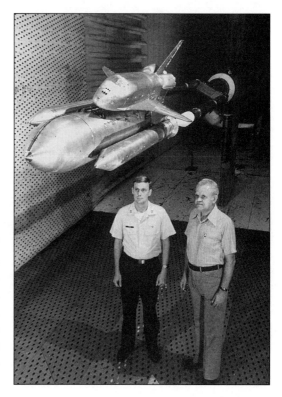

Captain William Tuck Jr., left, an Air Force test director, and Frank Urbaniak, an ARO Inc. engineer, examine a model of a space shuttle orbiter and launch vehicle prior to a transonic wind tunnel test at the Arnold Engineering Development Center, located at Arnold Air Force Base, TN, October 1, 1977. *(U.S. Department of Defense)*

which military service would be responsible for future management responsibility and operational relationships for communications, battlefield command and control, weather, and undefined major technology programs (Spires 1998, 172).

An additional noteworthy development in U.S. space policy that had military implications was the conclusion of the Apollo program and the development of the space shuttle also known as the Space Transportation System (STS) (Jenkins 1996; Heppenheimer 2002). The decision to construct the space shuttle was made by Nixon in January 1972 (Erickson 2005, 402).

The Air Force was initially skeptical about the space shuttle because of NASA's responsibility for its design and construction and due to questions about its long-term benefits. Air Force leaders initially saw the shuttle as a more cost-effective mechanism for launching larger and heavier satellites than could be done by then existing Atlas and Titan boosters. As the 1970s progressed, however, Air Force leaders came to see the shuttle as a multitasking vehicle that could preserve service interest in manned spaceflight following MOL's demise. This evolution in Air Force thinking about the shuttle was expressed in 1972 by Air Force secretary C. Robert Seamans, Jr. (1918–) who explained:

The shuttle offers the potential of improving mission flexibility and capability by on-orbit checkout of payloads, recovery of malfunctioning satellites for repair and reuse, or resupply of payloads on orbit thus extending their lifetime. Payloads would be retrieved and refurbished for reuse and improved sensors could be installed during refurbishment for added capability (Spires 1998, 181).

This rationale also became reflected in Air Force policy that the shuttle would help the Air Force fulfill its satellite surveillance and reconnaissance missions. Subsequent Air Force involvement with the shuttle program would see military requirements be incorporated into shuttle contractor design studies assessing technology, scope, timing, and cost. The Air Force would have influence in selecting launch sites and ensuring the shuttle met the technical requirements for launches with military payloads (Spires 1998, 181–184).

DOD Space Shuttle Support Operations Center (1977)

The antimilitary political and diplomatic sentiment prompting the passage of the ABM Treaty, concern over ongoing Soviet military augmentation, gradual space shuttle program development, and continuing displeasure at military space fragmentation prompted the Ford and Carter administrations to take a renewed look at space policy issues. The 1976 Soviet decision to resume antisatellite (ASAT) weapons testing, after a four-year moratorium, led to a number of U.S. policy developments that increased the role of space in U.S. military operational planning (Spires 1998, 188; Spires 2004, 1:9).

This increasing realization of space's growing military importance was reflected in a May 9, 1977 letter from Air Force chief of staff general David Jones (1921–) to Air Force command authorities. This document stressed that the Air Force affirmed that its primary responsibilities in space involve developing weapons systems, military operations, and defending the United States, protecting the free use of space by providing essential space defense capabilities, and serving as DOD's executive agent for liaison with NASA and cooperating and coordinating with that agency on activities of mutual interest (Spires 2004, 1:48).

A follow-up 1977 document to this letter saw Jones's sentiments elaborated in greater detail, presented an overview of other U.S. military services space missions, and provided a more explicit statement of Air Force military space policy and relationship with the space shuttle. Relevant document content stresses that Army and Navy space programs were limited to covering Army geodesic and land mapping efforts and ground communication terminal development and the Navy using space for long-haul communication and nuclear ballistic missile submarine navigation. The document went on to stress that Air Force space responsibilities included developing, purchasing, and launching all DOD launch vehicles; providing the only U.S. military capability for tracking Soviet satellites and for attacking hostile space systems; and developing, deploying, and operating space systems for tactical warning and surveillance (Spires 2004, 1:49–50).

Although this document did not produce any major follow-up initiative during 1977, it served as a keystone for stimulating discussion and action on subsequent space issues in the intermediate future (Spires 2004, 1:11).

Space Operations Center (1979)

During the late 1970s, Secretary of the Air Force Hans Mark (1929–) sought to create an operational orientation for space within the Air Force, which he believed would establish Air Force space preeminence within the U.S. space community. In June 1979, Mark sent a letter to Air Force chief of staff general Lew Allen (1925–) in which he urged Allen to more clearly define the Air Force's role as DOD's executive agent for space operations and to submit such a request to DOD. Mark believed that if the Air Force became the executive agent it could replace NASA as the shuttle's lead agency and become the only organization capable of determining future space transportation. Mark received authorization from Secretary of Defense Harold Brown (1927–) to develop an organizational plan for operating the DOD space system including proposing the establishment of a DOD Space Operations Center, but was unable to have the Air Force chosen as executive military space agent (Spires 2004, 1:11, 58).

Mark then proceeded to try to get the Air Force executive agent authorization from existing Joint Chiefs of Staff (JCS) publications with particular emphasis on JCS Publication 2 *United Action Armed Forces,* which described Air Force responsibility for national air defense (U.S. Joint Chiefs of Staff, 2001). The Air Force wanted updated versions of JCS Publication 2 to accept the term "aerospace" as part of Air Force defense responsibilities because it incorporated both air and space into air force mission responsibilities. Aerospace, as a term, had a controversial history in Air Force doctrinal development with

Hans Mark served as Secretary of the Air Force from 1979–1981. *(NASA)*

proponents and opponents of the term in Air Force leadership (Jennings 1990). However, the Air Force's judge advocate general (JAG) major general Walter D. Reed refused the Air Force's request to include aerospace within Air Force mission responsibilities because it would usurp secretary of Defense prerogatives to take such action (Spires 2004, 1:11–12, 59–60.

The Air Force achieved DOD executive agent status in 1981 as the following entry documents.

Draft DOD Directive 5160.32 Executive Agent for DOD Space Program (1981)

Air Force efforts to officially include space operations as a service mission component had been included in *Air Force Manual 1–1: Functions and Basic Doctrine of the United States Air Force* published February 14, 1979. This document asserted that space support, force enhancement, and space defense were the three missions Air Force space operations should execute. Space support operations involved launch and recovery activities, orbital support, and satellite surveillance and control. This document went on to assert that using space systems multiplied the effectiveness of surface, sea, and aerospace forces through conducting global surveillance, serving as penetration aids, delivering global communications capabilities, providing precise navigational and positioning data, and presenting detailed and current meteorological information (Futrell 1989; 2:690).

The Air Force's 1979 failure to achieve DOD executive agent for space status caused it to revise its efforts in this regard. This revision involved efforts to update the 1970 version of *DOD Directive 5160.32*. A proposed updated 1981 draft version of this directive proposed designating the secretary of the Air Force as executive agent for DOD space programs. Document compilers believed this official could serve as a single DOD contact source for military space activities and be able to coordinate with other military space entities. As "executive agent" the secretary of the Air Force could provide a centralized and equitable focus for space funding requirements, plans and programs, research and development, and space acquisition.

This proposal appeared at the onset of the Reagan administration, at a time when the new administration was beginning a major defense space policy review. Because of increasing momentum for creating an operational Air Force space command, key Air Force policymakers decided not to present this proposal although arguments supporting Air Force space executive agent authority appeared in future military space policy documents (Spires 2004, 1:12).

Sample features from this proposed revision of *Directive 5160.32* include the secretary of the Air Force being designated the executive agent for DOD space programs, the secretary of Defense being able to assign individual space systems segments to other DOD departments and agencies as appropriate, military satellite communications (MILSATCOM) responsibilities being assigned by the office of the secretary of Defense in accordance with

DODD (Department of Defense Directive) 5105.44, and other responsibilities for space systems and programs being assumed by the Air Force unless otherwise determined by the secretary of Defense (Spires 2004, 1:61).

MILSTAR Satellite (1982)

The late 1970s and early 1980s also saw military planners look for a strategic satellite system capable of supporting U.S. nuclear forces. The system that evolved out of these planners visions was MILSTAR, which was designed to avoid potential Soviet ASAT threats by orbiting in a supersynchronous orbit of 110,000 miles and operating in the extremely high-frequency range to provide additional bandwidth for space spectrum antijam techniques. On January 11, 1982 Deputy Secretary of Defense Frank Carlucci (1930–) sent a memorandum to the chairman of the joint chiefs of staff and military department secretaries directing them to give MILSTAR high priority in their service planning. A related DOD document on this subject called for initial MILSTAR operational capability by 1987 and a final operational capability by 1992 (Spires 2004, 2:1113, 1185, 1188).

MILSTAR represented the newest generation in a nearly four-decade old U.S. military satellite program (Arnold 2002). President Ronald Reagan (1911–2004) assigned MILSTAR

Artist's rendering of MILSTAR, a strategic satellite system launched in 1994. (U.S. Air Force)

"Highest National Priority" status in 1983, enabling it to proceed with few funding restrictions. The program experienced various cost overruns and bureaucratic administrative problems, which incurred congressional displeasure. These delays kept the first MILSTAR satellite from being launched until February 7, 1994 with fewer satellites, without a wide variety of survivability features, and with fewer ground control stations (Spires 2004, 2:1113; U.S. General Accounting Office 1992; U.S. General Accounting Office 1998).

Air Force Space Command Established (1982)

A far more important military space policy development than Air Force efforts to establish itself as DOD's executive space agent was the 1982 establishment of Air Force Space Command (AFSPACOM). Efforts toward such an organization with such an explicit mission focus within the Air Force had been ongoing for a number of years. An operational impetus toward such efforts was recognition that space counted for over 70% of military communications by the early 1980s and that all major U.S. military commanders relied upon satellites for command and control, intelligence, weather, navigation, and other crucial functions (Parrington 1989, 56). Preliminary steps in this regard included the inactivation of Aerospace Defense Command on October 1, 1979 and Mark's approval of the Air Force's decision to split the functions of Air Force Systems Command's Space and Missile Systems Organization (SAMSO) with the Ballistic Missile Organization and Space Mission (Spires 1998, 196).

Additional pertinent organizational changes saw the North American Air Defense Command (NORAD) Space Defense Center replaced with an operationally oriented center to be located near Cheyenne Mountain, Colorado. September 1981 saw the creation of the Directorate for Space Operations within the office of the Air Force's deputy chief of staff for Operations, Plans, and Readiness. Additional impetus to create an AFSPACOM came in late 1981 from Reagan administration efforts to modernize U.S. strategic nuclear forces. Further incentive for Air Force policymakers to promulgate an explicit space orientation came from Representative Ken Kramer (Republican of Colorado) (1942–) of Colorado Springs who introduced a resolution calling on the Air Force to rename itself the "aerospace force" and to create a separate space command (Spires 1998, 197–198, 201–202).

Air Force chief of staff general Lew Allen (1925–) wanted to control the process of centralizing Air Force space efforts as much as possible but had to contend with pressures from Congress as to the location of a space command and from other Air Force organizations concerned that a centralized space command might affect their corporate futures. During May 1982 Air Force secretary Verne Orr (1916–) appeared before Congress rejecting Kramer's proposal to call the Air Force the Aerospace Force and mentioned that a space command study was underway and nearly complete. On June 21, 1982 Allen announced that the new AFSPACOM would become effective on September 1, 1982 with headquarters at Colorado Springs (Spires 1998, 205; Futrell 1989, 2:697).

Air Force Space Command is responsible for centralizing Air Force space programs and assets and delivering them to operational users. The Command Post of the North American Air Defense Command (NORAD) Cheyenne Mountain Complex, April 1, 1984. Computer generated images are projected on two large display screens. *(U.S. Department of Defense)*

AFSPACOM was assigned responsibility for managing and operating space assets, centralizing planning, consolidating requirements, delivering operational support, and providing a closer interaction between research and development activities and Air Force space program operational users. AFSPACOM's commander was also charged with commanding NORAD and Aerospace Defense Command. May 1983 saw groundbreaking for a consolidated space operations center at Peterson Air Force Base near Colorado Springs, which would become responsible for controlling operational spacecraft missions and managing DOD space shuttle flights (Futrell 1989, 2:697).

Specific justification for AFSPACOM creation was described to a congressional committee as deriving from a Soviet threat in space, the United States' increasing dependence on space systems, an increasing national space resource commitment, the need to fully utilize the space shuttle to enhance manned space presence, and President Reagan's July 4, 1982 announcement that the U.S. space program's most important goal was strengthening national security (Futrell 1989, 2:698).

Orr provided a more lengthy explanation for AFSPACOM's creation emphasizing how increasing U.S. dependence on space and Soviet military policy developments were driving this U.S. decision:

As in the 1920s when we were just learning about the possible uses of airpower, today we are still learning how space based capabilities can contribute to our national defense posture. And *while some might view that space can be kept a weapons-free sanctuary free of military systems, history tells us that each time new technological opportunities present themselves, nations invariably employ them to avoid being placed in an inferior defense position.* Our nation will continue to pursue avenues to foster the peaceful use of space consistent with the President's national space policy. We and the Soviets are now… highly dependent on space for many military support functions, e.g., warning, communications and command and control. This dependence will undoubtedly grow. At a minimum then we must ensure that our space systems can operate in a hostile wartime environment, survive and continue our defense requirements. As national use of and investment in space increases, protection of our resources will be essential. Because such protection introduces the possibility of space-to-space, space-to-earth, and earth-to-space operations, it is in our national interest to be prepared to accomplish them. Prudent preparations such as ASAT, also give us a hedge against technological surprise, and ensure that we are not placed in a permanent position of disadvantage by Soviet initiatives (U.S. Congress, House Committee on Appropriations, Subcommittee on the Department of Defense 1983, 2:129–130).

Creation of AFSPACOM did not stop the desire of other armed services to develop their own space operational commands as evidenced by the Navy's 1983 decision to establish a Naval Space Command and long-standing Army space programs. The following year saw DOD accept a unified space command with Air Force, Army, Marine Corps, and Navy participation. A November 30, 1984 DOD press release announced activation of U.S. Space Command (USSPACECOM) as part of the military's growing emphasis on increasing cooperation between branches of the armed services, which included the emerging unified combatant command structure now part of U.S. military organizational efforts. This press release declared that this USSPACECOM would "better serve U.S. interests and the needs of our allies worldwide by providing an organizational structure that will centralize operational responsibilities for more effective use of military space systems" (Futrell 1989, 2:699–700; Locher 2002; Walker, Bernstein, and Lang 2003, B-1-B-53).

AFSPACOM remains a critical part of Air Force and U.S. military space policy planning a quarter century after its inception. It has experienced advances and setbacks during its institutional evolution such as management structure and acquisition practice problems and will continue to be a key player in formulating U.S. military space doctrine and policy (Stumborg 2006; U.S. General Accounting Office 1990; U.S. General Accounting Office 2000).

Military Space Doctrine (1982)

Formal activation of AFSPACOM provided further impetus to ongoing Air Force efforts to integrate space into official service military doctrine such as *Air Force Manual (AFM) 1.1* published in 1979. An example of such efforts to incorporate space power into

Air Force doctrinal practice came when the author of a document prepared for the 1981 Air Force Academy Military Space Doctrine Symposium asserted "military space doctrine should address... fundamental possibilities for space warfare now in the hope that we can plan more deliberately and prepare more decisively for the uncertain events that lie ahead." (Spires 1998, 206-207; Futrell 1989, 2:700).

Air Force efforts to incorporate space into its doctrinal documents had begun as far back as 1977 and culminated in the October 1982 release of *AFM 1.6 Military Space Doctrine* sponsored by General Charles A. Gabriel the new Air Force chief of staff (1928–2003). This document described space as the ultimate high ground, the outer reaches of the Air Force's operational medium, and an environment useful for conducting Air Force missions. It also asserted that aerospace power provided credible war-fighting capability from the battlefield to the highest orbit and that Air Force military interests included performing war-fighting missions with ground or space-based weapons systems that were consistent with national security requirements and overall national policy. Another crucial point of this document was that a modus operandi of U.S. space doctrine was ensuring free access to and transit through space for peaceful purposes for both military and civilian users. This required the United States possessing capable and prepared military capabilities so force could be used, if conflict was unavoidable, to achieve results favorable to the United States (Spires 1998, 206–207; Futrell 1989, 2:700).

Pertinent passages from this critical document outlining a military space policy role for the United States and how scientific and technological change now made this possible include:

> Space is the ultimate high ground. As the Air Force continues to lead in the development of space doctrine, strategy, and operations, great technical and management challenges lie ahead. The magnitude and direction of Soviet military space effort demand that we meet these challenges, employing the full range of aerospace assets in our nation's defense. . . Our scientific, technological, and industrial communities have established a resource base from which this nation can logically proceed with expanded space operations. Within that framework, our doctrine and strategy must evolve to provide the vision, focus, and direction to guide the development of future space programs, systems, and operational practice (Spires 2004, 1:65).

Additional explicit mission oriented tasks of how the Air Force will execute this emerging aerospace military doctrine stressed topics such as military space operations needing to contribute to U.S. interests in all environments, the Air Force needing to develop, operate, sustain, and deploy space systems to deter or resolve conflicts in favor of the United States, and being able to provide space-based surveillance, warning, and attack assessment to alert national command authorities and military commanders of potential attacks against the United States, its allies, and their forces (Spires 2004, 1:68).

An additional section of *AFM 1.6* includes various management, pedagogical, training, workforce, and general technological infrastructure requirements for implementing this doctrinal capability. These include promoting innovation to exploit emerging science and technology advances, making sure space programs are understood and fiscally sustainable, developing and maintaining pedagogical training programs for individual's leading space programs, and developing the required technology base, research and development programs, and acquisition policies to meet DOD, NASA, and other government space requirements (Spires 2004, 1:69).

Air Force Space Plan (1983)

Following the 1982 creation of AFSPACOM and publication that same year of *AFM 1.6,* the beginning of 1983 saw the Air Force seek to develop its own Air Force Space Plan. This document was published in March 1983 and described general military uses of space and identified four terms for space operations: space control, space support, force enhancement, and force application. Air Force Space Plan described space control as maintaining freedom of action in space and denying such autonomy to an enemy. Space support meant deploying, maintaining, and sustaining space equipment and personnel through space launch and orbital repair and recovery. Force enhancement encompassed defense support attributes including communication, navigation, and weather to enhance terrestrial and space-based forces. Force application involved performing combat operations in space.

Successful plan implementation proved problematic due to tension within Air Force organizations such as AFSPACOM and Air Force Systems Command over interpreting mission area functions. An additional problem with the plan occurred in October 1986 when the Air Force decided to separate AFSPACOM and USSPACECOM. This event saw AFSPACOM leadership going to a two-star general instead of a four-star general who did not have daily operational responsibility for crucial space resources, and reflected continuing disagreement within the Air Force on proper roles and missions and uncertainty about where space stood in Air Force policy planning (Spires 2004, 1:156–157).

Command Arrangement for Space (1983)

President Reagan's March 23, 1983 announcement about the proposed Strategic Defense Initiative (SDI) missile defense program provided critical support to planning and support for a unified space plan (Spires 1998, 218; Baucom 1992, 171–196). Following AFSPACOM's creation its commander general James Hartinger (1925–2000) proposed creating a unified command to centralize military space command activities, which received additional emphasis with the emergence of SDI. Gabriel agreed with Hartinger's objective and on June 7, 1983 these individuals provided the JCS with rationale for a unified command urging the JCS to seek presidential approval to take immediate action creating a unified space command to consolidate space control, space support, force application, and force enhancement operational control at Peterson Air Force Base, CO (Spires 2004, 1:481, 780).

This proposal was sent by Secretary of Defense Casper Weinberger (1917–2006) to national security advisor Robert McFarlane (1937–) on October 4, 1983, and in late November Weinberger requested presidential approval to establish a unified command for space on October 1, 1985 asserting that the JCS believed this would be the best way to ensure SDI's success. In late 1984, Reagan approved Weinberger's recommendation and US-SPACECOM was activated on September 23, 1985 (Spires 2004, 1:481, 780–781; Piotrowski 1987; Lambeth 2004).

Boost Surveillance and Tracking System and Space Surveillance and Tracking System (1984)

Concern over the aging Defense Support Program (DSP) satellite fleet in the early 1980s lead military planners to look at possible replacement systems to enhance the timeliness of U.S. warning and response to hostile ballistic missile launches (Richelson 1999, 95–109). During the early 1980s the Air Force studied a DSP replacement program called "Advanced Warning System," which was absorbed in 1984 by the Strategic Defense Initiative Organization (SDIO), which was the agency directed to implement SDI. SDI changed this program's name to Boost Surveillance and Tracking System (BSTS) while also creating a complimentary program the Space Surveillance and Tracking System (SSTS). Both of these programs were charged with developing ballistic missile surveillance, detection, tracking, and assessment capabilities with the Air Force ordered to develop relevant technology with long lead times, to prepare program plans, and to evaluate system conceptual designs and their survivability (Spires 2004, 2:1097).

A May 7, 1984 memorandum prepared for Orr set out requirements for BSTS and SSTS programs emphasizing assorted attributes including providing ballistic missile tactical warning/attack assessments; satellite attack warning/verification; satellite targeting for antisatellite operations; and SDI surveillance, acquisition, tracking, and kill assessment (SATKA). Orr's memorandum also stressed the importance of technology demonstration efforts and encouraged the Air Force to identify and proceed with developing relevant technologies such as long-life cryogenic refrigerators, focal plane array manufacturing technology, and radiation hardened electronics (Spires 2004, 2:1130–1131).

BSTS failed to reach deployment during the later 1980s due to immature technology and cost problems, while SSTS evolved and eventually was incorporated into an existing missile defense agency program (Smith 2005, 2; U.S. Missile Defense Agency 2006, 1).

Defense Space Launch Strategy (1984)

During July 1982, President Reagan confirmed that the space shuttle remained the United States' primary space launch vehicle. Despite this declaration, Air Force officials

A Delta II rocket in the Strategic Defense Initiative program lifts off beside its launch tower September 29, 1989. The 1984 Defense Launch Strategy sought to diversify U.S. military space launch capabilities by allowing such launches to be carried out by vehicles other than the space shuttle. *(U.S. Department of Defense)*

remained concern that there be an adequate supply of expendable boosters for military launching needs. This concern was articulated during 1983 by Air Force Systems Command Space Division commander lieutenant general Richard C. Henry (1925–), who was concerned about the imminent shutdown of Titan and Atlas rocket production lines and reliance on a costly shuttle fleet with reduced operational schedules. Henry argued that the shuttle was most suitable for missions where there was clear need for human intervention and that manned activity was not required for satellites sent to geosynchronous earth orbit. In Henry's view, the solution to this predicament was investing in a mixed fleet of expendable launch vehicles (ELVs) from both government and commercial service providers (Spires 2004, 2:736, 890–893).

NASA officials, placed on the defensive by Henry's concerns, defended their agency's relationship with the military saying the military had acquired experience with unmanned space systems while neglecting manned spaceflight. These officials went on to urge that DOD make optimum use of the manned spaceflight capabilities developed by NASA and lobbied against military attempts to use both the shuttle and commercial launch capabilities.

The military was not persuaded by these NASA entreaties and succeeded in convincing Weinberger to issue a Defense Space Launch Strategy, which was published on January 23, 1984 (Spires 2004, 2:737, 894).

The Defense Space Launch Strategy agreed with the military's desire to have military launches done by the shuttle and commercial service providers, although it said the shuttle remained the primary launch system for routine DOD payloads. It used a contingency planning scenario justifying this mixed launch strategy while seeking to look at longer term military space launch requirements by stressing the need for the United States to have complementary launch systems in the event of unanticipated technical or operational problems and to have a launch system suitable for operating in crisis or conflict situations if the U.S. mainland were directly attacked (Spires 2004, 2:895).

The Defense Space Launch Strategy went on to mention that while commercial ELVs were affordable and available for DOD space launch requirements into the early 1990s, other DOD launch capabilities to meet requirements beyond then must be evaluated and validated to ensure that future national security space missions were not restricted by inadequate launch capability (Spires 2004, 2:895–896).

The tragic January 28, 1986 explosion of the shuttle Challenger that resulted in the shuttle fleet being grounded for over two and a half years proved the wisdom of adopting this mixed ELV strategy (National Aeronautics and Space Administration, 2006, 2).

Blue Ribbon Panel on the Future of the Air Force in Space (1988)

The Challenger tragedy and subsequent Titan booster launch failures prompted the Air Force to reexamine their involvement with the shuttle and their commitment to space.

In 1987 Air Force secretary Edward C. Aldridge (1938–) issued a white paper that was very critical of Air Force space policy and leadership, arguing that it had not shown institutional purpose or responsibility toward space, that there had been few truly new Air Force space initiatives, and that the absence of strong aggressive Air Force space program advocacy has created a leadership vacuum that organizations such as the Office of the Secretary of Defense (OSD), SDIO, USSPACECOM, and other armed services are moving to fill (Spires 2004, 1:80, 158).

This white paper convinced Air Force chief of staff general Larry Welch (1934–) to establish a "Blue Ribbon Panel on Space Roles and Missions" consisting of senior representatives from major Air Force commands during the spring of 1988. Welch justified another space study based on significant space policy statements emanating from DOD, the White House, technical advances, SDI's potential, and friction and funding problems with other military services. Welch was also concerned that although the Air Force had played a critical space role for 30 years and received 50% of the U.S. space budget and 75% of DOD controlled space funding that it was uncertain about its future space mission. He believed that the commitment of Air Force leaders to institutionalize space responsibilities was not shared throughout the service. This lack of commitment, in Welch's opinion, stemmed from not understanding space systems and their potential and a multiple user approach to space systems, which weakened space in the military budget process (Spires 2004, 1:158–159).

Consequently, Welch directed his panel to examine the Air Force's future role in space and near and long-term commitments needed to achieve the requisite support for combatant commanders. The panel issued its report in August 1988, which said Air Force space policy should be revised and reflect realistic capabilities and aspirations. It reaffirmed the four mission functions described earlier in the October 1983 Space Command arrangement document, and it asserted that AFSPACOM must continue to play a central role as advocate, operator, and single manager for space support, while USSPACECOM should normalize its relationship with AFSPACOM by returning to it operational control of peacetime space assets (Spires 2004, 1:159).

Relevant report determinations include the assertion that space power will play as decisive a role in future combat operations as airpower currently does, that the evolution of space power from providing combat support to space weapons is approaching and will take years instead of decades, that the Air Force's future is inextricably linked to space, and that implementation of this updated role requires the Air Force's corporate commitment, broad involvement, and the vision to make it a reality (Spires 2004, 1:390–395; Spires 1998, 234–238).

During February 1989, Air Force headquarters issued plan to implement Blue Ribbon panel recommendations. This plan proclaimed "the Air Force *is and will be* responsible for the global employment of military power above the earth's surface." It charged AFSPACOM with developing a "Space Roadmap" for updating the Air Force Space Plan and integrating existing Air Force space operations. This roadmap was intended to project military space policy into the 21st century by linking space systems to war-fighting requirements, global strategy, and the four military mission control areas of space control, space support, force enhancement, and force application from the 1983 Air Force Space Plan. This implementation plan maintained that space power would achieve equal importance to airpower in future combat, that the Air Force must prepare for space power to evolve from combat support to encompass all military capabilities, and that this roadmap must produce a coherent Air Force space role (Spires 2004, 1:159).

Transitional Developments prior to the Clinton Administration (1989–1992)

The George H. W. Bush administration saw the final decline and collapse of the Soviet Union, which would appear to have ended the role Soviet military space policy would play in prompting U.S. military space programs. This would not be the case though, as a series of domestic and global events in the early 1990s influenced and accelerated U.S. efforts to develop a viable military space program.

A significant domestic event was the October 1, 1990 Air Force Systems Command transfer of its launch-related centers, ranges, bases, and Delta II and Atlas E missions to AFSPACOM, which was part of overall Air Force efforts to enhance the integration and normalization of space operations throughout the Air Force. This event also represented

Patriot Tactical Air Defense Missile System is an air defense guided missile system manufactured by Raytheon that gained fame in the Persian Gulf War as the "Scud killer." Reports after the war revealed the relative inaccuracy of the Patriot against Saddam Hussein's Scud missiles. *(U.S. Department of Defense)*

a major step forward in the Air Force assuming an operational war-fighting perspective on space (Spires 1998, 240–241).

The most important of these events enhancing space as a major military operational player was Operation Desert Storm, which saw the United States lead an international military coalition to drive Iraqi armed forces out of Kuwait during January–February 1991. This conflict saw space assets play a critical role in ensuring the success of coalition operations. Space assets were used to target Iraqi military capabilities; these targets were, in turn, destroyed by precision-guided munitions using satellite data to guide them to their targets. Coalition forces made use of satellite reconnaissance to track and attempt to destroy launched Iraqi Scud missiles using Patriot missiles. Furthermore navigation, early warning, and Desert Storm communication objectives were all advanced using space assets. In addition, postwar assessments determined that space-based weather operations were critical in areas in providing information about data sparse combat areas, that timely data delivery was critical for airborne, ground, and sea-based operations, that having mobile meteorological satellite control capability was critical for combat operational success, and that tactical users in the field should have access to weather data (U.S. Air Force Space

Command 1991, 1; U.S. Department of Defense 1992; 543–575, 801–809; Rip and Hasik 2002, 334–357; Chun 2001; 112, 198–205).

An assessment of space's role in Desert Storm was provided by AFSPACOM commander general Thomas Moorman (born approximately 1940–) who stressed:

Desert Storm was a watershed event for space systems. Satellites, and the ground systems and people trained to control them, played a crucial role in the outcome of the conflict. Space owned the battlefield. We had a robust on-orbit constellation and the inherent spacecraft flexibility to alter our operations to support specific needs of the terrestrial warfighter (Spires 1998, 260).

Desert Storm also served as culmination of gradual increases in military uses of space, which occurred during the 1980s. MILSATCOM were important in the 1982 British Falkland Islands campaign against Argentina, in the U.S. 1983 Operation Urgent Fury campaign in Grenada. Space systems also provided vital communications links and mission planning information in the 1986 Operation Eldorado Canyon bombing of Libya, GPS satellites were first used during Operation Earnest Will in 1988 to assist ships and helicopters conducting minesweeping operations in the Persian Gulf, and during 1989 satellites provided important communication links and weather data for Operation Just Cause in Panama (Spires 1998, 244–245).

Integrating space policy throughout the Air Force remained an ongoing service organizational challenge. An October 1991 report by the Air Force Office of Inspector General complained that the Air Force had failed to effectively normalize space within the service and reserve roles and missions issues throughout the broader military community. This document went on to maintain that Air Force space policy tenets received insufficient acceptance and that, despite Desert Storm's space accomplishments, the idea of space being a decisive factor in current and future combat operations was still viewed as excessively controversial and futuristic. The report also asserted that the Air Force had not accepted space as a critical component of mission planning or an equal partner with terrestrial and atmospheric components of the Air Force's mission (Spires 2004, 1:160).

Military assessments of space also recognized that, despite the successes of space-based assets during Desert Storm, many deficiencies remained before large-scale space-based military operations could be performed. Air Force analysts recognized that existing space systems were insufficient for tactical use, that ground personnel generally lacked the requisite equipment and training to make optimum use of space capabilities, and Air Force leaders recognized that they must provide leadership in efforts to modernize space infrastructure, achieve technical enhancements to space systems, and increase space awareness throughout their service and U.S. armed forces (Spires 1998, 260).

These efforts to achieve continued growth in military awareness of the space continued as the Clinton administration began in 1993 and were first reflected in the work of another blue ribbon panel report on the Air Force's future in space.

Blue Ribbon Panel on Air Force in Space in the 21st Century (1991)

Air Force chief of staff general Merrill McPeak (1936–) established a second blue ribbon panel during the fall of 1992 lead by Moorman to address internal space roles and missions while also examining how events such as Desert Storm affected current and future Air Force space roles and missions. The panel issued its report in January 1993, and it served as the beginning of a new assertiveness about space and declared that the Air Force would be key to national strategy of projecting military power rapidly and decisively with expeditionary forces and that space would provide the United States with "global eyes and ear" and corresponding reach and power capabilities (Spires 2004, 1:160–161).

Examples of major report recommendations, which covered a multifaceted array of mission responsibilities including the growing importance of battlefield information management and control, included: that the Air Force become the sole manager for DOD space acquisition and commit to reducing the cost of space systems; that the Air Force advocate and support national efforts to sustain the space industrial base; that the Air Force lead development of a new space-lift system for meeting unmanned military, civil, and commercial needs; that the Air Force lead a comprehensive effort to develop and operate ASAT and ballistic missile defense capabilities; and that the Air Force develop the doctri-

Gen. Merrill McPeak, Air Force Chief of Staff (1936–). McPeak served as Air Force Chief of Staff during the early 1990s overseeing transformations in Air Force operational capabilities and promoting the growing importance of space in military operations. *(U.S. Department of Defense)*

nal concepts and capabilities to gain battlefield information dominance and establish an Air Force Space Warfare Center, review DOD and intelligence community classification and information dissemination policies and practices, and make integrated aerospace employment a fundamental principle reflected in all Air Force education and training programs (Spires 2004, 1:400–414).

The Space Warfare Center recommended by the blue ribbon panel was activated on December 8, 1993 to advance Air Force and joint and combined space warfare through diverse innovation, testing, tactics, and development and training programs. This facility was renamed the Space Innovation and Development Center on March 8, 2006 (U.S. Air Force Space Command 2006, 1).

McPeak endorsed blue ribbon panel findings by the spring of 1993 and initiated another program to ensure the Air Force gained military space leadership, which was known as *Spacecast 2020,* described below (Spires 2004, 1:162).

Spacecast 2020 (1994)

Spacecast 2020 was a series of studies produced by Air University, the Air Force's professional military educational institution, during 1994 (U.S. Air University, Center for Strategy and Technology, 1994(a)). These studies sought to link existing and emerging space technologies in a coherent manner with national security missions. They also sought to reinforce Air Force space leadership and for that service to begin taking operational leadership of space (Carns 1995, 4–7).

Participants in this project included representatives from all U.S. military space commands, scientists, private sector industry, and the research community. Eighteen papers were produced by *Spacecast 2020* participants covering the broad categories of global presence, global reach, and global power. These papers stressed issues such as space transportation, the international economic competitiveness of the U.S. commercial space launch industry, and critical space industries and technologies in areas such as information architecture, space-based lasers with surveillance and counterforce capability, space-lift vehicles, and relevant professional military education (PME) requirements of a space-oriented military (Spires 2004, 1:162–163; Johnson 1993).

These reports were presented on June 22, 1994. The executive summary document stressed the traditional military importance of holding the high ground by maintaining that military space power provided unparalleled perspective and extremely rapid access to the earth's surface. Exploiting these advantages would have a major impact on intelligence, communications, command and control, navigation, force application, and other critical military operational aspects. It also mentioned that it provided the ability to "see over the next hill," which can reduce uncertainty and insecurity while promoting stability. This executive summary also contended that the United States needed to pursue a number of technological capabilities for optimal exploitation of space's high ground. These capabilities included existing ones, such as renewable space launch, to visionary or utopian capabilities, such as defending earth against asteroids in earth-intersecting orbits (Air University, Center for Strategy and Technology 1994(b), 3).

Numerous recommendations were made by *Spacecast 2020* participants in a variety of military operational areas. Two areas that are covered here include operational analysis and PME. Report compilers made the following recommendations for what they saw as the highest value space systems in these areas:

- Creating an integrated-demand architecture for capitalizing on global presence and providing the global view information required by military combatants and leaders.
- Developing a transatmospheric vehicle for space lift and global reach.
- Developing a multifunctional space-based laser system for global power counter-force and surveillance operations.
- Developing critical technologies contained within these systems including: high performance computing, micromechanical devices, and materials technology including various metals classes, ceramics, and carbon and ceramic composites (Air University 1994(b), 19–20).

Spacecast 2020 also examined the education and training that would be required for military space forces in the future. PME recommendations, whose relevance remains more than a decade, later include:

1. Protect future research sources by immediately stopping creation of print-only documents and publications at military educational and research institutions.
2. Begin to place all books and research papers online for easy access by military and civilian researchers.
3. Standardize, maintain, and enforce skills required in 2020 by requiring all PME participants to take technology orientation courses or test out of them.
4. Reinforce the status of PME higher learning institutions by designating them as centers for solutions to real-world problems. Incorporate more think-tank studies into military curriculum and take the experiences from *Spacecast 2020* and link them to all military and civilian education centers.
5. Encourage local units to develop their own PME and on-the-job training programs by recognizing such local program development as a pedagogical asset.
6. Continually monitor development of emerging technologies by regularly polling educational technology leaders.
7. Initiate PME system institutions by establishing direct links between military research institutions, laboratories, and staff colleges. Such links will enhance synergy between researchers, educators, and those using research results. Also flatten information distribution by sharing information at all organizational levels.
8. Prepare for future classrooms by reengineering them, including integrating more technology into classrooms and changing educational processes and methods.

9. Incorporate emerging technologies by taking advantage of civilian educational technological advances in interactive software and multimedia simulations.
10. Begin connecting individuals to the PME system by operating and linking education and training electronic bulletin boards at Air University and corresponding educational units in other services (Air University, Center for Strategy and Technology 1994(a), L-39-L-44).

Electronic access to *Spacecast 2020* is provided through Air University's Center for Strategy and Technology website (http://csat.au.af.mil/2020/) and the Federation of American Scientists website (http://www.fas.org/spp/military/docops/usaf/2020/).

New World Vistas (1995)

A complementary study to *Spacecast 2020* around this time period was *New World Vistas.* This study was commissioned by Secretary of the Air Force Sheila Widnall (1938–) and Air Force chief of staff general Ronald Fogleman (1942–), who directed the Air Force's Scientific Advisory Board (SAB) and other Air Force entities such as the U.S. Air Force Academy and Air University who participated in this endeavor to look at the Air Force's future. The initiative leading to what became a 15-volume compendium called *New World Vistas* was initiated in a two-page directive from Widnall and Fogleman to the SAB in November 1994. The study was inspired and influenced by the von Karman *New Horizons* study mentioned earlier in this chapter (Daso 1999, 70–71).

Widnall insisted that the report should examine the involvement of multiple services, simulation and modeling opportunities, and explore areas where drastic technological changes might affect the Air Force. A series of meetings were held at various locales in the United States during 1995 where panel participants brainstormed before presenting their report in December 1995 with public release beginning on January 31, 1996 (Daso 1999, 71–74).

SAB began preparing *New World Vistas* with the following assumptions about the existing technological and strategic environment. These included: the Air Force being required to fight at long distances from the United States with some operations being staged directly from the continental United States; the Air Force being prepared to fight or conduct mobility and special operations anywhere on short notice; that weapons are highly accurate, minimize collateral damage, and have minimal delivery and acquisition costs; the necessity of weapons delivering platforms to be lethal and capable of surviving hostile attacks; recognizing that future adversaries could be organized national militaries or terrorist groups; anticipating that targets could be fixed, mobile, or well-concealed and include geographic battlefields ranging from jungles to cities; the knowledge that adversary military capabilities will improve steadily and be difficult to anticipate; that the Air Force must detect and destroy chemical, biological, and nuclear weapons and their production centers; and that the number of Air Force personnel will decrease requiring optimization of individual performance (U.S. Air Force Scientific Advisory Board 1995, 5).

Sheila Widnall was President Bill Clinton's secretary of the Air Force from 1993 until 1997, the first woman to head a military service. *(U.S. Department of Defense)*

A key hypothesis of *New World Vistas* was that the realm of military conflict could shift from the earth's atmosphere into space and even the then emerging world of cyberspace. An outgrowth of this assessment was that national commercial communications and information systems will become increasingly interlinked with military counterparts and that advanced sensors and data-processing capabilities now give military commanders unprecedented detailed information on global operating conditions (Grier 1996, 20).

New World Vistas focused on specific technologies required to produce desired capabilities in the following six areas: Global Awareness, Dynamic Planning and Execution Control, Global Mobility in War and Peace, Projection of Lethal and Sublethal Power, Space Operations, and People. Where space operations are concerned SAB made a number of recommendations. These include using distributed satellite constellations relying on single or dual purpose satellites, reducing the time from satellite to launch to two years, using commercial vehicles to launch most military satellites, reassessing dedicated military systems like MILSTAR, examining different ways to protect satellite systems in the future, and ending the selective availability of Global Positioning System (GPS) satellites (U.S. Air Force Scientific Advisory Board 1995, 57–64).

More specific recommendations were provided in supplemental *New World Vistas* reports in areas such as information warfare, distributed satellite systems, communications, global positioning, space control, force projection, and related topics. Sample recommendations in these areas include: developing specific roadmaps to exploit commercial communications, positioning, environmental, and reconnaissance systems to assure their accessibility from daily peacetime operations through major regional conflicts; the Air Force developing and implementing a global terrestrial and satellite communications architecture built on DOD and commercial capabilities; possessing GPS systems with time transfer accuracies of a nanosecond or less to synchronize future communication and information; the Air Force ensuring that its most critical space assets are safe from attack by other nations, rogue groups, and major powers; the Air Force broadening the use of space to incorporate direct force projection against surface, airborne, and space targets; developing space munitions capable of precision strikes against surface and airborne targets; and working with other U.S. armed services to exploit virtual reality implementations to make space support more comprehensible to political leaders and war fighters by allowing these individuals to participate in a space-terrestrial operations continuum (U.S. Air Force Scientific Advisory Board 1996, vi–xi).

Rumsfeld Commission Ballistic Missile Defense (1996)

Iraq's use of Scud missiles during Operation Desert Storm, although failing to achieve military success for them, made U.S. and other international defense policymakers aware of emerging ballistic missile threats from developing countries following the Cold War (Nolan 1991; Chow 1993; Cunningham 1994).

This U.S. concern over missile proliferation focused on countries such as Iran, Iraq, India, Pakistan, and North Korea during the 1990s and was reflected in Section 721 of the fiscal year 1997 Intelligence Authorization Act. The act required the CIA to report to Congress every six months on foreign countries that had acquired dual-use (civilian and military) technologies that could be used to develop or produce weapons of mass destruction and the acquisition trends in such technologies by these countries (U.S. Central Intelligence Agency 1997, 1).

Congressional concern over what it saw as emerging ballistic missile threats to the United States from such countries was reflected in the fiscal year 1997 National Defense Authorization Act enacted on September 23, 1996. This legislation created a Commission to Assess the Ballistic Missile Threat to the United States to examine the characteristics and extent of this threat (National Defense Authorization Act for Fiscal Year 1997, 104–201).

This commission was chaired by former and future secretary of Defense Donald Rumsfeld (1932–). In its charter the Rumsfeld Commission was directed to scrutinize threats posed by ballistic missiles deployed on the territory of potentially hostile countries, launched from surface vessels, submarines, or aircraft operating off U.S. coasts, and deployed by potentially hostile countries on the territory of a third country to reduce the distance its ballistic missiles would have to travel to reach the United States. Additional commission responsibilities included examining the ability of existing and emerging powers to arm ballistic missiles with weapons of mass destruction; examining the domestic

Indian soldiers examine the giant cracks that appeared in the sun-baked ground on May 20, 1998 in Pokhran after India conducted nuclear bomb tests May 11–14, 1998. The tests raised fears of a nuclear arms race between India and Pakistan, who had fought three wars with each other in the last 50 years. This test amplified Rumsfeld Commission findings about the growing proliferation of ballistic missile technology. *(AFP/Getty Images)*

design, development, and production of nuclear materials and weapons by such states; reviewing the ability of these states to acquire relevant materials, technologies, and weapons through covert sales, transfer, or theft; and the U.S. intelligence community's current and future collection and analysis capabilities to warn of such threats (U.S. Commission to Assess the Ballistic Missile Threat to the United States 1998(a), *Report: Charter and Organization,* 1).

The Rumsfeld Commission released an unclassified version of its report in July 1998, which came in the aftermath of a year in which India and Pakistan tested nuclear weapons and Pakistan and Iran tested new ballistic missiles, demonstrating these countries' increasing missile design capability and sophistication (Towell 1999, 20). The nine commissioners reached the following unanimous conclusions in their assessment:

- Concerted efforts by a number of overtly or potentially hostile nations to acquire ballistic missiles with biological or nuclear payloads pose a growing threat to the United States, its deployed forces, and its friends and allies. These newer, developing threats in North Korea, Iran, and Iraq are in addition to those still posed by the existing ballistic missile arsenals of Russia and China, nations with which the United States is not now in conflict, but which remain in uncertain transitions. The newer ballistic missile-equipped nations' capabilities will not match those of U.S. systems for accuracy and reliability. However, they would be able to inflict major destruction on the United States within about five years of a decision to acquire such capability (10 years in the case of Iraq). During several of those years, the United States might not be aware that such a decision had been made.

• The threat to the United States posed by these emerging capabilities is broader, more mature, and evolving more rapidly than has been reported in estimates and reports by the intelligence community.

• The intelligence community's ability to provide timely and accurate estimates of ballistic missile threats to the United States is eroding. This erosion has roots both within and beyond the intelligence process itself. The community's capabilities in this area need to be strengthened in terms of both resources and methodology.

• The warning times the United States can expect of new, threatening ballistic missile deployments are being reduced. Under some plausible scenarios—including re-basing or transfer of operational missile, sea- and air-launch options, shortened development programs that might include testing in a third country, or some combination of these—the United States might well have *little or no warning before operational deployment* (U.S. Commission to Assess the Ballistic Missile Threat to the United States, *Report: Executive Summary* 1998(b), 1; U.S. Congress, House Committee on National Security, Research and Development Subcommittee 1998(b); U.S. Congress, House Committee on National Security 1998(a).)

Further illustration of the Rumsfeld Commission's concern over proliferating ballistic missiles was demonstrated on August 31, 1998 when North Korea launched a Taepo-dong missile capable of carrying a space satellite and with a range nearly sufficient to carry a small warhead to Alaska or Hawaii (Towell 1999, 20; Bermudez, Jr., 1998, 26).

Agreement Between NASA, NRO, and AFSPACOM (1998)

Achieving cooperation between military space agencies, and concomitantly civilian and military space agencies, has been a problem plaguing U.S. military space programs as shown in this chapter. The years 1995 and 1996 witnessed attempts between AFSPACOM and NASA to reach an agreement on exploring and exploiting future space launch activities and technologies, which came about in early 1997. AFSPACOM commander general Howell M. Estes III (born approximately 1943–), with approval of Air Force chief of staff Fogleman, concluded a memorandum of agreement with NASA administrator Dan Goldin (1940–), creating a partnership council between these two organizations effective February 28, 1997.

This council's mission was to improve interaction between these organizations to achieve more consistent long-range planning, more efficient resource allocation, increased technology partnerships, and more persuasive program advocacy. The AFSPACOM commander and NASA administrator were designated as cochairs as both organizations vowed to take the initiative in coordinating activities in areas of mutual interest (Spires 2004, 2:741).

An outgrowth of this increased cooperation between these organizations came in a supportive May 1, 1997 memorandum from Assistant Secretary of the Air Force (Space) and NRO Keith R. Hall. An April 8, 1998 partnership council meeting included Hall and resulted in expansion of the council to include NRO as a full partner. On November 23, 1998 a memorandum of agreement was signed by Goldin, Hall, and new AFSPACOM commander general Richard B. Myers (1942–), the future chairman of the JSC, that brought NRO into this partnership council. The following paragraph documents the purpose of this interagency partnership:

> The Partnership Council is established to expand cooperation between AFSPC, NRO, and NASA. This cooperation is intended to achieve efficiencies, risk reduction, and better understanding of plans and activities in areas of mutual interest. Improving the level of interaction between the organizations should lead to harmonized long-range planning, more efficient resource allocation, expanded technology partnerships, and more compelling advocacy of programs. Anticipated results might include: streamlining operations costs, cross utilization of facility capabilities, consolidation of redundant facilities, sharing of support services, and leveraging of science and technology investments (Spires 2004, 2:742, 954).

Aerospace Force: Defending America in the 21st Century (2000)

Additional effort to promote expanded aerospace integration occurred within the Air Force as the new century and millennium began. This was reflected in a task force study commissioned by Air Force chief of staff general Michael Ryan (born approximately 1943–) and Secretary of the Air Force F. Whitten Peters (1946–), which culminated in the May 9, 2000 release of the report *Aerospace Force: Defending America in the 21st Century.* This report sought to portray the Air Force moving into the 21st century as a seamless and integrated aerospace force whose mission encompassed both air and space operations while taking steps to increase the ongoing integration of what had been separate air and space power components. *Aerospace Force* also sought to describe the benefits of aerospace integration in supporting joint military, civilian, and commercial operations and applications (Spires 2004, 1:17, 106–107; Barry and Herriges 2000, 42–47).

The report began with definitions of aerospace, one of which was "the seamless operational medium that encompasses the flight domains of earth and space." It went on to describe "aerospace force" as encompassing air and space systems, the people using and supporting such systems, and having the entire range of capabilities to control and ex-

Gen. Michael Ryan served as Air Force Chief of Staff between 1997–2001. *(U.S. Department of Defense)*

ploit the aerospace theater. "Aerospace integration" was defined as a series of actions harmonizing air and space skills into an aerospace force capable of advancing multiple U.S. military forces in parallel, sequential, and mutually coordinated actions. "Aerospace power" was declared to be using lethal and nonlethal means by aerospace forces to reach tactical, strategic, and operational goals (U.S. Air Force 2000, 3).

An important part of this report was its description of aerospace power as having five key attributes: Speed, range, perspective, precision, and three-dimensional maneuverability. The characteristics of these attributes are listed below:

Speed: the ability to move rapidly across the theater of operation and achieve effects quickly. Through the integration of air, space, and aerospace systems, we can identify and attack mobile or concealed targets with breathtaking speed. The speed of our operations can overwhelm adversaries unable to keep pace.

Range: the ability to project power over great distances. The integration of air and space capabilities vastly expands the potential range of our forces and allows us to achieve objectives from greater distances or from orbit.

Perspective: the ability to perceive both friendly and hostile activity at a distance and in context. Commanders throughout history have sought to control the "high ground" because it provides perspective over the battlefield. Integrated aerospace systems combine the broad perspective of earth, provided by space-based platforms with the high fidelity of airborne platforms.

Precision: the ability to deliver discriminating, tailored effects. Highly accurate space-based navigation and timing systems, integrated with airborne platforms, already have increased dramatically the effective delivery of munitions anywhere and anytime. The ability to coregister targeting information in a common coordinate system will yield even greater precision.

Three-Dimensional Maneuverability: the ability to threaten the enemy through the movement of forces in the aerospace continuum. From its inception, airpower has presented the dilemma of defending against forces that fly over or around surface defenses. Through maneuvering in the third dimension, aerospace forces bypass traditional tactical and operational barriers and even terrestrial notions of sovereignty to pursue strategic, operational, and tactical objectives (U.S. Air Force 2000, 6–7).

Space Commission Report (2001)

Congressional concern over the effective utilization of U.S. military space assets, coordination, military education and training, and operations prompted the creation of a Commission to Assess U.S. National Security Space Management in the fiscal year 2000 defense-spending bill passed in 1999. Congress directed this commission, which would be chaired by Donald Rumsfeld, to examine how military space assets could be exploited to support U.S. military operations, existing interagency coordination processes for national security space capabilities, relationships between intelligence and nonintelligence aspects of national security space programs, how professional military educational institutions address military space issues, and potential costs and benefits of establishing a separate military department and service dedicated to national security space missions or a creation of a comparable corps within the Air Force with such a dedicated mission (National Defense Authorization Act for Fiscal Year 2000, 106–65, 511, 814–815).

The commission issued its report in January 2001 at the end of the Clinton administration. Commission members determined that the increasing U.S. dependence on space and the vulnerabilities involved in this dependence require space's recognition as a top national security priority, that DOD and the intelligence community are not arranged or focused to meet 21st century national space needs, that the secretary of Defense and director of Central Intelligence (DCI) must have a close and effective partnership for the intelligence community and national command authority to work together to pursue national security objectives, that space will become a medium of human conflict and that the United States must develop superior space capabilities to deter and defend against hostile attacks, and that investment in science and technology resources is a prerequisite if the United States is to remain the world's preeminent space-faring nation (U.S. Commission to Assess United States National Security Space Management and Organization 2001, 99–100).

Specific recommendations made by commissioners focusing on congressional organization and management expectations outlined in the commission's charter include the following:

- Provide for national level guidance that establishes space activity as a fundamental national interest of the United States.
- Create a process to ensure that the national level policy guidance is carried out among and within the relevant agencies and departments.
- Create conditions that encourage the DOD to develop and deploy systems in space to deter attack on and, if deterrence should fail, to defend U.S. interests on earth and in space.
- Create conditions that encourage the intelligence community to develop revolutionary methods for collecting intelligence from space.
- Account for the increasingly important role played by the commercial and civil space sectors in the nation's domestic and global economic and national security affairs.
- Develop a military and civilian cadre of space professionals within the DOD, the intelligence community, and throughout government more generally.
- Provide an organizational and management structure that permits officials to be agile in addressing the opportunities, risks, and threats that inevitably will arise.
- Ensure that the DOD and the intelligence community are full participants in preparing government positions for international negotiations that may affect U.S. space activities (U.S. Commission to Assess United States National Security Space Management and Organization 2001, xxx; U.S. Congress, Senate Committee on Armed Services, Subcommittee on Strategic 2002).

DOD Directive 5101.2 DOD Executive Agent for Space (2003)

The 2001 space commission also expressed its reaffirmation of existing *DOD Directive 5160.32* that the Air Force should remain the executive agent for space. The issuance of an updated order covering this—*DOD Directive 5101.2*—on June 3, 2003 reinforced existing policy and incorporated the space commission's wishes. This document again designated the secretary of the Air Force as the DOD's executive agent for space with responsibility for planning and programming major DOD space-system programs and acquisitions. The directive went on to describe space forces as "the space and terrestrial systems, equipment, facilities, organizations, and personnel necessary to use, and, if directed control space for national security." It maintained space power constituted "the total strength of a nation's capabilities to conduct and influence activities to, in, through, and from the space medium to achieve its objectives." The directive also described space systems as representing "All of the devices and organizations forming the space network. These consist of: spacecraft; mission package(s); ground stations; data links among spacecraft, ground stations, mission or user terminals, which may include initial reception, processing, and exploitation; launch systems; and directly related supporting infrastructure, including space surveillance and battle management/command, control, communications, and computers." (Spires 2004, 2:1215; *U.S. Department of Defense Directive 5101.2 2003; 2–4*).

Air Force Counterspace Operations Doctrine (2004)

A notable recent addition to the burgeoning literature of military produced space-policy documents is *Counterspace Operations: Air Force Doctrine Document 2–2.1* issued in August 2004. Issued in the aftermath of the conventional phase of 2003's Operation Iraqi Freedom, this document sought to further incorporate an aspect of space military operations into Air Force military doctrinal thought.

Chapters within this work seek to emphasize the general importance of counterspace operations, command and control of counterspace operations, space situation awareness including the relevant components of intelligence, surveillance, reconnaissance, environmental monitoring and command and control, characteristics of defensive and offensive counterspace operations, and planning and executing counterspace operations (U.S. Air Force, 2004, iii-iv).

Important foundational doctrinal hypotheses to Air Force counterspace operations include stressing that such operations are the means by which the Air Force achieves and maintains space superiority, that Air Force counterspace operations are intended to protect U.S. and allied military space capability while denying such capability to adversaries, and that the Air Force brings space expertise from a spectrum of military operations as a single service and in cooperation with other services through joint operations. Additional foundational doctrinal tenets include counterspace operations having offensive and defensive components depending on robust space situational awareness (SSA). Achieving SSA requires support from all levels of planners, decision makers, and operators representing terrestrial and space components. Defensive counterspace operations are required to preserve the U.S./allied ability to advantageously exploit space, offensive counterspace operations are required to prevent adversaries from exploiting space for their advantage, and counterspace operations must be conducted across war's tactical, operational, and strategic levels by all U.S. military forces (U.S. Air Force 2004, vii; Ziarnick 2004, 61–70).

This doctrinal document also stresses how hostile forces can conduct a wide spectrum of asymmetric attacks against U.S. space assets using various methods including:

- Ground system attack and sabotage using conventional and unconventional means against terrestrial nodes and supporting infrastructure.
- Radio frequency (RF) jamming equipment capable of interfering with space system links.

- Laser systems capable of temporarily or permanently degrading or destroying satellite subsystems, thus interfering with satellite mission performance.
- Electromagnetic pulse (EMP) weapons capable of degrading or destroying satellite and/or ground system electronics.
- Kinetic antisatellite (ASAT) weapons capable of destroying spacecraft or degrading their ability to perform missions.
- Information operations (IO) capabilities capable of corrupting space-based and terrestrial-based computer systems utilized to control satellite functions and to collect, process, and disseminate mission data (U.S. Air Force 2004, 4).

Air Force Doctrine 2–2.1 and the 2001 *Space Operations: Air Force Doctrine Document 2–2* (U.S. Air Force 2001) represent a growing emphasis on integrating military space into Air Force and military operational doctrine.

They conclude this review of six decades worth of military space policy documents representing multiple U.S. armed services with Air Force publications constituting the preponderance of U.S. military space policy doctrinal theory and policy statements. These documents demonstrate that determining the Air Force's and the U.S. military's proper operational military space policy mission and strategy remains an elusive concept and one which is still struggling to achieve resolution. This struggle will likely continue due to a variety of political and other constraints. Some of these constraints can be understood further by looking at presidential space policy directives and national space policy documents produced by the president under the organizational auspices of institutions such as the NSC.

Presidential Space Policy Directives/National Space Policy Documents

The most important U.S. Government space policy documents, whose scope covers both civilian and military aspects of space, are publications issued by the president through the Executive Office of the President (Dickenson 2005, 135–172), agencies such as the NSC (U.S. Department of State, Office of the Historian 1997; Zegart 1999; Best 2001), and the Office of Science and Technology Policy (OSTP) (Mann 2000, Herken 2000).

Although the OSTP serves as the president's primary science and technology advisor (U.S. National Archives and Records Administration 2006, 96), most military space policy documents issued by presidential administrations from Eisenhower to George W. Bush are issued by the NSC.

NSC documents setting forth the foreign and national security policies of individual presidential administrations have been produced by NSC staff and by DOD and State Department personnel. While some of these publications may be published in the *Federal Register,* the sensitive nature of this work can result in them remaining classified for decades. Upon declassification, these works can be found in presidential libraries, may be available on presidential library websites, and may be published by commercial publishers. These publications can go under a variety of names such as NSC Policy Papers during the Eisenhower administration, National Security Study Memoranda (NSSM) and National Security Decision Memoranda (NSDM) during the Nixon and Ford administrations, Presidential Review Directives and Presidential Decision Directives (PDDs) during the Clinton administration, and National Security Presidential Directives (NSPDs) during the George W. Bush administration. The number of these documents issued during individual presidential administrations varies with nearly 250 NSSMs issued during the Nixon-Ford administrations and at least 318 NSDMs issued during this same time period (Relyea 2005, 8–12; Dwyer 2002, 410–19).

The remainder of this chapter presents excerpts from selected presidential military space policy documents from the Eisenhower administration to the present. These documents cover military and diplomatic aspects of national security space policy. The authority of some may be enduring, while others may last for brief periods of time before being rescinded by subsequent presidential actions or policies. Brief contextual overviews are provided on the circumstances and events prompting the issuance of these documents.

Eisenhower Administration (1953–1961)

The emergence of space as a factor in U.S. national security policy, exemplified by the 1957 Soviet Sputnik satellite launch and the emergence of ICBMs as military weapons, are key contextual backdrops to Eisenhower administration space policy. One of the earliest U.S. Government national security space policy documents was *NSC 5520* "U.S. Scientific Satellite Programs" issued by the Eisenhower administration in 1955. This document observed that U.S. scientific programs should be motivated by the desire to preserve the United States' freedom of action in space and that no actions should take place in space research or international diplomatic negotiations that would restrict the United States' ability to engage in space research without the consent of other nations. This latter point became a crucial tenet of U.S. space policy (Lambakis 2001, 213). Eisenhower administration space policy documents reflected a tension between promoting peaceful uses of outer space while simultaneously seeking not to place restrictions on the United States' ability to use space for military or other purposes (Hall 1995, 58–72).

NSC 5520 went on to observe that establishing small scientific satellites could produce substantial benefit, that the first nation to launch a satellite would receive considerable international prestige, that the JSC believed a military intelligence application would benefit from constructing a large surveillance satellite, that a small satellite program could be developed from existing DOD missile programs, and that missile defense research would gain from experiences acquired in finding and tracking satellites (U.S. National Security Council 2006(a), 8–15).

The Soviet Union's October 4, 1957 launch of a Sputnik satellite produced drastic changes in U.S. policies toward space and its potential military implications (McDougall

Sputnik I, the first artificial satellite to successfully orbit the Earth, was launched by the Soviet Union on October 4, 1957. *(Bettmann/Corbis)*

1997, 141–194). August 18, 1958 saw the release of *NSC 5814* "Preliminary U.S. Policy on Outer Space," which sought to list multiple civilian and military uses of space along with relevant legal implications while also establishing outlines for international cooperation in space. In its efforts to retain optimal legal and political flexibility for the United States, *NSC 5814* advised against delineating a boundary between air and space to allow for liberal legal interpretation of what constituted "peaceful uses" of outer space (Lambakis 2001, 215–216).

This document also sought to list the numerous existing and potential military uses of outer space including ballistic missiles and missile defense systems, military reconnaissance, weather observation satellites, military communication satellites, electronic countermeasures or jamming satellites, navigation aids, manned defensive outer space vehicles, bombardment satellites, and manned lunar stations. It decided to not include missile and missile defense systems into U.S. space policy to avoid confusion about what was or was not a space vehicle. Particular emphasis was placed on the potential military intelligence value of reconnaissance satellites as this passage demonstrates:

20. Reconnaissance satellites are of critical importance to U.S. national security. Those now planned are designed: (a) to gather military intelligence data, weather

data, and information on the economic potential of the Sino-Soviet Bloc; and
(b) to detect the launching of a missile or air attack upon the United States or its
allies. Reconnaissance satellites would also have a high potential use as a means of
implementing the "open skies" proposal or policing a system of international armaments control (U.S. National Security Council 2006(a), iii, 30–31; Lambakis 218).

The next major Eisenhower administration space policy document was *NSC 5918/1* "U.S.
Policy on Outer Space" issued in early 1960 and intended to supersede *NSC 5814/1.* This
document acknowledged the space technology's civilian, military, and political implications and warned that the United States must take energetic steps to combat the perception that the United States had fallen behind the Soviet Union in space technology. It also
recommended a 60% increase in NASA's budget and said the United States should emphasize space projects with demonstrable results such as manned spaceflight (McDougall
1997, 205).

NSC 5918/1 went on to acknowledge that space represented "a new and imposing challenge," that recent Soviet space successes had caused them to experience substantial and
long-term prestige enhancement, and created an image of communist nations as a superior military power (U.S. National Security Council 2006(a), 58–59). An appropriate
U.S. response to these developments, according to *NSC 5918/1,* would involve the following actions:

> 31. Carry out energetically a program for the exploration and use of outer space by
> the U.S., based upon sound scientific and technological progress, designed: (a) to
> achieve that enhancement of scientific knowledge, military strength, economic
> capabilities, and political position which may be derived through the advanta-
> geous application of space technology and through appropriate international co-
> operation in related matters, and (b) to achieve and demonstrate an over-all U.S.
> superiority in outer space without necessarily requiring United States supremacy
> in every space of space activities (U.S. National Security Council 2006(a), 67).

Kennedy Administration (1961–1963)

The Kennedy administration began with the president not having a particular space
policy on the agenda but accepting the view that space would play a particularly important role in promoting national prestige and security. Soon after his administration
began, Kennedy sought to commit the United States to a manned landing on the moon by
the end of the decade, which he proposed in a May 25, 1961 address to a joint session of
Congress and which represents the defining moment of his space policy pronouncements
(U.S. Congress 1961, 8877–8882; McDougall 1997, 302–306).

His abbreviated administration also saw Kennedy take other policy actions that increased U.S. military activity in space and sought to expand international cooperation to

Dr. Wernher von Braun explains the Saturn Launch System to President John F. Kennedy. NASA Deputy Administrator Robert Seamans is to the left of von Braun. *(NASA)*

promote peaceful uses of outer space (Kay 1998, 573–586; Elliott, 1992). *National Security Action Memorandum (NSAM) 129* issued on February 23, 1962 sought to promote U.S.–Soviet cooperation in space exploration. In this document, Kennedy stressed his strong support for United Nations (UN) space science programs and directed National Security Advisor McGeorge Bundy (1919–1996) to work with NASA, the special assistant to the president for science and technology, and the State Department to develop concrete proposals and recommendations as ways for opening pertinent discussions with the Soviets (U.S. National Security Council 2006(a), 93).

May 26, 1962 saw the issuance of *NSAM 156*, which mentioned U.S. participation in various international negotiations on disarmament and peaceful uses of outer space. This document acknowledged that such negotiations could be lengthy and present the problem of what constitutes legitimate uses of outer space and whether space reconnaissance falls into this category. *NSAM 156* went to express this concern as follows:

> In view of the great national security importance of our satellite reconnaissance programs, I think it is desirable that we carefully review these negotiations with a view to formulating a position which avoids the dangers of restricting ourselves,

compromising highly classified programs, or providing assistance of significant military value to the Soviet Union and which at the same time permits us to continue to work for disarmament and international cooperation in space (U.S. National Security Council 2006(a), 95).

The year 1962 also saw the United States' desire to implement a satellite reconnaissance program, which is now known as Project Corona, even though there was concern that such a program would be controversial in some sectors of international opinion, and information about this program would have to be kept secret to maintain its prospects for operational success. The document *NSC Action 2454* "Space Policy and Intelligence Requirements" issued on July 10, 1962 recommended a U.S. satellite reconnaissance policy promoting the free and peaceful use of space, restricted the amount of publicly releasable information about U.S. reconnaissance activity, and proposed further international discussion of a possible agreement to prohibit satellites from carrying weapons of mass destruction (U.S. National Security Council 2006(a), iv).

U.S. diplomatic sensitivity to the implications of its reconnaissance satellite program is reflected by acknowledging Japan's reluctance to cooperate with NASA in establishing U.S. tracking facilities due to the suspicion that this could involve military activities, mentioning that groups in Zanzibar and Nigeria have argued that U.S. tracking stations in their countries were inconsistent with a nonaligned foreign policy, and recognizing that there is partial evidence that a Sino–Soviet campaign attributing sinister motive to U.S. satellite programs might receive sympathetic reactions from anti-U.S. elements and others concerned about increasing international tension (U.S. National Security Council 2006(a), 102).

This concern to demonstrate that U.S. space programs were of pacific intent was expressed in *NSAM 183* issued on August 27, 1962. This document reflected Kennedy's desire that such intentions be assertively voiced and defended at upcoming sessions of the UN General Assembly and Outer Space Committee. The document also directed the State Department to consult with DOD, the CIA, NASA, the Atomic Energy Commission, the Arms Control and Disarmament Agency, and the presidential science advisor to develop positions demonstrating that the United States intends to keep free from aggressive use and is interested in cooperating to promote space's peaceful scientific and technological purposes. *NSAM 183* also directed these agencies to demonstrate that distinguishing between peaceful and aggressive uses of space is not the same as distinctions between military and civilian uses, to build and maintain support for space reconnaissance's legality and propriety, to clarify that U.S. nuclear tests nor other space experiments were undertaken without proper scientific responsibility but as a response to previous Soviet tests, to explain that U.S. military space programs are defensive, and to stress that U.S. communication satellite policies conform to relevant international agreements (U.S. National Security Council 2006(a), 107).

Kennedy's own personal interest in promoting peaceful uses of outer space was reflected in *NSAM 192* issued on October 2, 1962. This document served as a follow up to *NSAM*

156 and *NSC Action 2454* and expressed his desire to be informed before the United States presented an initiative to the UN General Assembly or other international forum on proposals to ban weapons of mass destruction in outer space (U.S. National Security Council 2006(a), 111).

July 25, 1963 saw the Kennedy administration's final major space policy accomplishment with the signature of the Test Ban Treaty prohibiting nuclear weapons tests or other nuclear explosions underwater, in the atmosphere, or in outer space. The U.S. Senate ratified the treaty on September 24, 1963, and it entered into force on October 10 (U.S. Department of State, Bureau of Verification, Compliance, and Implementation, n.d., 1–5).

Johnson Administration (1963–1969)

The Vietnam War and its controversies served as the principal national security event of the Johnson administration. This did not prevent the United States from continuing to pursue some important space policy initiatives such as the growth and success of the Gemini and Apollo manned spaceflight programs (Rumerman 1998), declaring in 1964 that the United States was openly pursuing an ASAT capability to defeat Soviet bomb-carrying satellites like the fractional orbital bombardment system (Lambakis 2001, 223), and enhanced international cooperation in peaceful uses of outer space culminating in the 1967 OST (U.S. Department of State, Bureau of Verification, Compliance, and Implementation, n.d., 1–2).

Other noteworthy Johnson administration NSC national security space policy documents include *NSAM 285, NSAM 338,* and *NSAM 354. NSAM 285* "Cooperation with the USSR on Outer Space Matters" was issued on March 3, 1964. This memorandum sought to maintain a previously existing effort, begun with *NSAM 271* of November 12, 1963, to look for possible avenues to pursue peaceful space exploration with the Soviets and to monitor Soviet responses to U.S. space policy initiatives made at the UN (U.S. National Security Council 2006(a), 121).

NSAM 338 was written in response to the growing importance of the 1962 Communications Satellite Act, which lead to U.S. participation in the International Telecommunications Satellite Organization (INTELSAT) and saw satellite technology become increasingly important in facilitating global telecommunications. This September 15, 1965 document directed the Special Assistant to the President for Telecommunications to monitor U.S. policy assisting foreign communication satellite capability development and informing the president of any pertinent changes that may require his attention (U.S. National Security Council 2006(a), v-vi, 123).

NSAM 354 reflected the U.S. desire to cooperate with allied countries' space programs. This July 29, 1966 directive saw the United States encourage development of the European Launcher Development Organization (ELDO) (the predecessor the European Space Agency) and express the United States' willingness to cooperate with ELDO if it desired such cooperation. Johnson also directed DOD, NASA, and the State Department to take

Astronaut Edward White becomes the first American man to walk in space during the Gemini IV mission on June 9, 1965. *(NASA)*

the necessary actions to facilitate such cooperation (*National Security Space Project Presidential Decision: NSC Documents* 2006, vi, 125).

Nixon Administration (1969–1974)

The Nixon administration, responding to the sociopolitical strain and economic costs produced by the Vietnam War and "Great Society" social programs, decided the country was unable to afford large investments in manned space projects. This directional change was reflected in his March 7, 1970 speech announcing that U.S. space exploration would place greater emphasis on unmanned vehicles and a limited continuation of the Apollo program. In January 1972 Nixon announced the beginning of the partially reusable STS, which became known as the space shuttle. The early 1970s saw significant international arms control agreements with the Soviet Union such as the Strategic Arms Limitation Talks (SALT I) and the ABM treaty of 1972, which limited nuclear missile growth, implicitly recognized the value of space-based reconnaissance by including a vague prohibition against interfering with either side's "National Technical Means" capabilities, banned the deployment of space-based ABM components, and drastically limited ABM deployment (Lambakis 2001; 224; Hoff 1997, 92–132; U.S. Arms Control and Disarmament Agency 1996, 110–114).

The Nixon administration made some military space developments such as deploying longer lasting military satellites such as the KH-9 in 1971, which reduced space launch demand while also producing navigation, communications, and meteorological satellite enhancements (Lambakis 2001, 224). *National Security Decision Memorandum (NSDM) 72* issued on July 17, 1970 ordered an interagency group to review policy aspects and establish procedures for the United States to exchange technical data with foreign governments and agencies wanting to enter into cooperative space programs with the United States. This document also directed preparation of procedures for future European cooperation in U.S. space programs while taking measures to protect U.S. national interests (U.S. National Security Council 2006(a), 129).

Ford Administration (1974–1977)

The Ford administration saw Soviet military space advances emerge and engage the attention of U.S. policymakers. U.S. concern was manifested by Soviet ASAT advances and by a growing realization of the United States' increasing dependence on space assets for national security, with communications being a particular area of concern. Further demonstration of this vulnerability was provided by a Defense Science Board assessment, which maintained that ground segments of U.S. space systems were vulnerable in wartime. Lackadaisical Air Force and DOD interest in space defense prompted Ford to issue a number of NSDMs to address these concerns (Lambakis 2001, 225).

NSDM 333 issued on July 7, 1976 sought to deal with the vulnerability of U.S. military satellites and directed the Air Force to use money to make progress in space surveillance and space defense (Stares 1985, 153–156, 168–170). Although only some of this document has been declassified as of late 2006, its content demonstrates the importance of these concerns to administration policymakers. Document highlights include stressing the need to make improvements to enhance the technical survivability of U.S. space assets, the need for providing clear, reliable, and timely warning of attacks against U.S. satellites, and the critical importance of providing positive verification of interference with critical military and intelligence satellite capabilities (U.S. National Security Council 2006(b), 5).

Illustration of an ASAT (antisatellite) missile after being launched from an F-15. U.S. concerns over Soviet ASAT programs lead the Ford Administration to authorize U.S. development of comparable ASAT capabilities. *(U.S. Department of Defense)*

This directive eventually resulted in establishing a System Program Office and SAMSO within the Air Force. Both Nixon and Ford contributed to the gradual termination of the United States' nuclear ASAT program initiated during the 1960s. However, an early 1977 Ford administration document *NSDM 345* resulted in directing DOD to develop a miniature homing-vehicle ASAT weapon launched by an F-15 jet fighter to counter Soviet ocean reconnaissance capabilities and study possible arms control options (Stares 1985, 171; Lambakis 2001; 225).

NSDM 345 U.S. Anti-Satellite Capability was issued on January 18, 1977 and directed the secretary of Defense to acquire a non-nuclear ASAT capability, mentioned that this interceptor be capable of destroying low altitude satellites and nullifying 6–10 Soviet military satellites within a week, be able to electronically nullify critical Soviet military satellites at all altitudes, that such U.S. electronic satellite capability should be classified with compartmented security procedures used to protect its existence and operating characteristics, and that the director of the Arms Control and Disarmament Agency work with the secretaries of State and Defense and DCI to develop relevant diplomatic and military policies concerning ASAT systems, specifying the acts that would constitute interference with such systems (U.S. National Security Council 2006(a), 143–145).

Carter Administration (1977–1981)

The Carter administration produced a number of documents covering various aspects of U.S. civilian and military space policy. Although concerned with promoting expanded international arms control with the Soviet Union, it continued Ford administration policies detailed in *NSDM 345* for developing an ASAT weapons system in the belief that such a system could be used in arms control negotiations with the Soviets (Stares 1985, 180–182).

Carter directed his NSC Policy Review Committee, whose membership consisted of major national security policymakers and cabinet officials such as the secretaries of Agriculture, Commerce, and Interior, to conduct a thorough review of U.S. space policies, which produced the first comprehensive national space policy review since the Eisenhower administration. This group received its marching orders in *Presidential Review Memorandum (PRM) 23* issued on March 28, 1977. *PRM 23* charged this group to determine space's relative importance for U.S. civil, military, and national intelligence programs; establish current ground rules for balancing and controlling interactions between civil, military, and national intelligence sectors to achieve interrelated national security, political, economic, and arms control goals; make recommendations on necessary space policy practices the

Jimmy Carter and Leonid Brezhnev sign the second Strategic Arms Limitation Treaty (SALT II) treaty on June 18, 1979, in Vienna. The treaty was the culmination of a second round of talks between the U.S. and Soviet Union seeking to curtail further development of nuclear arms. This treaty would not be ratified by the U.S. Senate due to the intense opposition to it caused, in part, by the Soviet invasion of Afghanistan later that year. *(Jimmy Carter Presidential Library)*

U.S. needed to change or modify; and recommend how to address recommendations and directives contained in previous NSC space policy documents (U.S. National Security Council 2006(a), 147–148).

Presidential Directive (PD) 25 issued on December 14, 1977 designated the White House OSTP director to review experiments capable of affecting the environment. This document also required presidential approval for space launches of nuclear systems through the OSTP (*National Security Space Project Presidential Decisions: NSC Documents* 2006, 153).

The most important Carter administration space policy document was the National Space Policy document contained in *PD 37* issued May 11, 1978. Culminating the work initiated with issuance of *PRM 23* a year earlier, this document formally acknowledged a U.S. military space program, reaffirmed the importance of free access to space, ordered satellite reconnaissance for intelligence operations to remain classified, and stressed a national commitment to operate global remote-sensing operations to support national objectives. *PD 37* also mentioned that the United States should continue using space to defend itself, deter attack, and promote arms control agreements while also providing preliminary encouragement to domestic commercial exploitation of space assets to enhance national economic and technological growth. It also depicted space as an arena for enhancing land, sea, and air power and continued preexisting ASAT research and development programs although it did not outline a plan for integrating space weapons into national military strategy (Lambakis 2001, 226).

Additional *PD 37* contents stress that space systems are national property and have the right of passage through and operations in space without interference, that the United States will pursue space activities supporting its right of self-defense, that it will maintain a national intelligence space program, pursue space activities to increase scientific knowledge, develop useful civil space technology applications, maintain national leadership in space, and conduct international cooperative space-related activities that benefit the United States scientifically, politically, economically, and/or militarily (*National Security Space Project Presidential Decisions* 2006, 152).

Important *PD 37* intelligence and military components demonstrating the crisis contingency planning involved in national security policymaking include the United States having a space program to acquire information and data for formulating and executing foreign and military policies; supporting planning for and conducting military operations; providing warning to support crisis management and monitor treaties; protecting sensitive information; and supporting military operational requirements (*National Security Presidential Documents: NSC Documents Supplement: Newly Declassified Excerpts,* 2006, 7).

The next major Carter administration space policy directive was *PD 42* issued on October 10, 1978. This document's focus was on assigning a committee to review the possible release of selected photoreconnaissance imagery and ordering a review of separate DOD and NASA space shuttle activities for ways of achieving enhanced budgetary efficiency. Other directive provisions mentioned that U.S. space policy would be focused on what can most effectively be accomplished in space rather than on individual large-scale engineering initiatives, continuing the LANDSAT satellite development program, examining the potential for an integrated remote sensing system, achieving enhanced budgetary efficiencies in civilian and military meteorological satellite programs, possible combination of civilian and military oceanographic satellite programs, and ways of improving shuttle data link command and encryption between agencies such as the CIA, DOD, and NASA (U.S. National Security Council 2006(a), vii, 163–169; Mack 1990).

An additional noteworthy Carter administration space policy document dealt with the growing importance of remote sensing satellite capabilities in civilian and military operations. *PD 54* issued on November 16, 1979 enforced previously existing policies enumerated in *PD 37* and *PD 42* while defining three categories for remote sensing use. These categories were land, weather, and ocean programs. Overall directions of these programs involved separate classified activities having no civilian equivalents, joint or coordinated civil/military activities whose objectives could be achieved without jeopardizing national security, and integrating civil operational activities under civil agency management with coordination and regulation by an interagency board. In this latter instance, there would be no joint management and overall system convergence between classified space intelligence activities. *PD 54* also continued to separate DOD and Commerce Department polar-orbiting meteorological satellite programs (U.S. National Security Council 2006(a), vii, 171–173).

Reagan Administration (1981–1989)

The Reagan administration would see many significant and controversial changes in the direction of U.S. military space policy. The most important of these was SDI, which is described in greater detail in the Chapter 2. In August 1981 Reagan directed Dr. Victor H. Reis (born approximately 1935–), the assistant director of the OSTP, to conduct a national space policy review. This review was conducted by an interagency panel from various civilian and military agencies. Issues it was tasked with examining included: launch vehicle needs; whether existing space policy was sufficient to meet civil and military space program requirements; shuttle organizational responsibilities and capabilities; and potential space policy legislation (Stares 1985, 217).

In August 1981 the Reagan administration rejected a Soviet offer to discuss a space weapon treaty submitted to the UN General Assembly because of flaws administration policymakers saw in the treaty. The Reagan administration unveiled its strategic force modernization program to Congress during October and November 1981, which saw Secretary of Defense Casper Weinberger assert that the United States would continue pursuing an operational satellite system and stressed the need for the United States to have survivable early warning communication and attack assessment systems in the event of a nuclear war (Stares 1985; 217; U.S. Congress, Senate Armed Services Committee, Subcommittee on Strategic and Theater Forces 1982; U.S. Congress, Senate Committee on Foreign Relations 1981, 8–14).

Reagan administration NSC Documents were called *National Security Decision Directives (NSDD)* and the first military space policy oriented *NSDD* was issued November 13,

1981. *NSDD 8* designated the space shuttle as the primary space launch system for civil and military government missions. It went on to describe the shuttle as a national program requiring sustained commitment, that DOD would work with NASA to ensure that the shuttle was useful for defense missions, that national security missions would be integrated into shuttle launch schedules, and that launch priority will be given to national security missions (U.S. National Security Council 2006(a), 181).

The Reis review culminated in the July 4, 1982 issuance of a new U.S. national space policy statement *NSDD 42*, which superseded applicable Carter presidential directives and *NSDD 8*. *NSDD 42* declared the basic goals of U.S. space policy to be strengthening U.S. security; maintaining U.S. space leadership; obtaining economic and scientific benefits through space exploitation; expanding U.S. private sector investment and participation in civil space and space-related activities; promoting international cooperative activities if they are in the national interest; and cooperating with other nations in maintaining freedom of space (*National Security Space Policy Presidential Decisions: NSC Documents* 2006, 183).

Specific national security program objectives in *NSDD 42* included the following declarations:

> The United States will conduct those activities in space that are necessary to national defense. The military space program will support such functions as command and control, communications, navigation, environmental monitoring, warning, tactical intelligence, targeting, ocean and battlefield surveillance application (including an aggressive research and development program which supports these functions). In addition, military space programs shall contribute to the satisfaction of national intelligence requirements (U.S. National Security Council 2006(b), 8).

NSDD 42 also stressed that the United States would develop and deploy an operational ASAT system as soon as practical; that it would develop and maintain an integrated attack warning, notification, verification, and contingency reaction capability to effectively detect and react to threats to its space systems; that it would conduct research and planning and be prepared to develop and deploy space weapon systems to counter hostile space activities if conditions warranted; and that support of military operational requirements was a critical space intelligence mission (U.S. National Security Council 2006(b), 8–9).

Reagan's nationally televised March 23, 1983 address on ballistic missile defense marked the formal beginning of SDI and the controversy that the program produced. The authorizing program document for this was *NSDD 85* issued on March 25, 1983. A key excerpt from this document is this passage:

> I direct the development of an intensive effort to define a long-term research and development program aimed at an ultimate goal of eliminating the threat posed by nuclear ballistic missiles. These actions will be carried out in a manner consis-

tent with our obligations under the ABM Treaty and recognizing the need for close consultations with our allies. . . I further direct a study be completed on a priority basis to asses the roles that ballistic missile defense could play in future security strategy of the United States and our allies. . . (U.S. National Security Council 2006(a), 205).

May 16, 1983 saw the issuance of *NSDD 94 Commercialization of Space Launch Vehicles.* This document saw the United States encourage the development of a commercial expendable space launch industry to the extent that these operations were consistent with existing laws, regulations, and national security interests. The shuttle remained the primary U.S. Government launch system, and promoting the growth and international economic competitiveness of the U.S. space launch industry served as primary objectives of this document (U.S. National Security Council 2006(a), 207–214; Launius and Jenkins 2002; Scarborough 1991).

January 6, 1984 saw the issuance of *NSDD 119* concerning formal policy guidance for SDI. DOD was given formal program management responsibility and a key program emphasis was on technologies involving non-nuclear kill concepts. SDI program research concepts were to emphasize strategic defense concepts using nuclear devices as a hedge against Soviet attempts to escape ABM Treaty restrictions (U.S. National Security Council 2006(a), 216).

Additional provisions of *NSDD 119* were that the United States would begin a comprehensive program for developing and demonstrating critical technological concepts associated with ballistic missile defense; coordinating this program with other strategic defense programs and incorporating active and passive defense concepts; providing the option of a limited non-nuclear ballistic missile defense if a Soviet ABM breakout occurred; and the DCI increasing U.S. efforts to assess Soviet ballistic missile defense developments on an annual basis (U.S. National Security Council 2006(b), 10).

Opposition to SDI was particularly strong among congressional Democrats during this period. Many of these individuals sought to insert provisions restricting U.S. ASAT activities into appropriations bills, which achieved limited success. Congress did succeed in passing an amendment withholding procurement funds for ASAT weapons unless the president certified that the administration was actively exploring the possibility of negotiating with the Soviets and that the proposed ASAT tests were necessary. A March 31, 1984 administration report on this topic reviewed ASAT national security requirements and arms control possibilities. This document stressed that administration policy was to look for credible ASAT arms control opportunities but expressed acute skepticism about such negotiations with the Soviets because of concerns about verifying such agreements and about continuing Soviet ASAT programs (Lambakis 2001, 228–229; President of the United States 1984, 7–16).

NSDD 144 was the National Space Strategy issued on August 15, 1984. This document sought to establish national security space principles and develop corresponding

Space Shuttle Atlantis takes flight on its STS-27 mission on December 2, 1988. It was a classified Department of Defense mission. *(NASA)*

implementation guidelines with emphasis on civilian, commercial, and military aspects of space policy. Categories stressed in this document's coverage of national security space programs included maintaining assured access to space with emphasis on a supplemental launch system besides the space shuttle if the necessity for such a system arose; pursuing a long-term survivability program for national security space assets; stemming the flow of advanced space technology to the Soviet Union; studying possible space arms control options; insuring that DOD space and space-related programs support SDI, and maintaining a strong national security space technology program capable of supporting development of essential improvements and emerging capabilities (U.S. National Security Council 2006(a), 221–227).

NSDD 164, the National Security Space Launch Strategy, was issued on February 25, 1985. It sought to define DOD and NASA roles in maintaining the operational use of STSs. Additional directive provisions included telling the Air Force to purchase 10 ELVs and launching approximately 2 of them per year between 1988–1992, committing DOD to at least one-third of STS flights for the next 10 years; and directing DOD and NASA to conduct a joint study on developing a next generation STS to include manned and unmanned systems capable of meeting users requirements (U.S. National Security Council 2006(a), 229).

Another significant Reagan administration NSC space policy document was *NSDD 172* issued on May 30, 1985. This document involved methods and information to be used in making public presentations on SDI. Examples of factors to be presented in making the public case for SDI included stressing the changing nuclear strategic context between the United States and Soviet Union, emphasizing improvements in Soviet offensive and defensive weapons systems, ongoing Soviet research and development in advanced defense systems, Soviet noncompliance with existing arms control agreements such as the ABM Treaty, Soviet actions degrading the U.S. ability to verify their compliance with arms control agreements such as encrypting technical data emitted by their missiles during flight testing, and assessing the views of Soviet and allied countries about SDI (*National Security Space Policy Presidential Decisions: NSC Documents* 2006, 231–238).

The changing nature of nuclear deterrence from offensive forces to defensive forces and its potential implications for U.S.–Soviet strategic stability was a key point stressed in *NSDD 172*. This document stressed that long-term dependence on offensive nuclear forces may not serve as a stable deterrence basis and that continuing Soviet investment in offensive and defensive nuclear force capabilities could destroy nuclear deterrence's theoretical and empirical foundation. In response to this, it was essential for the United States to explore future options for ensuring deterrence and strategic stability in a way to counteract the destabilizing growth of Soviet offensive forces and transfer Soviet defense practices toward more stabilizing and mutually beneficial results, which *NSDD 172* contended could best be accomplished through SDI (U.S. National Security Council 2006(a), 235).

Additional *NSDD 172* talking points included outlining the aim of SDI as maintaining U.S.–Soviet strategic balance and ensuring stable deterrence instead of seeking superiority; that the United States would continue adhering to the ABM Treaty; the absence of preconceived ideas about what defensive options SDI research may generate; that it is premature to speculate on whether ground or space-based defensive systems would be recommended by SDI research; that this research is focused on defensive options for destroying attacking ballistic missiles before they reach their targets; that SDI is designed to enhance the security of U.S. allies; that consultation would occur with U.S. allies and the Soviets on possible missile defense system deployment; that SDI does not change the U.S. commitment to deterring war; that offensive nuclear forces and the potential of nuclear retaliation remain key deterrence elements; and eliminating nuclear weapons was an ultimate long-term U.S. goal, but that this required numerous changes in existing conventional and nuclear force quality, arms control, and confidence-building measures to occur (*National Security Space Project Presidential Decision: NSC Documents* 2006, 238–244; Rivkin, Jr. 1987).

The next major Reagan national security space policy directive was *NSDD 195* issued on October 30, 1985. This document was issued in preparation for U.S.–Soviet nuclear and space arms control negotiations in Geneva and directed SDI to adhere to ABM Treaty requirements while also proposing an "open laboratories initiative" with the Soviets as a vehicle for exploring research in strategic defense programs. Another significant space policy aspect of this directive was that the United States should propose and seek a Soviet commitment for exploring how a cooperative transition to more reliance on defenses should be achieved (U.S. National Security Council 2006(a), 251; Payne 1989).

Artist's concept of a space-based particle beam weapon attacking enemy missiles, 1986. *(U.S. Department of Energy)*

NSDD 164 was superseded by a subsequent space launch strategy directive issued on December 27, 1986. *NSDD 254,* issued in the aftermath of the January 28, 1986 shuttle Challenger tragedy, described launch policies for civil, commercial, and military missions. It announced that U.S. national space launch capability would consist of a mix of the space shuttle and ELVs. The directive went on to specify that this mix would be defined as being most capable of supporting the respective needs of these three launch types. National security launches were to use both the shuttle and ELVs and DOD was directed to acquire additional ELVs to maintain a balanced launch capability and provide access to space while maintaining east and west coast launch sites for these ELVs (U.S. National Security Council 2006(a), 253; Courter et al. 1994; U.S. Congress, House Committee on Science and Technology, Subcommittee on Space Science and Applications 1987; U.S. Congress, Office of Technology Assessment 1988).

Concern over a growing Soviet ASAT program caused the Reagan administration to begin efforts to remove congressional restrictions on testing ASAT capability in space. This concern resulted in the February 6, 1987 issuance of *NSDD 258* in which DOD and the Air Force requested funding to conduct relevant research and development efforts in this area and that further study of long-range U.S. ASAT requirements should continue (U.S. National Security Council 2006(a), 255–256).

A final noteworthy Reagan administration space policy document was *NSDD 293* on national space policy issued January 5, 1988. This document reaffirmed that the United States was committed to peacefully exploring and using outer space and that peaceful purposes allowed for military and intelligence-related activities in pursuit of national security and other goals, that the United States would pursue these military and intelligence activities to support its inherent self-defense rights and defense commitments to allies, that the United States rejected the claims of other nations to sovereignty over space or celestial bodies, that there can be limits on the fundamental right of sovereign nations to acquire data from space, and that the United States considers other national space systems to have the right to pass through and conduct space operations without interference (U.S. National Security Council 2006(b), 13–14).

This document went on to outline four basic DOD space mission areas including space support, force enhancement, space control, and force application. Space support guidelines stressed that military and intelligence space sectors could use manned and unmanned launch systems as determined by specific DOD or intelligence mission requirements. Force enhancement guidelines stressed that DOD would work with the intelligence community to develop, operate, and maintain space systems and develop appropriate plans and structures for meeting the operational requirements of land, sea, and air forces through all conflict levels. Space control guidelines stressed that DOD would develop, operate, and maintain enduring space systems to ensure freedom of action in space and deny such mobility to adversaries, that the United States would develop and deploy a comprehensive ASAT capability including both kinetic and directed energy weapons, and that DOD space programs would explore developing a space assets survivability enhancement program emphasizing long-term planning for future requirements. Where force application was concerned, this document proclaimed that DOD would, consistent with treaty requirements, conduct research, development, and planning to be prepared to acquire and deploy space weapons systems if national security conditions required them (U.S. National Security Council 2006(b), 15–16).

Projecting force from space was a particularly significant new facet of U.S. military space policy asserted in this document. This statement also reflected a belief in many governmental sectors that space was comparable to air, land, and sea war-fighting environments and that space combat operations should be pursued to defend national interests and enhance national security. *NSDD 293* culminated a period of significant growth in U.S. military space policy during the Reagan presidency. This administration saw AFSPACOM established in 1982 to consolidate space activities and link space-related research and development with operational space users. Army and Navy space commands were also created during this time and USSPACECOM was established in 1985 as a unified multiservice space command. Additional Reagan administration developments in military space policy included establishing a Space Technology Center at New Mexico's Kirtland Air

Force Base; forming a DOD Space Operations Committee, elevating NORAD's commander in chief to a four-star position and broadening that position's space responsibilities; creating a separate Air Force Space Division and establishing a deputy commander for Space Operations; constructing a consolidated Space Operations Center; creating a Directorate for Space Operations in the Office of the Deputy Chief of Staff/Plans and Operations in Air Force headquarters; establishing SDIO; and establishing a space operations course at the Air Force Institute of Technology (Lambakis 2001, 229–230).

George H.W. Bush Administration (1989–1993)

The beginning of the George H. W. Bush administration in 1989 saw some modification but overall continuity with Reagan administration military space policy directives. Although the first Bush administration's primary national security policy objectives would focus on the collapse of the Soviet bloc ending the Cold War and Operation Desert Storm, this administration still issued some significant documents reflecting the growing importance of space assets in military strategy and domestic and international economic activity.

George H.W. Bush administration NSC documents on space were called National Space Policy Directives (NSPDs). *NSPD 1*, also known as National Security Directive (NSD) 30, was issued on November 2, 1989. It essentially reaffirmed Reagan administration military space policy objectives while also emphasizing that U.S. space policy required continued American preeminence in space activities essential for achieving national security, scientific, technical, economic, and foreign policy objectives. It also called for supporting command and control, communications, navigation, environmental monitoring, warning, surveillance, and force application programs supporting national security program functions (U.S. National Security Council 2006(a), 262, 265).

The growing importance of commercial space launches in meeting military satellite requirements was reflected in *NSPD 2/NSD 46* issued on September 5, 1990. This directive gave United Boosters Inc. a license to participate in launches from Cape York, Australia if the Soviet Union agreed to provide international commercial market launch services only from Cape York for 10 years; if the Soviet Union and Australia observe Missile Technology Control Regime requirements; and if U.S. regulations on technology transfer to the Soviet Union are upheld. This document also allowed for additional participation in such launches by the European Space Agency and Australia if these aforementioned conditions were met (U.S. National Security Council 1990, 1–2).

NSPD 4 the National Space Launch Strategy was unveiled on July 10, 1991. This document declared that the National Space Launch Strategy had four components. These included ensuring that current space launch assets were satisfactory to meet government manned and unmanned space launch needs; developing a new unmanned but human usable space launch system to improve U.S. launch capability at lower costs and with enhanced responsiveness and mission performance; sustaining a strong space launch tech-

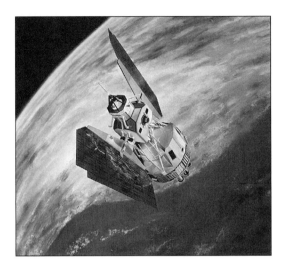

LANDSAT satellite orbits above the earth. This satellite system has civilian and military applications in areas such as remote sensing and detecting climate change. *(NASA)*

nology program to produce cost effective improvements in existing launch systems and developing advanced space launch capabilities for a new launch system, and actively considering commercial space launch needs and incorporating them into decision on improving launch facilities and vehicles (U.S. National Security Council 2006(a), 291; Bulloch 1994).

NSPD 5 dealt with LANDSAT remote sensing strategy and was issued on February 5, 1992. This directive ordered the preservation of LANDSAT satellites and acknowledged benefits of their use including their national security relevance. Policy goals contained in this directive declared that U.S. Government LANDSAT will have the following characteristics:

(a) Provide data which are sufficiently consistent in terms of acquisition geometry, coverage characteristics, and spectral characteristics with previous Landsat data to allow comparisons for change detection and characterization;

(b) Make Landsat data available to meet the needs of national security, global change research, and other federal users; and,

(c) Promote and not preclude private sector commercial opportunities in landsat-type remote sensing (U.S. National Security Council 2006(a), 298; Rawles 1989).

Additional *NSPD 5* stipulations include the government encouraging development of advanced remote sensing technologies in hope of reducing their cost and increasing performance quality to meet future government remote sensing needs; limiting federal regulations affecting private sector remote sensing activities to those affecting national security, foreign policy, and public safety; and maintaining an archive within the United States of existing and future LANDSAT data (U.S. National Security Council 2006(a), 299).

Bush also continued Reagan goals of using space combat systems to improve national security as demonstrated by moving SDI away from providing a comprehensive national ballistic missile defense shield and toward a program capable of providing the U.S. homeland, troops, and allies with limited protection against ballistic missile strikes (Lambakis 2001, 231).

Clinton Administration (1993–2001)

The Clinton administration saw continuation of the growth of the U.S. remote sensing industry, which began in the 1980s when Congress passed the 1984 Land Remote Sensing Commercialization Act removing many governmental restrictions on U.S. commercial satellites spatial resolution (Land Remote Sensing Commercialization Act, 98–451). Subsequent years saw foreign imagery suppliers dominate this market, which led Congress to pass the Land Remote Sensing Policy Act in 1992. This statute transferred governmental LANDSAT program management from the Commerce Department to DOD and NASA, acknowledged that full LANDSAT commercialization was not feasible in the foreseeable future and should not serve as a near-term national remote sensing policy goal, maintained that it was in the United States' long-term interest to maintain a permanent and comprehensive governmental archive of global LANDSAT and other remote sensing data, and declared that the private sector should be exclusively responsible for developing the remote sensing market and providing commercial value-added remote sensing services (Lambakis 2001; 231; Land Remote Sensing Policy Act, 102–555).

Consequently, the Clinton years would see significant growth in the commercial remote sensing imaging industry based on the belief that nurturing this industry would produce national security enhancements by promoting regional stability (Levy and Chodakewitz 1990; Monmonier 2002). The Clinton administration gave the Commerce Department jurisdiction over satellite exports in 1996, which Congress reversed in 1998 following fallout over revelations that U.S. companies had transferred sensitive satellite information to China (U.S. Congress, Senate Commerce on Commerce, Science, and Transportation 1999; Lambakis 2001, 232–233).

A number of NSC policy documents dealing with space were issued during the Clinton administration. These PDDs covered a variety of topics, with remote sensing applications being a particularly common characteristic of these documents. *PDD 23* was issued on March 10, 1994 and allowed for the release of remote sensing satellite images and associated technologies to the public under government regulation while seeking to secure national security information. A rationale behind this document was the belief that it would enable U.S. firms to compete more aggressively in the international remote sensing market, whose size was expected to increase from $400 million to $2 billion by the end of the century and in the space-based imagery sector, whose global market was estimated at being $15 billion by 2000 (U.S. National Security Council 2006(a), 311–312).

Decisions on limiting foreign access to commercial imagery due to possible national security concerns had to be made by the secretary of Commerce in consultation with the secretary of Defense and secretary of State, as necessary. Disagreements between these

Although the ruins of Troy have been explored for 130 years, archaeologists have only excavated 10% of the site. To help them, NASA scientists are exploring new ways of using remote sensing data. This image shows the original site of Troy and the surrounding area. Taken by the Advanced Land Imager (ALI) aboard the EO-1 satellite, the full-size image has a resolution of 10 meters. These and other sensors may help find the boundaries of a harbor near Trojan-war era Troy that has since filled with sediment, trace the route of a Roman aqueduct that carried water to the city 2,000 years ago, locate an ancient cemetery, and map the outer walls. (NASA)

cabinet officials could be appealed to the president. This document also stated that sensitive technology transfers could only be done according to a government-by-government agreement (*National Security Presidential Decisions: NSC Documents* 2006, 311–312).

The next pertinent Clinton space policy directive, issued in concert with the National Science and Technology Council (NSTC), was *PDD/NSTC 2* issued on May 5, 1994. This document combined civilian and military polar-orbiting satellites and directed that DOD, the Commerce Department, and NASA achieve this by October 1, 1994. A goal of this consolidation was reducing the cost of acquiring and operating polar-orbiting environmental satellites while satisfying civil and national security requirements. This reduced the number of these satellites from four to three, and satellite orbits were evenly spaced throughout the day to provide adequate data refreshing capability. *PDD/NSTC 2* also gave the United States the ability to deny critical environmental data to adversaries during a crisis or war to ensure that U.S. and allied military forces have exclusive access to this data (U.S. National Security Council 2006(a), 315, 319–320; U.S. Congress, House Committee on Science, Space, and Technology, Subcommittee on Space, 1994).

May 10, 1994 also saw the issuance of *PDD/NSTC 3* covering LANDSAT remote sensing strategy. This document stressed the importance of LANDSAT data to the military and the need for maintaining this data's continuity. It stressed that the U.S. Government should provide unenhanced data that was consistent in acquisition geometry, coverage characteristics, and spectral characteristics with previous LANDSAT data to permit quantitative comparisons allowing for change detection and characterization; making government-owned LANDSAT data available at the cost of users requests; and promoting and not excluding private sector commercial opportunities in LANDSAT-type remote sensing (*National Security Space Policy Presidential Decisions: NSC Documents* 2006, 323–324; Thomas 1999).

August 5, 1994 saw the Clinton administration issue its National Space Transportation Policy in *PDD/NSTC 4*. This document stressed that the U.S. space program was critical to achieving national security, scientific, technological, commercial, and foreign policy goals and that it was essential for the United States to have affordable, assured, and reliable access to space. DOD was named as the leading agency for developing ELVs and related technologies, NASA was designated the lead agency for improving the space shuttle and future generation reusable space systems, and the Commerce and Transportation Departments were charged with promoting domestic commercial space launch activities (Lambakis 2001, 232; U.S. General Accounting Office 1994; U.S. Congress, House Committee on Science, Space and Technology, Subcommittee on Space 1995).

Key national security space transportation aspects of this directive were that ELV improvements needed to be implemented in cooperation with the intelligence community, NASA, and the Commerce and Transportation departments while recognizing commercial space launch needs; DOD working with NASA could use the space shuttle for national security needs; and protecting space transportation assets used for national security missions will occur depending on their planned use in crisis situations and threats. This directive also allowed the United States to use foreign components, technologies, and certain launch services if such use is consistent with U.S. national security, foreign policy, and commercial space policy (*National Security Space Policy Presidential Decisions: NSC Documents* 2006, 329–330, 336).

PDD/NSTC 6 covering U.S. GPS policy was issued on March 29, 1996. This policy document defined the roles of agencies such as DOD and the State and Transportation Departments in administering U.S. GPS policy. DOD was authorized to continue as GPS's primary operator and maintenance agency and *PDD/NSTC 6* stressed that these agencies were to administer U.S. GPS resources to protect national interests and military use while also promoting civil, commercial, and scientific applications (*National Security Space Policy Presidential Decisions: NSC Documents* 2006, 309, 311; Black 1999; Pace et. al. 1995).

DOD was also charged with maintaining a Precise Positioning Service for use by the military and other authorized users; cooperate with the intelligence community and other appropriate departments and agencies to assess GPS national security implications; and develop measures to prevent hostile use of GPS while ensuring that the United States retains a military advantage without unnecessarily disrupting or degrading civilian GPS use. State Department GPS responsibilities include cooperation with appropriate departments and agencies; consulting with foreign governments and international government organizations on GPS issues and guidelines; coordinating interagency reviews of instructions to U.S. delegations to bilateral and multilateral GPS conferences; and coordinating reviews of international agreements on GPS issues. Transportation Department GPS responsibilities include serving as the lead U.S. agency for federal civil GPS matters; developing and implementing federal GPS augmentation for transportation applications; and cooperating with DOD and the State and Commerce Departments to provide leadership in promoting commercial applications of GPS technologies and of U.S. Government GPS augmentations as domestic and international transportation standards (*National Security Space Policy Presidential Decisions: NSC Documents* 2006, 347–348).

The last significant Clinton administration space policy document was its national space policy issued on September 19, 1996. *PDD 49* sought to promote peaceful uses of space without excluding military or intelligence uses. It went on to address national security, defense, and intelligence space guidelines while acknowledging the need to minimize space debris. This document stressed the importance of space assets in enhancing U.S. military operations, monitoring and responding to strategic military threats, and monitoring international arms control and nonproliferation agreements. It also directed the secretary of Defense and DCI to closely coordinate defense and space intelligence activities and integrate their supporting architectures as much as possible (U.S. National Security Council 2006(a), xi, 352).

PDD 49 made the following declaration about DOD space sector guidelines:

(c) DoD, as launch agent for both the defense and intelligence sectors, will maintain the capability to evolve and support those STSs, infrastructure, and support activities necessary to meet national security requirements. DoD will be the lead agency for improvement and evolution of the current ELV fleet, including appropriate technology development (U.S. National Security Council 2006(a), 353).

It also established a number of important intelligence space sector guidelines including ensuring that the DCI provide timely intelligence information to support various defense and foreign policy missions; that the DCI continue developing and applying advanced technologies for responding to a changing threat environment; that the nature, attributable collected information, and operational details of space intelligence activities remain classified; and that strict procedures are to be maintained to ensure that public discussion of satellite reconnaissance by executive branch personnel and contractors follows DCI guidance. In addition, *PDD 49* announced that the United States conduct satellite reconnaissance for peaceful purposes such as intelligence collection and monitoring arms control agreements; that this satellite reconnaissance include near real-time capability and be used to provide defense-related information for mapping, charting, and geodetic data that is provided to authorized federal agencies; that this data can be used to collect environmental data on natural or human-caused disasters; that the United States

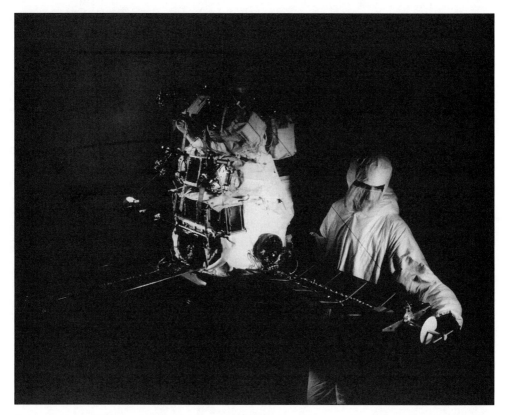

Scientist at Los Alamos National Laboratory with the Alexis satellite array, developed to de-tect nuclear weapons tests worldwide. The satellite was launched in 1993. Tracking nuclear proliferation by satellite surveillance remains a crucial U.S. intelligence and national security objective. *(U.S. Department of Energy)*

conduct overhead signals, measurement, and signature intelligence; and that the Energy Department has the ability to support space missions that may require using nuclear power (U.S. National Security Council 2006(a), 352–356, 362).

A recent assessment of Clinton administration space policy asserts that it was a low priority in their national security policymaking as evidenced by the president's limited rhet-oric on military space matters. Military space budgets were low and flat, and no progress was made on centralizing space policymaking and unifying military space objectives. Clinton ended the National Space Council begun under President Bush replacing it with the NSTC, whose mandate covered all science and technology issues, consequently dilut-ing its ability to influence military space policy. There was no fixed organizational space structure within DOD. A deputy undersecretary of Defense for Space Policy briefly ex-isted, but Secretary of Defense William Cohen (1940–) dissolved this position in 1997 and integrated it into the Command, Control, Communications, and Intelligence section of DOD's bureaucracy (Lambakis 2001, 234).

George W. Bush Administration (2001–2008)

The George W. Bush administration's foreign and national security policies have been irrevocably defined by the September 11, 2001 Al Qaeda terrorist attacks against the United States and the subsequent and controversial military interventions in Afghanistan and Iraq. The priority of responding to these attacks has occupied the preponderance of Bush administration national security policymaking. It has not kept this administration from engaging in efforts and promoting policies to strengthen the quality of U.S. military and intelligence space assets and to keep national security space policy in the minds of the domestic and international national security communities.

A significant indication of Bush administration military space policy was demonstrated by its December 13, 2001 announcement that it would withdraw from the ABM Treaty with the former Soviet Union effective in July 2002. The ABM Treaty had received significant criticism for the restrictions it placed on the United States' ability to construct ballistic missile defenses, whose need was becoming increasingly obvious as indicated by post–Cold War developments such as Iraqi use of Scud missiles during Operation Desert Storm, North Korea's 1998 flight testing of a ballistic missile over Japan and into the Pacific Ocean, and concerns documented in the 1998 Rumsfeld Commission report on ballistic missile defense. The Bush administration noted these concerns in explaining its reasons for withdrawing while pledging to continue working with Russia and other countries to combat weapons of mass destruction and their delivery components (U.S. Department of State 2001, 1–2; Ruse 2002; Bohlen 2003).

George W. Bush administration NSC policy documents are called National Security Presidential Directives (NSPDs). The first significant military space policy directive issued by this administration was *NSPD 23* issued on December 16, 2002, and it established national ballistic missile defense policy. Referring to the new security threats facing the United States since the 2001 terrorist attacks, this document directed the secretary of Defense to begin fielding an introductory suite of missile defense capabilities in 2004 and 2005. The missile defense system was to consist of ground and sea-based interceptors, additional Patriot missile defense units, and space-based sensors (U.S. National Security Council 2006(a), 365).

This document stated its desire to adhere to the National Missile Defense Act of 1999, which declared that U.S. policy was to deploy a national missile defense system capable of defending the United States against ballistic missile defense attack as soon as technologically feasible (National Missile Defense Act of 1999, 106–38). It then went on to describe the changing world strategic environment that requires ballistic missile defense.

Attributes of this evolving global strategic environment include the fact that hostile states that can sponsor terrorism are spending significant resources to develop ballistic missiles capable of hitting the United States with warheads that may carry biological, chemical, and nuclear weapons; the absence of effective U.S. and allied defenses against this threat makes it attractive to adversaries; Cold War era strategic logic does not apply to these new threats because the leaders of these emerging nations and forces are more risk-prone than leaders of the former Soviet Union and see WMD as weapons of choice instead of last resort; and that it is necessary for the United States to make progress in developing offensive and defensive infrastructures and capabilities to deal with these new threats (Federation of American Scientists n.d., 1–2).

NSPD 23 also sought to eliminate what it saw as artificial distinctions between national and theater missile defenses by vowing to develop and deploy defenses capable of defending the United States and its deployed forces along with friends and allies. This missile defense system now includes U.S. locations such as Fort Greely, Alaska and other domestic and international locations; includes ground, sea, and space-based components; and seeks the involvement of international allies such as NATO countries (Federation of American Scientists n.d., 3–5; U.S. Missile Defense Agency 2005).

NSPD 27, issued on April 25, 2003, addressed the continuing importance of remote sensing in its civilian and national security implications. Remote sensing space systems was defined in this document as covering technology, components, products, data, services, spacecraft, mission packages, ground stations, data links, and relevant command and control facilities. *NSPD 27* goals were providing guidance for licensing and operating U.S. commercial remote sensing space systems, U.S. Government use of commercial remote sensing space assets, foreign access to U.S. commercial remote sensing space capabilities, and government defense, foreign policy, and intelligence relationships with U.S. commercial remote sensing space capabilities (Federation of American Scientists 2003, 1).

According to this document, U.S. remote sensing policy is focused on advancing and protecting U.S. national security interests by maintaining U.S. leadership in remote sensing space activities and sustaining and developing the domestic remote sensing industry. *NSPD 27* maintained the United States would achieve this by making maximum practical use of U.S. commercial remote sensing capabilities for filling military, intelligence, foreign policy, homeland security, and civilian users' imagery and geospatial needs; focusing U.S. Government remote sensing systems on meeting needs that cannot be met by commercial providers for economic, national security, or foreign policy concerns; developing a long-term sustainable relationship between the federal government and domestic remote sensing industry, providing a timely and responsive regulatory framework for licensing operations and exports of commercial remote sensing systems; and enabling U.S. industry to be competitive in providing remote sensing space capabilities for foreign governments and commercial users if measures are taken to protect U.S. national security and foreign policy (Federation of American Scientists 2003, 1–2).

This document also established the National Imagery and Mapping agency (now National Geospatial Intelligence Agency) as the government agency responsible for acquiring and disseminating commercial remote sensing products and services for national security requirements and, in consultation with the secretary of State, for foreign policy requirements. It also specified that exports of sensitive or advanced information systems, technolo-

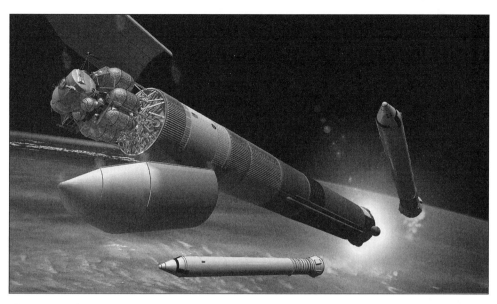

Illustration of the Ares V launch vehicle being developed to return astronauts to the moon by 2020. Ares V will use five RS-68 liquid oxygen/liquid hydrogen engines mounted below a larger version of the space shuttle's external tank, and two five-segment solid propellant rocket boosters for the first stage. *(NASA)*

gies, and components would be approved rarely and on a case-by-case basis in a consultative process involving the Secretaries of State and Defense and the DCI (Federation of American Scientists 2003, 4–6; Williamson and Baker 2004).

U.S. Space Transportation Policy was addressed in *NSPD 40* signed on December 21, 2004. This policy was introduced as a partial response to the January 14, 2004 U.S. Space Exploration Policy, which expressed its desire for human return to the moon by 2020 in preparation for additional human exploration of Mars and elsewhere. A focus of this document was achieving major transformation in U.S. space transportation capabilities and infrastructure by using the entrepreneurship and innovation of the U.S. private sector. *NSPD 40* articulated the importance of the United States being able to achieve rapid and dependable access to space by stressing the following steps the government would take to achieve such access, including making sure U.S. space transportation could provide reliable and affordable access to, transport through, and return from space; be capable of providing operationally responsive access to and use of space; developing space transportation capabilities facilitating human space exploration beyond low earth orbit; sustaining a focused technology development program from next-generation space transportation capacity to dramatically improve the reliability, responsiveness, and access cost of such transport; encouraging and facilitating the U.S. commercial space transportation industry for national security and civil transportation objectives; and sustaining and promoting the U.S. space transportation industrial base, infrastructure, and workforce to meet U.S. Government national security and civilian requirements (Federation of American Scientists 2005, 1–3; U.S. Congressional Budget Office, 2006).

This document also directed that the secretary of Defense and NASA administrator were responsible for assuring access to space, that DOD would be the national security sector launch agent responsible for developing and maintaining appropriate services and infrastructure for this activity, that the Evolved Expendable Launch Vehicle (EELV) program will be the keystone for space access for medium and large national and homeland security payloads, and that by 2010 DOD, the intelligence community, and NASA will evaluate EELV's long-term requirements, funding, management responsibilities, and infrastructure (U.S. Department of Defense, Office of the Assistant Secretary of Defense (Public Affairs) 2005, 1–7; Federation of American Scientists 2005, 3–4).

The most recent incarnation of U.S. national space policy documents as espoused by presidential administrations was issued on August 31, 2006. This document had not been assigned an *NSPD* number as of late November 2006. It restates a number of preexisting U.S. space policy goals, including stressing the U.S. commitment to peaceful exploration of space, rejecting other national or international claims to sovereignty over space or celestial bodies, and the importance of free and unimpeded right of passage in and through space. Additional U.S. space policy tenets asserted in this document are that the United States considers its space assets and ground supporting links to be vital national interests, that it will preserve its rights, capabilities, and freedom of action in space while dissuading and deterring others from restricting those rights or developing the ability to restrict those rights; that it will oppose new legal regimes or other restrictions seeking to prohibit or limit U.S. access to or use of space; that it will oppose arms control agreements or restrictions designed to limit its ability to use space for research, operations, and testing conductive to U.S. national interests; and that the United States wants to encourage a growing and entrepreneurial commercial space sector (U.S. Office of Science and Technology Policy 2006, 1–2).

This document went on to stress the significant and increasing dependence of U.S. national security on space assets. It reaffirmed how space capabilities supported the president and other senior executive branch policymakers in conducting foreign policy, homeland security, and national security responsibilities (U.S. Office of Science and Technology Policy 2006, 3). An additional noteworthy section of this document recognizes the creation of the position of Director of National Intelligence (DNI) to coordinate national intelligence activities as a result of the Intelligence Reform and Terrorism Prevention Act of 2004 (Intelligence Reform and Terrorism Prevention Act of 2004, 108–458).

National space policy goals prescribed for the DNI include establishing intelligence community objectives, intelligence requirements, and guidance for timely and effective collection, analysis, and dissemination; ensuring that this intelligence and data support defense policies including indication and warning, crisis management, and treaty compliance verification; providing intelligence collection and analysis of space-related capabilities to augment SSA; providing a strong foreign space intelligence and analysis collection capability for national and homeland security needs; and establishing and implementing policies and procedures to protect space intelligence collection and operational activities and declassify this information when it no longer needs to be protected (U.S. Office of Science and Technology Policy 2006, 4–5).

During June 2007, the Bush administration announced that it was working with Poland and the Czech Republic to set up ballistic missile defense systems in those countries. This was opposed by Russian president Vladimir Putin (1952–), who suggested Azerbaijan as a better location for this system. Discussion on this topic will influence U.S.–Russian relations for the foreseeable future (Hadley 2007).

These Bush administration military space policy priorities are likely to continue in the administration's final two years. Secretary of Defense Robert M. Gates (1943–), responding to advance questions submitted during his confirmation hearings, stated that he supported long-standing national policy on national rights of free passage to and through space, the right to protect the United States and its military from hostile space attacks, and his support for ongoing plans to develop and deploy ballistic missiles defenses (U.S. Congress, Senate Committee on Armed Services 2006(a), 48).

Conclusion

U.S. military space policy has come a long way during its six-decade history from von Karman's *Toward New Horizons* and Project Rand's *Preliminary Design of an Experimental World-Circling Spaceship* to today's accomplishments and challenges. Space has become an increasingly important factor in U.S. military policy and strategy and in national and international economic activity. The following statement by United States Strategic Command commander general James Cartwright (1949–) on March 16, 2005 before a Senate Armed Services Committee subcommittee graphically describes how crucial space has become to multiple aspects of contemporary life:

> The importance of the space mission to our national security cannot be overstated. The US economy, our quality of life, and our nation's defense are all linked to our freedom of action in space. For example, satellites are at the heart of routine financial activities such as the simple automatic teller machine operations or complicated international currency and stockmarket transactions. The telecommunications industry is heavily vested in space. Commercial airliners, container ships, trains, trucks, police, fire departments and ambulances have also become highly dependent upon space-based GPSs to enhance their ability to safely deliver people, goods and services. The fact is, our dependency on space increases every day—a fact not lost on our adversaries. This growing national dependence on space-based and

space-enabled capabilities establishes a true imperative to protect our space assets and our ability to operate freely in, and from, space (U.S. Congress, Senate Committee on Armed Services, Subcommittee on Strategic Forces, 2006(b), 88).

U.S. willingness to assertively defend its interests in space and opposing international restrictions on space activities has resulted in the United States being willing to stand against international opinion on some space policy issues. The 1967 OST still has a wide range of support within the international community. Formulaic UN General Assembly resolutions opposing what they see as an "arms race in outer space" are passed on a regular basis in that organization's debates. Both the United States and Israel were the only countries voting against this resolution on December 8, 2005 on the basis of their concerns that it would restrict their freedom of action in space (United Nations General Assembly 2005, 22–23).

This assertive defense of U.S. military space policy interests is set against a background of increasing concern about the nature of China's space program. U.S. policymakers have grown concerned that this program has military aspirations that may come to threaten U.S. military space interests and assets. The 2006 edition of DOD's annual report on Chi-

Chinese soldier stands guard near the China National Space Administration's *Shenzhou VI* space vehicle. The ship launched in October 2005, carrying two astronauts—China's second manned mission into space. *(AP/Wide World Photos)*

nese military power maintains that China continues pursuing an offensive ASAT system; that it can currently destroy or disable satellites by launching a ballistic missile or space-launched vehicle armed with a nuclear weapon; that it is improving its SSA, which will allow it to track and identify most satellites; that it continues to improve its space-based command, control, intelligence, surveillance, and targeting capabilities; and that it wants to acquire radio frequency weapons to defeat technologically advanced military forces (U.S. Department of Defense 2006, 31–35).

China's increasing economic affluence is also prompting it to become more assertive in international political and economic circles (Saunders 2006). This assertiveness has also made it more important to understand how China views space as a potential vehicle for asserting military power and promoting what it sees as vital national interests while recognizing that there are divergent views on emerging Chinese military strategy and policy (McCabe 2003; Murray and Antonellis 2003; Descisciolo 2005, 49–64).

Debate over the nature and intent of China's military power will occupy academics and policymakers for the foreseeable future. Chinese actions are important ways of determining their intent. Two incidents during the fall of 2006 and one in January 2007 caused concern about China's potential ability to negatively affect U.S. space assets. News reports revealed that China fired high-powered lasers at U.S. satellites flying over its territory in what can be seen as attempts to blind these craft. Such efforts could damage the effectiveness and operational ability of U.S. reconnaissance satellites and radar satellites. U.S. military officials are taking these incidents seriously enough to test ground-based lasers against their own spacecraft to determine their usefulness and develop space architectures strong enough to resist such attacks (Muradian 2006, 1–3).

Another incident of concern reflects China's increasing interest in waging information warfare, which can affect space-based assets given their heavy dependence on computer networks. During November 2006, Chinese hackers successfully penetrated and shut down the U.S. Naval War College computer network, forcing authorities to shut down that institution's email and official computer network including the website and prompting an investigation by the FBI and Naval Criminal Investigative Service (Gertz 2006; Thomas 2004).

On January 11, 2007, China destroyed a Feng Yun 1C polar-orbit weather satellite orbiting at an altitude of 865 kilometers (537 miles) from the earth using an ASAT system launched from its Xichang Space Center in Sichuan province. This test prompted protests from the United States, Japan, Australia, India, Canada, and other countries that have expressed displeasure with Chinese contentions that the test's intent was peaceful. U.S. military and defense policymakers have expressed concern over the test because it reveals major gaps in U.S. intelligence knowledge about Chinese weapons capabilities that could destroy or disable U.S. satellites responsible for handling nearly 90% of U.S. military communications. These officials are also concerned that the test shows that China's military warfighting and weapons capabilities are not a decade behind the United States as preexisting intelligence estimates maintained (British Broadcasting Corporation 2007; Gertz 2007).

Concern over Chinese military space capabilities and policies was also expressed during January 2007 in a report prepared for the government's U.S.-China Economic and Security Review Commission. This report reviews Chinese military literature and notes the publications of books in 2001, 2002, and 2005 by Chinese military officers that advocate various military-explicit uses of space. Examples of such uses include: developing ASAT weapons using land-based and satellite platforms; using space weapons to defeat the United States in a war over Taiwan; developing space weapons using an internally intense posture while maintaining a low profile international posture to maintain China's "good image"; developing an orbital network of concealed space strike weapons that would be used in a "crisis" or "emergency" without warning to deter and defeat the United States by jamming and attacking satellite ground stations; the necessity for China to formulate emergency crisis or response plans for space war preparation; and stating that surprise space attacks can have a huge psychological impact on opposing policymakers (Pillsbury 2007, 3, 10–12).

Although the U.S. military has made significant progress in developing its military and intelligence space capabilities, it still faces numerous problems in achieving the full potential of these capabilities. The military has been unable to achieve agreement on the best use of its space assets in military operations, and it has also had problems determining if there should be a separate military service dedicated to conducting space operations.

Proponents of a separate military service believe the time has come to create such a military branch (Gayl 2004), while opponents of this believe the Air Force has not developed enough space power theory and doctrine to drive a military effort in space (Moorehead 2004).

U.S. scientific, political, and military communities have achieved enough success to make space assets an essential component of U.S. national security architecture. Although there are significant budgetary, diplomatic, military doctrinal, organizational management, political, and technological challenges that remain to be effectively resolved, the United States will likely be able to create and sustain a primarily space-based military force during the first half of the 21st century. It is also possible that China, Russia, the European Union, and Japan may create comparable space-based military capabilities during this time period.

This debate will continue in the United States and other national militaries, U.S. political and governing circles, the domestic and international scholarly security studies community, and in international political forums such as the UN Office for Outer Space Affairs. The published literature in this field described in this book reveals strong arguments from proponents and opponents of a human military presence in space. Space's increasing importance in domestic and international economic activity, the importance of space to the United States, China, Russia, and other countries for military intelligence and surveillance, the emerging ballistic missile threat of Shabab and Taepo-dong missiles from rogue regimes such as Iran and North Korea, and global military history trends indicating expansion of military theaters from land, to sea, and air are inexorably expanding to include space despite naive utopian protestations from some participants in this debate. It will be imperative for 21st century national security policymakers to work to ensure that there are orderly and effective security architectures and internationally recognized procedures for ensuring free access to and movement through space, and that no totalitarian regimes or terrorist groups are able to impede the ability of countries or organizations to use space for disrupting commercial activities, intelligence, or national and homeland security operations. Achieving such freedom of space may require the United States to take unilateral or multilateral action to defend such access even if this may prove highly unpopular in certain sectors of world opinion. Space has become so important to domestic and international economic, intelligence, and security activity that the world cannot afford to surrender control of space to regimes or terrorist organizations opposed to market economics, the rule of law, and political pluralism.

References and Further Reading

Air University. Center for Strategy and Technology. 1994(a). "Professional Military Education (PME) in 2020." [Online article or information; retrieved 11/16/06.] http://csat.au.af.mil/2020/papers/app-1.pdf.

Air University. Center for Strategy and Technology. 1994(b). "SPACECAST 2020: Into the Future." [Online article or information; retrieved 11/16/06]. http://csat.au.af.mil/2020/monographs/exec-sum.pdf.

Anderson, F. W. 1981. *Orders of Magnitude: A History of NACA and NASA, 1915–1980.* Washington, D.C.: National Aeronautics and Space Administration.

Arnold, D. C. 2002. *Supporting New Horizons: The Evolution of the Military Satellite Command and Control System, 1944–1969.* Ph.D. diss. Auburn, AL: Auburn University.

Arnold, D. C. 2005. *Spying From Space: Constructing America's Satellite Command and Control Systems.* College Station, TX: Texas A&M University Press.

Barry, J. L. and D. L. Herriges. 2000. "Aerospace Integration, Not Separation." *Aerospace Power Journal* 14 (2): 42–47.

Baucom, D. R. 1992. *The Origins of SDI: 1944–1983.* Lawrence, KS: University Press of Kansas.

Bermudez, J. S., Jr. 1998. "North Koreans Test Two-Stage IRBM (Intermediate Range Ballistic Missile) Over Japan." *Jane's Defence Weekly* 30 (10): 26.

Berry, N. 2001. "Existing Legal Constraints on Space Weaponry." *Defense Frontier* 30 (2): 5–6.

Best, R. A., Jr. 2001. *The National Security Council: An Organizational Assessment.* Huntington, NY: Novinka Books.

Black, J. T. 1999. "Commercial Satellites: Future Threats or Allies?" *Naval War College Review* 52 (1): 99–114.

Bohlen, A. 2003. "The Rise and Fall of Arms Control." *Survival,* 45 (3): 7–34.

Boone, W. F. 1970. *NASA's Office of Defense Affairs: The First Five Years: December 1, 1962–January 1968.* Washington, D.C.: NASA History Office. [Online article or information; retrieved 10/31/06.] http://history.nasa.gov/HHR-32/HHR-32.htm.

Bowen, G. S. 2005. "Safeguard: North Dakota's Front Line in the Cold War." *Quest* 12 (1): 42–51.

British Broadcasting Corporation News. 2007. "Concern Over China's Missile Test," 1–3: January 19, 2007. [Online article or information; retrieved 1/23/07.] http://news.bbc.co.uk/2/hi/asia-pacific/6276543.stm.

Bulloch, C. 1994. "Commercial Launchers: What Military Boost?" *Interavia* 49 (July): 44–47.

Carns, M. P.C. 1995. "Spacecast 2020: A Commentary." *Airpower Journal* 9 (2): 4–7.

Chow, B. G. 1993. *Emerging National Space Launch Programs: Economics and Safeguards.* Santa Monica, CA: Rand Corporation.

Chun, C. K. S. 2002. *Aerospace Power in the Twenty-First Century: A Basic Primer.* Maxwell Air Force Base, AL: Air University Press.

Clarke, A. C. 1945. "Extra-Terrestrial Relays: Can Rocket Stations Give World-Wide Radio Coverage?" *Wireless World Radio and Electronics* 51 (10): 305–308.

Collins, M. J. 2002. *Cold War Laboratory: RAND, the Air Force, and the American State, 1945–1950.* Washington, D.C.: Smithsonian Institution Press.

Courter, J. 1994. "Military Space Policy: The Criticial Importance of New Launch Technology." *Strategic Review,* 22 (3)(Summer): 14-23.

Cunningham, J. 1994. "Third World Missile Proliferation Poses New Threats." *Journal of Social, Political, and Economic Studies* 19 (Summer): 131–148.

Daso, D. A. 1999. "New World Vistas: Looking Toward the Future, Learning From the Past." *Airpower Journal* 13 (4): 67–76.

Daso, D. A. 2000. *Hap Arnold and the Evolution of American Airpower.* Washington, D.C.: Smithsonian Institution Press.

Day, D. A., J. M. Logsdon, and B. Latell, eds. 1998. *Eye in the Sky: The Story of the Corona Spy Satellites.* Washington, D.C.: Smithsonian Institution Press.

Descisciolo, D. 2005. "China's Space Development and Nuclear Strategy." In *China's Nuclear Force Modernization,* 49–64. edited by L. Goldstein and A. S. Erickson. Newport, RI: Naval War College Press.

Dickenson, M. J. 2005. "The Executive Office of the President: The Paradox of Politicization." In *The Executive Branch,* edited by J. D. Aberbach and M. A. Peterson, 135–172. New York: Oxford University Press.

Dwyer, C. M. 2002. "The U.S. Presidency and National Security Directives: An Overview." *Journal of Government Information* 29 (6): 410–419.

Elliott, D. W. 1992. *Finding an Appropriate Commitment: Space Policy Development Under Eisenhower and Kennedy, 1954–1963.* Ph.D. diss. George Washington University, Washington, D.C.

Erickson, M. 2005. *Into the Unknown Together: The DOD, NASA, and Early Spaceflight.* Maxwell Air Force Base, AL: Air University Press.

Federation of American Scientists. 2003. *U.S. Commercial Remote Sensing Policy Fact Sheet,* 1–2, 4–5. [Online article or information; retrieved 11/29/06.] www.fas.org/irp/offdocs/remsens .html.

Federation of American Scientists. n.d. *National Security Presidential Directive/NSPD-23: National Policy on Ballistic Missile Defense,* 1–5. [Online article or information; retrieved 11/29/06.] www.fas.org/irp/offdocs/nspd/nspd-23.htm.

Federation of American Scientists. n.d. *U.S. Space Transportation Policy Fact Sheet,* 1–4. [Online article or information; retrieved 11/29/06.] www.fas.org/irp/offdocs/nspd/nspd-40.pdf.

Federation of American Scientists. Intelligence Resource Program. n.d. *Presidential Directives and Executive Orders.* [Online article or information; retrieved 10/18/06.] www.fas.org/irp/offdocs/direct.html.

Futrell, R. F. 1989. *Volume II: Ideas, Concepts, Doctrine: Basic Thinking in the United States Air Force 1961–1984.* Maxwell Air Force Base, AL: Air University Press.

Gayl, F. J. 2004. "Time for a Military Space Service." *U.S. Naval Institute Proceedings* 130 (7): 43–48.

Gertz, B. 2006. "Chinese Hackers Prompt Navy College Site Closure." *Washington Times,* November 30, 1–2. [Online article or information; retrieved 11/30/06.] www.washtimes.com/functions/print.php?StoryID=20061130–103049–5042r.

Gertz, B. 2007. "Officials Fear War in Space by China." *Washington Times,* January 24, 1–2. [Online article or information; retrieved 1/24/07.] www.washtimes.com/national/20070124–121536–8225r.htm.

Goodman, G. W., Jr. 2000. "Aerospace Force: US Air Force Sees its Future and Modernizes Itself to Get There." *Armed Forces Journal International* 138 (2): 48–58.

Gorn, M. H. 1992. *The Universal Man: Theodore von Karman's Life in Aeronautics.* Washington, D.C.: Smithsonian Institution Press.

Gorn, M. H., ed. 1994. *Prophecy Fulfilled: "Toward New Horizons" and Its Legacy.* Washington, D.C.: Air Force History and Museums Program.

Grier, Peter. 1996. "New World Vistas." *Air Force Magazine* 79 (3): 20–25.

Hadley, Stephen. 2007. "Press Gaggle by National Security Advisor Steve Hadley to the Travel Pool." June 7, 2007. [Online article or information; retrieved 6/11/07.] www.whitehouse.gov/news/releases/2007/06/print/20070607–4.html.

Hall, R. C. 1995. "The Eisenhower Administration and the Cold War: Framing American Astronautics to Serve National Security." *Prologue* 27 (1): 58–72.

Heppenheimer, T.A. 2002. *History of the Space Shuttle.* Washington, D.C.: Smithsonian Institution Press.

Herken, G. 2000. *Cardinal Choices: Presidential Science Advising from the Atomic Bomb to SDI.* Stanford, CA: Stanford University Press.

Hoff, J. 1997. "The Presidency, Congress, and the Deceleration of the U.S. Space Program." In *Spaceflight and the Myth of Presidential Leadership,* edited by R. D. Launius and H. E. McCurdy, 92–132. Urbana, IL: University of Illinois Press.

Intelligence Reform and Terrorism Prevention Act of 2004, Public Law 108–458, U.S. Statutes at Large 118 (2004), 3637–3872.

Jenkins, D. R. 1996. *The History of Developing the National Space Transportation System: The Beginning Through STS-75.* 2nd ed. Indian Harbour Beach, FL: D.R. Jenkins.

Jennings, F. W. 1990. "Doctrinal Conflict Over the Word Aerospace." *Airpower Journal* 4 (3): 46–59.

Johnson, D. J. 1993. *Space Launch Policies and Systems: A Presentation to SPACECAST 2020.* Santa Monica, CA: Rand Corporation.

Kay, W.D. 1998. "John F. Kennedy and the Two Faces of the U.S. Space Program, 1961–1963." *Presidential Studies Quarterly* 28 (3): 573–586.

Lambakis, S. 2001. *On the Edge of Earth: The Future of American Space Power.* Lexington, KY: University Press of Kentucky.

Lambeth, B. S. 2004. "A Short History of Military Space." *Air Force Magazine* 87 (12): 60–64.

Land Remote Sensing Commercialization Act, 1984. Public Law 98–451, U.S. Statutes at Large 98, 451–467.

Land Remote Sensing Policy Act, 1992. Public Law 102–555, U.S. Statutes at Large 106, 4163–4180.

Launius, R. D. 1994. *NASA: A History of the U.S. Civil Space Program.* Malabar, FL: Krieger Pub. Company.

Launius, R.D. and D.R. Jenkins, eds. 2002. *To Reach the High Frontier: A History of U.S. Launch Vehicles.* Lexington, KY: University Press of Kentucky.

Levy, L. J. and S. B. Chodakewitz. 1990. "The Commercialization of Satellite Imagery: Implications for Cross-Border Conflict." *Space Policy* 6 (August): 209–220.

Locher, J. 2002. *Victory on the Potomac: The Goldwater-Nichols Act Unifies the Pentagon.* College Station, TX: Texas A&M University Press.

Logsdon, J. 1992. *Legislative Origins of the National Aeronautics and Space Act of 1958: Proceedings of an Oral History Workshop Conducted April 3, 1992.* Washington, D.C.: NASA History Office.

Lonnquest, J. C. 1996. *The Face of Atlas: General Bernard Schriever and the Development of the Atlas Intercontinental Ballistic Missile, 1953–1960.* Ph.D. diss. Duke University, Durham, NC.

McCabe, T. R. 2003. "The Chinese Air Force and Air and Space Power." *Air and Space Power Journal* 17 (3): 73–83.

McDougall, W. A. 1997. *The Heavens and the Earth: A Political History of the Space Age.* Baltimore, MD: Johns Hopkins University Press.

Mack, P. E. 1990. *Viewing the Earth: The Social Construction of the Landsat Satellite System.* Cambridge, MA: MIT Press.

Mann, A. K. 2000. *For Better or for Worse: The Marriage of Science and Government in the United States.* New York: Columbia University Press.

Martinez, L. F. 1998. "Satellite Communications and the Internet: Implications for the Outer Space Treaty." *Space Policy* 14 (May): 83–88.

Monmonier, M. 2002. *Spying With Maps: Surveillance Technologies and the Future of Privacy.* Chicago: University of Chicago Press.

Moorehead, R. D. 2004. "Will We Need a Space Force?" *Military Review* 84 (4): 50–53.

Muradian, V. 2006. "China Attempted to Blind U.S. Satellites With Laser." *Defense News.com,* 1–3. [Online article or information; retrieved 11/30/06.] www.defensenews.com/story.php?F =2121111&C-america.

Murray, W. S., III and R. Antonellis. 2003. "China's Space Program: The Dragon Eyes the Moon (and Us)." *Orbis* 47 (4): 645–652.

National Aeronautics and Space Act of 1958, Public Law 85–568, U.S. Statutes at Large 72 (1958): 426.

National Defense Authorization Act for Fiscal Year 1997, Public Law 104–201, U.S. Statutes at Large 110 (1997), 2421, 2711–2714.

National Defense Authorization Act for Fiscal Year 2000, Public Law 106–65, U.S. Statutes at Large 113 (2000), 511, 814–815.

National Missile Defense Act of 1999, Public Law 106–38, U.S. Statutes at Large 113 (1999), 205.

Neufeld, J. 2005. *Bernard A. Schriever: Challenging the Unknown.* Washington, D.C.: Office of Air Force History.

Neufeld, M. J. 1996. *The Rocket and the Reich: Peenemunde and the Coming of the Ballistic Missile Era.* Cambridge, MA: Harvard University Press.

Neufeld, M. J. 2005. "The End of the Army Space Program: Interservice Rivalry and the Transfer of the Von Braun Group to NASA, 1958–1959." *Journal of Military History* 69 (3): 737–757.

Nolan, J. E. 1991. *Trappings of Power: Ballistic Missiles in the Third World.* Washington, D.C.: Brookings Institution.

Pace, S., G.P. Frost, I. Lachow, D.R. Frelinger, D. Fossum, D.K. Wassem, and M. Pinto et al. 1995. *The Global Positioning System: Assessing National Priorities.* Santa Monica, CA: Rand Corporation.

Parrington, A. J. 1989. "U.S. Space Doctrine: Time for a Change?" *Airpower Journal* 3 (3): 50–61.

Payne, K. 1989. "ICBMs, Arms Control, and the SDI." *Comparative Strategy* 8 (1): 55–71.

Pedlow, G. W. and D. E. Welzenbach. 1998. *The CIA and the U-2 Program, 1954–1974.* Washington, D.C.: Central Intelligency Agency, Center for the Study of Intelligence.

Pillsbury, M. 2007. *An Assessment of China's Anti-Satellite and Space Warfare Programs, Policies and Doctrines.* Washington, D.C.: U.S.-China Economic and Security Review Commission. [Online article or information; retrieved 2/6/07.] www.uscc.gov/researchpapers/2007/FINAL _REPORT_1–19–2007_REVISED_BY_MPP.pdf.

Piotrowski, J. L. 1987. "U.S. Space Command—Meeting National Security Needs in the Fourth Dimension." *Defense* (November-December): 43–47.

Portree, D. S. F. 1998. *NASA's Origins and the Dawn of the Space Age.* Washington, D.C.: NASA History Division, Office of Policy and Plans. [Online article or information; retrieved 10/30/06.] www.hq.nasa.gov/office/pao/History/monograph10/nasabrth.html.

Posey, R. 1998. "A Sudden Loss of Altitude." *Air and Space Smithsonian* 13 (2): 74–81.

Power, J. W. 1990. "Space Control in the Post–Cold War Era." *Airpower Journal* 4 (4): 24–33.

President of the United States. 1984. *U.S. Policy on ASAT Arms Control.* House Document 98–197. Washington, D.C.: U.S. Government Printing Office.

Project Rand. 1946. *Preliminary Design of an Experimental World-Circling Spaceship.* Santa Monica, CA: Douglas Aircraft Company. [Online article or information; retrieved 10/20/06.] www.rand.org/pubs/special_memoranda/2006/SM11827part1.pdf.

Rawles, J. W. 1989. "Commercial Imaging Comes Down to Earth." *Defense Electronics* 21 (April): 46–50.

Relyea, H. F. 2005. *Presidential Directives: Background and Overview.* Washington, D.C.: Library of Congress, Congressional Research Service.

Richelson, J. T. 1999. *America's Space Sentinels: DSP Satellites and National Security.* Lawrence, KS: University Press of Kansas.

Rip, M. R. and J. M. Hasik. 2002. *The Precision Revolution: GPS and the Future of Aerial Warfare.* Annapolis, MD: Naval Institute Press.

Rivkin, D. B., Jr. 1987. "SDI: Strategic Reality of Never-Never Land?" *Strategic Review* 15 (3): 43–54.

Rumerman, J. A. 1998. *Human Space Flight: A Record of Achievement, 1961–1998.* Washington, D.C.: NASA History Division. [Online article or information; retrieved 11/22/06.] http://purl .access.gpo.gov/GPO/LPS49039.

Ruse, M. A. 2002. "Reflections on the 1972 Antiballistic Missile Treaty and National Missile Defense." *Aerospace Power Journal* 16 (1): 69–76.

Saunders, P. C. 2006. *China's Global Activism: Strategy, Drivers, and Tools.* Washington, D.C.: National Defense University, Institute for National Strategic Studies. [Online article or information; retrieved 11/30/06.] www.ndu.edu/inss/Occasional_Papers/OCP4.pdf.

Scarborough, J. 1991. "The Privatization of Expendable Launch Vehicles: Reconciliation of Conflicting Policy Objectives." *Policy Studies Review* 10 (2–3): 12–30.

Schneider, M. B. 1971. "Safeguards, Sufficiency, and SALT." *Military Review* 51 (5): 24–33.

Smith, M. S. 2005. *Military Space Programs: Issues Concerning DOD's SBIRS and STSS Programs.* Washington, D.C.: Library of Congress, Congressional Research Service.

Sparling, W. P. 2003. "Cries of the Hunchback: Is Space a Theatre of War or a Sanctuary?" *Marines Corps Gazette* 87(5): 63–65.

Spires, D. N. 1998. *Beyond Horizons: A Half Century of Air Force Space Leadership.* Peterson Air Force Base, CO: Air Force Space Command.

Spires, D. N., ed. 2004. *Orbital Futures: Selected Documents in Air Force Space History.* 2 vols. Peterson Air Force Base, CO: United States Air Force Space Command.

Springer, A. M. 1999. "Securing the High Ground: The Army's Quest for the Moon." *Quest: The History of Spaceflight Quarterly* 7 (2): 34–38.

Stares, P. 1985. *The Militarization of U.S. Space Policy, 1945–1984.* Ithaca, NY: Cornell University Press.

Stumborg, M. F. 2006. "Air Force Space Command: A Transformation Case Study." *Air and Space Power Journal* 20 (2): 79–88.

Thomas, G. B. 1999. "External Shocks, Conflict and Learning as Interactive Sources of Change in U.S. Security Policy." *Journal of Public Policy* 19 (May/August): 209–231.

Thomas, T. L. 2004. *Dragon Bytes: Chinese Information War Theory and Practice from 1995–2003.* Fort Leavenworth, KS: Foreign Military Studies Office.

Towell, P. 1999. "Missile Defense Tug of War." *CQ Weekly*, 57 (1): 20–21.

United Nations General Assembly. 2005. *Official Records,* A/60/PV.61, December 8, 22–23. New York: United Nations General Assembly.

U.S. Air Force. 2000. *The Aerospace Force: Defending America in the 21st Century: a White Paper on Air Force Integration* 3, 6–7. [Online article or information; retrieved 11/20/06.] www.af.mil/shared/media/document/AFD-060726–029.pdf.

U.S. Air Force. 2001. *Space Operations: Air Force Doctrine Document 2–2.* [Online article or information; retrieved 11/20/06.] www.dtic.mil/doctrine/jel/service_pubs/afdd2_2.pdf.

U.S. Air Force. 2004. *Counterspace Operations: Air Force Doctrine Document 2–2.1.* [Online article or information; retrieved 11/20/06.] www.dtic.mil/doctrine/jel/service_pubs/afdd2–2–1.pdf.

U.S. Air Force. 2005. "Architect of Air Force Space and Missile Programs Dies." [Online article or information; retrieved 11/2/06.] www.af.mil/news/story.asp?storyID=123010834.

U.S. Air Force. 2006. "Defense Meteorological Satellite Program." [Online article or information; retrieved 11/7/06.] www.af.mil/factsheets/factsheet_print.asp?fsID=94&page=1.

U.S. Air Force Aeronautical Systems Center History Office. 2002. *Wright From the Start: Toward New Horizons,* 1–2. [Online article or information; retrieved 10/19/06.] www.ascho.wpafb.af.mil/START/CHAP7.htm.

U.S. Air Force Scientific Advisory Board. 1995. *New World Vistas: Air and Space Power For the 21st Century: Summary Volume.* Washington, D.C.: U.S. Air Force Scientific Advisory Board.

U.S. Air Force Scientific Advisory Board. 1996. *New World Vistas: Air and Space Power for the 21st Century: Space Applications Volume.* Washington, D.C.: U.S. Air Force Scientific Advisory Board.

U.S. Air Force Space Command. 1991. *Desert Storm "Hot Wash" 12–13 Jul 1991.* Peterson Air Force Base, CO. [Online article or information; retrieved 11/13/06.] www.gwu.edu/%7Ensarchiv/NSAEBB/NSAEBB39/document7.pdf.

U.S. Air Force Space Command. 2006. *Space Innovation and Development Center.* [Online article or information; retrieved 11/15/06.] www.afspc.af.mil/library/factsheets/factsheet.asp?id=3651.

U.S. Arms Control and Disarmament Agency. 1996. *Arms Control and Disarmament Agreements: Texts and Histories of Negotiations.* Washington, D.C.: U.S. Government Printing Office.

U.S. Central Intelligence Agency. 1970. *Intelligence Memorandum: Soviet ABM Defenses—Status and Prospects.* Washington, D.C.: Central Intelligence Agency.

U.S. Central Intelligence Agency. 1997. *Report of Proliferation-Related Acquisition in 1997.* [Online article or information; retrieved 11/17/06.] https://www.cia.gov/cia/library/reports/archived-reports-1/acq1997.html.

U.S. Commission to Assess the Ballistic Missile Threat to the United States. 1998(a). *Report: Charter and Organization,* 1. [Online article or information; retrieved 11/17/06.] www.fas.org/irp/threat/missile/rumsfeld/charter.htm.

U.S. Commission to Assess the Ballistic Missile Threat to the United States. 1998(b). *Report: Executive Summary,* 1. [Online article or information; retrieved 11/17/06.] www.fas.org/irp/threat/missile/rumsfeld/execsum.htm.

U.S. Commission to Assess United States National Security Space Management and Organization. 2001. *Report.* [Online article or information; retrieved 11/20/06.] www.fas.org/spp/military/commission/report.htm.

U.S. Congress. *Congressional Record.* August 6, 1969. Vol. 115, pt. 17: 22478–22479, 22483.

U.S. Congress. *Congressional Record.* May 25, 1971. Vol. 107, pt. 7: 8877–8882.

U.S. Congress. House Committee on Appropriations. Subcommittee on the Department of Defense. 1983. *Department of Defense Appropriations for 1984: Part 2.* Washington, D.C.: U.S. Government Printing Office.

U.S. Congress. House Committee on Government Operations. 1966. *Missile and Space Ground Support Operations: Twenty-Third Report.* House Report 89–1340. Washington, D.C.: U.S. Government Printing Office.

U.S. Congress. House Committee on National Security. Research and Development Subcommittee. 1998(a). *Ballistic Missile Threat Posed by Iran.* Washington, D.C.: U.S. Government Printing Office.

U.S. Congress. House Committee on National Security. 1998(b). *Findings and Conclusions of the Commission to Assess the Ballistic Missile Threat to the United States.* Washington, D.C.: U.S. Government Printing Office.

U.S. Congress. House Committee on Science and Technology. 1985. *Astronauts and Cosmonauts Biographical and Statistical Data [Revised-June 28, 1985].* Washington, D.C.: U.S. Government Printing Office.

U.S. Congress. House Committee on Science and Technology. Subcommittee on Space Science and Applications. 1987. *Assured Access to Space: 1986: Hearings, February 26–August 14, 1986.* Washington, D.C.: U.S. Government Printing Office.

U.S. Congress. House Committee on Science, Space, and Technology. Subcommittee on Space. 1994. *Convergence of Civilian and Defense Polar-Orbiting Satellites.* Washington, D.C.: U.S. Government Printing Office.

U.S. Congress. House Committee on Science, Space, and Technology. 1995. *National Space Transportation Policy.* Washington, D.C.: U.S. Government Printing Office.

U.S. Congress. Office of Technology Assessment. 1988. *Launch Options for the Future: A Summary.* Washington, D.C.: U.S. Government Printing Office.

U.S. Congress. Senate Committee on Aeronautics and Space Sciences. 1967. *Treaty on Principles Governing the Activities of States in the Exploration and Use of Outer Space, Including the Moon and Other Celestial Bodies: Analysis and Background Data.* Washington, D.C.: U.S. Government Printing Office.

U.S. Congress. Senate Committee on Armed Services. 2006(a). *Advanced Policy Questions for Dr. Robert M. Gates Nominee to be Secretary of Defense.* [Online article or information; retrieved 12/5/06.] http://armed-services.senate.gov/statemnt/2006/December/Gates%2012–05–06.pdf.

U.S. Congress. Senate Committee on Armed Services. Subcommittee on Strategic Forces. 2006(b). *Department of Defense Authorization for Appropriations for Fiscal Year 2006: PT 7: Strategic Forces.* Washington, D.C.: U.S. Government Printing Office.

U.S. Congress. Senate Committee on Armed Services. Subcommittee on Strategic. 2002. *Report of the Commission to Assess United States National Security Space Management and Organization.* Washington, D.C.: U.S. Government Printing Office.

U.S. Congress. Senate Committee on Armed Services. Subcommittee on Strategic and Theater Forces. 1982. *Strategic Force Modernization Programs.* Washington, D.C.: U.S. Government Printing Office.

U.S. Congress. Senate Committee on Commerce, Science, and Transportation. 1999. *Transfer of Satellite Technology to China.* Washington, D.C.: U.S. Government Printing Office.

U.S. Congress. Senate Committee on Foreign Relations. 1967. *Treaty on Outer Space.* Washington, D.C.: U.S. Government Printing Office.

U.S. Congress. Senate Committee on Foreign Relations. 1981. *Strategic Weapons Proposals.* Washington, D.C.: U.S. Government Printing Office.

U.S. Congress. Senate Special Committee on Space and Astronautics. 1958. *National Aeronautics and Space Act of 1958.* Senate Report 85–1701. Washington, D.C.: U.S. Government Printing Office.

U.S. Congressional Budget Office. 2006. *Alternatives to Future U.S. Space Launch Capabilities.* [Online article or information; retrieved 12/1/06.] http://purl.access.gpo.gov/GPO/LPS75737.

U.S. Department of Defense. 1992. *Conduct of the Persian Gulf War: Final Report to Congress.* Washington, D.C.: U.S. Department of Defense.

U.S. Department of Defense. 2003. *Department of Defense Directive 5101.2.* [Online article or information; retrieved 11/20/06.] www.dtic.mil/whs/directives/corres/pdf/51012.pdf.

U.S. Department of Defense. 2006. *Annual Report to Congress: Military Power of the People's Republic of China 2006.* Washington, D.C.: U.S. Department of Defense.

U.S. Department of Defense. Office of the Assistant Secretary of Defense (Public Affairs). 2005. "Air Force Press Conference on Evolved Expendable Launch Vehicle Program." [Online article or information; retrieved 11/29/06.] www.defenselink.mil/transcripts/2005/transcript.aspx?transcriptid=2256.

U.S. Department of State. 1997. *History of the National Security Council, 1947–1997.* Washington, D.C.: U.S. Government Printing Office.

U.S. Department of State. 2001. *ABM Treaty Fact Sheet: Announcement of Withdrawal from the ABM Treaty;* 1–2. [Online article or information; retrieved 11/29/06.] www.state.gov/t/ac/rls/fs/2001/6848.htm.

U.S. Department of State. Bureau of Verification, Compliance, and Implementation. n.d. "Treaty Banning Nuclear Weapons Tests in the Atmosphere, in Outer Space, and Under Water." 1–5. [Online article or information; retrieved 11/22/06.] www.state.gov/t/ac/trt4797.htm.

U.S. Department of State. Bureau of Verification, Compliance, and Implementation. n.d. "Treaty on Principles Governing the Activities of States in the Exploration and Use of Outer Space, Including the Moon and Other Celestial Bodies." 1–2. [Online article or information; retrieved 11/6/06.] www.state.gov/t/ac/trt/5181.htm.

U.S. Department of State. Office of the Historian. 1997. *History of the National Security Council, 1947–1997.* [Online article or information; retrieved 11/21/06.] http://purl.access.gpo.gov/GPO/LPS3006.

U.S. General Accounting Office. 1990. *Defense Reorganization: DOD's Efforts to Streamline the Space Command.* Washington, D.C.: U.S. General Accounting Office.

U.S. General Accounting Office. 1992. *Military Satellite Communications: Milstar Programs Issues and Cost-Saving Opportunities.* Washington, D.C.: U.S. General Accounting Office.

U.S. General Accounting Office. 1994. *National Space Issues: Observations on Defense Space Programs and Activities.* Washington, D.C.: U.S. General Accounting Office.

U.S. General Accounting Office. 1998. *Military Satellite Communications: Concerns with Milstar's Support to Strategic and Tactical Forces.* Washington, D.C.: U.S. General Accounting Office.

U.S. General Accounting Office. 2000. *Defense Acquisitions: Improvements Needed to Military Space Systems' Planning and Education.* Washington, D.C.: U.S. General Accounting Office.

U.S. Missile Defense Agency. 2005. *A Day in the Life of the BMDS.* [Online article or information; retrieved 11/1/06.] www.mda.mil/mdalink/html/video.html.

U.S. Missile Defense Agency. 2006. *Space Tracking and Surveillance System,* 1. [Online article or information; retrieved 11/9/06.] www.mda.mil/mdalink/pdf/stss06.pdf.

U.S. National Aeronautics and Space Administration. 2006. "Mission Archives: Shuttle Missions." [Online article or information; retrieved 11/10/06.] www.nasa.gov/mission_pages/shuttle/shuttlemissions/list_main.html.

U.S. National Aeronautics and Space Administration. Marshall Space Flight Center History Office. n.d. "Dr. Werner von Braun First Center Director, July 1, 1960–January 27, 1970." ; 1–2 [Online article or information; retrieved 10/27/06.] http://history.msfc.nasa.gov/vonbraun/bio.html; 1–2.

U.S. National Archives and Records Administration. 2006. *United States Government Manual 2006–2007.* Washington, D.C.: National Archives and Records Administration.

U.S. National Security Council. 1970. "Memorandum for Dr. Kissinger: A Safeguard Site at Washington for FY 71?" [Online article or information; retrieved 11/7/06.] www.gwu.edu/~nsarchiv/NSAEBB/NSAEBB60/abm03.pdf; 1–4.

U.S. National Security Council. 1990. [Online article or information; retrieved 11/1/07.] *National Security Directive 46: Cape York.* http://bushlibrary.tamu.edu/research/pdfs/nsd/nsd46.pdf.

U.S. National Security Council. 2006(a). *National Security Space Project Presidential Decisions: NSC Documents.* Compiled by Stephanie Feycock. Washington, D.C.: George C. Marshall Institute.

U.S. National Security Council. 2006(b). *National Security Space Project Presidential Decisions: NSC Documents Supplement: Newly Declassified Excerpts.* Compiled by R. C. Hall. Washington, D.C.: George C. Marshall Institute.

U.S. Office of Science and Technology Policy. 2006. *U.S. National Space Policy,* 1–2; [Online article or information; retrieved 11/29/06.] http://ostp.gov/html/US_NationalSpace_Policy.pdf.

Walker, J., L. Bernstein, and S. Lang. 2003. *Seize the High Ground: The Army in Space and Missile Defense.* Washington, D.C.: U.S. Army Center for Military History.

Wolf, R. I. 1987. *The United States Air Force: Basic Documents on Roles and Missions.* Washington, D.C.: United States Air Force Office of Air Force History. [Online article or information; retrieved 11/1/06.] http://purl.access.gpo.gov/GPO/LPS48765.

Zegart, A. B. 1999. *Flawed by Design: The Evolution of the CIA, JCS, and NSC.* Stanford, CA: Stanford University Press.

Ziarnick, B. D. 2004. "The Space Campaign: Space-Power Theory Applied to Counterspace Operations." *Air and Space Power Journal* 18 (2): 61–70.

2

U.S. Military Space Programs

T HROUGHOUT THE NEARLY five-decade history of U.S. military interest in space, there have been numerous space weapons defense programs the U.S. Government and military have embarked upon to increase U.S. capabilities in these areas. These programs were chosen because they were believed to be in accordance with existing or emerging national security needs and because they had the requisite political support and perceived scientific and technological prerequisites for success.

Each of these programs chronicled in this chapter achieved varying degrees of success with varying setbacks and have multifaceted organizational histories. These programs are not a comprehensive listing of relevant U.S. military space programs; rather, they have been chosen because they comprise a representative sampling of U.S. military space programs over the past five decades.

Project Corona

Project Corona served as the United States' first photoreconnaissance satellite system, operating from August 1960–May 1972 collecting both intelligence and mapping imagery (U.S. National Reconnaissance Office, n.d., 1). This program's provenance dates back to the Cold War and even to the Pearl Harbor attack. Because of the combination of the Pearl Harbor attack, the Soviet Union's development of atomic and hydrogen bombs, and the surprising 1950 North Korean invasion of South Korea, the U.S. realized it needed to gain the ability to conduct strategic reconnaissance of the Soviet Union and the territory of other potential U.S. adversaries (Day, Logsdon, and Latell 1998, 2–3).

Corona's programmatic origins stemmed from studies about the possible military uses of space done at the Rand Corporation think tank during the 1950s that became part of an Air Force reconnaissance satellite initiative known as Weapons System WS-117L in 1956. Following the aftermath of the 1957 Sputnik launch, the Eisenhower administration seized on Rand's idea of a photoreconnaissance satellite that would return exposed film to Earth in a reentry capsule instead of electronically; this idea was incorporated into WS-117L in 1957. President Eisenhower approved this plan in February 1958 giving the CIA the leading role in this program but managing it jointly with the Air Force in an arrangement comparable to that for the U-2 aerial reconnaissance plane (Day, Logsdon, and Latell 1998, 5–6; Greer 1973, 1–37).

President Eisenhower inspecting the capsule from Discoverer XIII in 1960–the first object ever ejected from an orbiting satellite and subsequently recovered. *(Dwight D. Eisenhower Presidential Library)*

The following passage from a September 14, 1960 CIA memorandum provides further explanation of Corona's military and intelligence value:

New equipment bearing upon the art of photographic interpretation has clearly expanded the quantity and quality of information derived from that photography. We have seen the extensive uses to which the material and the information derived there from can be put for strategic intelligence purposes, emergency war planning, intelligence purposes related to the responsibility of theater commanders, research and development requirements of the Department of Defense, and operational purposes of the military as well as intelligence operations. . . Its vast geographic coverage clearly enhances our ability to search for guided missile sites of all sorts, and will permit the identification of installations with which we have all become familiar. . . In addition to the uses for positive information on the USSR, it will materially assist in refining the targets for other collection programs and improving their potential (Ruffner 1995, 85–86).

Corona was a classified program whose funding was derived from off-budget resources possessed by the DCI, and noncompetitive bidding contracts for this project were negotiated with Lockheed by the CIA. The entire program and its key applications were classified top secret (Cloud 2001(a), 205). On August 26, 1960, Eisenhower decreed that all photography from Corona and future successor programs be covered by the highly restricted TALENT-KEYHOLE security protocols covering air and space reconnaissance systems in a directive to the secretary of State, secretary of Defense, attorney general, Atomic Energy Commission chair, and DCI (Ruffner 1995, 75).

The secretive NRO was created in 1961 to manage all U.S. aerial and space reconnaissance. NRO's existence was not publicly acknowledged until 1992 (Cloud 2001(a), 205; Cloud 2001(b), 237).

The first attempted Corona test launch was February 28, 1959, the first successful recovery of a Corona spacecraft from space was on August 12, 1960, and the first Corona image taken from space was on August 18, 1960, with many unsuccessful launch and recovery attempts complicating efforts during the program's early attempts to achieve viability (U.S. National Reconnaissance Office, n.d.; Greer 1973, 19–22). These satellites were launched from Cooke (later Vandenberg) Air Force Base (AFB) in California into near polar orbits. Using high-resolution strategic photography with panoramic cameras was Corona's key objective. The Keyhole (KH)-1 camera system, Corona's earliest, used one vertical panoramic camera, and the KH-2 and KH-3 cameras achieved incremental improvement. In the KH-4 camera system the satellite deployed pairs of tilted, longer-range, and higher resolution cameras rotated in synchronization. Later Corona cameras such as the KH-5 and KH-6 achieved greater spatial coverage and higher image calibration results as the program developed and evolved during the 1960s (Cloud 2001(b), 238–39; Greer 1973, 11).

Imagery derived from Corona photography produced numerous enhancements to U.S. knowledge of foreign military and intelligence trends and developments. An August 26, 1964 CIA National Intelligence Estimate (NIE) on China's Lop Nor nuclear test site in western China stressed that it thought this site could be ready for use in about two months, but believed that the Chinese did not have sufficient fissionable material to make a nuclear test within the next several months. The NIE concluded that China was unlikely to be able to conduct a nuclear test until after 1964, although the Chinese succeeded in conducting their first nuclear weapons explosion on October 16, 1964 (Ruffner 1995, 237–244; Nuclear Threat Initiative 2003, 1).

During the June 1967 Middle East War, Corona photographs were able to verify the damage Israeli air attacks had inflicted on Egyptian, Syrian, and Jordanian aircraft and prove that such claims were not exaggerated. Additional Corona accomplishments in the Middle East were providing proof during 1970 of Israeli–Egyptian cease-fire agreement compliance or violations following the 1967 war (Greer 1973, 37–38).

Corona conducted its 145th and final launch on May 25, 1972, and the final recovery of Corona imagery occurred on May 31, 1972 before the program was concluded due to emerging technological enhancements in satellite surveillance such as the Defense Support Program (DSP) satellites (Greer 1973, 38).

Quantitative measures of Corona's success include that it was the world's first photoreconnaissance satellite, achieved the first mid-air recovery of a vehicle returning from space, conducted the first mapping of Earth from space, provided the first stereo-optical data from space, and was the first reconnaissance program to fly 100 missions. Additional numerical accomplishments include improving imaging resolution from eight meters to six meters, individual images covering areas nearly 10-by-120 miles, taking over 800,000 images from space, and a collection consisting of 2.1 million feet of film (National Reconnaissance Office n.d., 2).

Corona's qualitative accomplishments are even more impressive. It provided U.S. policymakers with information on international security crises, trends, and developments such as the Russian and Chinese nuclear weapons programs, the 1967 Middle East War, Berlin Wall construction, the 1969 Soviet/Chinese border conflict, and the 1971 India/Pakistan War. Corona provided technical information about Soviet nuclear facilities and capabilities that made it possible for the U.S. to enter into arms control negotiations with the Soviets and to plan effective and cheaper weapons systems to use against U.S. adversaries. Most importantly, it gave U.S. policymakers sufficiently accurate information to enable the U.S. to get through the international crises of this period, while avoiding making erroneous calculations about enemy capabilities that could have produced serious consequences such as global military confrontation (Day, Logsdon, and Latell 1998, 226–229).

On February 22, 1995, President Bill Clinton issued Executive Order 12951 authorizing the public release and declassification of historical Corona imagery to the National Archives and Records Administration within 18 months (President of the United States 1995, 10789–10790). A section of the NRO website (www.nro.gov/corona/facts.html) includes examples of Corona imagery, Web casts, and other information on this vitally important program including biographies of key Corona personnel in the industrial, intelligence, and military communities.

The Soviet Union's response to Corona was the Zenit satellite reconnaissance program, which had its genesis in a January 30, 1956 governmental decree authorizing the development of an artificial satellite called Object D. After several years of trial and error the Soviets finally achieved successful space imagery photos from the Zenit 2-Kosmos 7 mission between July 28–August 8, 1962 (Gorin 1998, 158, 164; Siddiqi 2003, 250, 354). On March 10, 1964 the Soviet Ministry of Defense declared Zenit 2's space reconnaissance capability operational, although this capability was not limited to the satellite itself. Zenit satellites were initially launched from Tyuratam or Baikonur in what is now Kazakhstan, but beginning in 1966 the rockets carrying these satellites were launched from Plesetsk in northern Russia (Gorin 1998, 166).

These satellites initially remained in orbit for 8–12 days, although their orbital lifetimes would gradually increase. Consequently, the Soviets needed to launch many more of these satellites than the United States did, and they averaged 30 to 35 launches per year during the early 1970s, while the U.S. was averaging 6 to 10 launches annually. A key reason for the short lifespan of the Zenit satellites was their inability to eject individual film rolls to aircraft anywhere on Earth, in contrast with Corona. Zenit satellites and imagery had to be brought down within Soviet territory (Lindgren 2000, 125–126).

Zenit's data was used by numerous organizations within the Soviet military including its military intelligence service, the GRU, whose Satellite Intelligence Directorate interpreted and analyzed space photos. Additional Soviet photoreconnaissance users during this period included the Topographical Directorate of the Armed Forces General Staff and the Strategic Rocket Forces Commanding Staff. Topographical Directorate responsibilities included military mapping, and Intelligence Department responsibilities included using Zenit information for precision ICBM targeting. The Soviets also sought to disguise their military space missions by mixing military and civilian satellites and failed probes as part of the Kosmos program, which constituted approximately 95% of Soviet space missions at this time (Gorin 1998, 167).

The Zenit program did not have a clear end in the early 1970s like Corona but has probably evolved into current Russian military space satellite programs such as the Kobalt, Yenisey, Strela–3, and GLONASS systems described in Chapter 4 (Gorin 1998, 169; Center for Nonproliferation Studies 2005(?), 1–3).

Dyna-Soar

Project Dyna-Soar, which was an abbreviation of dynamic soaring, was an Air Force program with the collaboration of the National Advisory Committee on Aeronautics (NACA) (NASA's predecessor agency) in the later 1950s and early 1960s, which sought to give the Air Force a manned presence in space and serve as a military counterweight to NASA's emerging manned space program. The program's genesis began during the summer of 1952 when NACA directed its organizational laboratories to study issues and problems concerning high altitude supersonic flight (U.S. Congress, House Committee on Science and Technology 1985, 207). In the aftermath of the 1957 Sputnik launch, Air Force leaders became concerned with developing a reusable shuttle vehicle to perform orbital reconnaissance or serve as a strategic deterrent by conducting nuclear bombing missions. By December 1957 Dyna-Soar became possible through the consolidation of three previously existing Air Force research and development programs: Hywards, which covered a boost-glide vehicle; the high altitude reconnaissance system Brass Bell; and the Rocket Bomber rocket missile whose collective activities included testing piloted vehicles to obtain aerodynamic, structural, and human factor data and speeds and altitudes beyond the reach of the then cutting edge X-15 fighter plane. Dyna-Soar was intended to operate at an altitude of 350,000 feet and at a speed of 10,800 miles per hour as opposed to the X-15's altitude and speed ceilings of 250,000 feet and 4,000 miles per hour (Houchin 1999, 4–5; Spires 1998, 74; Spires 2004, 2:760–761).

A Dyna-Soar (Dynamic Soaring) vehicle clears the launch tower atop an Air Force Titan II launch vehicle in this 1961 artist's concept illustration. Originally conceived by the U.S. Air Force in 1957 as a manned, rocket-propelled glider in a delta-winged configuration, the Dyna-Soar was considered by Marshall Space Flight Center planners as an upper stage for the Saturn C-2 launch vehicle. *(NASA)*

A 1958 Air Force document provides a detailed description of Dyna-Soar's anticipated military potential stressing that the rocket engine would allow it to reach an altitude of 170,000 feet at a speed of nearly 18,000 feet per second. Additional Dyna-Soar attributes described by this document included the crew being able to monitor automatic system operation and make corrections as necessary, operate reconnaissance equipment and observe activities in areas it overflies, the ability to provide high-quality photographic, radar, and intelligence data, and perform extremely accurate strategic bombing at speeds and altitudes capable of providing significant protection against hostile fire (Spires 2004, 2:751–752).

A recent Air Force historical analysis of Dyna-Soar's technical and operational capabilities made the following assessment. This appraisal noted that Dyna-Soar could be pictured as an isosceles triangle, which would have a cylindrical fuselage for the pilot in front and a rear payload bay. Triangles attached perpendicularly to the main wing structure would provide aerodynamic surfaces for control and stability. Dyna-Soar would be launched by a modified ICBM or first-generation Saturn rocket and separate from that rocket upon reaching orbital velocity. The craft would conduct its mission on an orbital glide path around the earth then reenter the atmosphere by using retro-rockets to reduce its speed and have some flexibility to choose at which bases to land. This latter attribute gave it a heightened flexibility that craft in NASA's Mercury, Gemini, and Apollo programs did not have (Erickson 2005, 162–163).

Dyna-Soar's long-term viability would be seriously limited by the Eisenhower administration's belief that satellites should not be employed as offensive nuclear weapons systems or orbital bombs (Erickson 2005, 165). This belief would receive concrete policy reinforcement on January 26, 1960 in National Security Council Directive 5918 *US Policy on Outer Space,* which sought to emphasize civilian scientific space exploration and development activity while restricting military space activities to defense support and limiting offensive space weapons to study projects (Spires 1998, 80–81). This desire for predominantly peaceful uses of outer space by the Eisenhower administration was opposed by some members of Congress, the public, and Air Force officials who believed the Soviets would attempt to eliminate U.S. reconnaissance satellites through military means (Houchin 1988, 276).

An additional factor casting doubt on Dyna-Soar's future was Eisenhower's November 2, 1959 decision transferring control of the Saturn rocket system from the Air Force to the new National Aeronautics and Space Administration (NASA) over objections from the JCS. The Air Force's ability to develop the military super-booster rockets necessary for Dyna-Soar would also be diminished by the December 30, 1959 directive from Secretary of Defense Neil McElroy (1904–1972) transferring DOD space activities from ARPA to DOD's DDR&E, which required military space projects to compete with other military funding requests (Spires 1998, 79).

During the Kennedy administration, the increasing Dyna-Soar costs incurred the intense scrutiny of Secretary of Defense Robert McNamara (1916–), whose emphasis on systems management of DOD programs has been the subject of sustained historical and public policy analysis (Murdock 1974; Roherty 1970; Enthoven and Smith 2005). During January 1963, McNamara told the House Armed Services Committee that Dyna-Soar faced considerable technical problems with particular emphasis on its reentry capabilities. That same month, McNamara also directed DDR&E director Harold Brown (1927–), who later became secretary of Defense from 1977–1981, to examine Dyna-Soar's advantages and disadvantages in relationship to anticipated benefits from NASA's two-man Gemini program.

McNamara consulted with NASA administrator James Webb (1906–1992) in March 1963 on potential alternatives to spending $600 million on Dyna-Soar, which McNamara felt had vague military requirements. In October 1963, McNamara and Brown visited the Martin-Marietta factory in Denver to review progress on the X-20 aircraft and Titan III missile, and McNamara remained concerned with what he saw as the Air Force's apparent inability to answer what it wanted to do in space and its reasons for being in space (Stares 1998, 124). Both McNamara and Brown finished this Denver visit unconvinced that Dyna-Soar could perform either bombing or satellite inspection missions, and they remained convinced that existing unmanned systems such as Corona were more cost-effective for reconnaissance missions. The October 1963 U.S.–Soviet agreement renouncing weapons of mass destruction in outer space and growing international acceptance of reconnaissance satellites also facilitated Dyna-Soar's demise. All of these factors lead to Dyna-Soar's cancellation on December 10, 1963 (Spires 1998, 124; Houchin 1999, 13–14; Houchin 1988, 279).

Despite being cancelled, Dyna-Soar left an important legacy to influence future Air Force aerospace research and development. Air Force Secretary Eugene Zuckert (1911–2000) approved continuing 36 Dyna-Soar research programs in areas including advanced technology, hardware, and technical data, and specifically high-temperature material and fabrication processing enhancements that facilitated the development of spacecraft and large rocket boosters. Research from 2,000-plus hours of wind tunnel testing increased knowledge of aerodynamic stability and control and structural design problems.

Dyna-Soar also represented the first officially authorized military space-faring system and the only system that included an offensive mission capability. It led to the development of the Titan III space booster and its aerodynamic space operations emphasis would also influence design of the Space Shuttle in the 1970s.

Manned Orbiting Laboratory (MOL)

A 1961 Air Force proposal involving putting a continuous military force in space with piloted craft, manned surveillance, and space stations can be viewed as the provenance of the MOL (Posey 1998, 75). MOL received more formal DOD support in 1963 in the aftermath of Dyna-Soar's cancellation. It was envisioned as a way of determining human military usefulness in space. Both the Air Force and Navy participated in MOL, whose objectives included enhancing understanding of what individuals could do in space and how this capability could be used for defense purposes, developing technology and equipment to improve manned and unmanned space flight, and experimenting with this technology and equipment. The laboratory was designed to support two men in orbit for 30 days. DOD selected 17 astronauts for the program whose membership consisted of test pilots and graduates of the Aerospace Research Pilot School at Edwards AFB, California (U.S. Congress, House Committee on Science and Technology 1985, 208).

MOL's genesis dates from a December 10, 1963 announcement assigning responsibility for this program to the Air Force if the military could define and justify a military space mission NASA could not perform (Posey 1998, 75). The news release announcing MOL contained information on its projected mission and its relationship with NASA. This release mentioned that MOL would be connected to a modified Gemini capsule and launched into orbit by a Titan III booster. Astronauts would move to the laboratory upon reaching orbit and return to their capsule and the earth once their orbital assignments were completed. MOL was designed to permit space rendezvous with orbiting Gemini capsules delivering replacement crews if lengthy space laboratory operations were needed. MOL would use existing NASA tracking and control facilities for NASA and DOD space flight programs, and the laboratory would conduct military experiments involving manned equipment and instrumentation, if NASA desired, for scientific and civilian missions (Spires 2004, 2:848).

Between 1963–1965, MOL technical specifications were established. The station would consist of a modified Gemini capsule connected to a cylindrical module 10 feet in diameter and 42 feet in length. Approximately half of this structure would be a pressurized working area for the crew, and another unpressurized section would have life support equipment and a restartable rocket engine for orbital adjustments.

MOL would be launched by a Titan III to a 150-mile high orbit, and the astronauts would leave Gemini to move to their workplace. The astronauts would stay in orbit for a week or two with 30 days being the maximum time for such missions before returning to Gemini and heading back to Earth. While in orbit, MOL astronauts would watch and photograph activity in the Soviet bloc and inspect hostile satellites and destroy them if necessary. Proposed MOL experiments included using large optics in space, tracking Earth and space targets, electromagnetic intelligence surveys, multispectral photography, and post-strike target assessment using equipment such as the KH-10 camera (Posey 1998, 76).

MOL's launch site was initially set up at Cape Kennedy, Florida but was shifted to Vandenberg AFB, California to get better quality coverage of the Soviet Union. President Lyndon Johnson (1908–1973) announced approval of MOL on August 25, 1965 with an initial program budget of $150 million. Primary MOL contractors were Douglas, which was responsible for the laboratory canister; McDonnell for the Gemini capsule; and General Electric for space experiments. The Air Force hoped to launch the first unmanned MOL in 1968 with manned crews to follow soon after (Spires 1998, 129–130).

The Air Force placed high hopes on the MOL as its means of beginning and maintaining a manned military space presence as reflected in a 1965 program justification statement. This document contended that man was the key to the future in space, that MOL was a bridge from research and development experiments to being able to conduct traditional military operations in space, that new regions and technologies have been historically exploited for military advantage, and that MOL is needed to prevent hostile exploitation of space against the United States (Erickson 2005, 418).

This optimistic Air Force position on MOL stands in partial contrast to a 1964 statement by DDR&E Albert G. Hall (1914–1992). Hall argued that there was not a decisive case for manned space supremacy as a key component of military supremacy. He believed the United States should purchase insurance against the possibility of a manned operational system being required by the middle 1970s in the form of a flight test system to determine human effectiveness in performing desired military activities in space. Hall believed MOL should be directed to examining human ability to perform military operations in space while acknowledging that there was no clear consensus on the military significance of manned space technology (Erickson 2005, 420–421).

The Air Force was convinced there was a valid raison d'etre for manned military activity in space and that MOL was the mechanism for such activity. An excerpt from a 1964 document explicitly described MOL astronaut responsibilities:

The 2-man crew will discriminate, detect, point, track, evaluate, reprogram and command as appropriate in missions of reconnaissance, fly-by inspection, co-orbital inspection. . . and perform support tasks such as navigation, re-entry, etc. The reconnaissance mission tasks seem to be well conceived. . . They [the crew] examine the area photographs and look for targets and then program themselves on a suitable orbit to take high resolution photographs of targets of interest. High resolution photos are then taken of these targets (Erickson 2005, 465).

Over the next few years MOL would proceed to carry out several experiments as part of its prospective program development. A March 1965 Air Force operational document describes 12 of 14 declassified MOL experiments covering a daunting array of intelligence, military, and space science activities. Examples of these included measuring human ability to acquire and track predetermined ground targets under multiple conditions; measuring their ability to acquire and track satellite targets under multiple conditions; measuring the ability to detect surface targets and make cursory intelligence assessment; measuring the ability to make decisions and adjustments from electromagnetically emitted information; measuring crew members' ability to perform in-space maintenance; determining what human functions and tools are required to work outside of spacecraft; determining crew members' ability to use a remote control maneuvering unit; measuring human ability to navigate in space and geodetically survey uncooperative targets; determining crew members' ability to use radiometric and related equipment to perform military and scientific activities; measuring crew members' daily performance capabilities; measuring the physiological and biomedical factors of crew members under long-term orbital conditions such as weightlessness; and evaluating human capabilities to control, coordinate, and use sensors to detect, track, classify, and catalog sea targets (Erickson 2005, 467–468).

MOL achieved some substantive progress during its existence. In November 1966, the Air Force conducted a number of successful tests, including nine on-board experiments, using a Gemini capsule launched by a Titan IIIC rocket. By 1967 MOL planners completed design work on a basic Gemini–Titan MOL arrangement and a new West Coast launch facility and selected for training 12 astronauts from the Air Force, Navy, and Marine Corps (Spires 1998, 131).

Despite these positive developments, storm clouds emerged and lingered over MOL. There was concern in Congress that MOL duplicated NASA's Apollo Applications Program (APP) involving lunar exploration. This concern was reflected in a March 21, 1966 House Government Operations Committee report on these programs. This document asserted that NASA participation in MOL would achieve significant cost savings, that NASA's existing APP's fiscal year 1967 budget request of $100 million was almost as much as MOL's budget request, and that since both of these programs were research and development programs with unclear operational missions, that combining them would achieve significant savings (U.S. Congress, House Committee on Government Operations 1966, 46).

Besides concern over program duplication, other factors coincided to produce MOL's decline and termination. The Vietnam War's ongoing costs and the burgeoning financial drain of Great Society social programs reduced political support for the space program, and DOD and Apollo space programs experienced budget cuts. Space represented 20% of DOD's research and development budget, and astronautic programs constituted one-third of the Air Force's budget, and half of this expenditure involved MOL with what was the most expensive of Air Force research and budget development programs not directly related to the Vietnam War (Spires 1998, 133).

These factors and DOD's belief that national security space missions could be better accomplished with cheaper unmanned spacecraft resulted in MOL's cancellation on June 10, 1969, although the DOD acknowledged that MOL had been managed well and that excellent results had been achieved by program participants (Spires 1998, 133; Spires 2004, 2:860–862).

Sentinel and Safeguard Antiballistic Missiles

Both the Sentinel and Safeguard ABM programs represented governmental attempts to build ABM systems to counter a growing Soviet nuclear threat. Sentinel emerged in the 1960s from military efforts to develop an ABM system after abortive U.S.–Soviet attempts to limit ABMs in their overall arms control discussions. These efforts saw the Air Force evaluate the potential of using lasers to burn missile warheads in flight but determined they could not produce sufficient energy to damage a warhead. Army ballistic missile defense research emphasized developing radars encased in hardened structures along with a faster missile system named Sprint. The new radars and Sprint would be combined into a system called Nike-X and in 1966 military leaders recommended Nike be deployed to defend the entire United States against a Soviet ICBM attack (U.S. Centennial of Flight Commission 2003, 1).

Secretary of Defense Robert McNamara instead favored developing independently targetable reentry vehicles that would allow a single ABM to attack multiple targets. During 1967, McNamara agreed to begin working on a modified and scaled back version of Nike-X called Sentinel, which he felt should focus on Chinese rather than the Soviet ICBMs, since arms control negotiations with the Soviets were not progressing on this issue.

McNamara responded to Soviet intransigence on September 18, 1967 by announcing that the United States would begin deploying the small-scale Sentinel system to counter Chinese ballistic missiles (Haas 1988, 235; Bowen 2005, 44; U.S. Centennial of Flight Commission 2003, 1).

Sentinel's initial deployment plans called for 6 Perimeter Acquisition Radars, 17 Missile Site Radars, 480 Spartan missiles, 192 Sprint missiles with an additional missile site radar, and 28 Sprints planned for Hawaii. If fully deployed, Sentinel would have been capable of defending most of the continental United States, Hawaii, and parts of Alaska (Bowen 2005, 44).

The early months of the Nixon administration in 1969 were not a propitious time to advocate new defense weapons systems because of increasing public opposition to the Vietnam War and the fact that the Sentinel's interceptor missiles were nuclear armed. There was significant opposition to Sentinel for environmental and anti-Vietnam war reasons in some areas of the country. New England notably was a center of this activity, and Senator

The last of six production version Spartan missiles rises from Meck Island at Kwajalein Missile Range in the Marshall Islands on April 3, 1975. The 55-foot long Spartan was the long range interceptor of the Army's Safeguard Ballistic Missile Defense System. It had a range of several hundred miles and was designed to carry a nuclear warhead in the megaton range. *(Bettmann/Corbis)*

Edward Kennedy (Democrat from Massachusetts) (1932–) was a prominent figure in this opposition (Bowen 2005, 44).

This vociferous opposition caused the Nixon administration to further scale back the Sentinel program and rename it Safeguard. This new program would no longer be an area ABM system that would try to protect civilian and military assets but would serve as a point defense system intended to protect ICBM sites. The Nixon administration also wanted to retain an ABM system to use as a bargaining chip in arms control negotiations with the Soviet Union (U.S. Centennial of Flight Commission 2003, 2; Bowen 2005, 44).

Intensive debate and negotiation occurred between the Nixon administration and Congress over Safeguard's fate during the first few months of 1969 (Gross 1975). Critics of deploying Safeguard such as Senator Stuart Symington (Democrat from Missouri) (1901–

1988) stressed concerns about Safeguard's technical reliability, questioned whether the Soviet missile threat warranted deployment of such a weapons system, and felt that more emphasis should be placed on domestic social spending (U.S. Congress 1969, 22478–22479).

Proponents of deploying Safeguard such as Senator Henry Jackson (Democrat from Washington) (1912–1983), emphasized the need to counter the steady growth in Soviet nuclear missile development and deployment and potential instability in the Soviet leadership, which did not promote strategic stability between the two sides (U.S. Congress 1969, 22483).

In August 1969, Congress passed legislation funding 2 of 12 Safeguard sites with the Senate passage of this bill occurring by a margin of two votes (U.S. Congress 1969, 22498). President Richard Nixon (1913–1994) decided to deploy Safeguard, which would defend Minuteman ICBM sites at Grand Forks AFB, North Dakota and Malmstrom AFB, Montana, and these two sites were under construction in 1972 as ABM treaty negotiations were occurring with the Soviet Union (Bowen 2005, 44–45).

The Nixon administration was also interested in the possibility of using Safeguard to defend the National Command Authority in Washington, D.C. A January 24, 1970 NSC memorandum prepared for National Security advisor Henry Kissinger (1923–) stated that advantages of using Safeguard as a Washington ABM site would decrease the temptation for a third country or a crazed military commander trying to provoke a U.S.–Soviet nuclear exchange by knocking off the "head" of the United States and causing its other military limbs to lash out at its perceived assailant. This memorandum also argued that such a system would be the equivalent of the Galosh ABM system the Soviets were deploying around Moscow, that such deployment would be consistent with the administration's rationale for providing a missile defense system to protect civilian and military command and control authorities, and that work on a Washington ABM site could proceed without the Nixon administration having to take a definitive stand on the kind of area defense system it wanted to build.

This appraisal went on to acknowledge that there could be political problems with appearing to protect only the president and Congress while delaying population defense measures, that a Washington ABM would have limited regional coverage and might not include cities like Baltimore or Philadelphia, and that this system could not defend Washington against bomber attack (U.S. National Security Council 1970, 1–4).

These modest U.S. efforts to develop a limited ABM system stood in sharp contrast to extensive Soviet ABM programs. An August 1970 CIA assessment of Soviet ABM activities mentioned that eight launch sites in Moscow ABM defenses were operational in early 1970 and that eight Hen House radars were either operational or under construction and deployed in five locations on the Soviet Union's periphery to provide early warning of missile attack, with one of these radars being at Olenegorsk near Murmansk and the other at Skrunda in Latvia. This assessment went on to contend that these ABM sites and other radars provided warning of ICBM attacks from the northwest, China, submarine launch areas in the north, the western Pacific, and eastern Mediterranean. The CIA stressed that this coverage could not currently monitor submarine-launched missiles from the western Mediterranean, but that Soviet deployment of three to five additional radars could close this and other existing coverage gaps (U.S. Central Intelligence Agency 1970, 20; Schneider 1971, 26).

Original plans called for Safeguard deployment, beyond the North Dakota and Montana sites mentioned earlier, to the upper Midwest; central and southern California; Warren AFB, Wyoming; Whiteman AFB, Missouri; the Michigan–Ohio area; southern New England; Washington, D.C.; Dallas, Texas; and the Florida–Georgia area (Bowen 2005, 47).

The May 26, 1972 ABM Treaty between the United States and Soviet Union, coming after lengthy negotiations, would be the beginning of the end for Safeguard. This agreement limited both sides to construction of one limited ABM system to protect its national capital area and another to protect an ICBM launch area. Both of these sites had to be at least 1,300 kilometers apart to prevent creation of effective regional defense zones or the beginning of a nationwide ABM system. The Treaty also limited each side to no more than 100 interceptor missiles and 100 launchers at each ABM site while also imposing restrictions on both sides to limit qualitative improvements in their ABM technology such as not developing, testing, or deploying ABM launchers capable of launching multiple interceptor missiles simultaneously and prohibiting systems for rapidly reloading launchers (U.S. Department of State n.d., 1; Burr 2001; Baucom 1992, 91–113; Bulkeley and Brauch 1988).

The United States maintained one ABM site under the treaty at the Grand Forks, North Dakota locale mentioned earlier. The Army realized that this site would be overwhelmed in a large-scale missile attack but wanted to retain the Grand Forks site for a year to gain operational experience for potential future ballistic missile defense systems. Congress, however, remained opposed to potential ballistic missile defense systems, and on October 2, 1975, the House of Representatives voted to deactivate Safeguard; subsequently the JCS ordered program termination on February 10, 1976. Following material disposition, the site's nontechnical infrastructure was declared excess property and turned over to the Department of the Interior. In 1984, the Army reacquired this infrastructure to provide support for the new SDIO. The facility has never been demolished and remains under Army control, although there are no apparent plans to include it in ongoing U.S. ballistic missile defense programs during the George W. Bush administration (Bowen 2005, 50).

Defense Support Program (DSP) Satellites

Cancellation of Dyna-Soar and MOL and the ongoing success of Corona demonstrated the preeminence of reconnaissance satellites in U.S. military space policy as the 1970s began. The need to develop a satellite system with more technologically sophisticated capabilities to detect Soviet or other hostile military activities was apparent to U.S. policymakers at this time and would lead to the development of the DSP satellite program during this period.

What became known as DSP had its genesis during the 1960s when U.S. military policymakers realized the Missile Defense Alarm System (MIDAS) military radar missile-warning program was proving inadequate to provide timely warning of hostile ballistic missile launches against the United States. Such inadequacy resulted in MIDAS's January 1966 cancellation (Spires 2004, 2:975, 1084). In August 1966, DOD's DDR&E approved development of Program 949 to replace MIDAS. Program 949 was intended to serve as a means of providing the United States with early simultaneous warnings of threats to U.S. military assets from ICBMs and the Soviet's Fractional Orbital Bombardment Systems and Submarine Launched Ballistic Missiles (SLBM). During 1969, a security breach caused the Air Force to change the program designation to Program 647, which then became known as DSP (Spires 2004, 2:1095).

A formal DOD awarding of this program and military satellite warning programs to the Air Force occurred on September 8, 1970 when Deputy Secretary of Defense David Packard (1912–1996) issued DOD Directive 5160.32 "Development of Space Systems," whose partial contents included assigning functional responsibilities within the Office of the Secretary of Defense and armed services for developing and acquiring space systems, giving the Air Force responsibility for developing, producing, and deploying space systems for warning and surveillance of enemy nuclear delivery and launch vehicle capabilities, and DOD's Director of Defense Research and Engineering being responsible for monitoring space technology to limit technical risk and cost as well as preventing unwarranted program duplication (U.S. Congress, Senate Committee on Armed Services 1971, 2670).

The first DSP satellite was launched from Cape Canaveral, Florida on November 6, 1970 on a Titan III rocket. The satellite's payload was reportedly secret but information about its launch was covered in the *New York Times* and on a sign at a Cocoa, Florida bank (Richelson 1999, 64). A detailed description of DSP capabilities and early weaknesses is described in a recent Air Force analysis of military space programs. This appraisal mentioned that DSP satellites weighed 2,000 pounds and measured 23 feet in length and 10 feet in width. DSP satellites rotated six revolutions per minute so their telescopes were able to scan the earth. This assessment also noted that Air Force planners were concerned about the ability of DSP software to receive and process large amounts of data before transmitting that data almost instantaneously worldwide. Satellite managers also were concerned about coverage gaps due to unfavorable sensor angles over the pole, and they lobbied DOD officials for additional satellites to achieve enhanced coverage but were turned down in the 1970s due to budget constraints (Spires 2004, 2:1095).

Data and imagery acquired by DSP satellites were sent to a global network of ground stations whose locations included Buckley AFB, Colorado; Vandenberg AFB, California; Guam; Hawaii; and Nurrungar, South Australia, Australia. The Nurrungar facility assumed command and control responsibilities for DSP on May 19, 1971. While Nurrungar had no problem communicating with the DSP, it had problems communicating reliably with the

Artist's concept of the Defense Support Program satellite in space. *(U.S. Department of Defense)*

United States, but these were eventually resolved. Another problem Nurrungar and other Australian satellite intelligence facilities had to contend with during this period was opposition to their presence from some elements of the opposition Australian Labor Party (Richelson 1999, 67–68; Ball 1987; Ball and Richelson 1985, 178–181, 190).

Additional DSP technological enhancements occurred during the 1970s and beyond. During the mid-1970s, the longer than anticipated lifespan of the four orbiting DSP satellites allowed military engineers to equip unlaunched DSP satellites with enhanced infrared sensors providing more accurate missile launch count and launch point determination capability. During March 1980, Secretary of Defense Harold Brown approved a document authorizing the Air Force to continue with ongoing DSP improvements and work with the Defense Advanced Research Projects Agency (DARPA) on exploring future DSP enhancements. This development allowed for improvements to existing satellites as well as new DSP enhancements planned for the mid- to late 1980s.

Examples of these upgrades included a more sensitive MOSAIC optical sensor system to counteract scanning limitations from continually "staring" at the earth's surface and a Sensor Evolutionary Development program, which involved developing mercury-cadmium-telluride sensor cells to provide more infrared detectors with enhanced sensitivity. Additional DSP modifications during the early 1980s included improved ground station computers and software (Spires 2004, 2:1095–1096).

The first improved DSP satellite, Flight 12, was launched into orbit on December 22, 1984 by a Titan 34D Transtage rocket. Enhancements in this satellite included a modified star sensor, new power supplies for command encryption units, and an upgraded nuclear detection package. Plans at this time also called for future DSP launches to be performed by the Space Shuttle. These plans were delayed by the January 1986 shuttle Challenger tragedy and the failure of Titan 34D launches in August 1985 and April 1986. Consequently, DSP Flight 13 would not reach orbit until November 1987.

During June 1989, AFSPACOM launched the beginning of a new series of satellites to replace two older DSP satellites. Flight 14—measuring 33 feet in length, weighing over 5,200 pounds, and capable of deploying more powerful solar arrays—was the first enhanced DSP craft. November 1990 saw another satellite join its DSP cohorts in orbit, which included three operational satellites and two spares. One DSP satellite was located over the Indian Ocean at 70° E longitude and was responsible for monitoring Asian ICBM launches. The other two satellites concentrated on SLBM launches from a position of 70° W longitude over the South Atlantic and over the eastern Pacific at 135° E longitude (Spires 2004, 2:1096).

The August 1990 Iraqi invasion and conquest of Kuwait and the ensuing crises of Operations Desert Shield and Desert Storm gave DSP satellites an excellent opportunity to demonstrate their strategic warning value. During Operation Desert Shield, DSP satellites detected an accident at an Iraqi arms depot at As Shuaybah, which the Iraqis were using to supply their troops in southern Kuwait. U.S. analysts estimated that this explosion destroyed nine storage bunkers and eight storage buildings capable of supplying six Iraqi heavy divisions for three days of medium- to high-intensity combat. On January 28, 1991 coalition strikes on an additional Iraqi ammunition depot produced an explosion so large that it was acquired by DSP sensors, and both Israel and the Soviet Union asked the United States whether it had used tactical nuclear weapons in carrying out this airstrike (Richelson 1999, 173).

During military operations in Operation Desert Storm, DSP satellites were able to keep track of Iraqi Scud missile launches and send this information to Strategic Air Command's global communications network. This near instantaneous capability made it possible to provide U.S. forces in Saudi Arabia with rapid warning of these launches, which made it possible for them to get Patriot missiles armed and to suit up in chemical defense gear in case these Scuds carried chemical weapons (Kutnya 1998, 103).

The rapid success of U.S. and allied forces in Operation Desert Storm occurred because of many factors, with space intelligence playing a particularly important role. This was the first military conflict to make comprehensive use of space systems support, with DSP and other satellite assets assisting coalition ground, naval, and air forces for multi-faceted purposes such as communications, navigation, targeting, and search and rescue.

Soldier with gas mask in Saudi Arabia, 1990. Such protective equipment was used out of fears that Iraqi leader Saddam Hussein might order his forces to use chemical or biological weapons against coalition forces. *(Derek Hudson/ Sygma/Corbis)*

The official DOD report on this war used this language to describe the crucial support role played by DSP satellites:

> DSP was the primary Scud launch detection system during Operation Desert Storm. The DSP constellation and associated ground station processing provided crucial warning data of Scud launches. This data was disseminated by a variety of means. The national military command center used DSP data to provide military and civilian warning to Israel and the Gulf states (U.S. Department of Defense 1992, 176–177).

Positive appraisals of DSP's performance during Desert Storm were not limited to the United States. On November 5, 1991, Australian defense minister Robert Ray (1947–) told his country's Parliament how coalition forces used space systems during Desert Storm to provide weather data, navigational assistance, information on military forces geographic locations, and other intelligence information. Ray went on to mention how Australia's Nurrungar facility served as an important part of the DSP system and referred to DSP's role in detecting the launch of Iraqi Scud missiles and providing warning of this to civilian populations in Israel and Saudi Arabia. The minister concluded his remarks with the following prescient observation about Nurrungar's importance in ensuring national security and international stability:

> I trust that the important role played by the joint defence facility, Nurrungar, in the Gulf War will further enhance public appreciation of its significance in efforts to promote measures for maintaining peace and stability, both globally and regionally. If anything, facilities such as Nurrungar are likely to be more important in the post Cold War period. They not only provide intelligence and early warning at a time when the prospect of proliferation is increasing, but also their arms control and verification function will be of greater significance to the cause of world peace (Australia. Parliament, 1991, 2374).

Despite these positive accomplishments, concern arose over DSP in the early 1990s from DOD and Congress over the system's age, ability to meet emerging security threats, and program management. A 1993 private sector contractor report prepared for the Air Force's Space and Missile Systems Center in Los Angeles stressed its belief that DSP had been in a holding pattern for several years because the Air Force was interested in pursuing a replacement early warning system. This document also expressed concern that insufficient investment in DSP replacement programs or technologies was causing unnecessarily high production costs to maintain the existing DSP infrastructure. It also expressed its belief that upgrades to DSP capabilities must occur within the then existing political environment of reduced defense budgets, the then prevalent international strategic environment placing greater emphasis on regional conflicts and limited nuclear war potential instead of the protracted nuclear Cold War confrontation with the former Soviet Union, and an evolving security environment marked by proliferating tactical ballistic missiles to third world countries capable of threatening U.S. and allied forces (U.S. Congress, House Committee on Government Operations 1994, 284, 299).

Additional concern over DSP's ability to meet these emerging security threats at this time was also expressed by DOD personnel during testimony before the U.S. House Appropriations Committee during annual budget request hearings. This concern noted that DSP had significant weaknesses in its Tactical Warning and Attack Assessment (TW/AA) mission including its design for 1970's ICBM technology, that its data processing architecture prevented it from quickly transmitting warning messages to users, and being unable to track all potential targets because of limited system technological sensitivity (U.S. Congress, House Committee on Appropriations 1993, 391–392).

This DOD appraisal of DSP deficiencies went on to make the following analysis of system capabilities and weaknesses, emphasizing that it provided insufficient warning time about attacks from shorter and intermediate range missiles, that DSP sensors had limited sensitivity against many contemporary targets since it was designed to operate primarily in the short-wave infrared frequency band, and that DSP was vulnerable to solar outages because of seasonal variations in the sun's position relative to satellites. These cumulative shortfalls made DSP inadequate for meeting current and emerging threats to U.S. security from proliferated, dimly lit, and short-burning missiles (U.S. Congress, House Committee on Appropriations 1993, 392).

DSP program management concerns also were brought to the attention of DOD policy-makers and congressional oversight committees. A May 1993 General Accounting Office (GAO) report to the Acting Secretary of the Air Force Michael B. Donley said it was premature to upgrade DSP ground stations because the Air Force had not completed validation of operational requirements as required by various DOD and Air Force regulations. GAO also found the global processing capabilities in the planned DSP ground station upgrades might not be cost-effective. This global processing capability would theoretically permit the Air Force to process the data generated by all DSP satellites at a single ground station. The Air Force, however, announced it had no plans to reduce the number of DSP ground stations. This response, along with the incomplete technical requirements process for DSP global processing capabilities, led GAO to question the Air Force's plans to spend $95 million for upgrading these stations (U.S. General Accounting Office 1993(b), 1).

DSP's contractor was TRW, now Northrop Grumman Space Technology. Twenty-two DSP program satellites were launched as of November 25, 2005 with the most recent being in February 2004. A final DSP was delivered to the Air Force in May 2005. Each satellite can operate for up to 10 years (Smith 2005, 1). Despite its age and concerns over its ability to meet emerging ballistic missile threats, DSP has remained the United States' principal early warning satellite system, withstanding attempts to replace it with other programs such as the Advanced Warning System in the early 1980s; the Boost Surveillance and Tracking System in the later 1980s; the Follow-on Early Warning System in the early 1990s; and the Alert, Locate, and Report Missile System in the mid-1990s. These programs failed because of technology problems, high costs, and other affordability problems (U.S. General Accounting Office 2001, 5).

The Space-Based Infrared System (SBIRS) is the military's latest effort to develop a successor satellite reconnaissance and early warning program to replace DSP. Its troubled development and evolution are chronicled later in this chapter.

Strategic Defense Initiative (SDI)

The signing of international arms control treaties such as the 1972 ABM treaty and the SALT treaty that same year by the United States and the Soviet Union appeared to limit attempts to develop defenses against ballistic missile defense systems. These treaties also appeared to codify the doctrine of mutually assured destruction (MAD), which posited that the nuclear weapons arsenals of both sides would destroy U.S. and Soviet military assets and civilian populations, into the nuclear deterrence theory and policies of both of these countries and even into international law (Sokolski 2004, 137–174).

Although MAD had adherents in both the U.S. Government and military, it also had numerous critics. These critics gained particular ascendancy with the advent of the Reagan administration in 1981, which sought to reassert American strength in the international security environment in the aftermath of losing the Vietnam War and the failures of detente with the Soviet Union (Schweizer 2002; Winik 1996; Wirls 1992).

A team of advisors headed by former undersecretary of the Army Karl R. Bendetsen (1907–1989) briefed Reagan on their missile defense concerns in January 1982 and recommended that he initiate a national program to develop missile defenses for the United States (Council on Foreign Relations 2002, 3; Baucom 1992, 153–155).

This dissatisfaction with MAD as a moral and practical mechanism for dealing with what Reagan administration policymakers saw as a growing security threat from the Soviet Union's nuclear and conventional military forces was given additional impetus during the early 1980s. National defense controversies during the early years of the Reagan administration involved the proposal to develop the MX missile system as a means of upgrading the United States' then existing land-based ICBM arsenal while also exploring possible airborne or sea-based deployments of the MX. Dissatisfaction with the political bickering over this and other subjects during late 1982 and early 1983 resulted in Reagan administration policymakers researching the possibility of deploying defensive systems that could protect the continental United States and its allies from Soviet nuclear missiles (Weinberger 1990, 302–303; Baucom 1992, 171–196).

A crucial factor in this U.S. decision to explore ways of developing and deploying a defense system against nuclear missiles came from President Ronald Reagan (1911–2004). Reagan had grown particularly disillusioned with the MAD doctrine for both moral and military strategic reasons (Shultz 1993, 261–264). The following passage from Reagan's autobiography expresses his thoughts on this subject and how he proposed putting this evolving thinking into practical action:

> I came into office with a decided prejudice against our tacit agreement with the Soviet Union regarding nuclear missiles. I'm talking about the MAD policy— 'mutual assured destruction'—the idea of deterrence providing safety so long as each of us had the power to destroy the other with nuclear missiles if one of us launched a first strike. Somehow this didn't seem to me to be something that would send you to bed feeling safe. It was like having two westerners standing in a saloon aiming their guns at each other's head—permanently. There had to be a better way. Early in my first term, I called a meeting of the Joint Chiefs of Staff—our military leaders—and said to them: Every offensive weapon ever invented by man has resulted in the creation of a defense against it; isn't it possible in this age of technology that we could invent a defensive weapon that could intercept nuclear weapons and destroy them as they emerged from their silos? They looked at each other, then asked if they could huddle for a few moments. Very shortly, they came out of their huddle and said, "Yes, it's an idea worth exploring." My answer was, "Let's do it" (Reagan 1990, 547).

During February 1983, the JCS unanimously recommended a national security strategy placing heightened emphasis on strategic defenses (U.S. Army Space and Missile Defense

During his national security speech on March 23, 1983, President Ronald Reagan speaks to the nation regarding the Strategic Defense Initiative, proposing intensive research on a space-based antiballistic missile defense system that would destroy Soviet missiles before they reached their target. *(Ronald Reagan Presidential Library)*

Command n.d., 2). Following extensive consultations with his advisors and other administration policymakers, Reagan introduced his ideas to the public in a nationally televised address on March 23, 1983. This speech reviewed the status of U.S. relations with the Soviet Union and current and historical international security and arms control developments. Near the conclusion of this speech Reagan presented his revolutionary vision for altering the military strategic landscape with the following declaration:

> Let me share with you a vision of the future which offers hope. It is that we embark on a program to counter the awesome Soviet missile threat with measures that are defensive. Let us turn to the very strengths in technology that spawned our great industrial base and that have given us the quality of life that we enjoy today. What if free people could live secure in the knowledge that their security did not rest upon the threat of instant U.S. retaliation to deter a Soviet attack, that we could intercept and destroy strategic ballistic missiles before they reached our own soil or that of our allies?
>
> I believe this is a formidable, technical task, one that may not be accomplished before the end of this century. Yet, current technology has attained a level of so-

phistication where it's responsible for us to begin this effort. It will take many years, probably decades of effort on many fronts. There will be failures and setbacks, just as there will be successes and breakthroughs. And as we proceed, we must remain constant in preserving the nuclear deterrent and maintaining a solid capability for flexible response. But isn't it worth every investment necessary to free the world from the threat of nuclear war? We know it is (*Public Papers of the Presidents of the United States*, 1984, 442–443).

The first tangible policy step in implementing this lofty and controversial vision was directing National Security Advisor William P. Clark, Jr. (1931–) to formulate detailed instructions for implementing this program throughout relevant civilian and military departments in NSDD 85 on March 25, 1983 (Feycock 2006, 205). Reagan's ideas would become known as the Strategic Defense Initiative (SDI) because of the proposal's drastic impact on the U.S. and global strategic environment. The program's audacity and some overselling of its assets by proponents created a firestorm of domestic and international controversy causing many critics to call it "Star Wars." These critics, such as Senator Edward Kennedy, along with opponents in Congress and some elements in U.S. and international diplomatic and security circles, attempted to claim that SDI would militarize space, create a new arms race, violate the ABM Treaty, and demonstrate that the United States was no longer willing to defend its allies against nuclear missile attack. Such controversies plagued SDI and future U.S. ballistic missile defense programs in the years to come (Shultz 1993, 258–261; Weinberger 1990, 309; National Review 1988, 18; Lambeth and Lewis 1988, 755–770).

DOD moved quickly after Reagan's actions described in NSDD 85 by commissioning two studies on SDI's policy implications and technical feasibility. The policy study was headed by Undersecretary of Defense for Policy Fred Ikle (1924–) who delegated the authority to Paul Hoffman of Pan Heuristics, a Los Angeles policy research group, and the technology study was lead by former and future NASA administrator James Fletcher (1919–1991) (Weinberger 1990, 310). The Fletcher report was completed in February 1984 and recommended SDI research proceed in areas such as surveillance, acquisitions, and tracking; directed energy weapons; battle management, command and control, and communications; survivability, lethality, and threat vulnerability; and selected support systems (U.S. Army Space and Missile Defense Command n.d., 2; U.S. Congress, House Committee on Armed Services 1985).

Important elements of the March 1984 policy study included recognizing that advanced ballistic missile defense had the potential to reduce the military value of ballistic missiles and their importance in the strategic balance, while related technologies could give the Soviet Union an incentive for nuclear arms reductions; the Soviets continuing ongoing efforts to discredit ballistic missile defense systems; that the Soviets might change their behavior if they were convinced the United States was serious in its missile defense programs; the need to revise the ABM Treaty if a widespread missile defense system were to be deployed over the United States; and the Soviets increasing their dependence on defensive military systems. Additional findings of this study include ballistic missile defenses enhancing the possibility of deterring intentional nuclear attacks, providing greater safety against accidental nuclear weapons use or unintended nuclear escalation, and presenting new arms control opportunities if uncertainties about technical feasibility, costs, and Soviet response are resolved (U.S. Congress, Senate Committee on Foreign Affairs 1984, 103–105; Fought 1987).

SDI's formal beginnings date from NSDD 119 signed by President Reagan on January 6, 1984 and placed the program under DOD's leadership. Key elements of this document reflecting SDI's raison d'etre include DOD managing the program and the SDI program manager reporting directly to the secretary of Defense, SDI placing primary emphasis on technologies involving nonnuclear components, and research continuing on nuclear-based strategic defense concepts as a hedge against a Soviet ABM breakout (Feycock 2006, 216).

On March 27, 1984, Secretary of Defense Casper Weinberger (1917–2006) appointed Air Force lieutenant general James Abrahamson (1933–) as the first director of the Strategic Defense Initiative Organization (SDIO), which was given responsibility for developing SDI. Weinberger signed the SDIO charter on April 24, 1984, giving Abrahamson extensive freedom in managing the program (Federation of American Scientists n.d., 5).

A May 7, 1984 memorandum from Deputy Secretary of Defense William H. Taft IV (1945–) to the secretary of the Air Force provided additional direction and guidance on the mission and program management of SDI's boost and space surveillance tracking systems. SDI attributes mandated in this document included the ability to provide ballistic missile TW/AA; satellite attack warning/verification (SAW/V); satellite targeting for U.S. ASAT operations; and SDI surveillance, acquisition, tracking and kill assessment SATKA. Additional program mandates included program plans showing specific requirements, critical milestones, and costs along with alternative means of achieving these objectives (Spires 2004, 2:1130–1131).

SDIO was organized into five program areas covering SATKA, Directed Energy Weapons (DEW) Technology, Kinetic Energy Weapons (KEW) Technology, Systems Concept/Battle Management (SC/BM), and Survivability, Lethality, and Key Technologies (SLKT). SATKA program objectives included investigating sensing technologies capable of providing information to activate defense systems, conduct battle management, and assess force status before and during military engagements. A key SATKA challenge was developing the ability to discriminate among hostile warheads, decoys, and chaff during midcourse and early terminal phases of their trajectories (DiMaggio et al. 1986, 6–7).

The DEW program sought to examine the potential for using laser and/or particle beams for ballistic missile defense. DEW can deliver destructive energy to targets near or at light speed and are particularly attractive for using against missiles as they rise through the atmosphere. Successfully engaging missiles during these flight stages can allow missiles to be destroyed before they release multiple independently targeted warheads. Relevant weapon concepts studied under DEW included space-based lasers, ground-beam lasers using orbiting relay mirrors, space-based neutral particle beams, and endoatmospheric charged particle beams guided by low-power lasers (DiMaggio et al. 1986, 7–8).

KEW program applications involved studying ways of accurately directing fairly light objects at high speed to intercept missiles or warheads during any flight phase. Technologies being investigated by this program include space-based chemically launched projectiles with homing devises and space-based electromagnetic rail guns (DiMaggio et al. 1986, 8).

Research pertinent to SC/BM programs explores defensive architecture options allowing for deployment of extremely responsive, reliable, survivable, and cost-effective battle management and command, control, and communications systems. Factors examined in such programs must include mission objectives, offensive threat analyses, technical capabilities, risk, and cost (DiMaggio et al. 1986, 8–9).

SLKT program components seek to support research and technology development for improving system effectiveness and satisfying system logistical needs. Such survivability and lethality study efforts seek to produce information about expected enemy threats and the ability of SDI systems to survive efforts to destroy or defeat it. Relevant SLKT supporting technology research areas include space transportation and power, orbital maintenance, and energy storage and conversion. Pertinent SDI logistical research, under program auspices, is crucial for evaluating and reducing deployment and operational costs (DiMaggio et al. 1986, 10).

SDI achieved significant program and technical accomplishments over the next decade. A June 1984 Homing Overlay Experiment achieved the first kinetic kill intercept of an ICBM reentry vehicle, SDIO established an Exoatmospheric Reentry Vehicle Interceptor Subsystem (ERIS) Project Office in July 1984, and a High Endoatmospheric Defense Interceptor (HEDI) Project Office in October 1984. March 1985 saw Weinberger invite allied participation in U.S. ballistic missile defense programs, and in October 1985 National Security Advisor Robert McFarlane (1937–) introduced a controversial "broad interpretation" of the ABM Treaty, which asserted that certain space-based and mobile ABM systems and components such as lasers and particle beams could be developed and tested but not deployed (U.S. Army Space and Missile Defense Command, n.d. 2–3; U.S. Congress, Senate Committee on Armed Services, Subcommittee on Theater and Strategic Nuclear Forces 1986, 136–144).

During August 1986 the Army's vice chief of staff approved the U.S. Army Strategic Defense Command theater missile defense research program, and the following month this official also directed the establishment of a Joint Theater Missile Defense Program Office in Huntsville, Alabama to coordinate Army theater missile defense requirements. May 1987 saw the successful kinetic energy intercept by the Flexible Lightweight Agile Guided Experiment of a Lance missile, which was a high-velocity, low-altitude target. In July 1988 Hughes Aircraft delivered the Airborne Surveillance Testbed Sensor to the military, which was the most complex long-wavelength infrared sensor built at that time.

February 1989 saw President George H.W. Bush (1924–) announce that his administration would continue SDI developments; a June 1989 national defense strategy review

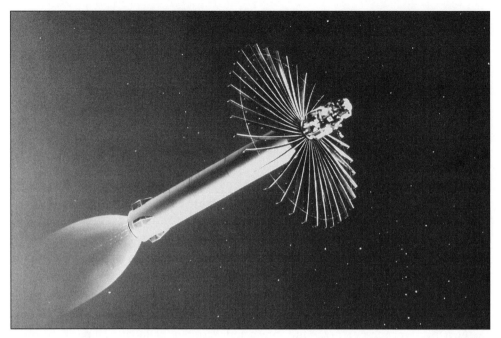

An artist's concept of the Army Homing Overlay Experiment (HOE) homing and kill vehicle preparing to intercept a mock nuclear warhead more than 100 miles above the mid-Pacific Ocean. The HOE sensor in the nose locks onto the target and the third stage axial propulsion motor maneuvers the vehicle onto a collision course. The 15-foot radial "net" opens to destroy the incoming warhead by impact at more than 15,000 feet per second. *(U.S. Department of Defense)*

concluded that SDI program goals were sound; SDIO approved an Endoatmospheric/ Exoatmospheric Interceptor program during summer 1990 to succeed HEDI; the first successful ERIS intercept took place during January 1991; and in June 1991 there were successful tests of the lightweight exoatmospheric projectile integrated vehicle strap down and free flight hover (U.S. Army Space and Missile Defense Command n.d., 3–4; U.S. Department of Defense 1989, 1–31).

SDI was able to achieve significant accomplishments during the 1980s and early 1990s as the list above demonstrates. The program remained controversial during its first decade before SDIO was renamed the Ballistic Missile Defense Organization (BMDO) by the Clinton administration on June 14, 1994 (U.S. Department of Defense 1994, 1).

Program expenditures remained a source of controversy for some congressional appropriators. SDIO's budget, according to a 1989 DOD report, was $3.8 billion for fiscal year 1989 representing 0.33% of the $282.4 defense budget for that year (U.S. Department of Defense 1989, 27). A 1992 congressional review of SDIO expenditures quantified that the organization had received $25 billion since 1984 for ballistic missile defense system research and development and that the Bush administration's proposed fiscal year 1992 budget estimated system acquisition costs to be $46 billion (U.S. General Accounting Office 1992(a), 10).

Changing SDI program objectives complicated SDIO's work and operational efficiency. SDI was originally intended to provide a massive system for defending the United States against Soviet ballistic missile attacks. During 1987 program objectives shifted from defending against massive missile strikes to deterring such strikes. The 1990 introduction of the Brilliant Pebbles space-based interceptor (see next entry) caused SDIO to change organizational direction again. A number of organizational realignments were implemented during September 1988 such as adding a chief of staff to oversee SDIO activities; adding a chief engineer to ensure multiple engineering tasks and analysis received top-level attention; and the creation of a Resource Management Directorate, which merged Comptroller and Support Services Directorates in an effort to enhance management efficiency (U.S. General Accounting Office 1992(a), 2; Federation of American Scientists n.d., 8).

Operation Desert Storm also heralded important changes in SDIO program activities. The use of Patriot missile batteries against Iraqi Scud missiles during this 1991 conflict achieved some success but with significant attending controversy over how successful the Patriot system had actually performed (U.S. Congress, House Committee on Government Operations, Subcommittee on Legislation and National Security 1993; Snodgrass 1993).

During his January 29, 1991 State of the Union address to Congress as this conflict raged, President Bush announced another SDI shift to the concept called Global Protection Against Limited Strikes (GPALS) as reflected in the following statement ". . . I have directed that the Strategic Defense Initiative program be refocused on providing protection from limited ballistic missile strikes, whatever their source. Let us pursue an SDI program that can deal with any future threat to the United States, to our forces overseas and to our friends and allies" (*Public Papers of the Presidents of the United States 1991*, 78).

This shift to GPALS came about as a result of a perceived decline in the Soviet missile threat and the emergence of tactical ballistic missile threats from Iraq and other third world countries. GPALS would have two ground-based and one space-based segment. One of the ground-based components would consist of sensors and interceptors to protect U.S. and allied missile forces overseas from missile attack. An additional ground-based segment would protect the United States from accidental or limited attacks of up to 200 warheads. GPALS spaced-based component would help detect and intercept missiles and warheads launched from anywhere in the world. SDIO sought to integrate these three segments to provide mutual coordinated support and required that each of these entities be designed to work together using automated data processing and communication networks (U.S. General Accounting Office 1992(a), 2–3).

This governmental emphasis on localized theater, as opposed to global strategic missile defense, was also reflected in the fiscal year 1991 congressional conference committee report on the defense budget issued October 24, 1990. This legislation called for the secretary of Defense to establish a centrally managed theater missile defense program funded at $218,249,000, required DOD to accelerate research and development on theater and tactical ballistic missile defense systems, and called for the inclusion of Air Force and Navy requirements in such a plan and the participation of these services (U.S. Congress, House Committee on Appropriations 1990, 117–118).

SDI and the concept of ballistic missile defense continued generating controversy throughout its first decade. Although SDIO was able to achieve relatively viable funding and enough operational successes to retain sufficient political support within DOD and in Congress to persevere as an organization, its organizational mission focus never remained constant. Contentiousness over whether there was even a need for SDI or ballistic missile defense was reflected in the following 1991 statements before House Government Operations Committee oversight hearings on SDI.

Opponents of SDI such as Federation of American Scientist's Space Policy Project director John Pike claimed that ballistic missile threats to the United States were examples of hyperbolic rhetoric, that SDI was too expensive, had numerous technical problems, and that its deployment could jeopardize international arms control. Pike described SDI as being a "Chicken Little" approach to existing threats, which would cost more than $100 billion instead of current projections of $40 billion. He also contended that SDI had significant computing and software problems, that its deployment would end the ABM Treaty and imperil arms control progress, and there was no compelling reason to deploy SDI based on the existing strategic environment (U.S. Congress, House Committee on Governmental Operations, Legislation and National Security Subcommittee 1992, 194).

Proponents of SDI such as Keith Payne of the National Institute for Public Policy emphasized how the Iraqi use of Scud missiles during Operation Desert Storm had drastically changed Cold War strategic assumptions about how ballistic missiles might be used in future military conflicts. These proponents stressed the threat to civilians from missiles that could carry chemical warheads, how normal life ended in cities threatened by Iraqi Scud attacks, how Iraqi conventionally armed missile attacks during the Iran–Iraq War caused nearly 2,000 deaths, forced the evacuation of urban areas like Tehran with ruinous economic consequences, and warned that such events could happen to U.S. and allied metropolitan areas due to ballistic missile proliferation (U.S. Congress, House Committee on Government Operations, Subcommittee on Legislation and National Security 1992, 284).

SDI supporters further stressed how the presence of ballistic missiles equipped with weapons of mass destruction in the hands of third world countries such as Iraq could drastically reduce the flexibility of U.S. leaders in responding to such threats. Examples of this reduced flexibility would involve U.S. leaders having to assess the possibility of third party ballistic missile strikes against U.S. forces, allies, or U.S. population centers, sufficient to limit the president's freedom of action to respond; emerging ballistic missile threats could have a debilitating effect on the U.S. capability to establish allied coalitions and respond to aggression as it did in Operation Desert Storm; and activities such as escorting threatened commercial shipping through hostile waters during the Iran–Iraq War or militarily evacuating U.S. citizens from foreign hot spots could become increasingly dangerous. Payne and other missile defense supporters stress that such defenses enable the United

States to maintain the credibility of its overseas security commitments and encourage the belief that the United States will not be deterred from defending its national interests and allies (U.S. Congress, House Committee on Government Operations, Subcommittee on Legislation and National Security 1992, 284–285).

SDIO continued its activities as the Clinton administration began in 1993. Ballistic missile defense was not high on the national security priorities of this administration as it took office (Lindsay and O'Hanlon 2001, 87). SDIO's initial institutional incarnation came to an end with DOD Directive 5134.9 on June 14, 1994, which established the BMDO as the organizational focal point for U.S. ballistic missile defense efforts. The now preponderant emphasis on developing defenses against theater ballistic missile threats, while also adhering to the ABM Treaty, was reflected in BMDO's mission, whose characteristics included deploying an effective and rapidly mobile theater missile defense system to protect forward-deployed and expeditionary components of U.S. and allied armed forces; defending the U.S. homeland against limited ballistic missile attacks; demonstrating advanced technology options for enhanced missile defense systems including space-based defenses and associated sensors; making informed decisions on development, production, and deployment of such systems in consultation with U.S. allies; and adhering to existing international agreements and treaty obligations while using nonnuclear weapon technologies (U.S. Department of Defense 1994, 1–2).

SDI may have been conceived and initially presented with idealistic fervor, but its inception was driven by profound and substantive dissatisfaction with the military and moral predicament of the United States being unable to defend its population and military interests against hostile ballistic missile attacks. SDI and its successor programs have survived and evolved into contemporary national missile defense programs because of their ability to pragmatically adapt to prevailing political, economic, and military environments facing the United States and its national security interests (Clagett 1996).

Brilliant Pebbles

Brilliant Pebbles is a program that experienced a brief life and achieved some technological success before its termination. The program's theoretical intellectual origins may be said to have begun around 1960 when DARPA's Project Defender missile defense technology inventory stressed the high defense value of using space-based interceptors to attack and destroy ICBMs while they were in their boost phase. During the 1980s, Brilliant Pebbles became a space-based interceptor program designed to be capable of destroying Soviet ICBMs during their boost phase, and would be capable of eliminating multiple Soviet warheads and decoys before they could be dispersed to multiple targets (Baucom 2004, 143–145).

In late 1986, Reagan and Secretary of Defense Casper Weinberger began entering a missile defense system into the overall defense acquisition process. This decision would eventually result in the September 1987 approval of the Strategic Defense System (SDS)

Phase I Architecture. This architecture consisted of six major subsystems including a space-based interceptor (SBI), a ground-based interceptor, a ground-based sensor, two space-based sensors, and a battle management system. SDS was intended to have a structure capable of producing further refinement of missile defense components that could be integrated into and improve overall system architecture in an iterative process.

An important change in SDS was SBI's replacement by Brilliant Pebbles. SBI was intended to be a large satellite housing several individual hit-to-kill interceptors. Several hundred SBIs were to orbit the earth and launch their interceptors at individual Soviet missiles in case of an attack, destroying these missiles during their boost phase. SBI's weaknesses were its projected $18–$30 billion cost and its large size making it an easy target for Soviet ASAT weapons (Baucom 2004, 152; U.S. Missile Defense Agency Historians Office n.d., 3–4).

Brilliant Pebbles came to be seen as a solution to this problem. SDIO officials believed Brilliant Pebbles could utilize advances in miniaturized sensors and computers to develop interceptors capable of operating without the sensors and communications infrastructure SBI required. These officials hypothesized that, because of Brilliant Pebbles, Soviet ASATs would have to contend with several thousand small and hard to find interceptors orbiting in constellations over strategically significant global regions instead of being able to confront several hundred large targets (U.S. Missile Defense Agency Historians Office n.d., 4).

Brilliant Pebbles was formally integrated into the SDS system in 1989 after Lt. General George L. Monohan, Jr. (1933–1993) became SDIO's second director. This decision made it possible to eliminate one constellation of space-based sensors achieving additional SDS cost reductions. The planned Brilliant Pebbles deployment would see the system consist of several large lightweight, low-cost, single hit-to-kill kinetic kill vehicles providing integrated sensors, guidance, control, and battle management. Individual Brilliant Pebbles interceptors would have their own sensors, computers, and thrusters to detect, track, and intercept hostile missiles. These interceptors weighed about 100 pounds and meant that SDIO no longer had to place 100,000-pound laser battle stations in orbit and could be launched by lighter medium-lift rockets (Missile Defense Agency Historians Office n.d., 4; U.S. National Aeronautics and Space Administration 1999, 5).

Additional Brilliant Pebbles attributes that were developed at the Energy Department's Lawrence Livermore National Laboratory (LLNL) include a wide-field-of-view telescope with a high-resolution multispectral sensor capable of viewing a land area the size of Virginia and individual buildings from 1,000 kilometers height, a multipurpose antenna capable of communicating with other space-based or ground platforms, two sets of thrusters and propellant tanks, and the ability to fly sideways or accelerate straight ahead (Foley 1988, 32–33).

Brilliant Pebbles' prospects, ironically, began declining just after the 1989 decision to integrate it into SDI program objectives. In June 1989, President George H.W. Bush issued National Security Directive (NSD) 14 on the SDI program. This document determined that SDI remained programmatically sound and directed Secretary of Defense Dick Cheney (1941–) to commission an independent review of SDI to see NSD 14 objectives carried out. This review was conducted by Ambassador Henry Cooper (1936–), who served as the chief U.S. negotiator at the defense and space arms control negotiations in Geneva. Cooper's report was submitted to the president on March 15, 1990 and contained a strong endorsement of Brilliant Pebbles, which its author believed was essential to SDI's success (Baucom 2004, 154–155; Missile Defense Agency Historians Office n.d., 4; U.S. General Accounting Office 1993(a), 29).

Cooper's report also emphasized that the most critical threats to U.S. security, in light of the Cold War's decline, would come from unauthorized or terrorist attacks with ballistic missiles and that U.S. forces would encounter increasing threats from shorter range theater ballistic missiles as ballistic missile technology and weapons of mass destruction proliferated. Cooper recommended that the SDI program shift its emphasis from preparing for a mass attack by thousands of Soviet warheads to developing defenses against limited ballistic missile attacks. He became SDIO's third director in July 1990 and began working to implement his report recommendations with Bush's January 1991 GPALS program announcement of this formal shift in U.S. missile defense policy (Missile Defense Agency Historians Office n.d., 4–5; U.S. Congress, Senate Committee on Armed Services 1992, 271–378).

Brilliant Pebbles received a mixed reception from congressional defense specialists during its existence, which was reflective of the often passionate congressional debate on SDI. Speaking before the Senate on August 4, 1990, Senator Malcolm Wallop (Republican from Wyoming) (1933–) praised what he saw as Brilliant Pebbles' very promising near-term interceptor technology and criticized an attempt by Senators Jeff Bingaman (Democrat from New Mexico) (1943–) and Richard Shelby (Democrat from Alabama) (1934–) to cut $200 million in Brilliant Pebbles program funding and transferring such funding to other SDI programs in New Mexico and Alabama, charging that this action turned SDI into a "technological welfare program" (U.S. Congress 1992, S12354–12355).

Some Democrats like then House Armed Services Committee chair representative Les Aspin (Democrat from Wisconsin) (1938–1995) and then Senate Armed Services Committee chair senator Sam Nunn (Democrat from Georgia) (1938–) were concerned that Brilliant Pebbles could have a negative effect on the ABM Treaty. Aspin and Nunn were also concerned about Brilliant Pebbles' effectiveness against low flying tactical missiles; that SDI's emphasis on this program was reducing spending for ground-based weapons, which they felt could be deployed faster to protect U.S. territory from ballistic missile attacks; and that the Soviets would see Brilliant Pebbles as part of U.S. plans to neutralize their nuclear forces, which, Aspin believed, would terminate possible Soviet interest in the then ongoing Strategic Arms Reduction Treaty (START), intended to reduce Soviet and U.S. strategic forces by 30% (Trowell 1991, 1836–1844).

Concerns over Brilliant Pebbles were expressed in a number of GAO reports during the early 1990s. A March 1991 assessment criticized SDIO for paying Brilliant Pebbles contractors to improve a design concept before LLNL had demonstrated that it would work. GAO further doubted LLNL's ability to complete a projected test program by the summer of 1993 because of the program's compression providing minimal time to account for near inevitable future problems. Lastly, the GAO emphasized that the program's flight test failed to achieve all of its objectives (U.S. General Accounting Office 1991, 6).

Another GAO report, issued a year after this initial assessment, was particularly critical of the computer simulations used by SDIO to design and implement Brilliant Pebbles' ability to defend against ballistic missiles as the following excerpt demonstrates:

> SDIO's estimates of effectiveness are based on computer simulations of various numbers of interceptors deployed against certain hypothetical ballistic missile attacks. SDIO has identified over 40 hypothetical attack scenarios, or threats, against the United States and its allies, which includes short-, intermediate-, and long-range ballistic missile attacks originating from all over the world and submarine launched attacks against the United States. SDIO has investigated many potential deployment schemes to identify a constellation that provides the optimum global protection against all threats. As of December 1991, SDIO had not evaluated through simulations the performance of Brilliant Pebbles against all identified threats (U.S. General Accounting Office 1992(b), 3).

This report also determined that these computer simulations included deployment decision assumptions that improved system performance with the increased deployment of Brilliant Pebbles. In addition, these SDIO simulations determined that Brilliant Pebbles constellations orbiting close to the equator would be most effective against missiles launched from the Middle East or Europe, while constellations orbiting over the North and South Poles would be most effective against attacks from Russia (U.S. General Accounting Office 1992(b), 4).

A September 1992 GAO report for the House Government Operations Committee analyzed seven flight tests of Brilliant Pebbles interceptors. This analysis mentioned that SDIO asserted that five of these tests were successful and two unsuccessful but GAO determined that SDIO inaccurately described the results in four of the seven tests (U.S. General Accounting Office 1992(c), 2).

These negative performance management reports and an evolving U.S. emphasis on developing more limited forms of ballistic missile defense during the early 1990s took its toll on Brilliant Pebbles. This was accelerated with the conclusion of the first Bush administration and the emergence of the Clinton administration in 1993. In November 1992, SDIO announced that Brilliant Pebbles would be removed from DOD's acquisition process. SDIO also transferred the program to the Air Force effective December 18, 1992, and new contracts in January 1993 converted Brilliant Pebbles into an "advanced technology demonstration" program. February 2, 1993 saw Aspin, now President Bill Clinton's (1946–) secretary of Defense, issue SDI program budget guidance by reducing Brilliant Pebbles to an anemically funded technology base program. Later DOD budget guidance for Brilliant Pebbles saw its budget reduced 25%, and it became the Advanced Interceptor Technology (AIT) program in March 1993.

Brilliant Pebbles' demise became official on December 1, 1993 when BMDO acting deputy director James D. Carlson issued an order ending the program due to budgetary constraints, although he thought the program had made progress given historical investments in it (Baucom 2004, 183–185).

Space-Based Infrared System (SBIRS)

The Space-Based Infrared System (SBIRS) is intended to replace DSP and serve as the United States' critical missile defense and early warning capability during the 21st century. Its program areas, including the existing DSP, SBIRS High, and the Space Tracking and Surveillance System (STSS), are described in greater detail in Chapter 3. The SBIRS High program component is expected to detect a missile launch, determine its course, and warn appropriate ground forces in 10–20 seconds as opposed to the 40–50 seconds required by DSP (U.S. Air Force Space Command n.d., 1; Smith 2006, 3–4).

This program's troubled history originated in 1994 when DOD consolidated its existing infrared space programs and selected SBIRS as its preferred "system of systems" approach

Space-Based Infrared System satellite acts as missile defense and as an early warning system. *(Lockheed Martin)*

to dealing with space reconnaissance and surveillance (Smith 2005, 2; U.S. General Accounting Office 2003(b), 7). Lockheed Martin and Northrop Grumman were awarded a $2.16-million contract to build SBIRS High in 1996. DOD increased the contract to $4.18 billion in September 2002, which does not include the cost of three of the five projected satellites (Smith 2005, 3).

SBIRS's initial purpose was serving as an acquisition program for supporting national and theater missile defense by tracking missiles throughout their flight and being able to discriminate warheads from decoys in supporting a missile defense mission. During 1998, the SBIRS program office had to be restructured based on an Air Force directive to delay satellite launches by two years to fund other DOD priorities. According to GAO, this contributed to program instability since the contractor was required to stop and restart activities and devise interim solutions that would not normally have occurred (U.S. General Accounting Office 2003(a), 6). Negative cost and schedule trends, along with performance estimates, caused DOD to take the program off an acquisition track and return it to a long-term technology development track. These concerns caused Congress to transfer SBIRS program management from the Air Force to the Ballistic Missile Defense Organization (now Missile Defense Agency) in October 2000 (U.S. General Accounting Office 2003(b), 7).

Congressional concerns about SBIRS program costs and technical problems were reflected in committee budget authorization reports, as shown in this 2001 House Appropriations Committee report denying the Air Force's $93,752,000 program request and replacing it with $30 million. The committee report noted:

> The Committee notes that the SBIRs High development program is facing serious hardware and software design problems. These programs are driving significant program shortfalls in all years, totaling more than $500 million. A recent GAO report notes that sensor jitter and inadequate infrared sensitivity as well as an issue of stray sunlight have plagued the program and are driving cost increases and schedule delays. Program officials have indicated that there are currently unbudgeted payload redesign activities and that schedule variances experienced to date portend serious schedule impacts ahead. The program office also reports "inconceivable software code growth" with an "overwhelming" number of discrepancy reports in ground mission software. The program is achieving "at best 1/2 of the estimated software development productivity" required to meet its schedule. Given these issues, the Committee believes it is prudent to defer satellite hardware procurement to provide additional time for development (U.S. Congress, House Committee on Appropriations 2001, 140).

Although SBIRS has continued in ensuing years, its viability and programmatic efficiency remain the subject of concern with DOD as well as in Congress. A May 2003 report by the Defense Science Board and Air Force Scientific Advisory Board, which also focused on space acquisition programs, maintained that cost had replaced mission success as the key factor in managing space development programs such as SBIRS; that unrealistic estimates produced unrealistic budgets and undeliverable programs; that undisciplined program definition and uncontrolled system growth requirements increased costs and schedule delays; that government capabilities to lead and manage the space acquisition progress have seriously eroded because of excessively surrendering such authority to industry during the 1990s; and that industry has failed to implement best management practices in programs such as SBIRS (U.S. Defense Science Board 2003, 2–4).

An October 2003 GAO report on SBIRS asserted that the program remained at substantial risk of cost and schedule increases despite recent restructuring (U.S. General Accounting Office 2003(a), 2). Delivery of a SBIRS High sensor for launch on one satellite was delayed until August 2004 due to electromagnetic interference between the sensor and other spacecraft equipment. Launch of the first SBIRS satellite for geosynchronous orbit has slipped repeatedly and is now expected in 2008 (Smith 2005, 4).

A September 30, 2005 DOD report observed that SBIRS's high costs had increased from $9,613,300 to $10,638,100 (a 10.7% increase) during the preceding year (U.S. Department of Defense, Acquisition Resources and Analysis 2005, 3). DOD requested $756 million for SBIRS for fiscal year 2006 (October 1, 2005–September 30, 2006). The House Appropriations Committee report on this legislation described the program as "extremely troubled" and complained that program costs had increased from $4 billion–$10 billion, while the Senate Appropriations Committee report cut SBIRS funding by $100 million given its protracted accounting and management problems (Smith 2005, 4; U.S. Congress, House Committee on Appropriations 2005, 181; U.S. Congress, Senate Committee on Appropriations 2005, 219).

SBIRS retains sufficient support with DOD and Congress to linger on, but its historic and ongoing cost control, management, and technical problems make predicting its future problematic.

References and Further Reading

Australia. Parliament. Senate. 1991. *Hansard.* November 5, 2374. [Online article or information; retrieved 9/29/06.] http://parlinfoweb.aph.gov.au/piweb/view_document.aspx?ID=82522&TABLE=HANSARDS.

Ball, D. 1987. *A Base for Debate: The US Satellite Station at Nurrungar.* Sydney and Boston: Allen & Unwin.

Ball, D. and J. Richelson. 1985. *The Ties That Bind: Intelligence Cooperation Between the UKUSA Countries, the United Kingdom, the United States of America, Canada, Australia, and New Zealand.* Boston: Allen & Unwin.

Baucom, D. R. 1992. *The Origins of SDI: 1944–1983.* Lawrence, KS: University Press of Kansas.

Baucom, D. R. 2004. "The Rise and Fall of Brilliant Pebbles." *Journal of Social, Political, and Economic Studies* 29 (2): 143–190.

Bowen, G. S. 2005. "Safeguard: North Dakota's Front Line in the Cold War." *Quest* 12 (1): 42–51.

Bulkeley, R. and H. G. Brauch. 1988. *The Anti-Ballistic Missile Treaty and World Security.* Mosbach, Germany: AFES Press.

Burr, W., ed. 2001. *The Secret History of the ABM Treaty: National Security Archive Briefing Book No. 60.* Washington, D.C.: George Washington University.

Center for Nonproliferation Studies. 2005. "Current and Future Space Security Russia: Military Programs," 1–3. [Online article or information; retrieved 9/8/06.] http://cns.miis.edu/research/space/russia/mil.htm.

Clagett, C. A. 1996. *Funding Star Wars: Senate Hearings and the Strategic Defense Initiative, 1984–1993.* Ph.D. diss. University of Maryland-College Park, College Park, Maryland.

Cloud, J. 2001(a). "Hidden in Plain Sight: The Corona Reconnaissance Satellite Program and Clandestine Cold War Science." *Annals of Science* 58 (2): 203–209.

Cloud, J. 2001(b). "Imaging the World in a Barrel: CORONA and the Clandestine Convergence of the Earth Sciences." *Social Studies of Science* 31 (2): 231–251.

Council on Foreign Relations. 2002. *Chronology of National Missile Defense Programs,* 3. [Online article or information; retrieved 10/3/06.] www.cfr.org/publication/10443/chronology_of _national_missile_defense_programs.htm.

Day, D. A., J. M. Logsdon, and B. Latell, eds. 1998. *Eye in the Sky: The Story of the Corona Spy Satellites.* Washington, D.C.: Smithsonian Institution Press.

DiMaggio, C., A. F. Manfredi, Jr., and S. A. Hildreth. 1986. *The Strategic Defense Initiative: Program Description and Major Issues.* Washington, D.C.: Library of Congress, Congressional Research Service.

Enthoven, A. C. and K. W. Smith. 2005. *How Much is Enough: Shaping the Defense Program 1961–1969.* Santa Monica, CA: Rand Corporation.

Erickson, M. 2005. *Into the Unknown Together: The DOD, NASA, and Early Spaceflight.* Maxwell Air Force Base, AL: Air University Press.

Federation of American Scientists. n.d. *Missile Defense Milestones 1944–1997.* [Online article or information; retrieved 10/4/06.] www.fas.org/spp/starwars/program/milestone.htm.

Feycock, S., comp. 2006. *National Security Space Project Presidential Decisions: NSC Documents.* Washington, D.C.: George C. Marshall Institute.

Foley, T. M. 1988. "Brilliant Pebbles Testing Proceeds at Rapid Pace." *Aviation Week and Space Technology* 129 (20): 32–33.

Fought, S. O. 1987. *SDI: A Policy Analysis.* Newport, RI: Naval War College Press.

Gorin, P. A. 1998. "Zenit: The Soviet Response to Corona." In *Eye in the Sky: The Story of the Corona Spy Satellites,* edited by Day, D.A., J.M. Logsdon, and B. Latell, eds., 157–172. Washington, DC: Smithsonian Institution Press.

Greer, K. E. 1973. "Corona." *Studies in Intelligence Supplement* 17 (Spring): 1–37.

Gross, B. W. 1975. *An Analysis of the Debate in the United States Senate of the Safeguard Antiballistic Missile System.* Ph.D. diss. Philadelphia: Temple University.

Haas, S. C. 1988. "Reassessing Lessons from the ABM Treaty." *International Affairs* 64 (2): 233–240.

Houchin II, R. F. 1988. "The Diplomatic Demise of Dyna-Soar: The Impact of International and Domestic Political Affairs on the Dyna-Soar X-20 Project, 1957–1963." *Aerospace Historian* 35 (4): 274–280.

Houchin II, R. F. 1999. "Hypersonic Technology and Aerospace Doctrine." *Air Power History* 46 (3): 4–17.

Kutyna, D. J. 1998. "Indispensable: Space Systems in the Persian Gulf War." 103-128. In *The U.S. Air Force in Space: 1945 to the Twenty-First Century: Proceedings Air Force Historical Foundation Symposium Andrews AFB, Maryland September 21–22, 1995,* edited by R. C. Hall and J. Neufeld. Washington, D.C.: U.S. Air Force History and Museums Program.

Lambeth, B. and K. Lewis. 1988. "The Kremlin and SDI." *Foreign Affairs* 66 (4): 755–770.

Lindgren, D. T. 2000. *Trust But Verify: Imagery Analysis in the Cold War.* Annapolis, MD: Naval Institute Press.

Lindsay, J. M. and M. E. O'Hanlon. 2001. *Defending America: The Case for Limited National Missile Defense.* Washington, D.C.: Brookings Institution Press.

Murdock, C. A. 1974. *Defense Policy Formation: A Comparative Analysis of the McNamara Era.* Albany: State University of New York Press, 1974.

Nuclear Threat Initiative. 2003. "China's Nuclear Testing," 1. [Online article or information; retrieved 9/8/06.] www.nti.org/db/china/testpos.htm.

Posey, R. 1998. "A Sudden Loss of Altitude." *Air and Space Smithsonian* 13 (2): 74–81.

President of the United States. 1995. "Executive Order 12951 of February 22, 1995: Release of Imagery Acquired by Space-Based National Intelligence Reconnaissance Systems." *Federal Register* 60 (39): 10789–10790.

Public Papers of the Presidents of the United States: Ronald Reagan 1983 Book 1-January 1 To July 1, 1983. 1984. Washington, D.C.: U.S. Government Printing Office.

Public Papers of the Presidents of the United States: George Bush 1991 Book 1-January 1–June 30, 1991. 1992. Washington, D.C.: U.S. Government Printing Office.

Reagan, R. 1990. *An American Life.* New York: Simon and Schuster.

Richelson, J. T. 1999. *America's Space Sentinels: DSP Satellites and National Security.* Lawrence, KS: University Press of Kansas.

Roherty, J. M. 1970. *Decisions of Robert S. McNamara: A Study of the Role of the Secretary of Defense.* Coral Gables, FL: University of Miami Press, 1970.

Ruffner, K. C., ed. 1995. *Corona: America's First Satellite Program.* Washington, D.C.: CIA History Staff, Center for the Study of Intelligence.

Schneider, M. B. 1971. "Safeguard, Sufficiency, and SALT." *Military Review* 51 (5): 24–33.

Schweizer, P. 2002. *Reagan's War: The Epic Story of His Forty-Year Struggle and Final Triumph Over Communism.* New York: Doubleday.

Shultz, G. P. 1993. *Turmoil and Triumph: My Years as Secretary of State.* New York: Charles P. Scribner's Sons.

Siddiqi, A. A. 2003. *Sputnik and the Soviet Space Challenge.* Gainesville, FL: University Press of Florida.

Smith, M. S. 2005. *Military Space Programs: Issues Concerning DOD's SBIRS and STSS Programs.* Washington, D.C.: Library of Congress, Congressional Research Service.

Smith, M. S. 2006. *Military Space Programs: Issues Concerning DOD's SBIRS and STSS Programs.* Washington, D.C.: Library of Congress, Congressional Research Service.

Snodgrass, D. E. 1993. *Attacking the Theater Mobile Ballistic Missile Threat.* Maxwell Air Force Base, AL: School of Advanced Airpower Studies, Air University. [Online article or information; retrieved 10/6/06.] http://purl.access.gpo.gov/GPO/LPS39550.

Sokolski, H. D., ed. 2004. *Getting MAD: Nuclear Mutual Assured Destruction, Its Origins and Practice.* Carlisle Barracks, PA: U.S. Army War College, Strategic Studies Institute.

"The Space Factor." 1988. *National Review,* 40 (24): 18.

Spires, D. N., ed. 1998. *Beyond Horizons: A Half Century of Air Force Space Leadership.* Peterson Air Force Base, CO and Maxwell Air Force Base, AL: Air Force Space Command and Air University Press.

Spires, D. N., ed. 2004. *Orbital Futures: Selected Documents in Air Force Space History.* 2 vols. Peterson Air Force Base, CO: Air Force Space Command.

Trowell, P. 1991. "Bush Carries On Fight for SDI, But Space Weapons in Doubt." *Congressional Quarterly Weekly Report* 49 (27): 1836–1844.

U.S. Air Force Space Command. n.d. *Space-Based Infrared Systems (SBIRS),* 1. [Online article or information; retrieved 10/2/06.] www.afspc.af.mil/library/factsheets/factsheet.asp?id=3675.

U.S. Army Space and Missile Defense Program Command. n.d. *SMDC History: A Non-Nuclear Approach.* [Online article or information; retrieved 10/3/06.] www.smdc.army.mil/Historical/SMDCTimeline2_ANon-NuclearApproach.doc.

U.S. Centennial of Flight Commission. 2003. "Spaceflight: Ballistic Missile Defense"; 1 [Online article or information; retrieved 9/22/06.] www.centennialofflight.gov/essay/SPACEFLIGHT/missile_defense/SP39.htm.

U.S. Central Intelligence Agency. 1970. *Intelligence Memorandum: Soviet ABM Defenses—Status and Prospects.* Washington, D.C.: Central Intelligence Agency.

U.S. Congress. *Congressional Record,* 1969. (August 6)(115)(17): 22478–22479, 22493, 22498.

U.S. Congress. *Congressional Record,* 1992. (August 4)(136)(105): S12354-S12355.

U.S. Congress. House Committee on Appropriations. 1990. *Making Appropriations for the Department of Defense: Conference Report to Accompany H.R. 5803.* House Report 101–938. Washington, D.C.: U.S. Government Printing Office.

U.S. Congress. House Committee on Appropriations. 2001. *Department of Defense Appropriations Bill, 2002 and Supplemental Appropriations, 2002.* House Report 107–298. Washington, D.C.: U.S. Government Printing Office.

U.S. Congress. House Committee on Appropriations. 2005. *Department of Defense Appropriations Bill, 2006.* House Report 109–119. Washington, D.C.: U.S. Government Printing Office.

U.S. Congress. House Committee on Appropriations. Subcommittee on the Department of Defense. 1993. *Department of Defense Appropriations for 1994: Part I.* Washington, D.C.: U.S. Government Printing Office.

U.S. Congress. House Committee on Armed Services. 1985. *Strategic Defense Initiative [SDI] Program.* Washington, D.C.: U.S. Government Printing Office.

U.S. Congress. House Committee on Government Operations. 1966. *Missile and Space Ground Support Operations: Twenty-Third Report.* House Report 89–1340. Washington, D.C.: U.S. Government Printing Office.

U.S. Congress. House Committee on Government Operations. Legislation and National Security Subcommittee. 1992. *Strategic Defense Initiative: What Are the Costs, What Are the Threats?* Washington, D.C.: U.S. Government Printing Office.

U.S. Congress. House Committee on Government Operations. Legislation and National Security Subcommittee. 1993. *Performance of the Patriot Missile in the Gulf War.* Washington, D.C.: U.S. Government Printing Office.

U.S. Congress. House Committee on Government Operations. Legislation and National Security Subcommittee. 1994. *Strategic Satellite Systems in a Post–Cold War Environment.* Washington, D.C.: U.S. Government Printing Office.

U.S. Congress. House Committee on Science and Technology. 1985. *Astronauts and Cosmonauts Biographical and Statistical Data [Revised-June 28, 1985].* Washington, D.C.: U.S. Government Printing Office.

U.S. Congress. Senate Committee on Appropriations. 2005. *Department of Defense Appropriations Bill, 2006.* Senate Report 109–141. Washington, D.C.: 2005.

U.S. Congress. Senate Committee on Armed Services. 1971. *Fiscal Year 1972 Authorization For Military Procurement, Research and Development, construction and Real Estate Acquisition For the Safeguard ABM and Reserve Strengths.* Washington, D.C.: U.S. Government Printing Office.

U.S. Congress. Senate Committee on Armed Services. 1992. *Department of Defense Authorization For Appropriations For Fiscal Year 1993 and The Future Years Defense Program: Part 7 Strategic Forces and Nuclear Deterrence.* Washington, D.C.: U.S. Government Printing Office.

U.S. Congress. Senate Committee on Armed Services. Subcommittee on Strategic and Theater Nuclear Forces. 1986. *Strategic Defense Initiative.* Washington, D.C.: U.S. Government Printing Office.

U.S. Congress. Senate Committee on Foreign Relations. 1984. *Strategic Defense and Anti-Satellite Weapons.* Washington, D.C.: U.S. Government Printing Office.

U.S. Defense Science Board. 2003. *Report of the Defense Science Board/Air Force Scientific Advisory Board Joint Task Force on Acquisition of National Security Space Management Programs.* Washington, D.C.: Defense Science Board. [Online article or information; retrieved 10/2/06.] www.acq.osd.mil/dsb/reports/space.pdf.

U.S. Department of Defense. 1989. *Strategic Defense Initiative: Progress and Promise.* Washington, D.C.: U.S. Department of Defense.

U.S. Department of Defense. 1992. *Final Report to Congress: Conduct of the Persian Gulf War.* Washington, D.C.: U.S. Department of Defense.

U.S. Department of Defense. 1994. *Department of Defense Directive 5134.9.* Washington, D.C.: U.S. Department of Defense.

U.S. Department of Defense. Acquisition Resources and Analysis. 2005. *Selected Acquisition Report (SAR): Summary Tables As of Date: September 30, 2005.* [Online article or information; retrieved 10/2/06.] www.acq.osd.mil/ara/am/sar/2005-SEP-SST.pdf.

U.S. Department of State. n.d. *Treaty Between the United States of America and the Union of Soviet Socialist Republics on the Limitation of Anti-Ballistic Missile Systems; 1.* [Online article or information; retrieved 9/22/06.] www.state.gov/www/global/arms/treaties/abm/abm2.html.

U.S. General Accounting Office. 1991. *Strategic Defense Initiative: Need to Examine Concurrency in Development of Brilliant Pebbles.* Washington, D.C.: U.S. General Accounting Office.

U.S. General Accounting Office. 1992(a). *Strategic Defense Initiative: Changing Design and Technological Risk Create Significant Risk.* Washington, D.C.: U.S. General Accounting Office.

U.S. General Accounting Office. 1992(b). *Strategic Defense Initiative: Estimates of Brilliant Pebbles Effectiveness Are Based on Many Unproven Assumptions.* Washington, D.C.: U.S. General Accounting Office.

U.S. General Accounting Office. 1992(c). *Strategic Defense Initiative: Some Claims Overstated for Early Flight Tests of Interceptors.* Washington, D.C.: U.S. General Accounting Office

U.S. General Accounting Office. 1993(a). *Ballistic Missile Defense: Evolution and Current Issues.* Washington, D.C.: U.S. General Accounting Office.

U.S. General Accounting Office. 1993(b). *Defense Support Program: Ground Station Upgrades Not Based on Validated Requirements.* Washington, D.C.: U.S. General Accounting Office.

U.S. General Accounting Office. 2001. *Defense Acquisitions: Space-Based Infrared System-low at Risk of Missing Initial Deployment Date.* Washington, D.C.: U.S. General Accounting Office.

U.S. General Accounting Office. 2003(a). *Defense Acquisitions: Despite Restructuring, SBIRS High Program Remains at Risk of Cost and Schedule Overruns.* Washington, D.C.: U.S. General Accounting Office.

U.S. General Accounting Office. 2003(b). *Missile Defense: Alternate Approaches to Space Tracking and Surveillance System Need to Be Considered.* Washington, D.C.: U.S. General Accounting Office.

U.S. Missile Defense Agency Historians Office n.d. *Ballistic Missile Defense: A Brief History,* 3–4. [Online article or information; retrieved 10/10/06.] www.mda.mil/mdalink/html/briefhis .html.

U.S. National Aeronautics and Space Administration. 1999. *X-33 History Project Fact Sheet #4: The Policy Origins of the X-33 Part IV: The New World Disorder,* 5. [Online article or information; retrieved 10/10/06.] www.hq.nasa.gov/pao/History/x–33/facts_4.htm.

U.S. National Reconnaissance Office. n.d. *Corona Fact Sheet,* 1–2. [Online article or information; retrieved 9/7/06.] www.nro.gov/corona/facts.html.

U.S. National Security Council. 1970. "Memorandum for Dr. Kissinger: A Safeguard Site at Washington for FY 71?"; 1–4. [Online article or information; retrieved 9/22/06.] www.gwu.edu/ ~nsarchiv/NSAEBB/NSAEBB60/abm03.pdf.

Weinberger, C. 1990. *Fighting for Peace: Seven Critical Years in the Pentagon.* New York: Warner Books.

Winik, J. 1996. *On the Brink: The Dramatic, Behind-the-Scenes Saga of the Reagan Era and the Men and Women Who Won the Cold War.* New York: Simon and Schuster.

Wirls, D. 1992. *Buildup: The Politics of Defense in the Reagan Era.* Ithaca, NY: Cornell University Press.

3

Space Weaponry Development

THIS CHAPTER SEEKS to describe the multifaceted variety of space weapons and related applications being developed by the U.S. military. Emphasis is being placed on U.S. military research and development efforts in this arena because the United States is the principal nation conducting substantive scientific technological research in this area and because significant portions of this research are publicly accessible on U.S. military and government websites. This research is produced by a variety of U.S. military agencies including the Missile Defense Agency (MDA) and U.S. Air Force component organizations including AFSPACOM, the Air Force Space and Missile Systems Center, and the Air Force Office of Scientific Research.

Programs described in subsequent sections of this chapter include information about program capabilities and historical organization if available and relevant.

Active Denial System

The Active Denial System (ADS) is an Advanced Concept Technology Demonstration program conducted under the joint auspices of the Air Force Research Laboratory (AFRL) at Kirtland, AFB, New Mexico and the DOD Joint Non-Lethal Weapons Directorate. Using cutting edge technology, ADS seeks to provide unprecedented nonlethal striking power with a range greater than that provided by small arms. ADS works by projecting a focused beam of millimeter waves to produce an unbearable heating sensation on an enemy's skin repelling the individual without causing injury. These waves are produced at a frequency of 95 gigahertz traveling at light speed to penetrate skin to a depth of less than 1/64th of an inch. Such capability enables U.S. forces to stop, deter, and repel advancing forces using nonlethal force while also minimizing collateral damage.

Advanced Electro-Optical System

The Advanced Electro-Optical System (AEOS) is a 3.67-meter telescope space surveillance system that seeks to enhance the collection and quality of space data at Hawaii's Maui Space Surveillance Complex facility. AEOS is used primarily for DOD space surveillance missions, but the telescope is also used by the U.S. academic and scientific community.

Its origins began in the middle 1980s when the Air Force was attempting to develop a ground-based laser ASAT capability. The Maui location proved attractive to facility

The Phillips Laboratory Advanced Electro-Optical System (AEOS) is the Department of Defense's largest optical telescope supporting the Air Force Space Command space surveillance mission. *(U.S. Department of Defense)*

planners due to its maritime location, 10,000-foot altitude, clear visibility, near equatorial location, and a stable physical environment as an ideal site for observing space objects. Collaborative work in support of Vandenberg AFB (California) Western Test Range, the Barking Sands Missile Range on Kauai Island, Hawaii, and restricted airspace in this section of the Pacific Ocean further enhanced the site's ability to meet its space tracking mission. The 3.67-meter telescope was added to previously existing Maui Space Surveillance Complex facilities including a 1.6-meter telescope, 1.2-meter twin telescopes, a laser beam director, a beam director/tracker, and the ground-based Electro-Optical Deep Space Surveillance System, whose capabilities were augmented by close proximity to the Maui High Performance Computing Center.

At its inception, AEOS's mission was supporting space testing and tracking missions for SPACECOM, which had historically favored radar-based imaging techniques over electro-optical methods. The latter systems could produce photographic images, unlike radar, and these images are more user friendly to human eyes than images produced through radar signatures. Anticipated benefits from AEOS and the enhanced Maui Space Surveillance System included mission payload assessment and space object identification for AFSPACOM, adaptive optic research for AFRL, and use by government agencies and national and international astronomy communities.

Effective in fall 1995, AEOS retained its research and development mission for Air Force Material Command, while its AFSPACOM mission emphasized space intelligence, space tracking, and space control. The space tracking responsibilities required detecting and tracking space objects that would produce metrics of space objects for a catalog being developed of these objects by the Air Force. AEOS space control activities demand high-resolution imagery and good signature data to ensure positive identification of individual space objects.

Advanced Extremely High Frequency System

The Advanced Extremely High Frequency System (AEHF) is a joint-service satellite communications system providing secure, survivable, and jam-resistant communications for high-priority military land, sea, and air assets. AEHF is among the newest generation of military satellites, and its first launch is expected in April 2007.

Once fully deployed, AEHF will consist of three satellites in geosynchronous earth orbit that will be capable of servicing up to 4,000 networks and 6,000 terminals and have 100 times the capacity of 1990's vintage MILSTAR satellites. AEHF satellites will provide continual 24-hour coverage of the earth between altitudes of 65° N and 65° S. It will allow NSC and Unified Combatant Commanders to contact their tactical and strategic forces at all conflict levels through nuclear war and support their attaining information superiority. AEHF provides connectivity throughout the spectrum of combat missions including land, air, and naval warfare; special operations; strategic nuclear operations; strategic defense; and space operations and intelligence. It also gives war fighters broadcasting, data networking, voice conferencing, and strategic reporting capabilities, and represents a multinational effort involving British, Canadian, and Dutch partners.

Additional AEHF attributes include consisting of three segments: space (satellites), terminals (users), and mission control and associated communications links. These particular links provide communications in specified data speeds from 75 bits per second to nearly 8 megabits per second. AEHF satellites are capable of responding directly to service requests from operational commanders and user terminals while providing real-time point-to-point connectivity and network services on a priority basis.

Lockheed Martin Space and Strategic Missiles serves as the primary contractor. An AEHF satellite will weigh 13,500 pounds at launch and 9,000 pounds in orbit, and each satellite has an estimated 14-year design life and costs approximately $477 million.

Advanced Research and Global Observation Satellite

The Advanced Research and Global Observation Satellite (ARGOS) is the largest Air Force research and development satellite. Weighing almost three tons, ARGOS is responsible for handling DOD payloads that cannot be flown on the space shuttle or smaller launch vehicles due to complexity, size, and mission duration constraints. ARGOS's mission is spending three years in orbit collecting crucial science data on the earth's global environment for top military space programs.

Examples of research functions performed by ARGOS include investigating electric propulsion, orbital debris distribution, space radiation effects, the effect of upper atmospheric conditions on the security of Army communication systems design, magnetic storm prediction, and identification of plumes and atmospheric wakes of launch and orbital vehicles.

Aegis Ballistic Missile Defense

Aegis Ballistic Missile Defense (ABMD) serves as the sea-based component of the MDA's ballistic missile defense system. Aegis destroyers patrol, detect, and track ICBMs and report tracking data to the missile defense system. Such capability shares tracking data to inform other missile defense sensors and provides fire control data to ground-based midcourse defense interceptors at Fort Greeley, Alaska and Vandenberg AFB, California. It is possible for Aegis to reliably track data across eight time zones to enhance missile defense situational awareness and missile targeting and engagement capabilities.

Aegis cruisers and long-range surveillance and track destroyers are given the capability to intercept short- and medium-range ballistic missiles and to distinguish between missiles carrying individual and multiple warheads. Operational capability for Aegis cruisers is scheduled for late 2006.

As of July 2006, 11 of 15 long-range surveillance and track destroyer installations have been completed and all Aegis long-range surveillance and track destroyers are expected to be upgraded with engagement capability by 2009. Anticipated future capabilities include increasing precision track data from radar signal processing upgrades to augment long-range surveillance and track and engagement capabilities and gaining the ability to defend against Intermediate Range Ballistic Missiles (IRBMs) and ICBMs.

Aerospace Engineering Facility

The Air Force's Aerospace Engineering Facility (AEF) is located at Kirtland AFB, New Mexico. AEF's mission is serving as a single facility for space experiment integration, verification, and testing. AEF personnel test components and payloads, integrating them for space flights, and near space flights such as high altitude balloons.

Encompassing 16,500 square feet, AEF is designed to provide vibration, shock, acceleration, environmental, and thermal variation testing for flight components and their payloads under realistic launch and orbital environments. AEF includes a 60-foot tall, 4,500-square-foot laboratory for assembling and testing space flight hardware, three environmental chambers, and a thermal vacuum chamber capable of housing components up to 9 feet long. Additional facility capabilities consist of three vibration tables capable of exerting 42,000 pounds of force on small satellites of up to 500 pounds, and the ability to conduct electromagnetic compatibility and susceptibility testing within a copper screen room to determine whether satellites and space experiments can survive launch and orbit.

Airborne Laser

The Airborne Laser (ABL) is a collaborative program between the MDA, the Air Force, the AFRL's Directed Energy Directorate, Boeing, Lockheed Martin, and Northrop Grumman Space Technologies. The ABL program office was formed in 1993, and in November 1996 the Air Force awarded a $1.1 billion contract to the three companies listed above to develop a laser capable of finding, tracking, and hitting targets such as ballistic missiles.

Air Force testing with lasers dates back to the 1960s and has produced mixed results. During 1967 scientists invented the first gas dynamic laser, which used nitrogen and water vapor and influenced the belief that a laser could be used as an antimissile system,

Airborne Laser aircraft in flight. *(Missile Defense Agency)*

although testing this belief would prove to be a protracted process. Between October and December 1972, technicians fired a ground-based 100-kilowatt carbon dioxide laser propagating 10.6 microns against various stationary targets. Successful results from these tests saw the Air Force look at firing a laser at a moving airborne target. On November 13, 1973, the laser was shot at a 12-foot-long radio-controlled aerial drone in attempt to knock it out of the air. The drone fell but the results were not as intended since the laser beam burned the drone's aluminum skin frying the control system instead of igniting the drone's fuel tank.

Continued testing occurred throughout the 1970s and early 1980s when an ABL Laboratory plane (a KC-135) shot down a Sidewinder air-to-air missile over California's China Lake on May 26, 1983. Concern that these tests did not reflect real world battle conditions and that the laser was impractical resulted in it being ignored during the late 1980s.

ABL's fortunes revived during the 1990–1991 Persian Gulf War when Iraqi forces began firing Scud theater ballistic missiles at U.S. troops and their allies. Intervening technological advances also facilitated enhancements in ABL capabilities as the gas dynamic laser was replaced by a Chemical Oxygen Iodine Laser (COIL) that was more powerful than the gas dynamic laser, more compact in size, and capable of producing a lethal beam over long distances. The Air Force decided to replace the gas dynamic laser with COIL, whose modules are installed on the rear of a Boeing 747–400 plane. ABL is also enhanced by having an optical system capable of projecting a beam over hundreds of kilometers and compensating for atmospheric disturbances potentially existing between the aircraft and its target. Between July and December 2002, ABL aircraft made 14 flights logging over 60 flight hours, and it is based at Edwards AFB, California.

ABL continues to undergo research and development. Effective system requirements continue to include:

- Being housed aboard a stable platform capable of staying aloft for hours above weather systems whose clouds could refract its laser beams and nullify its effectiveness;
- Having sensors capable of locating a ballistic missile just after launch and holding the missile's track long enough for other missile defense system operations to become active;
- Possessing a computer system capable of tracking dozens of missiles and prioritizing them so the most threatening is targeted first;
- Possessing a highly developed optical system capable of measuring the thermal disturbance between the aircraft and target and being capable of directing an energy beam capable of compensating for clear-air obstacles;
- Having the ability to focus the killer beam on a rapidly rising target that may be traveling at speeds of Mach 6 or greater, and keeping the energy shaft in place long enough to burn a hole in the missile's metal skin; and
- Having a laser powerful enough to be lethal at distances of hundreds of kilometers.

Air Force Research Laboratory Directed Energy Directorate

The Air Force Research Laboratory Directed Energy Directorate (AFRLDED) is located at Kirtland AFB, New Mexico. DED employs over 800 people and develops directed energies such as high-energy lasers and high-powered microwaves while also working with advanced optics and imaging technologies. During 2004, these DED employees worked with a budget of approximately $309 million in a 670,000-square-foot working space, focusing on integration and transition research technologies in military systems used by various operational commands.

DED work focuses on six major emphasis areas. These include directed energy technologies protecting the U.S. population and resources; giving military field commanders more information about space assets; exploiting the global advantages and uses of high-power lasers; emphasizing the tactical roles of lasers; using radio frequency and high-power microwave technologies for electronic attacks capable of eliminating enemy threats without causing physical destruction, and examining "exotic" directed energy research that doesn't fall into the preceding five areas.

DED research is carried out by three technical divisions focusing on high-power microwaves, lasers, and optics. The High-power Microwave Division manages the research and development of high-power microwave technologies including those capable of protecting against hostile microwave systems. Such systems can identify weapons concealed in buildings or turn away attacking forces without using lethal force. The Laser Division performs cutting edge research and development of transformational technologies including semiconductor, gas, chemical, and solid-state lasers such as the COIL laser used by the ABL. Optics Division research stresses improving optical and imaging systems and improving the United States' ability to view space objects along with developing high-energy technologies to accurately direct high-energy lasers to their targets. This particular division operates DOD's largest and most sophisticated telescope facilities conducting experiments at Kirtland's Starfire Optical Range, the North Obscura Peak on White Sands Missile Range, New Mexico, and Hawaii's Maui Space Surveillance Site.

Work done by these three divisions is then taken over by DED's Technology Applications Division, which takes the developed technologies and transitions to other war-fighting organizations, while also looking for potential DOD needs and developing opportunities for transferring directed energy systems to relevant DOD entities.

Antisatellite (ASAT) Weapons

ASAT weapons are generally designed to destroy or disable satellites of hostile powers. The initial objective of U.S. ASAT weapons was to counter orbiting nuclear weapons, which was a threat that failed to materialize. Initial problems with planned early ASAT weapons were that since they were nuclear-armed they would likely damage U.S. satellites as well as their intended Soviet targets. Limitations on early ASAT guidance systems made it possible to place such weapons only within a few miles of their target. An additional complication from this inaccurate ASAT targeting and dependence on nuclear armament was the widespread impact of electromagnetic pulse from the detonation of these weapons. An upper atmospheric ASAT test in 1962 activated burglar alarms and darkened streetlights in Hawaii several hundred miles from the test site while also disabling several U.S. satellites in the area.

A number of ASAT weapon systems were tested by various branches of the U.S. military during the 1950s and 1960s. Beginning in 1959, the Air Force's Bold Orion program launched rockets from a B-47 bomber as part of an ASAT program. During 1962, the Navy conducted two Hi-Ho ASAT weapons tests from an F-4 jet fighter. The Army's Nike-Zeus program during this period initially began as an ABM system but evolved into more of an ASAT system because of its ineffectiveness as an ABM. The United States' first ASAT intercept occurred on May 23, 1963 from Kwajalein Island in the Pacific Ocean. The Air Force tested and deployed several THOR rockets for ASAT tests, and these became operational on Johnston Island in the Pacific in 1964 and had greater range than Nike-Zeus. These tests occurred at least 16 times between 1964–1970 before the system was retired in 1976.

The Air-Launched Miniature Vehicle (ALMV) was the principal U.S. ASAT program during the early 1980s. ALMV was launched from an F-15 fighter by a small two-stage rocket and carried a heat-seeking miniature homing vehicle that would destroy its target by direct impact at high speed. An advantage of this system was its enabling the F-15 to bring the ALMV under its targets ground track, as opposed to a ground-based ASAT, which must wait for a target satellite to overfly its launch site. An operational force of over 100 interceptors was originally planned for the ALMV program but cost overruns by 1986 had seen the program's estimated cost skyrocket from $500 million to $5.3 billion. The Air Force scaled the program back by two-thirds in 1987, and it was cancelled by the Reagan administration in 1988 after encountering continuing cost overruns, testing delays, and homing guidance system problems.

In February 1989, the Kinetic Energy Anti-Satellite Joint Program Office was established and the Army was given leadership of this program in December 1989. The purpose of this program was developing a ground-based interceptor capable of destroying satellites by homing in and colliding with them. This interceptor would reach satellites in low earth orbit at ranges of up to several thousand kilometers. Upon reaching the target, the interceptor would extend a sheet of Mylar plastic, called a "kill enhancement device," that would strike the target and neutralize it without destroying the satellite.

In August 1992 a Kinetic Energy integrated technology experiment demonstrated the ability to intercept reentry vehicles in the atmosphere using a homing seeker and non-nuclear warhead, and in August 1997 a successful hover test of a prototype kinetic energy ASAT kill vehicle occurred.

An air-to-air left side view of an F-15 Eagle aircraft releasing an anti-satellite (ASAT) missile during a test, 1985. *(U.S. Department of Defense)*

Air Force officials have expressed concern that the kinetic energy ASAT could create debris and endanger other U.S. space assets. DOD has not requested funding for this program for several years, but Congress added money for this program into the defense budget for fiscal years 1996–1998, 2000–2001, and 2004.

There has been renewed congressional interest in ASAT weapons since the 104th Congress (1995–1996), and some funding for such programs has occurred even though there are variant viewpoints within DOD and individual armed services on the suitability of these programs for U.S. national security interests. A May 18, 2005 *New York Times* article asserted that a forthcoming national space policy being developed by the Bush administration was bringing the United States closer to deploying offensive and defensive space weapons. A legislative amendment introduced by Representative Dennis Kucinich (Democrat from Ohio) to ban the use of weapons to damage or destroy objects in orbit was rejected by the House by a vote of 302–124 on July 20, 2005.

Despite supporting some ASAT programs, Congress has been skeptical about the ability of the Air Force to manage the costs and goal schedules of these programs and expressed concern about relationships between classified and unclassified space activities and about defense space acquisition programs.

U.S. ASAT research programs are likely to continue but with acute skepticism about their viability and costs, Congress is likely to keep a tight rein on their funding.

Atlas II Launch Vehicle

The Atlas II is designed to launch payloads into low earth orbit, geosynchronous transfer orbit, or geosynchronous orbit. Atlas vehicles have been used by NASA as a space launch vehicle since 1958 and by the U.S. Army Signals Corps since the Eisenhower administration. Atlas was also initially deployed as an ICBM with the first vehicle being placed on alert at Vandenberg AFB, California by the 576th Strategic Missile Squadron on October 31, 1959. In May 1988, the Air Force selected General Dynamics (now Lockheed Martin) to develop the Atlas II to carry Defense Satellite Communications Systems payloads for commercial users because of Atlas I launch failures in the late 1980s.

The final West Coast Atlas II launch occurred in December 2003 by the 30th Space Wing at Vandenberg AFB, and subsequent launches are carried out by the 45th Space Wing at Cape Canaveral AFS, Florida.

Ballistic Missile Defense System

The U.S. Ballistic Missile Defense System (BMDS) is directed by the MDA within DOD. On December 17, 2002, President George W. Bush directed DOD to field a defense system capable of countering the ballistic missile threat to the U.S. homeland and to forces deployed by the United States and its allies. MDA is charged with developing a BMDS that will eventually address all three phases of a hostile ballistic missile's flight path and defend against ballistic missiles of all ranges.

The three phases of a ballistic missile's flight trajectory are the boost phase, midcourse phase, and terminal phase. During the boost phase, which occurs just after launch, the missile is easiest to detect and track because missile exhaust fumes are bright and hot. This phase, however, is the most difficult phase in which to engage a missile because the intercept window is only 1–5 minutes. The midcourse phase occurs when the hostile missile's booster burns out and it begins coasting in space toward its target. This phase may last as long as 20 minutes, which allows several opportunities to destroy the incoming missile before it reenters the atmosphere, and debris remaining after the intercept burns up after entering the atmosphere. During the terminal phase, the missile reenters the atmosphere. This is the last opportunity to intercept the warhead before it reaches its target. Intercepting a warhead is difficult and the least desirable time because there is little margin for error and because the intercept will occur so close to the intended missile target.

Ballistic Missile Defense System Interceptors

This capability has been developed by MDA to provide a next-generation mobile, multi-use intercept capability to destroy medium-range ballistic missiles, intermediate-range ballistic missiles, and ICBMs during their boost, ascent, and midcourse flight phases. The interceptor's mobile capability is used during the boost and ascent phases where hostile missiles are destroyed shortly after launch before they can release their weaponized payloads and countermeasures. This interception capability may also be used during the midcourse phase when the missile is no longer thrusting and follows a more predictable glide path, allowing for a longer time to track and engage the target.

This particular system is deployed close to threats on mobile land launchers or on sea-based platforms including surface ships and submarines. Interceptor system design and performance approach are for booster, kill vehicle, and mobile fire control. System risk is reduced through demonstration testing and robust engineering and integration, while interceptor fire control equipment interfaces with the overall BMDS. The interceptor uses existing BMDS sensors as well as additional overhead sensors to obtain threat-tracking data. Deployment for these interceptors is estimated in 2014 and 2015.

Beam Weapons

Beam weapons are also called directed energy weapons and they consist of lasers, high-powered microwaves, and particle beams. They can be used for air, ground, sea, and space warfare. The ABL, described earlier in this chapter, is one example of a beam weapon. An additional example of beam weapons researched by the United States for over two decades includes the Army's Tactical High Energy Laser (THEL) at White Sands, New Mexico, which has demonstrated the ability to heat high-flying rocket warheads and blast them with enough energy to make them self-detonate using a high-energy deuterium fluoride chemical laser.

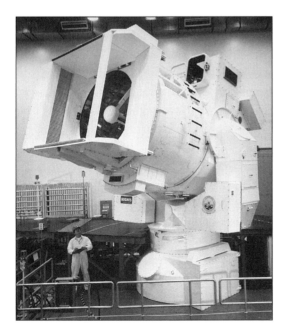

The Navy's high energy laser beam director built by Hughes Aircraft Company for use in high energy laser research and development. The experimental pointing and tracking system is designed to track targets in flight and direct a high power laser beam to selected aimpoints. *(U.S. Department of Defense)*

Active Denial Technology is another example of beam weapons and it presents a non-lethal way for using millimeter-wave electromagnetic energy to stop, deter, and turn back advancing adversaries. Such technology has been supported by the Marine Corps and seeks to use millimeter wave beams to heat an enemy's skin and cause severe pain and make them flee the area. Work at Los Alamos National Laboratory involving the Navy also uses free-electron laser work in the terahertz frequency range.

U.S. military beam research initiatives continue although limited funding and uncertain political support for these programs makes their future uncertain.

Chemical Oxygen-Iodine Laser

The Chemical Oxygen-Iodine Laser (COIL) is the world's shortest wavelength and high-power chemical laser-emitting light with a wavelength of 1.315 micrometers and a power range of 1–40 kilowatts. It is used in the ABL laser described earlier. COIL is developed at the AFRL's DED facility and was invented in 1977. Other significant milestones in COIL's development include the 1982 demonstration of the world's highest power subsonic gas flow, the 1984 demonstration of supersonic gas flow, the 1989 demonstration of a high-power (700 watts) continuous wave frequency doubling capability, and the 1992 demonstration of high-power COIL pulsing using magnetic gain switching.

Command, Control, Battle Management, and Communications

Command, Control, Battle Management, and Communications (CCBMS) are essential characteristics of the U.S. BMDS program. They deliver layered defense through networking and unifying individual element components (sensors, weapons systems, and fire control) with military commands globally. CCBMS also allows the president, secretary of Defense, and tactical and strategic level combatant commanders to systematically plan battles, watch conflicts unfold, and dynamically direct or adjust networked sensors and weapons to systems to effectively engage ballistic missile threats at any time and place.

MDA successfully delivered an introductory foundation for an integrated-layered defense emphasizing situational awareness, basic planning, and network architecture at the end of 2005. Ongoing and future MDA goals for CCBMS include completing the foundation for fielding common situational awareness, deliberative planning capability for all leadership levels, advanced battle management capability to control and direct sensor weapon-system combinations and global network management by late 2007, expanding geographically, and incorporating additional sensors and weapons capable of planning and adjusting real-time fighting ability to attain highest kill probability against any range of threats between now and 2009.

Communication/Navigation Outage Forecasting System

The Communications/Navigation Outage Forecasting System (CNOFS) is produced by the AFRL's Space Vehicles Directorate. CNOFS's objective is detecting active scintillations in the ionosphere that are naturally occurring irregularities leading to communication signal fluctuations. Such scintillations are responsible for decreased satellite-to-ground message work capacity and delayed signal acquisition. CNOFS alerts users of impending UHF and L-band satellite communication outages that affect certain satellite communication frequencies and terrestrial communications between satellite equipment.

CNOFS collaborative partners include NASA, the Naval Research Laboratory, the University of Texas, the National Polar Orbiting Environmental Satellite System, General Dynamics, and Orbital Sciences. CNOFS satellite assets include a radio beacon, GPS receiver for remote ionospheric sensing, ion velocity and neutral wind monitors, vector electric field instrument, and planner Langmuir Probe.

Communications Satellite Sabotage

Communications satellite sabotage occurs when satellites are attacked through the use of nuclear explosions or more targeted attacks such as space mines, which occur when nations or terrorist organizations target satellites used for civilian or military communications or intelligence purposes by seeking to destroy or disable them. Responses to such potential attacks and sabotage include producing a variety of satellite platforms for system redundancy against potential targeters, giving satellites substantial operational autonomy, choosing satellite orbits beyond the reach of most threats, having satellite orbits go through several orbital planes to preclude predictable targeting, hardening the satellites, installing ASAT attack warning sensors, and making the satellites orbit frequencies and paths irregular.

Cryocoolers: Cool Infrared Sensors to Enable Space Intelligence, Surveillance, Reconnaissance and Situation Awareness

Cryocoolers are small simply designed refrigerators operating at very low temperatures, which compress and expand gas such as helium to lower the temperature of critical satellite payload elements such as sensors. AFRL's Space Vehicles Directorate conducts cryocooler research to develop cryogenic refrigeration technology so satellite infrared sensors can be cool enough to enhance missile detection, conduct intelligence gathering, and enable space situational awareness. Cryocoolers help these sensors function in space's cold environment by enabling them to accurately identify distant objects in space or on the land through their heat signatures, which are often referred to as spectral footprints.

Historical satellite refrigerators had an approximate 1-year lifespan, weighed around 1,000 pounds, and could only generate approximately 0.5 watts cooling. In contrast, the Cryocooler has an estimated 10-year lifespan, weighs approximately 11 pounds, and can generate up to 20 watts cooling power.

Defense Meteorological Satellite Program (DMSP)

The Defense Meteorological Satellite Program (DMSP) has been responsible for collecting military data for U.S. military operations for four decades. Two operational DMSP satellites are in polar orbits of about 458 nautical miles at all times. DMSP's Operational Linescan System serves as the primary weather sensor providing continuous visual and infrared imagery of cloud cover covering 1,600 nautical miles. Other satellite sensors measure atmospheric vertical profiles of moisture and temperature. Military weather forecasters use this data to detect developing weather patterns and track existing weather systems such as severe thunderstorms and hurricanes over remote areas.

DMSP satellites also measure local charged particles and electromagnetic fields to examine the ionospheric impact of ballistic missile early warning radar systems and long-

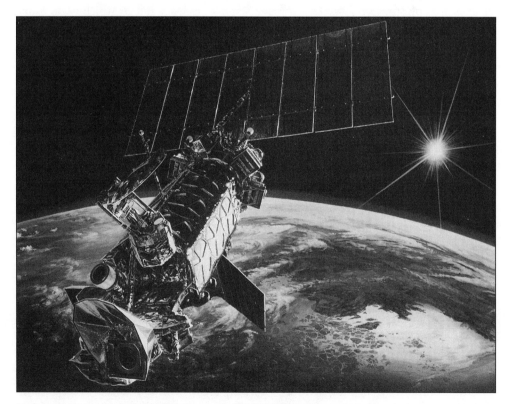

Defense Meteorological Satellite Program (DMSP) illustration. *(U.S. Air Force)*

range communications. Such data is also used to monitor global auroral activity and to predict space-environment effects on satellite operations.

President Clinton directed DOD and the Commerce Department to consolidate their previously separate polar-orbiting weather satellite programs in July 1994. DMSP operations were transferred to the Commerce Department in Suitland, Maryland in June 1998. The National Oceanic and Atmospheric Administration's Office of Satellite Operations provides command, control, and communication support for DMSP and the Space and Missile Systems Center of Los Angeles AFB is responsible for developing and acquiring DMSP systems.

DMSP-derived data is received by tracking stations at New Boston AFS, New Hampshire; Thule AFB, Greenland; Fairbanks, Alaska; and Kaena Point, Hawaii who transfer this electronically to the Air Force Weather Agency at Offutt AFB, Nebraska. Specially equipped tactical units can also receive this data directly from satellites. DMSP satellites weigh approximately 2,545 pounds including a sensor payload of 592 pounds, are just over 14 feet long without the solar panels deployed, have a power plant of 10 panels generating 2,200 watts of power, and are launched by a medium evolved expendable launch vehicle. Lockheed Martin Missiles and Space is the primary DMSP contractor.

Defense Satellite Communications System

The Defense Satellite Communications System (DSCS) is used for high priority command and control communication including wartime information exchange between defense officials and battlefield commanders. DSCS is also used by the military to transmit space operations and early warning data to various systems and users.

The system has been in use since its first launch in 1982. DSCS is built with single and multiple beam antennas that provide highly flexible coverage. A single steerable dish antenna provides an increased power spot beam that can be customized to suit the needs of different size user terminals. DSCS Phase III satellites can resist jamming and consistently exceed their projected ten-year design life.

Members of the Air Force's 50th Space Wing's 3rd Space Operations Squadron at Schriever AFB, Colorado provide satellite command and control for all DSCS satellites. AFSPACOM operates 13 Phase III DSCS satellites orbiting at an altitude of over 22,000 miles. Each satellite uses six super high-frequency transponder channels capable of delivering secure voice and high-rate data communications. DSCS III assets also include a single-channel transponder capable of disseminating emergency-action and force-direction messages to nuclear capable forces.

Lockheed Martin Missiles and Space is the primary contractor for this 2,716-pound satellite, which costs $200 million per unit. DSCS's power plant consists of solar arrays generating an average of 1,500 watts, its dimensions are 6 six feet long and high, 7 feet wide, and an overall 38-foot span with solar arrays deployed.

Defense Support Program

The Defense Support Program (DSP) satellites provide early warning of ballistic missile launches, space launches, and nuclear detonations from their geosynchronous orbits. DSP satellites use an infrared sensor to detect heat from missile and booster plumes against the earth's background. During 1995 technological enhancements were made to ground processing systems, increasing their ability to detect smaller missiles to give enhanced warning of attack by short-range missiles against U.S. and allied forces overseas. These enhanced features have been incorporated into the DSP's successor Space-Based Infrared System (SBIRS).

The first DSP satellite was launched in 1970. Over the years, DSP has become an important part of the U.S. early warning defenses. During Operation Desert Storm, DSP detected the launch of Iraqi Scud missiles and warned coalition forces in Saudi Arabia and Israel along with Israel's civilian population. The 460th Space Wing at Buckley AFB, Colorado with affiliate units elsewhere is responsible for operating DSP satellites and providing warning to appropriate authorities.

Delta II Launch Vehicle

The Delta II Launch Vehicle serves as an expendable launch medium-lift vehicle for launching Navstar GPS satellites into orbit so these satellites can provide navigational data to military users. The Delta II also launches civil and commercial payloads into low-earth, polar, geosynchronous transfer, and stationary orbits.

Delta's launch vehicle history began in 1959 when NASA's Goddard Space Flight Center awarded a contract to the Douglas Aircraft Company to produce and integrate 12 space launch vehicles. Delta component parts included the Air Force's Thor IRBM for its first stage and the Navy's Vanguard launch vehicle for the second stage. The inaugural Delta launch occurred from Cape Canaveral AFS, Florida, on May 13, 1960. In January 1987 the Air Force awarded a contract to McDonnell Douglas, now Boeing, to construct 18 Delta IIs for launching Navstars, which had originally been designed to be launched on the space shuttle, and the Delta remains the Air Force's only launch platform for launching and orbiting GPS satellites.

The first Delta II was successfully launched at Cape Canaveral on February 14, 1989 and Delta has successfully launched over 270 military, civil, and commercial craft since 1960. Historically significant Delta launches include the Telstar I international satellite in 1962, the first geosynchronous orbit satellite Syncorn II in 1973, and the first commercial communications satellite COMSAT 1 in 1965.

Delta II is launched primarily from Cape Canaveral, but it is also launched at Vandenberg AFB, California. The AFSPACOM's 45th Space Wing headquartered at Patrick AFB, Florida and the 30th Space Wing at Vandenberg AFB are the military organizations responsible for Delta II launches.

Demonstration and Science Experiments (DSX) Satellite

The Demonstration and Science Experiments (DSX) Satellite is being produced by AFRL's Space Vehicles Directorate. Scheduled for launch in 2008, DSX is being designed to conduct basic research to enable DOD spacecraft to successfully operate in medium earth orbit (MEO) with its harsh radiation environment. This satellite's military benefits include enhancing understanding of MEO and its "slot region," which is a highly desirable area for future space surveillance and high-speed communication. It will also perform research needed to evaluate DOD's ability to actively regulate agitations in the space meteorological environmental that cause accelerated degrading of critical space assets.

Areas of DSX experimentation include:

- Wave Particle Interaction, which researches the physics of very low frequency (VLF) transmissions in the magnetosphere and characterizes the capability of natural and man-made VLF waves to reduce space radiation;
- Space Weather Experiment, which characterizes and models the space radiation environment in MEO, which is a desirable orbital area for future DOD and commercial missions;
- Space Environmental Effects, which investigates and characterizes space weather effects on spacecraft electronics and materials.

Directed Energy Weapons

See Beam Weapons

Early Warning Radar Service Life Extension Program

The Early Warning Radar Service Life Extension Program (EWRSLEP) is an Air Force program to replace 1970s–1980s era computer systems used in the Solid State Phased Array Radar System (SSPARS) providing the military with missile early warning and space surveillance capabilities. These mission capabilities are provided by the PAVE Phased Array Warning System (PAWS) at Cape Cod AFS, Massachusetts; Beale AFB, California; Clear AFS, Alaska; and by Ballistic Missile Early Warning System Radars at Thule AFB, Greenland and the British Royal Air Force Base at Flyingdales, UK. A key factor prompting this program is the increasing inability of original equipment managers to repair or produce spare parts for original SSPARS equipment.

Solid state module tests, the Flyingdales' radio control computer, the network-processing unit 8-Mb micromemory instruction board, tape and disk drive peripherals for the digital module test set/radar controller and main mission processor, and the solid state phased-array radar-training system will be the main EWRSLEP parts replaced as a result of this program.

Electromagnetic Pulse

Electromagnetic pulse (EMP) involves the electromagnetic radiation from a nuclear explosion caused by recoiling electrons and photoelectrons from photons scattered in a nuclear devices materials or a surrounding medium. Resulting electric and magnetic fields can combine with electrical/electronic systems to produce damaging current and voltage surges, which can also be produced by nonnuclear means.

EMP attacks could disrupt or destroy the electric, electronics, energy, financial, tele-communications, transportation and other infrastructures in the United States or other countries. Concern over this possibility caused Congress to create an EMP Commission in 2000, and this commission's report issued in 2004 recommended that the United States take aggressive steps to harden civilian and military infrastructures that could be vulnerable to EMP including space-based assets while also using intelligence, interdiction, and deterrence to thwart EMP attacks against U.S. national interests.

Evolved Expendable Launch Vehicle (EELV)

The EELV seeks to enhance the reliability of U.S. space access by making space launch vehicles more affordable and reliable. Boeing Delta IV and Lockheed Martin Atlas V

Atlas V expendable launch vehicle with the New Horizons spacecraft poised for launch. *(NASA)*

launchers are the chief EELV component parts, and their operability improvements over predecessor systems include a standardized payload interface, standardized launch pads, and increased off-pad processing.

Initial EELV program activity dates from the November 1996 completion of the Low Cost Concept Validation program emphasizing competition in preliminary design and risk reduction demonstration. Four $30-million contracts were awarded to companies such as Boeing and Lockheed Martin during this period. Two $60-million 17-month contracts were awarded to Boeing and Lockheed Martin after this initial phase and subsequent development agreements with these contractors run through September 30, 2007 with launch agreements lasting until September 30, 2012.

Forward Deployable Radars

These radars are part of BMDS's efforts to detect ballistic missiles in their early flight stages and provide precise tracking information for missile defense system use. Radar will provide high-resolution, X-band class, phased-array radar that will acquire, track, discriminate, classify, identify, and estimate the trajectory parameters of hostile missiles and missile components, and pass this information to other BMDS tracking assets downstream. These radars can be transported by air, ship, or rail and are also deployed with command and control interface, a radar support trailer, generators, and supply containers.

Development plans for this system include four forward deployed units to protect the United States from ICBM and IRBM threats with an initial search and track capability being available in 2006 and discrimination enhancements being added in 2007.

Global Positioning System (GPS)

The GPS is one of the key elements in the U.S. military space arsenal as well as serving as a system with significant civilian applications. Its involvement in U.S. military activities dates from its testing period from approximately 1978–1985, and its influence on U.S. military operations has continually increased.

GPS is a series of orbiting satellites providing navigation data to military and civilian users globally, and it is operated by the 50th Space Wing at Schriever AFB, Colorado. These satellites orbit the earth every 12 hours emitting continual navigational signals. Users with proper equipment can receive these signals to determine time, location, and velocity. The accuracy of GPS signals is such that time can be calculated to within a millionth of a second, velocity within a fraction of a mile per hour, and location to within 100 feet. GPS receivers can be used in aircraft, ships, land vehicles, and be hand carried.

Around-the-clock navigation services provided by GPS include:

- Extremely accurate three-dimensional location information including latitude, longitude, and altitude with velocity and precise time

- A common global grid, which can easily be converted to any local grid
- Passive all-weather operational capability
- Support of an unlimited numbers of users and areas
- Support of civilian users at slightly lower accuracy levels.

GPS includes a suite of 24 satellites consisting of six planes with a minimum of four satellites per plane. Delta II expendable launch vehicles are used to launch GPS satellites from Cape Canaveral into circular orbits nearly 11,000 miles above the earth. GPS's design life is 7.5 years, and it transmits signals on two different L-band frequencies.

During its recent history, GPS has already had significant impact on U.S. military operational activities. During the 1990–1991 Persian Gulf War, U.S. and allied troops made heavy use of GPS to navigate the featureless Arabian Desert. Use of GPS increased substantially during Operations Enduring Freedom and Iraqi Freedom. During Iraqi Freedom, GPS satellites facilitated the delivery of 5,500 GPS-guided Joint Direct Attack Munitions to within 10 feet of their targets and with minimal collateral damage. This represented nearly one-fourth of the 29,199 bombs and missiles released against Iraqi targets by coalition forces during the course of this campaign. GPS continues to play a crucial role in air, ground, or sea operations by helping ensure military personnel that they and their equipment are on time and accurately on target.

Rockwell International, Lockheed Martin, and Boeing serve as GPS's largest contractors. GPS power plant includes solar panels generating 800 watts and Block IIF panels generating 2,450 watts. The height and weight ranges of individual GPS systems are 2.4–3.4 meters and 1,705–2,217 kilograms.

Ground-Based Electro-Optical Deep Space Surveillance

Ground-Based Electro-Optical Deep Space Surveillance (GEODSS) is carried out by AFSPACOM's Joint Space Operations Center Mountain (JPSOC-MTN) within Cheyenne Mountain AFS near Colorado Springs. GEODSS is responsible for tracking nearly 10,000 man-made objects in Earth orbit. These objects consist of active satellites and debris from rocket bodies or historical satellite breakups. More than 2,500 of these objects, including geostationary communication satellites, are in deep-space orbits ranging from 10,000–45,000 kilometers from the earth.

GEODSS missions are performed using a one-meter telescope equipped with highly sensitive digital camera technology called "Deep STARE." Each GEODSS detachment has three telescopes that can be used individually or collectively. Individual telescopes are able to view objects under conditions 10,000 times dimmer than the human eye can detect. Deep STARE can track multiple satellites in its viewing field, and the telescopes take rapid electronic snapshots that show up as tiny streaks on the monitoring recipient's console. Computers measure these streaks and use the data to calculate the current position of an orbiting satellite and this information is sent instantaneously to JPSOC-MTN. Beginning in 2004, Deep STARE began upgrading its capabilities so GEODSS can track objects as small as a basketball more than 20,000 miles from the earth.

Ground-Based Midcourse Defense

Ground-Based Midcourse Defense (GBMD) is part of the BMDS system of sensors, radars, and ground-based interceptors capable of shooting down ICBMs during their midcourse flight phase. GBMD hits the incoming missile by ramming the warhead at a speed of approximately 15,000 miles per hour to destroy it, which has proven successful in flight tests.

The three system components are sensors, ground-based interceptors, and fire control and communications. GBMD uses various sensors and radars to acquire information on missile launches and track, discriminate, and target incoming warheads. Such information is provided to the ground-based interceptor prior to launch and during flight to help find the missile and close in on it.

A ground-based interceptor consists of a three-stage solid fuel booster and exoatmospheric kill vehicle. Once launched, the booster missile carries the kill vehicle to the target's predicted location in space. Upon release from the booster, the 152-pound kill vehicle uses in-flight data received from ground-based radars and its own on-board sensors to close in and destroy the target using the force of impact.

Fire control and communications serves as GBMD's central nervous system connecting the hardware, software, and communications systems required for planning, tasking, and controlling GBMD.

Interceptor missiles are deployed at Fort Greely, Alaska, and Vandenberg, AFB, California with more deployments planned for 2006. Fire control centers have been established in Alaska and Colorado and a global system of existing early warning radars, including one at Shemya Island in Alaska's Aleutian Islands, has been upgraded to support flight tests and provide tracking information if a hostile missile attack occurs. A powerful mobile sea-based X-Band radar is nearly complete and expected to be fully incorporated into BMDS during 2006.

Ground Station Attacks

Ground station attacks are military attacks made from space or other venues on land-based satellite tracking stations by lasers, or assaults against these facilities by natural disasters or man-made weapons systems such as cruise missiles, ground attacks, bombs, artillery, and sabotage. The consequences of attacks on satellite ground stations would have severe military and civilian repercussions. It would not be possible for the military to get early warning information and track hostile missile launches, and the ability to get

High-Frequency Active Auroral Research Program array in Alaska. *(U.S. Department of Defense)*

accurate battlefield intelligence information and assessment would be severely compromised. The ability to do precision strikes would be restricted and increased collateral i.e., civilian, damage would likely occur, and mapping would have to revert to paper maps and compasses.

Civilian consequences of attacks or sabotage on satellite ground stations or their spaceborne infrastructure would include not being able to use pagers, cell phones, personal digital assistants, radio, or television. Land, sea, and aircraft using GPS for precise location and navigation information would not have the most current information, mapmakers could not update maps with current information, weather satellite information could not be updated, emergency responders could not respond as quickly to disasters, and many credit card transactions would no longer be possible since businesses could not verify personal credit quality.

High-Frequency Active Auroral Research Program

The High-Frequency Active Auroral Research Program (HAARP) is jointly managed by AFRL's Space Vehicles Directorate and the Navy's Office of Naval Research. HAARP is responsible for providing expanded new capabilities for conducting experimental research involving high-power radiowave interactions in the ionosphere and space and related military system applications.

Relevant programs involve assessing the possibility of exploiting emerging ionosphere-radio technology for next generation communications, radar, and navigation systems. HAARP radio and optical diagnostic instruments give real-time data on geophysical parameters characterizing the ionosphere and magnetosphere and include observations of the earth's magnetic field, electron densities, and radio wave absorption under normal conditions and solar-related disturbances. Facility diagnostic instruments ultimately provide a ground-based space weather station. Further information on HAARP can be found at www.haarp.alaska.edu.

High-Power Microwaves

Air Force high-power microwave research focusing on the weapons potential of this technology is centered in the High Power Microwave Division (HPMD) of AFRL/DED at Kirtland AFB, New Mexico. Research conducted here sees scientists exploring ways for generating high-power microwave energy and accurately delivering that energy to intended targets. Applications of this research include efforts assessing the effects of high-power microwaves on various targets and reviewing the feasibility of installing high-power microwave systems on various Air Force platforms.

While a typical household microwave oven generates less than 1,500 watts of power, AFRL's HPMD works with equipment generating millions of watts of power. Once microwaves encounter modern microelectronic systems, the microwave's heat and power can cause these systems to burn out or function incorrectly and such heavy reliance on electronic components in contemporary weaponry enhances the desirability of high-power microwave weapons.

High-power microwaves can be used in command and control warfare to suppress hostile air defenses, tactical aircraft, or unmanned aerial vehicles. HPMD research focuses on the following technology areas: source and antenna development, beam development, vulnerability efforts, high-power microwave modeling and simulation efforts, active denial technology, and the vehicle stopper program. Source and antenna research and development emphasizes narrow and wide-band high-powered microwaves capable of focusing ultrawide radiation into a conical beam with a single degree beam width.

Beam development initiatives seek to produce technology making it possible to steer microwave beams into an extremely narrow region. Division vulnerability efforts evaluate the effects of high-power microwaves on U.S. weapons and seek to protect these systems from microwave threats. High-power microwave modeling and simulation efforts seek to investigate the effectiveness of this technology in disabling targets. Active denial technology involves high-power microwaves that penetrate less than 1/64th of an inch into human skin to stimulate individual pain sensors enough to deter them from aggressive action. The vehicle stopper program works with the Justice Department to explore how radio frequency devices can stop vehicles without using lethal force and without injuring suspects or bystanders.

Innovative Space-Based Radar Antenna Technology (ISAT) Flight Demonstrator

The Innovative Space-Based Radar Antenna Technology (ISAT) Flight Demonstrator is a collaborative program between AFRL, DARPA, NASA's Langley Research Center and Jet Propulsion Laboratory, and private sector contractors Boeing, Raytheon, Lockheed Martin, and Harris Corporation. ISAT's anticipated launch date is 2010, and the program seeks to deploy a large system (up to 300 yards) of electronically scanning radar antennas flying 5,700 miles above the earth's surface and providing ground target detection for U.S. forces. It will weigh over five tons and serve as the forerunner of next generation U.S. intelligence, surveillance, and reconnaissance (ISR) space assets. These ISR capabilities will facilitate tracking and identifying targets with precise resolution and scanning in multiple areas of interest to warfighters.

Joint Surveillance Target Attack Radar (JSTAR)

Joint Surveillance Target Attack Radar (JSTAR) is an airborne battle management, command and control, and ISR platform housed on a Boeing EC-8 aircraft. JSTAR's mission is providing theater ground and air commanders with ground surveillance to support offensive operations and facilitate the delay, disruption, and destruction of enemy forces.

EC-8 radar and computer subsystems gather and display detailed battlefield ground force information, which is relayed in almost real time to Army and Marine Corps ground stations and other command, control, computers, communications, and intelligence (C4I) nodes. System antenna can be tilted on either side of the aircraft to develop a 120°-viewing field covering nearly 50,000 square kilometers and detecting targets at more than 250 kilometers.

JSTAR originated with Air Force and Army programs to develop, detect, locate, and attack enemy armor beyond the range of forward area troops. The first two JSTARs were deployed in Operation Desert Storm in 1991 with later deployments including supporting NATO troops over Bosnia-Herzegovina in 1996, Operation Enduring Freedom, and Operation Iraqi Freedom. Northrop Grumman serves as JSTARS's primary contractor. The aircraft has a flight ceiling of 12,802 meters, optimum orbit speed of 390–510 knots, can fly for nine hours without refueling, and has a flight crew of 4, plus 15 Air Force and 3 Army specialists, although the crew size varies depending on the mission.

Large Membrane Mirrors

Large membrane mirrors are another research focus of AFRL/DED. This program seeks to explore the use of new lightweight membrane materials in large optical quality telescope designs. The program seeks to develop a large aperture, high-resolution, space-deployable laser projection system capable of reducing optic payload weights by at least 50% and with comparable launch cost decreases. The principal applications of these mirrors will be on a space-based surveillance satellite or high-altitude imaging platform on aircraft such as dirigibles to enhance battlefield situational awareness for military commanders (U.S. Air Force Research Laboratory 2004(b), 1–2).

Laser Effects Test Facility

The Laser Effects Test Facility (LETF) is part of AFRL/DED and conducts experiments for the laboratory, DOD, the Energy Department, other government agencies, U.S. industry, and universities. LETF has a variety of laser capabilities including a 50,000-watt carbon dioxide electric discharge coaxial laser and other lasers covering the electromagnetic spectrum from ultraviolet to far infrared wavelengths.

Facility optic inventory capabilities permit tailoring laser beam spot size and irradiance to various configurations. Data acquisition systems can record more than 64 data channels per computer at rates exceeding 300 kilohertz per channel. These systems are augmented by cutting edge diagnostic equipment such as infrared cameras measuring spatial and temporal temperature distributions in interested targets.

LETF's Reflectance Laboratory analyzes physics laser-material interactions and makes it possible to acquire accurate coupling data during the laser's interaction with a target and resulting target surface property changes. This laboratory also can perform coupling measurements in a vacuum, which reduces target surface oxidation during laser interactions.

LG-118A Peacekeeper

The LG-118A Peacekeeper ICBM served as one of the United States' key nuclear weapons systems from its December 1986 deployment until it was deactivated on September 19, 2005. The Peacekeeper's first successful test flight saw it travel 4,190 miles from Vandenberg AFB, California to drop six unarmed reentry vehicles at the Kwajalein Missile Test Range in the Pacific Ocean. The first Peacekeepers were deployed at Warren AFB, Wyoming in December 1986 and reached a full operational capability of 50 missiles in December 1988.

Missile capabilities included delivering 10 independently targeted warheads on a four-stage rocket system consisting of a boost system, post-boost vehicle system, and reentry system. The boost system contained four rocket stages launching the missile into space. Each of these stages were mounted atop one another and fired successively. The post-boost vehicle system consisted of a maneuvering rocket and a guidance and control system riding atop the boost system. The reentry system at the top of the missile included the deployment module, up to 10 cone-shaped reentry vehicles, and a shroud responsible for protecting the reentry vehicles during ascent. The shroud was topped with a nose cap containing a rocket motor separating it from the deployment module.

LGM-30G Minuteman III Missile

The LGM-30G Minuteman III Missile has served as the primary land-based ICBM of the U.S. nuclear missile arsenal since the early 1960s. (L is a DOD designation for a silo-launched missile, G refers to surface attack, and M refers to guided missile). The Minuteman arsenal was created in response to the weaknesses of slow reacting, liquid-fueled, remotely controlled ICBMs used previously. In contrast, the Minuteman is quick reacting, inertia guided, and a highly survivable part of the United States' nuclear weapons triad of land, air, and sea-based missiles.

These weapons are dispersed in hardened silos to protect against attack and connected to an underground launch control center through a hardened cable system. Two-member launch crews perform constant alert in the launch control systems, and various communication systems provide the U.S. National Command Authority with reliable and almost instantaneous contact with the launch crew. If command capability is lost between

Sgt. Stephen M. Kravitsky inspects an LGM-30G Minuteman III missile inside a silo about 60 miles from Grand Forks Air Force Base, North Dakota, 1989. *(U.S. Department of Defense)*

the launch control center and remote missile launch facilities, specially designed E-6B airborne launch control center aircraft automatically assume command and control of the isolated missile(s).

The current Minuteman force has 500 ICBMs located at Warren AFB, Wyoming; Malstrom AFB, Missouri; and Minot AFB, North Dakota. A life extension program focusing on replacing the aging guidance system, remanufacturing rocket propellant motors, replacing standby power systems, repairing launch facilities, and installing updated survivable communications and command and control capabilities is expected to maintain Minuteman reliability into the 21st century.

The Minuteman's range exceeds 6,000 miles, its flight ceiling is 1,120 kilometers, its top speed is 24,000 kilometer per hour, Boeing is the primary contractor, Thikol, Aerojet-General, and United Technologies Chemical Systems Division are rocket motor stage contractors, and Minuteman's prelaunch height is 18 meters.

MILSTAR Satellite Communications System

The MILSTAR Satellite Communications System serves as a joint-service satellite communications system providing secure, jam resistant, and global communications for meeting crucial wartime requirements for high priority military users. MILSTAR satellites link command authorities with various resources including ships, submarines, aircraft, and ground stations.

The five operational MILSTAR satellites are positioned in geosynchronous orbits, weigh approximately 4,536 kilograms, and have a projected 10-year life span. Individual MILSTAR satellites serve as a smart space switchboard directing traffic from terminal to terminal anywhere significantly reducing ground control switching requirements. MILSTAR establishes, maintains, reconfigures, and disassembles required communications circuits as needed by users. Satellite terminals provide encrypted voice, data, teletype, or fax communications while striving to provide interoperable communications among Air Force, Army, and Navy MILSTAR terminals.

The first MILSTAR launch was February 7, 1994 aboard a Titan IV EELV and the most recent launch was April 8, 2003. AFSPACOM's Space and Missile Systems Center at Los Angeles AFB, California is responsible for developing and acquiring MILSTAR space and mission control components. The Electronics Systems Center at Hanscom AFB, Massachusetts handles the Air Force portion of MILSTAR terminal segment development and acquisition. The 4th Space Operations Squadron at Schriever AFB, Colorado is responsible for providing real-time satellite platform control and communications payload management.

Lockheed Martin Missiles and Space serves as MILSTAR's primary contractor. Each satellite is powered by solar panels generating 8,000 watts, weighs about 4,536 kilograms, and costs $800 million each. MILSTAR payloads include low data rate communications delivery capabilities ranging from 75 bits per second to 2,400 bits per second and medium data rate communications ranging from 4.8 kilobits per second to 1,544 megabits per second.

Minotaur Space Launch Vehicle

The Minotaur space launch vehicle is produced for the Air Force's Space and Missile Center by Orbital Sciences Corporation. Minotaur seeks to provide low-cost and reliable solutions for launch services for government-sponsored payloads. System features include inertia-guided four-stage solid rocket propulsion, comprehensive payload support including power, telemetry, sequencing, deployment, attitude control and recovery, horizontal satellite integration to simplify launch operations, 18-month mission response including payload integration and launch by Orbital crews, and the ability to launch from sites in Alaska, California, Florida, and Virginia.

Near-Space Access Program: High-Altitude Balloons and Tethered Aerostats

The Near-Space Access Program uses high-altitude balloons and aerostats such as dirigibles to conduct research, development, testing, and evaluation for the Air Force, DOD, additional government agencies, universities, and industries. The Near-Space Access

Program is run by the High-Altitude Balloon and Tethered Aerostat Group in AFRL's Space Vehicles Directorate. High-altitude balloons and aerostats are useful instruments for space environment qualification; meteorological measuring; optical, infrared, ultraviolet, and radar surveillance; radio and laser communications; and target simulation.

These instruments provide low-cost, nonpolluting, vibration-free, and highly reliable platforms capable of delivering quick response times, long-duration flights, limitless configurations, nearly unlimited launch sites, and completely recoverable payloads. Balloons may be used for simulating low-earth orbit and geosynchronous satellites by utilizing repeatable stratospheric wind patterns.

North Oscura Peak

North Oscura Peak is an AFRL facility in the northern part of the Army's White Sands Missile Range, New Mexico. North Oscura is designed to assemble and evaluate advanced sensor, tracking, and atmospheric compensation systems. From the summit of this 8,000-foot-high peak, a 30-inch telescope is used to send and receive laser light to and from the Salinas Peak about 35 miles away. Instrumentation is then used to measure the degree to which the earth's atmosphere distorts this laser light. Mirrors capable of changing their shapes can be used to compensate for any distortions that may occur during the laser light transmission.

Research gained from this testing benefits the ABL. While the ABL is designed to operate at altitudes around 40,000 feet, North Oscura Peak tests occur between 8,000–9,000 feet. Denser air at these lower test elevations makes it possible to take acquired data and scale it to the higher altitudes and longer ranges envisioned for the ABL. Lasers used at North Oscura include a 30-watt tracking laser, a 30-watt adaptive optics beacon laser, and a 3-watt scoring laser.

Nuclear Weapons in Space

From a strictly scientific technical standpoint, the explosion of a nuclear weapon in space would result in the fallout being dispersed over the universe instead of on the earth. Since there is no air in space, electromagnetic waves would be freed with radioactive particles, and the intensity of this effect decreases the farther away one gets from the explosion (U.S. Department of Energy, Argonne National Laboratory, n.d., 1). During the early years of the space age, both the United States and Soviet Union showed some interest in the possibility of placing nuclear weapons in space. International political sentiment was strongly against this and resulted in both these countries signing the United Nations Treaty on Outer Space in 1967, which banned the positioning and use of nuclear weapons and other weapons of mass destruction in outer space. Although this treaty has been in existence for nearly four decades, its enforcement provisions are nonexistent, and it remains possible for a nation or terrorist organization to use EMP or other means to place mass destruction weapons in orbit.

Patriot Advanced Capability–3

The Patriot Advanced Capability–3 is an Army weapons program that is part of the U.S. BMDS system. Patriot is capable of countering ballistic missiles and airborne threats including aircraft, unmanned aerial vehicles, and cruise missiles. It provides short-range point defense for crucial civilian and military assets, defends deployed troops, and provides ongoing missile defense coverage for rapidly maneuvering forces.

Patriot is mounted on wheeled vehicles and includes launchers carrying several interceptors along with advanced radars providing 360° battlefield coverage. It directly hits targets to destroy them, is linked to BMDS's CCBMS infrastructure, and can be rapidly deployed to global hotspots.

The Army is responsible for producing and further development of Patriot and the Medium Extended Air Defense System, which is a cooperative venture between the United States, Germany, and Italy to develop a mobile and transportable air and missile defense system. The MDA maintains responsibility for ensuring Patriot's interoperability and integration into BMDS.

PAVE PAWS Radar System

The PAVE PAWS Radar System is an AFSPACOM radar system. PAVE is an Air Force program name while PAWS refers to "Phased Array Warning System." Three 21st Space

Mike Badman, a security policeman with the 6th Space Warning Squadron, Cape Cod Air Station, Massachusetts, patrols the perimeter of the PAVE PAWS facility in 1996. *(U.S. Department of Defense)*

Wing squadrons are responsible for operating this system's missile warning and space surveillance capabilities. PAVE PAWS radars are located at Cape Cod AFS, Massachusetts; Beale AFB, California; and Clear AFS, Alaska. PAVE PAWS is also responsible for earth-orbiting satellite detection and tracking and information concerning ballistic missile and satellite detection is forwarded from PAVE PAWS to U.S. Strategic Command's Missile Warning and Space Control Center at Cheyenne Mountain Air Station, Colorado, the National Military Command Center, and U.S. Strategic Command.

Mechanical radar must be physically aimed at a space object to track and observe it. PAVE PAWS uses phased array antenna technology, which is in a fixed position and part of an exterior building wall. Aiming this kind of radar is done by electronically controlling the timing/phase of incoming and outgoing signals. By controlling the signal phasing through the many segments of the antenna system it is possible to allow the beam to be quickly projected in different directions. This drastically reduces the time required to change beam direction from one point to another, which permits nearly simultaneous tracking of multiple targets without losing surveillance responsibility. The large fixed antenna array enhances system sensitivity and tracking accuracy through a better quality beam.

Overall operational activity is automated, only requiring human involvement for monitoring, maintenance, and final checking on warning validity before the information is transferred to Cheyenne Mountain.

Personnel Halting and Stimulation Response

Personnel Halting and Stimulation Response (PHASR) is a rifle-sized laser weapon system using two nonlethal laser wavelengths to deter, prevent, or limit an opponent's effectiveness. This is accomplished by a laser light illuminating hostile forces and temporarily limiting their ability to see the laser source. PHASR can be operated by a single individual and includes a self-contained power source. This weapon uses one visible wavelength diode-powered laser and one mid-infrared wavelength.

ScorpWorks, which is part of AFRL/DED, designed PHASR for military and law enforcement applications, and AFRL/DED's Human Effectiveness Directorate works to ensure its safe operation and study its biological effects.

RAD6000 Computer

This computer is used by AFRL's Space Vehicles Directorate, and it serves as the first radiation-hardened 32-bit microprocessor containing over one million transistors. The RAD600 is capable of withstanding the harsh space radiation environment and operating reliably over long-term missions focusing on controlling data stream telemetry between spacecraft and ground controllers.

Ongoing radiation bombardment produces unwanted electrical charges inside transistors and can reach the point where the transistor can no longer control electron flow.

This can cause overcharged transistors to shut down and the resulting electronics failures can terminate missions and cost millions of dollars. Both DOD and NASA used to pay $50–$100 million in development and manufacturing costs for each processor. RAD6000 processing module costs, in contrast, range from $500,000–$2 million and is available as off-the-shelf hardware.

Air Force and industry collaboration on this system has increased the lifespan of spacecraft electronic systems. More than 60 Air Force, DOD, NASA, and commercial space systems use this technology and over 90% of satellites launched today rely on these radiation-hardened processors.

Relay Mirror Technology

Relay Mirror Technology program research is conducted at AFRL/DED and seeks to use a dual-mirror instrument in air or space to transfer laser energy from one part of the earth to another. Low earth orbit relay-mirror satellites can be used to relay laser energy from one point to another providing global light speed capability to war fighters. This works by directing a laser beam at a "receive mirror," which collects the beam, passes it to a beam control system that optically refines the beam, then refocuses and retransmits it to a second mirror transcending the limits of Earth's curvature.

Program goals include identifying and developing crucial technologies required to produce a relay demonstration mirror in the near future. Relay mirror technology and technical synergy with other airborne or space-based directed energy systems are key program emphases instead of laser source development. Technologies that must be examined to achieve program objectives include space vehicle design, vibration and thermal management, attitude control, large-angle slewing and momentum control of a multibody system. The system must be able to precisely point, acquire, and track the laser source and targets, and large, lightweight, and potentially deployable mirrors must be developed along with optical coatings and techniques to control jitter and optical aberrations.

Satellite Countermeasures

Satellites may take a variety of actions to deter, defeat, or reduce the effects of hostile actions taken against them by hostile weapon systems. These include increasing the number of satellites in orbit (although this is more costly than other mitigating measures), redesigning satellites to reflect radar signals weakly or evade such signals, taking electronic countermeasures such as jamming or blinding hostile satellites, using nuclear weapons such as ICBMs and Submarine Launched Ballistic Missiles (SLBMs), developing non-nuclear interceptor spacecraft, space mines, developing ground-based directed energy or kinetic energy weapons to use, establishing and defending protected zones around specific satellites, and giving individual satellites self-defense capabilities.

Possible diplomatic satellite countermeasures include negotiating limitations on the hostile use of satellites and establishing restrictions on potentially provocative activities in space such as unexplained close approaches to foreign satellites and irradiating foreign satellites with direct energy beams.

Scintillation Network Decision Aid

The Scintillation Network Decision Aid (SCINDA) is a computer program developed by AFRL's Ionospheric Hazards Branch for AFSPACOM. SCINDA predicts communication satellite outages in the equatorial region caused by naturally occurring ionospheric disruptions. These disruptions can cause satellite signals to rapidly fluctuate or scintillate at or near the earth's surface. This development is most intense during the night within 20° of the earth's magnetic equator, which occupies over one-third of the earth's surface. Such scintillation affects radio signals and seriously disrupts communication and navigation satellites.

SCINDA has been developed to inform operational users when and where scintillation is likely to take place. Fourteen SCINDA sensors are installed in South America, southeast Asia, and southwest Asia. These sensors measure scintillation data from existing GPS and geostationary beacon satellite links and ionospheric drift speeds are measured and stored at remote sites. AFRL researchers retrieve this information via the Internet every 15 minutes, and this information is compiled to make simple bicolor maps of equatorial disturbances and related areas of likely communication outages. These maps provide scientists with enhanced understanding of how such scintillation structures develop and provide situational awareness to satellite communication operators.

An additional four to six stations are planned during 2006–2007, and these will be concentrated primarily in Africa's equatorial regions where AFRL is participating in a United Nations Basic Space Science Initiative to deploy space weather sensors for the International Heliophysical Year.

Sea-Based X-Band Radar

Upon integration into the U.S. BMDS, Sea-Based X-Band radar will track, discriminate, and assess incoming target missiles and enhance the MDA's ability to conduct vigorous and operationally realistic tests of BMDS's GBMD.

Sea-Based X-Band radar includes advanced X-band radar with a mobile oceanic and semisubmersible platform giving BMDS a discrimination capability to cover anywhere in the world. It is located on a high-tech semisubmersible oil drilling platform, which is twin-hulled, self-propelled, and remains stable in high winds and unsettled sea conditions. The radar's ocean-spanning mobility allows it to be positioned as needed to provide radar coverage of possible threat launches from any location.

This system is 240 feet wide and 390 feet long, covers more than 289 feet from keel to the top of its radar dome, and displaces nearly 50,000 tons. It will be staffed by an approx-

Sea-Based X-Band radar is a U.S. system designed to track, discriminate, and assess characteristics of hostile ballistic missiles. *(Missile Defense Agency)*

imately 75-person crew who will live and work in an area housing living quarters, work areas, storage, power generation, a bridge, and control rooms while also providing requisite floor space and infrastructure for supporting the radar antenna array, command, control, and communication assets, and an In-Flight Interceptor Communication System Data Terminal.

System construction and assembly were completed in two Texas shipyards and sea-trials were conducted in the Gulf of Mexico. It will be based at Adak, Alaska upon deployment.

Solar Mass Ejection Imager

The Solar Mass Ejection Imager (SMEI) was produced to detect, track, and forecast the arrival at Earth of coronal mass ejections (CMEs), which are responsible for all severe space weather. Since the January 2003 launch of the Coriolis satellite, which carries SMEI, it is possible to track CMEs from sun to Earth orbit and beyond from an orbit 840 kilometers above the earth. SMEI provides scientists with enhanced understanding of CMEs and longer lead times to predict and understand their detrimental effects on spacecraft and ground systems.

SMEI was designed and constructed by scientists and engineers from AFRL, the University of California-San Diego, Boston College, Boston University, and the United

Kingdom's University of Birmingham with additional financial support provided by the Air Force and NASA. Imagery produced by SMEI is available on the National Solar Observatory Web site, www.nso.edu.

Space-Based Infrared Systems (SBIRS)

The SBIRS is one of AFSPACOM's highest priority space systems and is intended to provide the United States with critical missile defense and early warning capability for the 21st century. SBIRS includes three individual space constellations and an evolving ground component: the existing DSP, SBIRS High, and the Space Tracking and Surveillance System (STSS). The four mission areas supported by SBIRS include missile warning, missile defense, technical intelligence, and battle-space characterization.

DSP was described earlier in this chapter and has served the United States for over 30 years and for approximately the past decade has given military theater commanders missile-warning notification. This notification, initially, occurred through the Attack Launch and Early Reporting to Theater (ALERT) system before transitioning to SBIRS. The SBIRS Missile Control Station at Buckley AFB, Colorado became operational on December 18, 2001 and enhances national infrared space capability by consolidating command and control and data-processing elements from divergent legacy systems into a centralized and modern facility.

SBIRS High consists of four geosynchronous satellites, two highly elliptical orbit satellites, and associated ground hardware and software. It is expected to have greater sensor flexibility and sensitivity than DSP since it possesses scanning and staring sensors while DSP only has scanning sensors. This enhanced capability means SBIRS High is expected to take only 10–20 seconds to detect a missile launch, determine its course, and warn appropriate ground forces while DSP would take 40–50 seconds to accomplish these tasks.

STSS is a capabilities-based system managed by MDA, which will track tactical and strategic ballistic missiles. STSS sensors are designed to operate across long- and short-wave infrared and the visible light spectrum. These wavebands are intended to allow STSS sensors to acquire and track missiles during their boost and midcourse phases. Launch of the first satellite is expected in 2006.

Space-Based Radar

Space-Based Radar (SBR) is a defense acquisition program inaugurated in 2001 whose objective is deploying by 2008 space-borne ability for theater military commanders to track moving targets. SBR emphasizes maturing technology and developing an ISR system capable of offering Ground Moving Target Identification (GMTI), Synthetic Aperture Radar (SDR), and Digital Terrain and Elevation Data (DTED) covering large portions of the earth (land and sea) on an ongoing basis. An SBR system incorporates battlefield tasking and control to enhance near real-time SBR product availability to the theater. SBR gives military forces a deep look and nonintrusive access to currently inaccessible areas of interest without jeopardizing personnel or resources.

A constellation of SBR satellites is needed to satisfy these demanding operational requirements. These satellites must offer day/night, all-weather, near continuous, global GMTI search/track and high-resolution imagery, direct theater downlink of overhead GMTI and imagery collection, and precision DTED collection.

Space Countermeasures Hands On Program (Space CHOP)

Space Countermeasures Hands On Program (Space CHOP) is a DOD program designed to emulate terrorist and asymmetric threats to U.S. military and critical national infrastructure systems. The program occurs three to four times per year at Kirtland AFB, New Mexico and involves a select group of junior military officers and civilian federal employees using open source Internet databases and libraries to seek out potential weaknesses in current and future DOD space systems or other critical government agency systems.

The beginning of each of these sessions sees Space CHOP identify rules of engagement to participants, and client and events are coordinated, for precautionary reasons, with the customer's security organization and other relevant security entities. The stimulated terrorist team gives a status briefing for the customer halfway through the mission. Upon mission completion, the customer agency receives a formal and classified presentation and report including a listing of simulated terrorist team findings in open source resources.

Governmental and military entities providing consultation to CHOP include U.S. Strategic Command, the Air Force's Space Warfare Center and Space Battlelab, the Navy's Space and Warfare Systems Center, MDA, NASA, Naval Postgraduate School, the FBI, and U.S. Customs and Border Protection.

Space Mines

Space mines are microsatellites capable of having military and non-military uses. Military applications of space mines would allow a satellite with maneuver capability to approach a target satellite at varying ranges and explode to destroy or disable a satellite. Peaceful uses of these microsatellites include observation and communication. It is technologically easy to produce these weapons but using space mines to destroy or disable space assets such as satellites can create space debris along with having serious political, diplomatic, and international security repercussions.

Space Tracking and Surveillance System (STSS)

The STSS is a MDA program using space-based sensors that are part of BMDS for detecting visible and infrared light such as that produced by a ballistic missile.

STSS will initially consist of two research and development satellites that are scheduled to be launched into low earth orbit in 2007, and a ground segment will be developed to operate these satellites. System requirements include passing missile-tracking data to missile defense interceptors with requisite accuracy and timeliness so they can intercept incoming missile targets. Later program components include taking lessons learned from the initial deployment and testing in 2008 to make necessary STSS upgrades, fielding a constellation of operational STSS satellites for global missile tracking beginning in 2012, and achieving enhancements in satellite lifetime, producibility, and the ability to process and communicate missile tracking data to interceptors in 2012.

TacSat–2 Micro Satellite

The TacSat–2 Micro Satellite is produced by AFRL's Space Vehicles Directorate and is designed to demonstrate and meet TacSat–2 objectives including being able to test a ready-launch spacecraft within 15 months of receiving the authority to begin the project, launching within one week of being called from storage, performing on-orbit checkout within a day, conducting efficient operations and downlinking data directly to the required theater, and providing this theater with images containing tactically significant resolution.

This satellite is scheduled for 2006 launch into a sun-synchronous orbit of 350-kilometer altitude at a 97.3° circular inclination. Besides AFRL, participating organizations include DOD's Space Test Program, Naval Research Laboratory, Army Space Program Office, AFSPACOM, and NASA components including the Jet Propulsion Laboratory.

Artist's rendition of the TacSat-2 Micro Satellite. *(U.S. Air Force)*

Telescope and Atmospheric Compensation Laboratory

The Telescope and Atmospheric Compensation Laboratory (TACLAB) is part of the Starfire Optical Range at Kirtland AFB, New Mexico. This facility features optics, electronics, computer, and mechanical laboratory space emphasizing equipment design, construction, and testing before integrating with telescopes and other experimental hardware. The laboratory houses a series of optical mounts such as telescopes and beam directors capable of tracking low-earth orbit satellites, and these mounts possess large-scale, high-performance adaptive optical systems.

Additional system instrumentation includes smaller telescopes, beam directors, multiple laser systems, and assorted optic, electronic, and mechanical laboratories. TACLAB work specialties include technological experimentation in real-time atmospheric compensation, atmospheric turbulence physics, and target acquisition, pointing, and tracking.

Terrorism

Space may become a forum for terrorism just as terrorist activities occur in the ground, air, and sea. Possible examples of space terrorism could include destroying satellites and other space-based objects or creating obstacles that hinder their normal operations and seizing and using space-based objects to enhance communications among terrorists. Terrorists may use space-based assets to attack urban targets such as high-rise apartments and major transportation and economic hubs including drinking water infrastructures, postal delivery, computer networks, research centers located near large urban areas, chemical facilities, nuclear reactors, and petroleum storage facilities.

Providing security for these facilities against such scenarios must become part of the homeland security, critical infrastructure planning, and antiterrorism responsibilities policymakers engage in during the years to come.

Theater or Terminal High-Altitude Area Defense (THAAD)

Theater or Terminal High-Altitude Area Defense (THAAD) is the BMDS component responsible for providing a rapidly transportable and forward deployable capability of intercepting and destroying ballistic missiles inside or outside of the atmosphere when they are in the final or terminal phase of their flight.

THAAD system characteristics include truck-mounted launchers, interceptors containing eight interceptors per launcher, x-band radars, and fire control and communication units. The launchers are highly mobile and capable of storing, transportation, and firing interceptors and reloading rapidly. The interceptor is designed to intercept targets in and out of the atmosphere using hit-to-kill lethality. The x-band radar is the world's largest mobile band and provides searching, tracking, discrimination, and fire control updates to the interceptor. The fire control and communications units serve as a data management backbone linking THAAD components together and to external BMDS units. The entire system can be transported by land, sea, and air and be airlifted anywhere within hours.

During 2006, the MDA hopes to build, test, and verify THAAD's initial capability, conduct four tests at White Sands Missile Range, New Mexico by the end of 2006, continue system planning and conducting soldier training, and continue planning for transitioning system operations to the Army.

310th Space Group

The 310th Space Group is the Air Force Reserve's sole space organization and is located at Schriever AFB, Colorado, where it was activated on September 4, 1997 and reports to the 10th Air Force. The mission of the 310th is providing command and control for DOD and Commerce Department satellites, supporting the Air Operations Center and the Commander, Space Air Forces (COMSPACEAF), supporting space asset testing and evaluation, and providing security for terrestrial based 14th Air Force assets. Additional 310th responsibilities include supporting GPS, DSP, and DMSP operations.

Organizational components of the 310th include the 6th Space Operations Squadron at Schriever responsible for operating DMSP satellites, the 7th Space Operations Squadron at Schriever responsible for supporting GPS and DSP satellites, the 8th Space Warning Squadron at Buckley AFB whose responsibilities include SBIRS, and the 9th Space Operations Squadron at Vandenberg AFB, which gives COMSPACEAF the ability to command and control space forces by providing force status, intelligence data, and battle space awareness.

Additional 310th components include the 14th Test Squadron at Schriever, which supports the Space Warfare Center by testing and evaluating space assets, Schiever's 19th Space Operations Squadron, which supports GPS launch, modernization, and operation, Schriever's 26th Space Aggressor Squadron, which is responsible for supporting adversary space capability simulations and conducting exercises, training, and testing to increase US space force quality, the 310th Security Forces Squadron at Schriever, which is responsible for providing AFSPACOM ground asset security, and the 310th Communications Flight at Peterson AFB, which enhances AFSPC's Network Operations and Security Center by providing command, control, and situational awareness for AFSPC communications system and assets.

Titan IVB

The Titan IVB is a space booster used by the Air Force and launched from Vandenberg AFB, California and Cape Canaveral, Florida. It consists of a liquid-fueled core and two large solid rocket boosters, and the liquid core ignites approximately two minutes after launch.

A seven-year journey to the ringed planet Saturn begins with the liftoff of a Titan IVB/Centaur carrying the Cassini orbiter and its attached Huygens probe, October 15, 1997. *(NASA)*

System origins date back to October 1955 when the Air Force awarded the Glenn L. Martin Company (now Lockheed Martin) a contract to build an ICBM, which became known as the Titan I becoming the United States' first two-stage ICBM. Additional system upgrades occurred over ensuing decades and the Titan IVB first flew on February 23, 1997 with an upgraded rocket possessing a new guidance system, flight termination system, ground checkout system, solid rocket motor upgrade, and 25% thrust capability increase.

Titan IVB has a height of just over 62 meters, its motors provide 1.7 pounds of thrust per motor at liftoff, it can carry up to 21,682 kilograms into low-earth orbit, 5,761 kilograms into geosynchronous orbit when launched from Cape Canaveral, and up to 17,599 kilograms into low-earth polar orbit when launched from Vandenberg. The Titan IVB can also carry up to 2,381 kilograms into geosynchronous orbit if it uses an inertial upper stage.

Wideband Gapfiller Satellites

Wideband Gapfiller Satellites (WGS) were scheduled to be first launched between October 1, 2005–September 30, 2006 though the first launch did not occur until October 10, 2007. WGS is responsible for providing flexible and high-capacity military communications and drastically increased communications bandwidth available to U.S. forces.

This capability will be compatible with terrestrial portions of the Defense Information Systems Network while also being compatible with existing and programmed x and Ka-band terminals. WGS will eventually consist of five satellites in geosynchronous orbit. Boeing Satellite Systems serves as the primary contractor and each of these satellites has an approximate cost of $300 million.

XSS-10 Microsatellite

The XSS-10 Microsatellite is an AFRL experimental microsatellite first launched on January 29, 2003 from Cape Canaveral. It weighs about 65 pounds and is the first in a series of future microsatellites the Air Force wants to use for inspection, rendezvous, docking, and up-close maneuvering around space objects. Key XSS technologies include a lightweight propulsion system, guidance, navigation, and control capability, a miniaturized communications system, using primary lithium polymer batteries, and an integrated camera and star sensor.

XSS-11 Microsatellite

The XSS-11 Microsatellite is also produced by AFRL and was launched for the first time on April 11, 2005. It weighs approximately 100 kilograms and program goals include giving the XSS-11 military applications such as space servicing, diagnostics, maintenance, space support, and performing efficient space operations. The XSS-11 is expected to increase AFSPACOM's future missions by reducing the size and complexity of future space ground stations.

YAL-1A Attack Laser

The YAL-1A Attack Laser is the world's first laser-armed combat aircraft, and it is a conversion of a Boeing 747–400F aircraft. This project, involving the MDA, the Air Force, Boeing, Lockheed, and TRW, has been under development since 1992, and its goal is creating a laser to destroy hostile ballistic missiles during their vulnerable boost phase. Unique YAL-1A features include infrared heat detectors first used on the Navy's F-14 Tomcat jet fighter; a turbopump, capable of filling a household swimming pool in ten minutes, circulating laser fuel through a megawatt class laser; two solid-state kilowatt class lasers; the COIL liquid and gas-fueled high-energy laser; and a beam-steering configuration incorporating adaptive optics science. YAL-1A marks the first time these systems are installed and used as an integrated weapons system, and system testing occurred at Edwards AFB, California during 2004 and 2005.

References and Further Reading

Beason, D. 2005. *The E-Bomb: How America's New Directed Energy Weapons Will Change the Way Future Wars Will Be Fought.* Cambridge, MA: Da Capo Press.

Bingham, T. P. 2004. "Ground Radar Surveillance and Targeting." *Joint Force Quarterly* 35 (October): 88–94.

Boeing Corporation. 2007. "Boeing Advanced Military Satellite Begins On-Orbit Checkout." [Online article or information; retrieved 10/25/07.] www.boeing.com/news/releases/2007/q4/071011a_nr.html.

Bolkcom, C. and S. A. Hildreth. 2005. *Airborne Laser (ABL): Issues for Congress.* Washington, D.C.: Library of Congress, Congressional Research Service.

Bouchard, J. F. 1999. "Guarding the Cold War Ramparts: The U.S. Navy's Role in Continental Air Defense." *Naval War College Review* 52 (3): 111–135.

Brearley, A. 2005. "Faster Than A Speeding Bullet." *Astropolitics* 3 (1): 1–34.

Cady, S. E. 1982. "Beam Weapons in Space." *Air University Review* 33 (4): 33–39.

Covault, C. 2003. "USAF Technology Satellite Plays Tag With GPS Delta." *Aviation Week and Space Technology* 158 (5): 39.

David, L. 2006. *Beam Weapons Almost Ready for Battle,* MSNBC, January 11, 2006. [Online article or information; retrieved 8/1/06.] www.msnbc.msn.com/id/10805240/.

Dunn, D. H. 1997. *The Politics of Threat: Minuteman Vulnerability in American National Security Policy.* New York: St. Martin's.

Engel, J. A. 2003. *The Missile Plains: Frontline of America's Cold War: Historic Resource Study, Minuteman Missile National Historic Site, South Dakota.* Omaha: National Park Service.

Evans, D.L. ed. 1995. *Spaceborne Synthetic Aperture Radar: Current Status and Future Directions.* Washington, D.C.: NASA Scientific and Technical Information Office.

Fabey, M. 2006. "Spy Sats Seek Relevance in War on Terror." *Defense News* 21 (14): 1.

Ferguson, J. 2002. "NATO, Europe, and Theater Missile Defense." *Canadian Military Journal* 3 (1): 45–52.

Fernandez, A. J. 2004. *Military Role in Space Control: A Primer,* 9, 13. Washington, D.C.: Library of Congress, Congressional Research Service.

"Frontlines." 2005. *Air Force Times,* 66 (4) 6–7.

Globalsecurity.org, *Anti-Satellite Weapons-Overview,* (1993?): 1–9; [Online article or information; retrieved 7/27/06.] www.globalsecurity.org/space/systems/asat-overview.htm.

Goodman, Jr., G. W. 2000. "Layered Protection: New US Theater Missile Defense Systems Will Be a Far Cry From the Patriots of the Gulf War." *Armed Forces Journal International* 138 (4): 44–49.

Gray, C. 1993. "Space Power Survivability." *Airpower Journal* 7 (4): 27–42.

Gregorian, R. 1993. "Global Positioning Systems: A Military Revolution for the Third World?" *SAIS Review* 13 (1): 133–148.

Lacomme, P., Hardange, J.P., Marchais, J.C., and Normant, E. 2001. *Air and Spaceborne Radar Systems: An Introduction.* Norwich, NY: William Andrew Publishing.

Lambakis, S. 2001. "Space Weapons: Refuting the Critics." *Policy Review* 105 (February-March): 41–51.

Lawes, I. 2006. "Land Force Air and Missile Defence: Dealing With the Complexities of Future Warfighting." *Australian Army Journal,* 3 (2): 109–122.

McKenna, T. 2005. "Lost in Space: Could Space-Based Weapons Help Protect Military Satellite Capability?" *Journal of Electronic Defense* 28 (1) 40–48.

Moltz, J. C., ed. 2003. *New Challenges in Missile Proliferation, Missile Defense, and Space.* Monterey, CA: Center for Nonproliferation Studies.

Neufeld, J. 1990. *The Development of Ballistic Missiles in the United States Air Force, 1945–1960.* Washington, D.C.: Office of Air Force History, United States Air Force.

Neufeld, M. J. 2006. "'Space Superiority': Werner von Braun's Campaign for a Nuclear-Armed Space Station, 1946–1956." *Space Policy* 22(1): 52–62.

Orbital Sciences Corporation. 2006. *Fact Sheet: FORMOSAT-3/COSMIC: Constellation Observing System for Meteorology, Ionosphere and Climate (COSMIC),* 2; [Online article or information; retrieved 10/25/07.] www.orbital.com/NewsInfo/Publications/FORMOSAT-3_Fact.pdf.

Reiss, Major R. J., Jr. 2005. "Space Games: Scripted Exercises Fail to Address Threats to U.S. Satellite Capabilities." *Armed Forces Journal* 142 (12): 28–30.

Richelson, J. T. 1999. *America's Space Sentinels: DSP Satellites and National Security.* Lawrence, KS: University Press of Kansas.

Rip, M. R. and J. M. Hasik. 2002. *The Precision Revolution: GPS and the Future of Aerial Warfare.* Annapolis, MD: Naval Institute Press.

Roberd, R. M. 1984. "Introducing the Particle-Beam Weapon." *Air University Review* 35 (5): 74–84.

Rogers, M. E. 1997. *Lasers in Space: Technological Options for Enhancing U.S. Military Capabilities.* Maxwell Air Force Base, AL: Air War College, Center for Strategy and Technology.

Singer, J. 2003. "U.S. Seeks to Target Satellites From Ground." *Defense News* 18 (29): 38.

Smith, M. S. 2005. *U.S. Space Programs: Civilian, Military, and Commercial,* 9, 13–14. Washington, D.C.: Library of Congress, Congressional Research Service.

Smith, M. S. 2006. *Military Space Programs: Issues Concerning DOD's SBIRS and STSS Programs,* 3–4. Washington, D.C.: Library of Congress, Congressional Research Service.

Spires, D. N. and R. W. Sturdevant. 1997. "From Advent to Milstar: The U.S. Air Force and the Challenges of Military Satellite Communications." In *Beyond the Ionosphere: Fifty Years of Satellite Communication,* edited by A. J. Butrica, 65–78. Washington, D.C.: NASA.

U.S. Air Force. 2003. *The Airborne Laser: Frequently Asked Questions,* 1–6. [Online article or information; retrieved 10/25/07.] www.kirtland.af.mil/shared/media/document/AFD-070404-23.pdf.

U.S. Air Force. 2005(b). *Fact Sheet: Defense Meteorological Satellite Program,* 1–2. [Online article or information; retrieved 8/2/06.] www.af.mil/factsheets/factsheet_print.asp?fsID=94&page=1.

U.S. Air Force. 2005(c). *Fact Sheet: Defense Satellite Communications System,* 1.[Online article or information; retrieved 8/2/06.] www.af.mil/factsheets/factsheet_print.asp?fsID=95&page=1.

U.S. Air Force. 2005(d). *Delta II Launch Vehicle,* 1–2. [Online article or information; retrieved 8/3/06.] www.af.mil/factsheets/factsheet.asp?fsID=97.

U.S. Air Force. 2005(e). *Global Positioning System,* 1. [Online article or information; retrieved 8/8/06.] www.af.mil/factsheets/factsheet_print.asp?fsID=119&page=1.

U.S. Air Force. 2005(f). *Fact Sheet: E-8C Joint Stars,* 1–2. [Online article or information; retrieved 4/24/00.] www.af.mil/factsheets/factsheet_print.asp?fsID=100&page=1.

U.S. Air Force. 2005(g). *Milstar Satellite Communications System,* 1–2. [Online article or information; retrieved 8/21/06.] www.af.mil/factsheets/factsheet_print.asp?fsID=118&page=1.

U.S. Air Force. 2006. *Defense Support Program Satellites,* 1–2. [Online article or information; retrieved 8/24/06.] www.af.mil/factsheets/factsheet.asp?id=96.

U.S. Air Force. Operations Analysis Office. 1962. *100 MT Weapons in an Orbital Bombardment System.* Washington, D.C.: Headquarters, United States Air Force, Operations Analysis Office.

U.S. Air Force Research Laboratory. 1999. *New Space Propulsion System Launched.* [Online article or information; retrieved 10/25/07.] www.pr.afrl.af.mil/press/articles/esex991a.htm.

U.S. Air Force Research Laboratory. 2002(a). *Advanced Electro-Optical System,* 1–2. [Online article or information; retrieved 10/25/07.] www.kirtland.af.mil/shared/media/document/AFD-070404-030.pdf.

U.S. Air Force Research Laboratory. 2002(b). *Chemical Oxygen-Iodine Laser (COIL).* 1–2. [Online article or information; retrieved 10/25/07.] www.de.afrl.af.mil/Factsheets/COIL.pdfkirtland.af.mil/shared/media/document/AFD-070404-034.pdf.

U.S. Air Force Research Laboratory. 2002(c). *High power Microwave,* 1–3. [Online article or information; retrieved 8/18/06.] www.de.afrl.Factsheets/HPM.pdf.

U.S. Air Force Research Laboratory. 2002(d). *Laser Effects Test Facility.* [Online article or information; retrieved 10/25/07.] www.kirtland.af.mil/shared/media/document/AFD-070404-037.pdf.

U.S. Air Force Research Laboratory. 2002(e). *North Oscura Peak,* 1–2. [Online article or information; retrieved 10/25/07.] www.kirtland.af.mil/shared/media/document/AFD-070404-041.pdf.

U.S. Air Force Research Laboratory. 2003. *Telescope & Atmospheric Compensation Laboratory (TACLab),* 1–2. [Online article or information; retrieved 10/25/07.] www.kirtland.af.mil/shared/media/document/AFD-070404-046.pdf.

U.S. Air Force Research Laboratory. 2004(a). *Directed Energy Directorate,* 1–2. [Online article or information; retrieved 10/25/07.] www.kirtland.af.mil/shared/media/document/AFD-070404-035.pdf.

U.S. Air Force Research Laboratory. 2004(b). *Large Membrane Mirrors,* 1–2. [Online article or information; retrieved 10/25/07.] www.kirtland.af.mil/shared/media/document/AFD-070404-038.pdf.

U.S. Air Force Research Laboratory. 2005(a). *Active Denial System: Advanced Concept Technology Demonstration,* 1–2. [Online article or information; retrieved 10/25/07.] www.kirtland.af.mil/shared/media/document/AFD-070404-026.pdf..

U.S. Air Force Research Laboratory. 2005(b). *Aerospace Engineering Facility,* 1. [Online article or information; retrieved 10/25/07.] www.kirtland.af.mil/shared/media/document/AFD-070404-093.pdf..

U.S. Air Force Research Laboratory. 2006(a). *Personnel Halting and Stimulation Response (PHaSR),* 1. [Online article or information; retrieved 10/25/07.] www.kirtland.af.mil/shared/media/document/AFD-070404-043.pdf.

U.S. Air Force Research Laboratory. 2006(b). *Relay Mirror Technology,* 1–2. [Online article or information; retrieved 10/25/07.] www.kirtland.af.mil/shared/media/document/AFD-070404-044.pdf.

U.S. Air Force Research Laboratory. Space Vehicles Directorate. 2003. *Near-Space Access Program: High-Altitude Balloons and Tethered Aerostats,* 1–2. [Online article or information; retrieved 10/25/07.] www.kirtland.af.mil/library/factsheets/factsheet.asp?id=7890.

U.S. Air Force Research Laboratory. Space Vehicles Directorate. 2005(a). *Demonstration and Science Experiments (DSX) Satellite,* 1. [Online article or information; retrieved 10/25/07.] www.kirtland.af.mil/shared/media/document/AFD-070404-096.pdf.

U.S. Air Force Research Laboratory. Space Vehicles Directorate. 2005(b). *High Frequency Active Auroral Research Program,* 1. [Online article or information; retrieved 10/25/07.] www.kirtland.af.mil/shared/media/document/AFD-070404-097.pdf.

U.S. Air Force Research Laboratory. Space Vehicles Directorate. 2005(c). *AFRL's RAD6000 Computer,* 1. [Online article or information; retrieved 10/25/07.] www.kirtland.af.mil/shared/media/document/AFD-070404-100.pdf.

U.S. Air Force Research Laboratory. Space Vehicles Directorate. 2005(d). *Solar Mass Ejection Imager: New Tool for Space Weather!,* 1. [Online article or information; retrieved 10/25/07.] www.kirtland.af.mil/shared/media/document/AFD-070404-102.pdf.

U.S. Air Force Research Laboratory. Space Vehicles Directorate. 2005(e). *XSS-10 Micro Satellite,* 1. [Online article or information; retrieved 10/2507.] www.kirtland.af.mil/shared/media/document/AFD-070404-107.pdf.

U.S. Air Force Research Laboratory. Space Vehicles Directorate. 2005(f). *XSS-11 Micro Satellite,* 1. [Online article or information; retrieved 10/25/07.] www.kirtland.af.mil/shared/media/document/AFD-070404-108.pdf.

U.S. Air Force Research Laboratory. Space Vehicles Directorate. 2006(a). *The Communications/Navigation Outage Forecasting System (C/NOFS),* 1. [Online article or information; retrieved 10/25/07.] www.kirtland.af.mil/shared/media/document/AFD-070404-094.pdf.

U.S. Air Force Research Laboratory. Space Vehicles Directorate. 2006(b). *Cryocoolers: Cool Infrared Sensors to Enable Space Intelligence, Surveillance, Reconnaissance and Situational Awareness,* 1. [Online article or information; retrieved 10/25/07.] www.kirtland.af.mil/shared/media/document/AFD-070404-095.pdf.

U.S. Air Force Research Laboratory. Space Vehicles Directorate. 2006(c), *Innovative Space-Based Radar Antenna Technology (ISAT) Flight Demonstrator,* 1. [Online article or information; retrieved 10/25/07.] www.kirtland.af.mil/shared/media/document/AFD-070404-098.pdf.

U.S. Air Force Research Laboratory. Space Vehicles Directorate. 2006(d). *Scintillation Network Decision Aid (SCINDA),* 1–2. [Online article or information; retrieved 10/25/07.] www.kirtland.af.mil/shared/media/document/AFD-070404-101.pdf.

U.S. Air Force Research Laboratory. Space Vehicles Directorate. 2006(e). *The Space Countermeasures Hands On Program (Space CHOP),* 1. [Online article or information; retrieved 10/25/07.] www.kirtland.af.mil/shared/media/document/AFD-070404-103.pdf.

U.S. Air Force Research Laboratory. Space Vehicles Directorate. 2006(f). *TacsSat–2 Micro Satellite,* 1. [Online article or information; retrieved 10/25/07.] www.kirtland.af.mil/shared/media/document/AFD-070404-105.pdf.

U.S. Air Force Space and Missile System Command. 2001. *Space-Based Radar (SBR),* 1. [Online article or information; retrieved 10/25/07.] www.losangeles.af.mil/library/factsheets/factsheet.asp?ID=5308.

U.S. Air Force Space and Missile Command. 2004. *Factsheet: Advanced Extremely High Frequency System,* 1–3. [Online article or information; retrieved 10/25/07.] www.losangeles.af.mil/library/factsheets/factsheet.asp?id=5319.

U.S. Air Force Space Command. 2003. *Early Warning Radar Service Life Extension Program,* 1. [Online article or information; retrieved 10/25/07.] www.afspc.af.mil/news/story_print.asp?id=123071186.

U.S. Air Force Space Command. 2004(a). *LGM-30G Minuteman III,* 1–2. [Online article or information; retrieved 10/25/07.] www.afspc.af.mil/libary/factsheets/factsheet.asp?id=3655.

U.S. Air Force Space Command. 2004(b). *310*th *Space Group,* 1–2. [Online article or information; retrieved 10/25/07.] www.afspc.af.mil/library/factsheets/factsheet.asp?id=3644.

U.S. Air Force Space Command. 2005(a). *Evolved Expendable Launch Vehicle,* 1. [Online article or information; retrieved 8/8/06.] www.afspc.af.mil/library/factsheets/factsheet_print.asp?fsID =3643&page=1.

U.S. Air Force Space Command. 2005(b). *LG-118A Peacekeeper,* 1–2. [Online article or information; retrieved 10/25/07.] http://space.au.af.mil/factsheets/peacekeeper.htm.

U.S. Air Force Space Command. 2006. *Ground-Based Electro-Optical Deep Space Surveillance,* 1. [Online article or information; retrieved 10/25/07.] www.af.mil/factsheets/factsheet.asp?ID =170.

U.S. Air Force Space Command. n.d.(a). *Pave Paws Radar System,* 1–2. [Online article or information; retrieved 8/22/06.] www.afspc.af.mil/library/factsheets/factsheet.asp?id=3656.

U.S. Air Force Space Command. n.d.(b). *Space Based Infrared Systems (SBIRS),* 1–2. [Online article or information; retrieved 8/24/06.] www.afspc.af.mil/library/factsheets/factsheet.asp ?id=3675.

U.S. Air Force Space Command. n.d.(c). *Wideband Global Satcom Satellite (WGS),* 1–2. [Online article or information; retrieved 10/25/07.] www.afspc.af.mil/library/factsheets/factsheet.asp ?id=5582.

U.S. Army. Space and Missile Defense Command. 1998. *SMDC History-New Frontiers,* 1, 4. [Online article or information; retrieved 7/28/06.] www.smdc.army.mil/Historical/SMDC Timeline3_NewFrontiers.doc.

U.S. Army. Space and Missile Defense Command. 2002. "A Day Without Space: Ensuring It Doesn't Happen." [Online article or information; retrieved 8/17/06.] www.smdc-armyforces .army.mil/SpaceJournal/Article.asp?AID=15.

U.S. Army. Space and Missile Defense Command. n.d. *SMDC History: A Non-Nuclear Approach,* 2. [Online article or information; retrieved 7/28/06.] www.smdc.army.mil/Historical/ SMDCTimeline2_ANon-NuclearApproach.doc.

U.S. Commission to Assess the Threat to the United States from Electromagnetic Pulse (EMP) Attack. 2004. *Volume I: Executive Report,* 1: 11–13, 15, 28. 32, 40, 44, 46–48.

U.S. Congress. House Committee on Government Operations. Subcommittee on Legislation and National Security. 1993. *Performance of the Patriot Missile in the Gulf War.* Washington, D.C.: U.S. Government Printing Office.

U.S. Congress. House Committee on Science and Technology. Subcommittee on Science, Space, and Technology. 1994. *The Global Positioning System: What Can't It Do?* Washington, D.C.: U.S. Government Printing Office.

U.S. Congress. Office of Technology Assessment. 1984. *Directed Energy Missile Defense in Space.* Washington, D.C.: U.S. Government Printing Office.

U.S. Congress. Office of Technology Assessment. 1985. *Anti-Satellite Weapons, Countermeasures, and Arms Control.* Washington, D.C.: U.S. Government Printing Office.

U.S. Congress, Senate Committee on Commerce, Science, and Transportation. 1994. *Weather Satellite Convergence.* Washington, D.C.: U.S. Government Printing Office.

U.S. Congressional Budget Office. 2004. *Alternatives for Boost-Phase Missile Defense.* Washington, D.C.: U.S. Congressional Budget Office.

U.S. Defense Science Board. 2003. *Report of the Defense Science Board/Air Force Scientific Advisory Board Joint Task Force on Acquisition of National Security Space Programs,* 30–31. Washington, D.C.: U.S. Defense Science Board.

U.S. Department of Commerce. National Telecommunications Information Administration. 1996. *A Technical Report to the Secretary of Transportation on a National Approach to Augmented GPS Services.* Boulder, CO and Washington, D.C.: National Telecommunications and Information Administration and U.S. Department of Transportation.

U.S. Department of Energy. Argonne National Laboratory. n.d. *Nuclear Weapons in Space.* [Online article or information; retrieved 8/22/06.] www.newton.dep.anl.gov/askasci/gen01/ gen01086.htm.

U.S. Department of State. Bureau of Arms Control. n.d. *Treaty on Principles Governing the Activities of States in the Exploration and Use of Outer Space, Including the Moon and Other Celestial Bodies,* 1–2; [Online article or information; retrieved 8/22/06.] www.state.gov/t/ac/trt/ 5181.htm.

U.S. Government Accountability Office. 2004. *Defense Acquisitions: Space-Based Radar Needs Additional Knowledge Before Starting Development.* Washington, D.C.: U.S. Government Accountability Office.

U.S. Missile Defense Agency. 2006(a). *Fact Sheet: Aegis Ballistic Missile Defense,* 1. [Online article or information; retrieved 7/27/06.] www.mda.mil/mdalink/pdf/aegis.pdf.

U.S. Missile Defense Agency. 2006(b). *The Ballistic Missile Defense System,* 1. [Online article or information; retrieved 8/1/06.] www.mda.mil/mdalink/pdf/bmds.pdf.

U.S. Missile Defense Agency. 2006(c). *Ballistic Missile Defense System Interceptors,* 1. [Online article or information; retrieved 8/1/06.] www.mda.mil/mdalink/pdf/bmdint.pdf.

U.S. Missile Defense Agency. 2006(d). *Command, Control, Battle Management, and Communications,* 1. [Online article or information; retrieved 8/2/06.] www.mda.mil/mdalink/pdf/ c2bmc.pdf.

U.S. Missile Defense Agency. 2006(e). *Forward Deployable Radars,* 1. [Online article or information; retrieved 8/8/06.] www.mda.mil/mdalink/pdf/fdr.pdf.

U.S. Missile Defense Agency. 2006(f). *Ground-Based Midcourse Defense,* 1. [Online article or information; retrieved 8/17/06.] www.mda.mil/mdalink/pdf/gmd06.pdf.

U.S. Missile Defense Agency. 2006(g). *PATRIOT Advanced Capability–3,* 1. [Online article or information; retrieved 8/22/06.] www.mda.mil/mdalink/pdf/pac3meads.pdf.

U.S. Missile Defense Agency. 2006(h). *Sea-Based X-Band Radar,* 1. [Online article or information; retrieved 8/24/06.] www.mda.mil/mdalink/pdf/sbx.pdf.

U.S. Missile Defense Agency. 2006(i). *Space Tracking and Surveillance System,* 1. [Online article or information; retrieved 8/25/06.] www.mda.mil/mdalink/pdf/stss06.pdf.

U.S. Missile Defense Agency. 2006(j). *Terminal High Altitude Area Defense,* 1. [Online article or information; retrieved 8/28/06.] www.mda.mil/mdalink/pdf/thaad.pdf.

U.S. National Research Council. 2004. *Terrorism: Reducing Vulnerabilities and Improving Responses: U.S.-Russian Workshop Proceedings,* 6–7. Washington, D.C.: The National Academies Press. [Online article or information; retrieved 8/28/06.] www.nap.edu/openbook/0309089719/ html.

4

Other Countries' Space Weapons Programs

THE UNITED STATES is not the only country to have a space weapons or defense program. Other countries have made efforts to achieve space weapons or defense systems to further what they consider as national security objectives. This chapter seeks to chronicle the efforts made by these countries in this regard. The countries whose space weapons and defense systems receive the most coverage are Russia and the former Soviet Union, China, and European countries, focusing on those that are members of the European Union.

Russia/Soviet Union

Besides the United States, no nation has invested as much effort or as many resources in developing space weapons and defenses as the former Soviet Union and its national successor the Russian Federation. For the purposes of historical distinction, the term "Russian" is used to describe the military astronautics programs of the Russian Federation since 1991 and "Soviet" is used to describe Russian national space programs for 1991 and earlier.

Russian efforts to develop a military space program began during the concluding stages of World War II when they sought, along with the United States, to gain information about the German V-2 rocket program, which introduced the world to the military potential of rockets and guided missiles (Neufeld 1996; Bille and Lishock 2004, 23–25, 56–72, 100–114; McDougall 1997, 41–62, 237–293).

Soviet interest in German space program assets began before the Germans surrendered to the Red Army. There is vague evidence suggesting that the Soviet government had acquired recent intelligence on a German missile development program in 1935. In a July 13, 1944 letter, British prime minister Winston Churchill (1874–1965) told Soviet leader Joseph Stalin (1879–1953) of a German rocket weapon being tested in Poland and asked Stalin to instruct his advancing forces to preserve any equipment they found and allow British personnel to examine this equipment. Stalin granted this request and Soviet troops entered the German rocket test site at Blizna on August 6 and sent samples of the German's A-4 missile back to the Soviet Union for further inspection (Russian Space Web 2006(a), 1–4; Siddiqi 2003(a), 1–22).

This Soviet interest in military applications of space built on preexisting and ongoing work by Soviet scientists such as Konstantin Tsiolkovsky (1857–1935) and Sergey Korolev (1907–1966). Tsiolkovsky was a rural math teacher enthralled by the idea of human travel beyond the atmosphere. In 1895 he wrote on the possibility of an artificial satellite and discussed the basics of space flight and orbital mechanics in articles published in 1903 and 1911. In later work he reached the conclusion that it would take the power and speed of a rocket engine to boost a satellite beyond the earth's atmosphere and concluded that a combination of liquid hydrogen and liquid oxygen (LOX) would be the best way to fuel such access to space. Tsiolkovsky was supported by the Bolshevik regime, which seized power in the 1917 revolution; his writings were published by the Soviet government, and his work played a key role in motivating future Soviet research in astronautics (Bille and Lishock, 6–8; Harford 1997; Zak 2002, 62–69).

Korolev was working in a Soviet military supported research and development center during the 1930s. He survived being arrested during the Stalinist purges on a specious charge of "sabotage" and endured some time in the Gulag before ending up working for the NKVD, the Soviet secret police during World War II's later years. While working for the NKVD, Korolev designed his first long-range rockets with warheads designed to be carried 40 miles. He was involved in conducting assessments of captured German rocketry equipment and went on to play key roles in the development of the Soviet Union's ballistic missile and artificial satellite programs, which culminated in the 1957 Sputnik launch (Bille and Lishock, 56–72; Siddiqi 2003(b), 470–501).

Soviet developments in this area over the next decade underwent numerous changes and began with a July 23, 1945 government decree establishing three development bureaus that would each be responsible for creating missiles with different ranges and fuel propellants. A March 13, 1946 decree signed by Stalin distributed rocket technology responsibilities among several governmental ministries and created a special government committee on reactive technology to oversee these military astronautic efforts (Russian Space Web 2006(b), 3, 6; Siddiqi 2003(a), 23–47).

Soviet research efforts were assisted by teams of German scientists captured in the aftermath of World War II, and Soviet rocket research programs were concentrated at Kapustin Yar, which was chosen for its relative proximity to Stalingrad (Volgograd). On October 18, 1947 the first German A-4 rocket was launched at Kapustin Yar and flew for approximately 209 kilometers before landing 30 kilometers to the left of its intended target with the rocket disintegrating before crashing and not leaving a hole in the ground upon impact (Russian Space Web 2006(c), 1–2; Siddiqi 2003(a), 54–56).

Subsequent years saw incremental increases in Soviet military astronautics skills and technology. Under Korolev's leadership and with the assistance of their captured German slave labor force, the Soviets launched their version of the German A-4, which they called the R-1, from Kapustin Yar on October 18, 1948. This missile reached its target area nearly 288 kilometers from the launch site (Russian Space Web 2006(d), 1–2).

Russian aeronautical engineer Sergey Pavlovich Korolev. *(Bettmann/Corbis)*

Lessons learned from this initial launch were applied to the successor R-2 missile and included improvements such as making the upper position fuel tank part of the rocket's external structure. The R-2 was launched from Kapustin Yar on September 21, 1949 signifying significant improvement in Soviet ballistic missile knowledge and expertise while also indicating maturation in the nascent Soviet aerospace industry (Russian Space Web 2006(e), 1–2; Siddiqi 2003(a), 73).

Korolev became the chief developer of Soviet long-range ballistic missiles on April 26, 1950, and the R-1 was officially incorporated into the Red Army's arsenal on November 25, 1950, and the R-2 became part of the Red Army's weapons stockpile on November 27, 1951 (Russian Space Web 2006(f), 2). Further development in the Soviet's ballistic missile arsenal involved the R-5 missile, which was first launched on March 15, 1953 and received formal Soviet government approval to proceed with production on April 10, 1954. The R-5's significance is that it represented the first Soviet rocket capable of flying over 1,000 kilometers and that it was capable of carrying a nuclear warhead. This missile's flight control system included aerodynamic and gas rudders, which prevented it from rolling on its main axis after launch. A U.S. CIA assessment at this time could not confirm nor deny Soviet guided missile production (Russian Space Web 2006(g), 1–2; Bluth 1992; Cochran, Norris, and Bukharin 1995; Bolonkin 1991; U.S. Central Intelligence Agency 1954).

This growth in Soviet missile flight range exceeding 1,000 kilometers meant that the Kapustin Yar facility would no longer work due to its proximity to population centers on the Volga River. Consequently, the Soviet military began looking for a new missile range flight test site. A key requirement for this new test range was the desire of missile program scientists to deploy a series of guidance antennas that would have unobstructed views of the missile during its flight. Korolev directed his associates to search various regions in the Soviet Union and rejected the area adjacent to Kapustin Yar and the Stavropol Region west of the Caspian Sea due to their proximity to population centers, countries such as Iran, and mountains (Russian Space Web 2006(h), 1).

On March 17, 1954, the Soviet Minister's Council issued a decree directing several government agencies including the Ministry of Defense and Ministry of Aviation Industry to search for a long-range missile test site and report their findings by March 1, 1955. Following several months of investigation, the Soviet commission decided to select the remote Central Asian village of Tyuratam in what is now Kazakhstan to build their missile test range. Key factors in selecting Tyuratam were the area's geographic isolation and proximity to railroads connected to other areas of the Soviet Union.

Tyuratam is an isolated and desolate region whose summer climate can include dust storms and temperatures up to 122°F and winter snowstorms and temperatures as low −13°F. The commission presented its recommendations to the government on February 4, 1955, and the Politburo agreed soon after this, issuing a formal decree authorizing construction at Tyuratam on February 12, 1955. Work soon began on making this site, which would become known as the Baikonaur Cosmodrome, the center of Soviet missile testing and space launches in the years to come (Russian Space Web 2006(h), 2–6; Siddiqi 2003(a), 135–138).

On June 21, 1956, the Red Army incorporated the nuclear tipped R-5 missile into its arsenal. With a range of nearly 1,200 kilometers, this became the first "strategic" ballistic missile in the Soviet arsenal although later arms control classification would place it in the Intermediate Range Ballistic Missile (IRBM) category. R-5 development began in 1952, and the ultimate result was a single-stage missile with a height of 20 meters, which was shaped like a cylinder instead of a cigar. The R-5 was powered by a single engine that used a 92% mix of alcohol with water as fuel and LOX as an oxidizer while yielding thrust of 43.8 tons. This missile's flight control system consisted of aerodynamic and gas rudders, which prevented the missile from rolling on its main axis during flight (Russian Space Web 2006(g), 1–2; Siddiqi 2003(a), 99–101).

Soviet missile and military striking power increased exponentially with the August 21, 1957 launch of the R-7 missile. With a range of 8,500–8,800 kilometers, the R-7 was the first Soviet ICBM. The R-7 had a two-stage rocket, weighed 280 tons when full, and was capable of carrying a single 3–5 megaton nuclear warhead. As a weapon the R-7 reached obsolescence quickly, but descendants of its launch capability are still in use launching Russian manned spacecraft into orbit (Russian Space Web 2006(i), 1–2; Siddiqi 2003(a), 135–143).

These initial Soviet accomplishments in space were only of interest to observers in relevant scientific disciplines and military and intelligence fields and had limited public impact. This obscurity would be eliminated by the October 4, 1957 launch of the world's first artificial satellite Sputnik as part of the International Geophysical Year from July 1957–December 1958. Sputnik's launch, while primarily being a boost for Soviet propaganda, also created acute concern in the United States about its space efforts and the possible national security implications Sputnik's launch might have on U.S. national security policies. It also transformed the U.S. educational system, which began placing increased emphasis on science and technology training as it sought to rise to meet the perceived Soviet technological challenge presented by Sputnik (U.S. National Academies 2005, 1; Launius, Logsdon, and Smith 2000; MacInnis 2003; Siddiqi 2003(a); Portree 1998; NASA History Office 2007; Killian 1977; U.S. Central Intelligence Agency 1958, 2–6).

One assessment of Soviet military space policy describes the impact of Sputnik and other early Soviet space accomplishments as follows:

> The Soviet leadership under Khrushchev certainly recognized the potential of the space programme as a focus of national unity and pride. It was presented as peaceful in nature and as conductive to the promotion of peace.
>
> Soviet achievements in space were also used as diplomatic tools in relations with neutral and Third World countries, and Soviet astronauts were frequently sent on tours to promote the image of the Soviet Union. Obviously the space programme was useful as a propaganda tool not only abroad, but also at home. Achievements in space which demonstrated Soviet missile capability bolstered Khrushchev's arguments for reliance on the strategic missile as the major factor in Soviet security (Bluth 1992, 221).

This growth in Soviet military space accomplishments also saw the Soviet government seek to share this technology with ideologically compatible nations. On December 6, 1957, the Soviets decided to provide China with the production license for the predecessor R-2 missile, whose development began in 1949 and had a range of 600 kilometers in what can be viewed as an early instance of weapons of mass destruction proliferation (Russian Space Web 2006(e), 1).

A key post-Sputnik development in Soviet military space policy was the December 17, 1959 Soviet government decree establishing the Strategic Missile Forces, which gave this organization control of all ballistic missiles within the Soviet Union. Headed by Marshall Mitrofan Nedelin (1902–1960), who would be killed during an October 24, 1960 explosion of a missile at Baikonaur, the Strategic Missile Forces were also responsible for handling launching, tracking, and communications operations for Soviet spacecraft and ensuring

Soviet premier Nikita Khrushchev (center) and cosmonauts Valentina Tereshkova and Lt. Colonel Valery Bykovsky, acknowledge cheers of crowds during welcoming celebrations from atop Lenin's Mausoleum in Red Square on June 22, 1963. *(Bettmann/Corbis)*

that the Soviet military and Ministry of Defense would be the preeminent drivers of Soviet space policy for several decades (Siddiqi 2003(a), 211–212, 256–258).

These expanded Soviet military space responsibilities were financed by an augmented Soviet military budget, which increased an estimated 40% between 1957–1962. Some of this budget was allocated for a partially deployed ABM system near Leningrad, which was abandoned in 1962 although another ABM system called Galosh would eventually be deployed near Moscow (Mathers 1998, 38–40).

This military preeminence in the Soviet space program was described in an early 21st century assessment. This appraisal contended that the military was and remains the focus of Soviet space power. It went on to assert that the rockets launching Sputnik and Yuri Gagarin were ICBM derived and that the Soviet space program was politically motivated with its purpose being to display Soviet power to the world (Mowthorpe 2002, 25).

Further illustration of the military's ongoing centrality in Soviet space policy is illustrated by the September 30, 1963 Ministry of Defense deployment of an ICBM missile site near Plesetsk, located near the community of Mirny about 400 miles northeast of St. Petersburg, to shorten the time and distance required to launch missiles to North America. Besides being used for missile launches, the Plesetsk site was also a center for intelligence satellite launches for at least three decades (Russian Space Web 2006(j), 1–4; Siddiqi 2003(a), 72; Federation of American Scientists n.d.(a), 1).

Additional Soviet military space developments during 1963 included the November 1 launch of the Polet 1 satellite, which was the first satellite to maneuver in space by changing orbits, an essential capability for performing antisatellite operations (Siddiqi 2003(a), 72). Just over a month later on December 19, the Zenit reconnaissance satellite, which had been under development since 1958, was launched giving the Soviets the ability to monitor other nations' military activities from space and a counterpart to the United States' Corona satellite reconnaissance program (Siddiqi 2003(a), 250; Gorin 1998, 157–170).

The evolving organizational structure of the Soviet military space program was reflected in the October 1964 creation of the Central Directorate of Space Assets (TSUKOS) within the Ministry of Defense. TSUKOS was separated from the Strategic Missile Forces Chief Directorate of Reactive Armaments and now reported directly to the Strategic Missile Forces commander-in-chief. This reorganization now made TSUKOS the primary client for all Soviet space program assets giving it the authority to approve relevant program specifications. TSUKOS was now given authority over two component organizations: the Center for Leading the Development and Production of Space Armament Assets, which served as a research and development facility, and the Center of the Command Measurement Complex, which was responsible for overseeing the space program's national tracking, communications, and flight control stations (Siddiqi 2003(a), 380).

This same 1963–1964 time period also saw two commands established within the Soviet military dealing with space warfare and defense programs. The PRO command was given responsibility for detecting, intercepting, and destroying enemy ballistic missiles, while the PKO command was responsible for antispace defense including destroying enemy space weapons and assets (Federation of American Scientists n.d.(b), 1). The October 27, 1967 launch of a Tsyklon–2 rocket capable of carrying antisatellite weapons from Baikonaur is evidence of Soviet intent to deploy such weaponry (Russian Space Web 2006(k), 6).

This willingness to assert national military power in space was also being reflected in Soviet military doctrinal statements. A recent analysis of the 1968 *Soviet Military Strategy* makes the following appraisals of Soviet military space policy. It maintained that this policy sought to create space weapons systems to enhance overall military combat effectiveness; to prevent other countries from using space; and for developing strategic offensive systems for space war fighters. Soviet space policy objectives also encompassed protecting tactical and strategic strike capabilities; preventing hostile space use for military, political or economic gain; and giving the Soviets unrestricted access to space assets. Such assessment went on to maintain that the Soviets made extensive use of photoreconnaissance satellites for surveillance; early warning; support for troop deployment and targeting; intelligence gathering; strike assessment; and targeting U.S. and North Atlantic Treaty Organization (NATO) supply lines, communication links, and space systems (Mowthorpe 2002, 27; U.S. Defense Intelligence Agency 1984).

Soviet military space doctrinal thought during this 1960's chronological timeframe also consisted of diverse strands of opinion on the efficacy and feasibility of ballistic missile defenses. Individuals representing the viewpoints of personnel in the Strategic Missile Forces and naval submarines viewed wars involving missile defenses as being ones in which their service branches would be the principal participants, and they estimated that such wars would be relatively short in duration. In contrast to these perspectives, there were those who argued that future wars would be more protracted and involve the increased integration and involvement of all levels of Soviet strategic defense planning and cooperation such as antiaircraft, antimissile, and civil defense programs. Such debates characterized Soviet military and political planning on space warfare and defense issues during the 1960s and beyond (Mathers 1998, 44–55).

During the 1960s and 1970s, the Soviets made extensive efforts to develop ASAT with some recognition of these efforts occurring as early as 1962. Between 1968 and 1982 an ASAT was tested 20 times in space. During each test, a dedicated target vehicle was launched into low earth orbit by rockets from Baikonur and Plesetsk. The intercepting ASAT was launched from these sites and attempted to reach the intended target after either one or two revolutions around the earth. The interceptor weighed 1,400 kilograms and had a diameter of 1.8 meters and length of 4.2 meters, while the intended target was a 650-kilogram polyhedron with a 1.4-meter diameter (Federation of American Scientists n.d.(c), 1; U.S. Central Intelligence Agency 1962, 4).

Launch opportunities occurred as the target satellite's orbital plane passed over Baikonur twice a day, but only one daily launch opportunity actually existed to prevent possible launches toward China, which would have caused considerable problems for Soviet testers and policymakers. The time between launch and target intercept was 90–200 minutes after launch. Once the target was within range, the ASAT was maneuvered into desired attack position and a conventional warhead was exploded to destroy the target (Federation of American Scientists n.d.(c), 1).

Five of the initial seven ASAT tests between 1968–1971 were judged successful with tests being conducted at altitudes ranging from 230 to 1,000 kilometers above the earth's surface. Thirteen more tests were conducted between 1976–1982 in efforts to achieve a faster intercept profile and evaluate a new acquisition sensor. Two of these subsequent tests attempted to reach the target in one revolution around the earth but were unsuccessful, while two of this series of attacks achieved success adhering to the two revolution standard. In addition, some missions during this latter time frame are believed to have employed optical or infrared scanners for target acquisition instead of a radar seeking scanner and are believed to have failed in their missions (Federation of American Scientists n.d.(c), 1).

These Soviet military space efforts had, by the early 1980s, produced a significant infrastructure of programs in areas such as meteorology, communications, navigation, reconnaissance, surveillance, targeting, and antisatellite missions. In June 1981 a mobile command center of the Strategic Missile Forces began operational patrols, and in November 1981 the Main Directorate of Space Assets was transferred from the Strategic Missile Forces to report directly to the Ministry of Defense. A 1983 U.S. Defense Department as-

Launch of Soyuz T-6, June 24, 1982.
(Roger Ressmeyer/Corbis)

sessment of Soviet military space programs contended that the Soviets could launch the initial prototype of a space-based laser ASAT system in the late 1980s or early 1990s and that space-based ABM systems could be tested in the 1990s but would not become operational until the next century (U.S. Department of Defense 1983, 65, 68; Russian Space Web 2006(k), 8).

This report went on to emphasize that the then existing Soviet space launch rate was four to five times larger than the United States' then current space rate, that the Soviet payload weight placed into orbit was 10 times greater than the United States, and that future Soviet space deployments would expand their military global command, control, and communications capabilities and potential to communicate with ground, sea, and air armed force components (U.S. Department of Defense 1983, 69).

A later edition of a regular Defense Department report on Soviet military capabilities during the 1980s reiterated the importance of Soviet military space operations by emphasizing the presence of the Krasnoyarsk ballistic missile radar system. This facility, located 3,700 kilometers from Moscow and 750 kilometers from the Mongolian border, violated the 1972 ABM Treaty between the United States and Soviet Union because it exceeded treaty provisions allowing the Soviets to build an ABM facility only in the Moscow area and because it was not located on the Soviet Union's periphery and pointed outward, which the ABM Treaty required for early warning radars. Additional Soviet ABM Treaty violations involved developing components giving them the ability to construct individual mobile ABM sites within months instead of the period of several years normally required to construct ABM systems (U.S. Department of Defense 1986, 41, 45).

By the late 1980s, the Soviets had begun the GLONASS global navigation satellite system as their equivalent to the United States' GPS system. GLONASS had an announced fleet of 9–12 satellites with the potential ability to be upgraded from two to three dimensional reconnaissance capability and orbit 18–24 satellites. The Soviets also continued developing and deploying radar-carrying satellite systems. While designed for mapping polar formation ice, these satellites also enhanced the Soviet naval abilities to conduct operations in icebound areas by expediting northern sea route navigation and routing ships from western USSR naval yards to ports in the Pacific.

Soviet literature also indicated that military applications of remote sensing, oceanography, meteorology, and geodesy were stressed in cosmonaut activities. Possible implications of such research may have been enhancing the accuracy of directed energy weapons, repairing friendly satellites, and inspecting and disabling enemy satellites (U.S. Department of Defense 1988, 63–64).

Enhancing the ability of their satellites to conduct surveillance and targeting of adversary military forces also characterized Soviet military space operations. Their radar ocean and electronic intelligence (ELINT) ocean reconnaissance satellites were used to locate and target U.S. and allied military forces. Soviet ASAT capabilities allow them to deny or inhibit an enemy's use of vulnerable satellite systems and gave them the ability to attack and potentially destroy satellites in near-earth orbit. The Soviets also concluded 27 months of continuous manned presence in space in April 1989 through use of the Mir space station in another indication of a national commitment to maintain an ongoing presence in space (U.S. Department of Defense 1989, 54–56; Collins 1989, 129–143).

A key development in Soviet military space historical efforts was the Soviet Union's response to President Reagan's proposed ballistic missile defense system called the Strategic Defense Initiative (SDI). A 1983 CIA analysis correctly predicted that the Soviets would try to use assorted political, propaganda-related, and diplomatic means, negotiating strategies, and active measures to disrupt SDI. For example, the Soviets claimed that SDI would violate the ABM Treaty, produce threats to international security and stability, and other purported dangers (U.S. Central Intelligence Agency 1983, 1; Fitzgerald 1987; Dewolf 1989; and Simon 1990).

A 1985 CIA assessment estimated the costs of Soviet space programs at approximately $26 billion and stressed that this program's size and depth gives them the greatest potential in the competition for space and that the size of Soviet efforts compensated for the inefficiency and technological deficiencies marking many individual Soviet space programs. This appraisal went on to predict that Soviet efforts to acquire space technology would increase given heightened military-technological competition with the United States and that the Soviets had acquired and would continue to try to acquire relevant tech-

Russian space station Mir in 1996. *(NASA)*

nologies in areas such as space-based lasers, directed-energy weapons, and antimissile defense systems from U.S., Western European, and Japanese sources. Additional information sources in these fields of interest to the Soviets would include NASA documents and NASA-funded contractor studies (U.S. Central Intelligence Agency 1985, 1–3).

A series of political upheavals began affecting the Soviet space program starting with the collapse of Soviet satellite regimes in Eastern Europe in 1989 and the eventual 1991 collapse of the Soviet Union and its replacement by the Russian Federation (Zelikow and Rice 1995; Brandon 1992; Falk and Szentes 1997; Aslund and Olcott 1999; Szporluk 2000). Initially, these events had limited effect on Soviet military space programs. The 1991 U.S. Defense Department assessment of Soviet military capabilities, issued in the aftermath of the failed August 1991 coup attempting to restore traditional Soviet power, acknowledged that Soviet space launch rates in 1989–1990 were 15% below what they were between 1980–1988. This report went on to mention that Soviet space launches remained more than double U.S. launches, that this declining launch rate had not degraded Soviet military space capabilities, and that the Soviets still had over 170 operational satellites in orbit and that these satellites were increasing in sophistication and had longer life spans (U.S. Department of Defense 1991, 41–42; U.S. Department of Defense 1990).

At the same time, a 1991 assessment on the future of Soviet space programs by the Library of Congress' Congressional Research Service predicted that the future of Soviet space programs was questionable given the societal transformation occurring in the Soviet Union at this time.

> The political future of the Soviet space program remains in doubt as the Soviet Union undergoes political and economic upheaval. Although the Soviets are much more open about the space program today, it is still almost impossible to understand clearly how much is being spent on space and exactly on what is being spent. Revelations about past Soviet space programs—particularly the unsuccessful program to send cosmonauts to the Moon in the late 1960s—are becoming commonplace, but plans for future programs are murky. Rising dissent among the Soviet populace and some government officials against the space program is evidenced by complaints ranging from space spending as a waste of scarce government resources, to environmental damage to areas around Soviet launch sites from years of launch operations (Smith 1991, 6).

The late 1991 collapse of the Soviet Union and its replacement by the Russian Federation produced significant changes in Russian space programs including those devoted to space warfare and defense. Between 1990 and 1995, Russian civilian space programs experienced an 80% budget reduction, and military space programs saw their budget slashed by 90%. Besides these draconian budget reductions stemming from the Russian Federation's constricted fiscal resources, the Russian government's practice of not giving final budget approval to current year budgets until mid-spring means all governmental agencies must survive on monthly handouts based on previous years' allocations. This caused lower level subcontractors to demand advance payment for delivering goods resulting in production stoppages by prime contractors. In addition, the Russian Space Agency (RSA) 1994–1995 budget suffered because of the need to finance Russian military operations in Chechnya (Twigg 1999, 70; Nguyen 1993, 413–423).

RSA was created by President Boris Yeltsin in February 1992 and was given responsibility for coordinating entities involved in Russia's civil space program while also coordinating efforts with the Ministry of Defense in cases such as satellite communications, where space missions have civilian and military applications. Declining government purchases of Russian space launch vehicle services have also forced this industry to market their products and services abroad (U.S. Central Intelligence Agency 1992, 2–3).

The ability of Russia's space launch industry to market these services abroad and retain some level of international economic and technological competitiveness was seriously restricted by Russia's declining economic position. This economic decline was most dramatically affected by precipitous space workforce reductions. Between 1991–1994, the Russian aerospace industry lost 115,000 engineering and technical personnel along with 90,000 industrial workers. The head of RSA estimated in late 1994 that only 100,000 of 360,000 aerospace industry workers would still be employed in that industry. Additional evidence of deterioration in this industry during this time is demonstrated by an aging workforce. More than half of research and design aerospace personnel were over 55, almost a third were 45–55, and only 1% were under 35 with many of these younger workers seeking more lucrative careers in other industries (Oberg 2002, 56–57; U.S. Congress, House Committee on Science 1998, 513).

Russia's military space programs were not immune to this deteriorating and spasmodic funding situation, which negatively impacted space research, industrial infrastructure, and combat training. Vladimir Ivanov, the Commander of Russian Military Space Forces in 1996, stated that his units only received 8% of their budget allowances for research and development, 20% for purchasing equipment, and 6% for capital construction. Military space force staffing was cut in half between 1990–1997, and launch and technical complexes and ground-based guidance systems were wearing out after two to three decades of use with no prospect of financial support to enhance the quality of these systems or replace them (Twigg 1999, 70).

The Russian Army General Staff chief announced in early 1997 that Russian capability to monitor global rocket launches was seriously degraded and that 60% of deployed monitoring satellites were beyond their normal service lives with no prospects of replacement because these products were no longer being produced. A report in the Russian press also mentioned that one military officer from the Strategic Missile Forces believed that this degradation in satellite monitoring capability increased the chances of Russia making an accidental nuclear strike against the United States (Twigg 1999, 70).

The disintegration of the Soviet Union also placed some Russian space launch facilities into new countries such as Azerbaijan and Kazakhstan and compelled the Russian Federation to seek agreements with these countries to have continued access to these facilities. In January 1994, Russia negotiated an agreement with Kazakhstan for a 20-year lease to the Baikonur Cosmodrome and agreed to pay the Kazakhs an annual rent of $115 million. An April 1994 agreement with Latvia to lease the Skrunda missile early-warning radar station for $5 million per year lasted until August 1998 when it was moved to Baranovichi, Belarus. Another agreement with Kazakhstan in October 1996 provided Russia with access to the Kapustin Yar missile test site for $26.5 million per year. Russia also signed a preliminary agreement with Azerbaijan in August 1997 for access to the Garbala early-warning radar station for an undetermined price and duration. Each of these agreements recognizes that host countries retain formal legal control over these facilities and specifies Russian rights and obligations in using these facilities (Cooley 2000/01, 113–116).

Despite these significant post-Soviet setbacks, the Russian Federation still retains a partially viable space program and remains interested in military uses of space. The Russian Space Forces (VKS) were created in June 2001 to increase the use of space for Russia's military information gathering requirements (Center for Nonproliferation Studies 2005?(a), 1).

Russian Space Forces commander colonel general Vladimir Popovkin said Russia had approximately 60 military satellites in orbit in late 2004, which is two-and-one-half times fewer than were in orbit in 1990, but that these satellites are newer and a greater percentage of them are functioning within their normal operational lives. Russia has five kinds of

GIOVE-A atop the Soyuz launcher on pad six at Baikonur Cosmodrome in Kazakhstan. This facility has served as the primary Soviet/Russian space launch center for five decades. *(European Space Agency)*

imagery reconnaissance satellites in use: Kometa, Kobalt, Yenisey, Araks (Arkon), and Neman. Kometa satellites update military topographic and mapping data by photographing large areas. The Kobalt provides detailed photo-reconnaissance data and is believed to have 20 retrievable film capsules to deliver the exposed film while still in orbit. Yenisey satellites take high-resolution wide format photographs of the earth's surface and remain in orbit for about one year and use film capsules to preserve their images. Araks and Neman satellites relay their images digitally. An Araks satellite with an estimated three-year life span was launched in July 2002, and a Neman satellite with a projected one-year life span was launched in August 2003, but neither of these satellites functioned successfully (Center for Nonproliferation Studies 2005?(b), 1).

Russia currently possesses four dedicated military communication satellites: Strela–3, Molniya–3K, Geizer, and Raduga. Strela–3 receives and transmits communications from isolated areas and serves as the central communications system for the Main Intelligence Directorate, while Molniya satellites are used for general purpose military communications. Following the July 2005 launch failure of a Molniya–3, Popovkin announced that its production would end and that it would be replaced by a new communications satellite. The Geizer serves as a relay satellite for data gathered by Araks and Neman satellites, while

Raduga satellites provide real-time military communications services including leadership and strategic forces communication (Center for Nonproliferation Studies 2005?(b), 2).

Russian navigation satellite assets also include the Parus and GLONASS systems. Parus provides navigation and communication services for the Russian Navy and the GLONASS system, which is similar to the United States GPS, is under development with 11 of these operational in mid-2004 with hopes of having 24 operational satellites by 2010 (Center for Nonproliferation Studies 2005(b), 2).

Additional Russian military satellite assets cover ballistic missile early warning, space monitoring, ballistic missile defense, and ASAT capabilities. Their early warning network consists of ground-based and satellite-based systems. The ground-based stations are located throughout the former Soviet Union although not all post-Soviet successor governments have cooperated with Russian efforts to maintain and upgrade these facilities. Oko and Prognoz satellites, which are launched into elliptical and geostationary orbits are the satellite components of Russia's ballistic missile early warning network. The last known test of a Russian ASAT took place in 1982, and the 2001–2002 edition of *Jane's Space Directory* described Russian ASAT programs as "inactive" (Center for Nonproliferation Studies 2005(b), 3; Fitzgerald 1994, 457–476; Menshikov 2000, 36–39; Kornukov 2001, 6–12; Zhuk 2003, 209–216).

The Russian space launch industry remains active in the international space launch market. Launches are conducted by Russian Space Forces at Baikonur in Kazakhstan, Plesetsk, and the Svobodnyy Cosmodrome in eastern Russia. Russia hopes to modernize Plesetsk and Svobodnyy to enhance its national launch infrastructure and save money for the space program. It has been working on upgrades at Plesetsk since 2001 and in October 2003 prioritized its work there with Popovkin announcing in August 2005 that Russia wanted all military launches conducted from Plesetsk by 2010. Additional upgrading of Svobodnyy will not occur until 2010, and this site allows rockets to be launched to solar-synchronous and polar orbits without crossing over foreign countries. In June 2005, Russian defense minister Sergei Ivanov repeated Russia's commitment to lease Baikonur from Kazakhstan through 2050 (Center for Nonproliferation Studies 2005(c), 1–2).

Russia has entered into international commercial launch partnerships with the United States, the European Space Agency, and numerous other countries and commercial entities. Its U.S. partnership, called International Launch Services, was established in 1995 and is responsible for 50% of the global space services market (Center for Nonproliferation Studies 2005(c), 2).

During August 2005, Russia and China engaged in joint military exercises lasting for a week, which may indicate increasing security cooperation between these two countries in space and other military arenas (Hyodo 2005, 1–5).

Russian military space efforts have experienced considerable success and failures during their nearly six-decade existence. It remains an important global player in military space endeavors, and Russia's increasing oil and natural gas revenues give it the opportunity to increase its investment in civilian and military space programs. The Kliper moon launch spacecraft of 2006 may be an indication of this enhanced Russian space investment (Russian Space Web 2007, 1–2). The Russian Federation still retains significant military space interests and assets that may increase given future international security trends such as the increasing power of China, problematic relations with the United States and NATO, and the threat of a nuclear Iran, consequently reinforcing the importance of space as a national security priority in the minds of Russian policymakers.

China

As China has grown in economic prosperity and overall national assertiveness since the 1949 Communist revolution, its view of national security interests has expanded to include space. A 1967 U.S. Government assessment stressed that a Chinese ICBM system could be deployed in the early 1970s and potentially as early as 1970–1971, that Chinese national resources could probably support moderate and increasing ICBM deployment through 1975, and that China was likely to launch a satellite as soon as possible for political benefit (U.S. Central Intelligence Agency 1967, 2).

The genesis of China's military space programs began in 1956 when it acquired two Soviet R-1 missiles, which were copies of German cryogenic liquid-propellant V-2 missiles of World War II provenance. The following year China acquired the more advanced R-2 missiles from the Soviets, and these had greater range and a larger payload than the R-1 while also using storable liquid propellants. Besides providing the ballistic missiles, the Soviets also gave China the R-2's blueprints and provided advisors to assist in developing a copy of the R-2, which enabled the Chinese to produce and deploy these missiles.

Chinese engineers and students received aeronautical engineering training at the Moscow Aviation Institute and gained experience with more advanced Soviet missiles such as the SS-3 and SS-4, and their knowledge of these missiles was also facilitated by making copies of restricted notes on these weapons. The 1960 Sino–Soviet ideological split ended such cooperation, but the Chinese used the knowledge gained from this brief cooperation and would later acquire from U.S.-trained scientists to expand the growth and progress of their military space programs (U.S. Congress. House Select Committee on U.S. National Security and Military/Commercial Concerns With the People's Republic of China 1999, 1:176–177).

Chinese ballistic missile and space programs grew significantly because of the influence of Qian Xuesen (1911–) who is considered the progenitor of China's ballistic missile force. A Shanghai native, Qian left China during the Japanese occupation in 1935 and emigrated to the United States where he received a master's degree from the Massachusetts Institute of Technology and a Ph.D. from the California Institute of Technology. During his time at Cal Tech, Qian worked with a rocket research group at the Guggenheim Aeronautical Library where his work focused on aviation engineering theory, supersonic and transonic aerodynamics, and thin shell stability theory for ballistic missile structures (House Select Committee on U.S. National Security and Military/Commercial Concerns With the People's Republic of China 1999, 1:177).

Qian later went on to work at the Jet Propulsion Laboratory and because of his work reputation and quality, he was recruited to join the U.S. Army Air Force in developing its long-range missile programs. He was commissioned as a colonel and began working on the Titan ICBM. However, during the 1950s, allegations arose that he was spying for China. He lost his security clearance, was removed from working on U.S. ballistic missiles, and eventually returned to China in 1955 with four other colleagues from the Titan design unit (House Select Committee on U.S. National Security and Military/Commercial Concerns With the People's Republic of China 1999, 1:178).

Following his return to China, Qian and his associates applied their U.S.-derived knowledge to China's nascent ballistic missile programs. He became the chief project manager in all of China's ballistic missile programs and served as the lead designer of the CSS-4 nuclear ICBM targeted at the United States. Qian also served as the first director of China's Fifth Academy, which is responsible for China's aeronautics and missile development research and is now called China Aerospace Corporation. In 1958 he presented his ideas for satellite development to Communist Party leaders. During 1962 Qian began training Chinese scientists to design and develop satellites including the Dong Fang Hong–1 satellite, which was the first Chinese satellite launched. Qian was personally commended for his satellite work by Mao Zedong and other Chinese Communist leaders, awarded the honorary rank of lieutenant general in the People's Liberation Army (PLA) for his ballistic missile program development work, and in 1991 President Jiang Zemin awarded him with a "State Scientist of Outstanding Contribution," which is the highest national honor a Chinese scientist can receive (House Select Committee on U.S. National Security and Military/Commercial Concerns With the People's Republic of China, 1:179; Descisciolo 2005, 52).

The first Chinese satellite launch was in 1970 using a CSS-3 ICBM launch package, which weighed 380 pounds and stayed in orbit for 26 days. A second successful satellite launch took place on March 3, 1971. Three unsuccessful attempts were made launching longer range and more powerful Long March rockets in 1973 and 1974 before achieving success in 1975. Most subsequent Chinese satellite launches have been of communications, weather, remote sensing, navigation, or scientific satellites, which may have military applications or dual civilian and military applications (Smith 2005, 1; House Select Committee on U.S. National Security and Military/Commercial Concerns With the People's Republic of China 1999, 1:200–201).

In 1974 China launched a series of satellites whose focus involved programs covering remote sensing and microgravity research, and over subsequent decades Chinese space capabilities have grown to encompass communication satellites, groups of launching rockets, a modern space launch complex, and an increasing list of customers for its launch services (Patterson 1995, 3).

In February 1975 the State Council of China approved a report on developing Chinese satellite communications outlined by the State Planning Commission and the National Defense Science and Technology Commission, which facilitated communication satellite development into national plans (Patterson 1995, 4).

AsiaSat 2 sits atop Long March 2E rocket ready for lift-off at the Xichang Space Center launch pad November 28, 1995. *(Manuel Ceneta/AFP/Getty Images)*

These civilian space endeavors were also balanced with a desire to enhance China's military capabilities in space. A 1974 CIA estimate mentioned that China's ICBM arsenal had the ability to hit U.S. forces in Asia and that China wanted to increase the range and striking power of those forces so they could strike the Soviet Union west of the Ural Mountains and the continental United States while also improving the survivability of their nuclear deterrent (U.S. Central Intelligence Agency 1974, 1–5).

China developed the Long March 3 rocket in 1977 to meet requirements for launching communications satellites into geosynchronous orbit and began developing the Long March 4 rocket during the late 1970s to launch meteorological satellites into sunsynchronous orbits for military and civilian purposes. China also began entering the commercial space launch industry around 1986, which proved to be fortuitous timing for them because of the temporary suspension of U.S. space launches following that year's space shuttle Challenger tragedy. This temporary moratorium on U.S. launches was reflected in U.S. policy changes allowing China to launch U.S. manufactured satellites if China signed agreements with the United States on competitive pricing, liability, and protection of U.S. technology. The China Great Wall Industry Corporation vigorously markets Chinese launch services, and revenues earned from Chinese commercial launches are shared between two government organizations, the Commission of Science, Technology, and Industry for National Defense (COSTIND) and the Chinese Aerospace Corporation (CASC) (House Select Committee on U.S. National Security and Military/Commercial Concerns With the People's Republic of China 1999, 1:206–207; Thompson and Morris 2001, 5).

China's nuclear capabilities expanded considerably in 1980 when it successfully tested the DF-5 ICBM, which was capable of reaching the continental United States and in 1982 it successfully tested its first submarine-launched ballistic missile (Roberts 2003, 3).

China's launch site infrastructure also began taking shape in the 1980s. Three of these facilities are responsible for managing Chinese launch capabilities as of late 2005. Xichang, in southeastern China near Chengdu, was opened in 1984 and is responsible for primarily launching communication satellites into geostationary orbit above the equator. Jiuquan or Shuang Cheng-tzu, located in the Gobi Desert, is China's first launch site and launches an assortment of spacecraft including those of China's human space-flight program. Taiyuan, south of Beijing, opened in 1988 and is used for launches into polar orbits, and its satellites include those used for weather and other earth observation assignments (Smith 2005, 1).

Two men monitor a simulated rocket launch at the command and control center in Xichang, China. Mission control is six kilometers from the launch pad. *(Roger Ressmeyer/Corbis)*

President Ronald Reagan's 1983 inauguration of the SDI ballistic missile defense program had a significant impact on Chinese views of the global security environment. Initial Chinese reaction was cautious with some officials asserting that SDI was an understandable and appropriate attempt to counter Soviet attempts to gain strategic superiority. As time evolved, China began distinguishing between ballistic missile defense research and deployment, favoring the former but opposing the latter. Debate over Chinese nuclear doctrine intensified within Chinese military and political circles with there being some evidence that this debate instigated a Chinese move from what could be called "minimum deterrence," to nuclear threats, to a more vigorous posture called "limited deterrence" (Roberts 2003, ES-2; Glaser and Garrett 1986, 28–44).

The end of the Cold War, collapse of the Soviet Union, and declining U.S. interest in SDI seemed to indicate to the Chinese that ballistic missile defense was a less salient issue to U.S. security interests. Ballistic missile defense received new impetus from the 1990–1991 Persian Gulf War and its aftermath, which saw the United States gain renewed interest in theater missile defense (TMD). Chinese policymakers began to worry about the potential consequences of U.S. TMD deployments in East Asia, which were being taken in response to large-scale enhancement of Chinese theater missile forces with Taiwan and its national independence being the primary target of these Chinese missiles (Roberts 2003, ES-3).

In the late 1990s and the early 2000s, the Chinese government launched a concerted campaign against U.S. missile defense plans. Such U.S. responses were propelled by the 1998 North Korean test of a long-range missile that overflew Japan and instigated a U.S. policy decision to deploy a national missile defense system as soon as possible. China claimed that ballistic missile defense was a threat to the viability of its nuclear deterrent, jeopardized what it saw as strategic stability, would reverse "progress" made in deescalating the nuclear "arms race," would ignite nuclear and missile proliferation and an arms race in space, consolidate alleged American global hegemony, exacerbate the Taiwan problem, expand Japan's East Asian regional security role, and deepen U.S. East Asian involvement, whereas China wishes such involvement reduced (Roberts 2003, ES-3; Lee 2001, 85–120; Bermudez 1999; Gertz 2000, 38–43).

U.S. concerns over Chinese space capabilities were enhanced by charges of Chinese espionage at the U.S. Department of Energy (DOE) laboratories and involving thefts of sensitive U.S. space technologies from corporations such as Loral and Hughes. A U.S. House of Representatives select committee chaired by Rep. Christopher Cox (Republican from California) was charged with examining these allegations and released its unclassified three-volume public report in June 1999. Report findings indicated that China had stolen design information on the United States' most advanced nuclear weapons as well as U.S. missile technology and used it for Chinese ballistic missile applications, that this stolen technology was applicable to Chinese ballistic missiles and space-lift rockets, and that U.S. satellite manufacturers had transferred missile design information and technology to China without obtaining legally required U.S. Government licenses.

The Cox Report also revealed that this illicitly obtained information and technology improved the reliability of current and future Chinese rockets and missiles whose uses can include military communications and reconnaissance satellites, space-based sensors, space-based weapons, and satellites for state-of-the-art command and control and sophisticated intelligence collection capabilities. The report also mentioned that China had proliferated missile and space technology to countries as diverse as Iran, Pakistan, Saudi Arabia, and North Korea and other incidents that the report could not disclose without adversely affecting national security (House Select Committee on U.S. National Security and Military/Commercial Concerns With the People's Republic of China 1999, 1:ii, xii, xiv–xv, xvii, xxxvii, 1:172–232, and 2:2–217; Smith 2001, 7-10).

The 1990s saw additional noteworthy developments in Chinese military space programs. In 1992, Chinese President Jiang Zemin approved Project 921 inaugurating a manned space program, and in 1993 PLA chief of staff Chi Haotian visited Russia's Star City cosmonaut training center near Moscow beginning greater bilateral Sino–Russian space cooperation, which continues to the present. In 1999 the Shenzhou 1 rocket, which is an upgraded version of Russia's Soyuz rockets, was unveiled, in 2000 the Chinese launched Beidou 1 as their first navigation satellite, and in October 2003 China's first manned mission was launched on the Shenzhou 5 rocket carrying Lt. Col. Yang Liwei as China's first astronaut on a flight lasting 21 hours and 14 orbits, and which may also have deployed a military intelligence satellite (Descisciolo 2005, 53–54, 60, 62).

The 1990s and early years of the 21st century have also seen Chinese military literature place increasing importance on using space as an arena for military conflict and as an area of military research. Laser radars have become a Chinese military research priority. The Chinese have experimented with lidars, which are similar to radar in that they use laser light reflected from targets and received by optical lenses to locate targets. Lidars use an intensively widened beam to acquire a target, and the beam is reduced to a pencil beam to enhance target calculations. Particular emphasis has been placed by the Chinese on CO_2 lasers, and they have also conducted research on a higher powered laser radar, which has space tracking ability (Stokes 1999, 110–111; Feigenbaum 2003; Pillsbury 2000, 363–375).

China has augmented its military space capabilities by secretly acquiring U.S. Patriot missile technology after the 1990–1991 Persian Gulf War, seeking to develop an electromagnetic missile capable of causing severe disruptions to the electronic systems of attacking aircraft and missiles, developing military doctrine advocating the physical destruction of adversary reconnaissance platforms, and developing ballistic missile defense programs capable of countering missiles with a range of 2,500 kilometers (Stokes 1999, 112–115; Frieman 2001, 163–185).

A detailed critique of Chinese military space policy and doctrine is presented in a recent U.S. Army War College assessment, which argues that literature from China's Academy of Military Science, COSTIND, and CASC has supported China developing a military space capability since the 1991 Gulf War. These Chinese organizations recognize the United

States' high reliance on military space systems as a potential "Achilles heel." These and comparable appraisals go on to mention that the PLA and Chinese defense industries are developing active and passive counterspace measures that are being integrated into Chinese military doctrine such as the belief that it is easier to develop ASAT weapons instead of ballistic missile defenses and developing camouflage standards for its deployed missiles to counter foreign optical, infrared, and radar satellite systems (Stokes 1999, 117–118; Johnson-Freese 2003, 259-265; Mulvenon et al. 2006, 67–76; Scobell 2003).

China, as an increasingly important international political, economic, and military power, has sought to reassure the global community that its purposes in space are benign. In 2000, the Chinese government released *China's Space Activities* as a white paper that sought to describe and explain Chinese space policies. This document asserted China sought to adhere to existing international agreements on peaceful uses of outer space and that its overall national space policies aims are:

- to explore outer space and learn more about the cosmos and the earth;
- to utilize outer space for peaceful purposes, promote mankind's civilization and social progress, and benefit the whole of mankind; and
- to meet the growing demands of economic construction, national security, science and technology development and social progress, protect China's national interests, and build up the comprehensive national strength (China Internet Information Center 2000, 1).

The 2002 Chinese defense policy statement also asserted that China opposed weaponizing outer space, theater ballistic missile defense in northeast Asia with particular opposition to any such defense for Taiwan, and that it regretted the U.S. decision to abrogate the ABM Treaty (China Internet Information Center 2002, 2–3). The 2004 version of this document made a brief reiteration of Chinese rhetoric about the peaceful uses of outer space with no additional elaboration (China Internet Information Center 2004, 2; Zhang 2005, 6–11).

Despite these Chinese rhetorical protestations of peaceful space policy intent, the United States remains very concerned about the nature of Chinese military space policy and overall military power. This concern was most vividly expressed in the 2000 defense-spending budget passed in 1999, which required the Defense Department to prepare annual reports for Congress on Chinese military power and strategy (An Act to Authorize Appropriations for Fiscal Year 2000 and for Military Activities of the Department of Defense for Military Construction, and for Defense Activities of the Department of Energy, to Prescribe Personnel Strengths, for Such Fiscal Year for the Armed Forces, and for Other Purposes. Public Law 106–65. 113 U.S. Statutes at Large 2000, 781–782).

The 2000 edition of this report noted that while China had the ability to launch military photoreconnaissance satellites, their technology was obsolescent by Western standards. This report went on to mention that the China–Brazil Earth Resources satellite launched in October 1999 could help Chinese efforts to develop better military reconnaissance satellites and that China and Russia had 11 joint space projects including those involving cooperative manned space activities (U.S. Department of Defense 2000, 14–15).

This report's 2002 edition noted improvements in China's command, control, communications, computers, and intelligence (C4I) capabilities thanks to negotiations with the Belarusian firm Agat to produce relevant battle management software and that China has purchased new space systems such as over-the-horizon radar to increase its ability to detect, monitor, and target western Pacific naval activity. In July 2001, a five-year Sino–Russian cooperation agreement was signed in which these countries established organizations to jointly develop a regional missile defense system and create programs to develop new generation high-tech weapons and equipment (U.S. Department of Defense 2002, 4–5).

In 2003, this report stressed that China likely had thorough knowledge of U.S. and foreign space operations due to open-source information on U.S. space systems and operations, that China had acquired technical assistance applicable to developing laser radars to track and image satellites, that it may have the ability to damage optical sensors on satellites that are vulnerable to laser damage, and that it still desired to develop an ASAT system between 2005–2010 (U.S. Department of Defense 2003, 36).

The 2004 edition of this report detailed additional Chinese military space warfare enhancements but also acknowledged that it still lacked information about the motivations and decision making behind China's policy making in this area because of the considerable secrecy surrounding Chinese national security policy making and the reluctance of Chinese leaders to engage in genuine transparency on these issues (U.S. Department of Defense 2004, 7).

The 2006 edition of this Pentagon report noted continuing Chinese interest in developing radiofrequency, laser, and ASAT weapons, mentioned that China would eventually deploy satellites with advanced imagery, reconnaissance, and earth resource systems capabilities for military purposes to supplement existing coverage with Russian and Western technology. This report also acknowledged that China had launched its second manned space mission on October 12, 2005 with its two-person crew returning safely five days later after performing experiments in space for the first time. There was also acknowledgement of press reports stating that China wants to perform its first space walk in 2007, rendezvous and dock spacecraft between 2009–2012, and have a manned space station by 2020 (U.S. Department of Defense 2006, 32–34).

Besides its launch facilities at Jiuquan, Taiyuan, and Xichang, China maintains an advanced telemetry, tracking, and command network including eight domestic ground-tracking stations, foreign ground-tracking stations in Kiribati in the South Pacific and Namibia, four tracking ships, and two space control facilities. It also established a Space Target and Debris Observation and Research Center in March 2005 to help prevent space

Chinese astronauts Fei Junlong (L) and Nie Haisheng wave as they walk to the launch tower of the Jiuquan Satellite Launch Center in northwest China's Gansu Province on October 12, 2005. *(China Newsphoto/Reuters/Corbis)*

debris strikes against satellites and manned spacecraft (Center for Nonproliferation Studies 2006(a), 1–2).

China's three Beidou 1 navigation satellites, the most recent being launched in May 2003, are believed to have the capability to improve the accuracy of China's long-range weapons and data available to its military forces. The Zi Yuan remote satellites that are part of the China–Brazil Earth Resources Program are believed to have an estimated three- to nine-meter resolution and are considered useful for military purposes despite Chinese assertions that they are used for civilian purposes. There is some evidence that China wants to upgrade its satellites so they have one-meter resolution capability, which may enable them to have the ability to broadcast military data such as maps and enemy force deployments to small field stations (Center for Nonproliferation Studies 2006(b), 1).

China is clearly intent on becoming a major political, economic, and military participant in space. Whether this involvement is benign or has assertive or even hostile military intent toward the United States or other countries is the subject of considerable debate (Lele 2005, 67-75; Lim 2004, 30-39; McCabe 2003, 73-83; Murray and Antonellis 2003, 645-652; Saunders 2005, 21-23). Nevertheless, keeping track of Chinese military space trends and developments and related regional security developments such as its January 2007 destruction of a polar-orbiting weather satellite (British Broadcasting Corporation 2007, 1–3) and related regional security developments such as North Korea's efforts to develop ballistic missiles (Bennett 2004, 79–108) will become increasingly important for the foreseeable future for U.S. and other international military policymakers and for those studying international security trends and developments. These trends, as described in this section on China, make it likely that China will become the primary competitor to U.S. military space policy aspirations in the years and decades to come.

Europe

Many European countries including France, Germany, and the United Kingdom have sought to develop indigenous national space programs and have achieved varying degrees of success with these programs. The growing importance of the European Union (EU) in continental politics and policymaking has influenced European efforts to work together to achieve cooperative solutions to various public policy issues. Civilian space policy and military space policy have gradually become a greater part of this trend, and the concluding section of this chapter will examine the factors shaping historical and contemporary European military space policy.

A 2003 review of European space policy produced under the auspices of the European Union's Institute for Security Studies makes the following appraisal of space policy in European integration.

Space developments have been independent of the general process of European integration... different civilian and military bodies, either exclusively national or acting through various partnerships, have contributed to defining space policy and developing industrial activities. The European Space Agency has become the main authority in the European space industry. However, the growing role of the European Union, the development of military space activities, and changes in the industrial sector are new features that have to be taken into account along with the internal evolution of the national space sectors in individual European member countries (Silvestri 2003, 11):

Following World War II, the United Kingdom secretly began development of the Blue Streak intermediate range ballistic missile program in 1955 and in 1959 began cooperation with the United States on the Ariel scientific satellite, but the British rejected a 1958 proposal to cooperate on space technology with other European nations. Intellectual and policy changes within Britain's then governing Conservative Party would result in the decision to pursue greater cooperation with Europe during the 1960s, and the British would began turning away from the idea of developing their own nationally unique military space capability (Madders 1997, 5–25).

The first attempts for more unified Western European space policy collaboration began during the 1960s. The European Launcher Development Organization (ELDO) began when its convention was signed on March 29, 1962 by Australia, Belgium, France, West Germany, Italy, the Netherlands, and the United Kingdom to give these countries a collaborative space launch capability; it began operations on February 29, 1964 (Madders 1997, 41–55; de Maria 1993; Krige 1994).

Just over two months later, European countries signed a convention creating the European Space Research Organization (ESRO) on June 14, 1962. Signatories to this pact were Belgium, Denmark, France, West Germany, Italy, the Netherlands, Spain, Sweden,

Switzerland, and the United Kingdom, and ESRO began operations on March 20, 1964 (Madders 1997, 41–42; Krige 1994). ESRO's mission was to promote peaceful space research and technology collaboration among European states. Its infrastructure would eventually include the European Space Technology Center (ESTEC) in Delft and later Noordwijk, the Netherlands where research, design, development, integration, and testing activities would be handled; an adjacent European Space Laboratory would carry out ESTEC research programs; the European Space Data Center at Darmstadt, West Germany would coordinate tracking, telemetry, and command stations; a sounding rocket facility at Kiruna, Sweden; and the European Space Research Institute (ESRIN) in Frascati, Italy, the responsibility of which was theoretical space science work (Madders 1997, 55–61).

This arrangement in which ELDO and ESRO served as dual European space policy agencies continued for another decade. Dissatisfaction with this arrangement among Western European countries resulted in the replacement of these two agencies with the European Space Agency (ESA) in 1975. This dissatisfaction with European space policy agencies began as early as 1966 when arguments began to be made that there were too many European space organizations and that there needed to be more cost-effective use of these organizations and their capabilities. This desire for greater space policy uniformity was given increased impetus by the 1971 British entry into the European Common Market, which demonstrated a heightened determination by that country to play an enhanced role in European affairs. This move was further accelerated by Michael Heseltine, the British official responsible for space policy. He sought to enhance coordination of British national space capabilities by urging that similar initiatives be taken at the European level (Krige, Russo, and Sebesta 2000, 23).

Continental negotiations to begin revising the organizational structure of European space agencies began in 1971 and continued until 1975. The Convention creating the ESA was signed on May 30, 1975 by Belgium, Denmark, France, West Germany, Italy, the Netherlands, Spain, Sweden, Switzerland, and the United Kingdom. Ireland signed the Convention on December 31, 1975, Canada became a cooperating state in December 1978, Austria signed an Association Agreement with ESA in October 1979, and ESA officially came into existence when France deposited its ratification instrument on October 30, 1980 (Krige, Russo, and Sebesta 2000, 23; Krige and Russo 2000; Bonnet and Manno 1994; Zabusky 1995).

In its founding charter ESA described its institutional mandate as follows:

> The purpose of the Agency shall be to provide for and to promote, for exclusively peaceful purposes, cooperation among European states in space research and technology and their space applications, with a view to their being used for scientific purposes and for operational space applications (Madders 1997, 180).

An important application of ESA's civilian space capabilities was its development of the Ariane launch vehicles, which were first test launched in 1979 and began operational

Ariane 5G ready to lift off from Europe's Spaceport in Kourou, French Guiana in 2004. *(European Space Agency)*

launches in 1982. ESA reached an agreement with France to launch these vehicles from a preexisting French launch facility in use since 1964 at Kourou in French Guiana in northeast South America. Kourou is approximately 500 kilometers north of the equator and this location makes it highly suitable for launching satellites into geostationary transfer orbit, which requires few changes to a satellite's trajectory. Kourou's location also enables launches to benefit from the "slingshot" effect of the energy created by the earth's rotation speed around the axis of the north and south poles, which enhances launcher speed consequently saving fuel and money while extending satellite life. Through spring 2004, the ESA had spent 1.6 billion euros developing and enhancing Kourou's ground facilities and infrastructure (Smith 2001, 8; Krige, Russo, and Sebasta 2000, 18–22; European Space Agency 2004, 1–2).

Although ESA began with a strictly civilian mission and orientation, geopolitical developments in the 1980s caused European countries to began looking at possible military and defense applications of space and how ESA might be able to play a role in supporting national military space policies that might have the potential to become European in scope.

Impetus for this reexamination of ESA's civilian-only charter was influenced by President Ronald Reagan's proposed SDI in 1983, which caused some European political figures to see space as having military as well as political applications. A leading European leader responding to this thinking was French president François Mitterand (1916–1996).

In a February 7, 1984 speech in the Netherlands, Mitterand asserted that if Europe were capable of launching a manned space station enabling it to observe, react, and deter possible threats it would enhance European defense and be a response suitable to what he saw as emerging military realities (Scheffran 1999, 92).

The Western European Union (WEU), a European intergovernmental organization concerned with national security (Western European Union 2002) issued a 1984 report advocating an increased military component for European space activities. This prescient document maintained that space would play a leading role in future warfare, that the force projection capability differences between space-faring and non-space–faring nations would be similar to the difference between nuclear and nonnuclear nations, and that ESA should look at developing ASAT and missile defense capabilities (Scheffran 1999, 92–93).

Further support for European military space programs came from reports produced by the German Society for Foreign Policy during the late 1980s and 1990. These studies recommended that satellites be used for applications such as reconnaissance, communications, early warning, disarmament verification, and surveillance of emerging security threats such as ballistic missiles (Scheffran 1999, 93).

WEU issued an additional report on ballistic missile defense in November 1992 that sought to build on its 1984 findings. This report acknowledged Europe was not threatened by ballistic missile attack from the former Soviet Union, but stressed the emerging danger of proliferating ballistic missile technology and the absence of security of nuclear, biological, and chemical warheads stored on the territory of former Soviet republics that were now part of the Commonwealth of Independent States. WEU went on to warn that numerous third world countries in the Mediterranean and Middle East were making concerted efforts to acquire ballistic missiles capable of reaching Europe and that European countries should work on developing ballistic missile defenses (Scheffran 1999, 96–97).

Despite these WEU warnings of the growing military importance of space to European countries and the increasing security threat from ballistic missile technology proliferation, European countries and the European Union have been slow to take substantive steps to address these situations. A 1999 British analysis for this slow European response to space's increasing military importance provides useful background, guidance, and context.

There are three fundamental reasons why a European perspective differs significantly from that of either the United States or the United Kingdom. The first is Europe's fragmentation; because Europe is not a unitary body, the development of any European policy requires the agreement—or at least the tacit consent—of a number of different states, each with their own political agendas to be taken into account. Secondly, the historical background to the development of space research and activity differs within Europe. Historically, the driving force behind the early days of space activity in the United States, and to a large extent in the United Kingdom, was the military. However, this motivating factor has not been the case at the European level. The originators of European space research were scientists rather than the military or politicians (McLean 1999, 47).

An additional decisive factor prompting a lackadaisical European response to military space issues concerns the European national security relationship with the United States and the NATO alliance.

Finally, reliance on the United States is a fundamental reason. The security architecture of Western Europe stems from the North Atlantic Treaty. The transatlantic partnership that is at the heart of NATO is the bedrock of European security, and, within the NATO framework, each of the member states contributes to the security of the others. In terms of military space capability, the United States undoubtedly has the greatest panoply of space assets, and the European members of NATO have seen little reason to duplicate such assets. With a few exceptions, the European allies have been content to assume that, when necessary, U.S. military space capability would be activated (McLean 1999, 47).

Some European military thinkers have recognized the need for Europe to develop an expanded military space capability. There is general acknowledgement that European countries possess the individual national and collective industrial and space science capabilities to develop such a capacity, including ballistic missile defenses. Further, it is also recognized that a European theater missile defense system under NATO auspices should include sensors for early warning and surveillance of ballistic missile attack and missile launch, an interceptor to destroy ballistic missiles at any stage of flight, and necessary battle management and C4I capabilities to handle requisite data processing, communications, and information dissemination skills for ballistic missile defense (Schmidt and Verschuur 1997, 3–5).

The 1990s and early years of the 2000s saw some tentative steps towards expanded European military space capabilities. One example of this is the Galileo satellite system. The European Commission (EC), the European Union's executive organization, proposed Galileo in 1999 for radio-navigation purposes with the project being jointly funded by EU and ESA. In May 2003, these two organizations removed barriers to the Galileo's development (European Commission 2003, 013).

Although publicized as a civilian satellite, Galileo has military applications. An analysis of this system by the European Union's Institute for Security Studies mentions that Galileo's position, navigation, and timing (PNT) capabilities enable it to provide military planners and commanders the ability to achieve greater management effectiveness of infrastructure, troops, and munitions. Galileo's global coverage also makes it possible for its services to be offered or sold to interested parties, which could produce unintended consequences and produce troubling security implications for the EU and its allies (Lindstrom and Gasparini 2003, 4).

The importance of global navigation satellite systems (GNSS) such as Galileo in managing military applications helps U.S. and allied militaries work together in a variety of operational and logistical capacities including positioning and directional information and guiding munitions to intended targets. One analysis describes how GNSS systems such as Galileo or the United States' GPS satellites can influence combat operations.

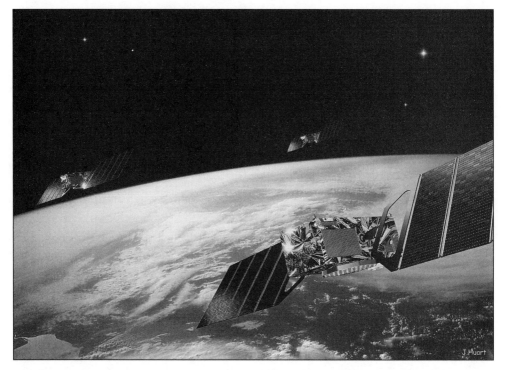

Artist's concept of the European Space Agency's Galileo satellite system. *(European Space Agency/ J. Huart)*

The capability to synchronize the movement of different units on the battlefield from space, air, sea, and land provides the current and future field commander with unprecedented area awareness. Combined with the accurate weapons guidance provided by GNSS, there is improved strike effectiveness that may minimize the amount of collateral damage caused during an operation. The possibility to strike from a distance reduces risks to military personnel involved in operations. The use of navigation and positioning technology may also reduce the risk of accidents due to friendly fire. Likewise, PNT services can lower risks to personnel operating or patrolling around unmarked borders where boundary transgressions can have dire implications (Lindstrom and Gasparini 2003, 7).

The EU hopes to have launched and deployed a total of 30 Galileo satellites and affiliated ground stations by 2008. An additional belief of EU policymakers is that Galileo assets will benefit increasing international demand for global satellite services and derivative products, which they believe will increase 25% a year and create 100,000 skilled jobs by 2020 (European Commission 2003, 014).

Concern over Galileo's military capabilities has been expressed by some in the U.S. military. One assessment asserts that Galileo reflects a European belief that they should have greater independence from the United States in space policy and that Europe believes Galileo has superior performance capabilities than GPS, that it is more accurate and reliable, and that it has fewer design vulnerabilities than GPS. This same assessment also asserts that Galileo gives Europe an economic opportunity to obtain international satellite market share from the United States and become the global standard in this industry (Beidleman 2005, 150).

Additional concerns expressed by the author of this critical assessment of Galileo's military capabilities as applied to U.S. security are that Galileo could interfere with GPS signals and nullify U.S. navigational warfare capabilities, that Galileo's encryption program has questionable security, and that Galileo's projected widespread international usage and participation could increase future hostile use of Galileo against U.S. national interests (Beidleman 2005, 150–151).

In anticipation of such concerns the United States and EU announced in January 2004 that they were working on a GPS/Galileo cooperation agreement, which would enable Galileo to meet its performance requirements while protecting U.S. and NATO national security needs by separating the signals emitted by Galileo and GPS military services (United States Mission to the European Union 2004, 1–2). Agreement between these parties on this subject was reached and signed at a U.S.–EU conference in Shannon, Ireland on June 26, 2004 (United States Mission to the European Union 2006, 1).

Another European space program with military aspects is the Global Monitoring for the Environment and Security (GMES) initiative. GMES was initiated in 1998 to create an operational system for providing and using space-based information. GMES seeks to establish an independent European capability for Earth observation and monitoring by collaboratively pooling national and multilateral European space assets. An example in this latter category is a 2000 Franco–German decision to develop an independent joint military satellite system. GMES will support both civil and military national satellites used for military purposes by enhancing imagery and mapping capacities (Center for Nonproliferation Studies 2006(c), 1; Fiorenza 2000, 46).

Further official EU support for GMES was provided at the Gothenberg Summit in June 2001 when the European Council called for establishing GMES by 2008. GMES was set up as a collaborative venture between the European Commission and ESA to provide independent, operational, and relevant support in various objectives with its military applications stressing the importance of supporting the EU's Common Foreign and Security Policy (CFSP) and providing early warning capabilities (European Commission 2003, 015–016; Silvestri 2003, 12).

Besides these tentative European forays into military and intelligence uses of space that can augment existing national military space capabilities, the EU has also sought to promote disarmament in space. The following series of quotations by prominent EU policymakers reflects such inconsistent European thinking on military uses of space. EU Research commissioner Phillippe Busquin made the following observations on March 19, 2003 advocating an expanded European military space presence:

> Security must be a key element of a European space policy. The global tensions that we face today are an irrefutable argument for investing in effective space program to meet our security needs, be they civil or military. If China is able to send

astronauts into space by the end of this year, there should be no reason why Europe cannot develop the space assets that are fundamental to any credible security policy. We have the technological know-how in Europe, but we need to better organise ourselves to define our ambitions and realise them (Center for Nonproliferation Studies 2006(d), 3).

A February 16, 2004 statement by ESA director Jean-Jacques Dordain commented that the distinction between civilian and military space systems made limited sense because the same satellites could be used for both purposes. He went on to assert that defense was the primary force stimulating the development of space systems offering civilian benefits while contending that European civil institutions played the primary role in European security and defense (Center for Nonproliferation Studies 2006(d), 2).

An additional illustration of what can be seen as contradictory European attitudes toward military uses of space was reflected by Ambassador Chris Sanders to a United Nations committee on October 19, 2004. Sanders said the EU was aware of the international community's increasing involvement in space initiatives, which he said should be for peaceful purposes to prevent an "arms race" in space and that the EU believed that the UN's Conference on Disarmament was the only multilateral international organization for negotiating space disarmament agreements (Center for Nonproliferation Studies 2006(d), 1).

An effort to lessen the confusing and contradictory nature of European attitudes toward space military applications was provided in a report produced by the Austrian think-tank the European Space Policy Institute (ESPI). ESPI's November 2005 report *A New Paradigm for European Space Policy: A Proposal* features a number of useful recommendations for bringing greater coherence to European military space programs. These recommendations include enhancing national capability coordination and reducing duplication in military communications' C4Is; breaking down barriers between military and civilian space programs and between ESA programs and security-oriented national or multinational programs; recognizing that an enhanced military program would be beneficial to dual technology aspects of space science and technology and achieve cost efficiencies for civil and military applications; allowing technology developed for civil programs such as meteorological satellites to be used for defense applications while also considering that restrictions placed on civil programs may limit their defense utility; and increasing European commitment to space-based applications with liberally defined defense and security missions. Examples of such missions would include treaty verification, disaster and environmental monitoring, and space surveillance (European Space Policy Institute 2005, 19; McLean 1995, 239–248; Logsdon 2002, 271–280; Peter 2005, 265–296; Gleason 2006, 7–41).

The ESPI report went on to assert that EU space policy should consider how the European space industry would benefit from an expansion of defense and security space programs since participating companies would receive benefits from dual use technology and cost savings by developing common platforms and components. The report also stressed its belief that general European industrial revenues would increase as a result of heightened spending in defense and security space programs (European Space Policy Institute 2005, 23).

European military space efforts will probably experience incremental growth because of the desire of some European leaders to achieve greater independence from U.S. military space policies and overall U.S. national security policies. These leaders will have to struggle against other individual leaders and countries who are more comfortable with U.S. military space policy leadership and do not wish any alterations to reduce the strength of the NATO alliance. Programs such as Galileo and GMES are likely to continue and will gradually increase some European military space capabilities in areas such as threat detection and surveillance.

The ongoing reluctance of many European nations to surrender national security sovereignty to the purported European Common Foreign and Security Policy and conflicting EU stances on whether space should be militarized will continue and make it difficult to produce a unified European military space policy posture. This lack of European security policy cohesion may prove particularly detrimental if Iran's nascent nuclear program develops into a credible security threat to Europe and may have other negative consequences for collective European security and the security of individual European countries. Given the increasing economic and international security importance of space, it is imperative that European nations work collaboratively with the United States or develop their own effective space security architecture or face the prospect that space could be controlled by nations and interests hostile to democratic governance, political pluralism, and free market economics.

References and Further Reading

An Act to Authorize Appropriations for Fiscal Year 2000 and for Military Activities of the Department of Defense for Military Construction, and for Defense Activities of the Department of Energy, to Prescribe Personnel Strengths, for Such Fiscal Year for the Armed Forces, and for Other Purposes. Public Law 106–65. 113 U.S. Statutes at Large (2000), 781–782.

Aslund, A. and M. B. Olcott, eds. 1999. *Russia After Communism.* Washington, D.C.: Carnegie Endowment for International Peace.

Beidleman, S. W. 2005. "Galileo vs. GPS: Balancing for Position in Space." *Astropolitics: The International Journal of Space Power and Policy* 3 (2): 150–151.

Bennett, B. 2004. "Weapons of Mass Destruction: The North Korean Threat." *The Korean Journal of Defense Analysis* 26 (2): 79–108.

Bermudez, Jr., J. S. 1999. *A History of Ballistic Missile Development in the DPRK.* Monterey, CA: Center for Nonproliferation Studies.

Bille, M. and E. Lishock. 2004. *The First Space Race: Launching the World's First Satellites.* College Station, TX: Texas A&M University Press.

Bluth, C. 1992. *Soviet Strategic Arms Policy Before SALT.* Cambridge, UK: Cambridge University Press.

Bolonkin, A. 1991. *The Development of Soviet Rocket Engines (For Strategic Missiles)*. Falls Church, VA: Delphic Associates.

Bonnet, R. M. and V. Manno. 1994. *International Cooperation in Space: The Example of the European Space Agency*. Cambridge, MA: Harvard University Press.

Brandon, Henry., ed. 1992. *In Search of a New World: The Future of U.S.-European Relations*. Washington, D.C.: Brookings Institution.

British Broadcasting Corporation News. 2007. "Concern Over China's Missile Test," 1–3; January 19. [Online article or information; retrieved 1/23/07.] http://news.bbc.co.uk/2/hi/asia-pacific/6276543.stm.

Center for Nonproliferation Studies. 2005?(a). "Current and Future Space Security: Russia." [Online article or information; retrieved 6/7/06.] http://cns.miis.edu/research/space/russia/.

Center for Nonproliferation Studies. 2005?(b). "Current and Future Space Security: Russia Military Programs." [Online article or information; retrieved 6/7/06.] http://cns.miis.edu/research/space/russia/mil.htm.

Center for Nonproliferation Studies. 2005?(c). "Current and Future Space Security: Russia: Launch Capabilities." [Online article or information; retrieved 6/7/06.] http://cns.miis.edu/research/space/russia/launch.htm.

Center for Nonproliferation Studies. 2006(a). "China: Launch Capabilities." [Online article or information; retrieved 6/12/06.] http://cns.miis.edu/research/space/china/launch.htm.

Center for Nonproliferation Studies. 2006(b). "China: Military Programs." [Online article or information; retrieved 6/12/06.] http://cns.miis.edu/research/space/china/mil.htm.

Center for Nonproliferation Studies. 2006(c). "European Union: Military Programs." [Online article or information; retrieved 6/20/06.] http://cns.miis.edu/research/space/eu/mil.htm.

Center for Nonproliferation Studies. 2006(d). "European Union: Arms Control Proposals and Statements." [Online article or information; retrieved 6/20/06.] http://cns.miis.edu/research/space/eu/arms.htm.

China Internet Information Center. 2000. *China's Space Activities*. [Online article or information; retrieved 6/12/06.] www.china.org.cn/e-white.

China Internet Information Center. 2002. *China's National Defense in 2002*. [Online article or information; retrieved 6/12/06.] www.china.org.cn/e-white/20021209/VII.htm.

China Internet Information Center. 2004. *China's National Defense in 2004*. [Online article or information; retrieved 6/12/06.] www.china.org.cn/e-white/20041227/X.htm.

Cochran, T. B., R. S. Norris, and O. A. Bukharin. 1995. *Making the Russian Bomb: From Stalin to Yeltsin*. Boulder, CO: Westview Press.

Collins, J. M. 1989. *Military Space Forces: The Next 50 Years*. Washington, D.C.: Pergamon-Brassey's.

Cooley, A. 2000/01. "Imperial Wreckage: Property Rights, Sovereignty, and Security in the Post-Soviet Space." *International Security* 25 (3): 113–116.

de Maria, M. 1993. *The History of ELDO*. Noordwijk, the Netherlands: ESA Publications Division.

Descisciolo, D. 2005. "China's Space Development and Nuclear Strategy." In *China's Nuclear Force Modernization,* edited by L. J. Goldstein and A. S. Erickson. Newport, RI: Naval War College Press, 52. [Online article or information; retrieved 6/9/06.] http://purl.access.gpo.gov/GPO/LPS65977.

DeWolf, H. G. 1989. *SDI and Arms Control.* Washington, D.C.: National Institute for Strategic Studies. [Online article or information; retrieved 6/9/06.] http://purl.access.gpo.gov/GPO/LPS31603.

European Commission. 2003. *White Paper: Space: A New European Frontier for an Expanding European Union: An Action Plan for Implementing the European Space Policy.* [Online article or information; retrieved 6/16/06.] http://ec.europa.eu/comm/space/whitepaper/pdf/spwhpap_en.pdf.

European Space Agency. 2004. "Europe's Spaceport Launchers." [Online article or information; retrieved 6/15/06.] www.esa.int/SPECIALS/Launchers_Europe_s_Spaceport/.

European Space Policy Institute. 2005. *A New Paradigm for European Space Policy: A Proposal.* Vienna: European Space Policy Institute.

Falk, R. and T. Szentes, eds. 1997. *A New Europe in the Changing Global System.* Tokyo and New York: United Nations University Press.

Federation of American Scientists. n.d(a). "Plesetsk Cosmodrome 62.8 N 40.7 E." [Online article or information; retrieved 6/2/06.] www.fas.org/spp/guide/russia/facility/plesetsk.htm.

Federation of American Scientists. n.d(b). "Russia and Anti-Satellite Programs." [Online article or information; retrieved 6/2/06.] www.fas.org/spp/guide/russia/military/asat/.

Federation of American Scientists. n.d(c). "Co-orbital ASAT." [Online article or information; retrieved 6/5/06.] www.fas.org/spp/guide/russia/military/asat/coorb.htm.

Feigenbaum, E. A. 2003. *China's Techno-Warriors: National Security and Strategic Competition from the Nuclear to the Information Age.* Stanford, CA: Stanford University Press.

Fiorenza, N. 2000. "Joint Eyes in the Sky: European Military Cooperation Reaches into Space." *Armed Forces Journal International* 138 (1): 46.

Fitzgerald, M. C. 1987. *The Soviet Military on SDI.* Alexandria, VA: Center for Naval Analyses.

Fitzgerald, M. C. 1994. "The Russian Military's Strategy for 'Sixth Generation' Warfare." *Orbis* 38 (3): 457–476.

Frieman, W. 2001. "The Arms Control and Ballistic Missile Defense Costs of a Chinese Conflict." In *The Costs of Conflict: The Impact on China of a Future War,* edited by A. Scobell, 163–185. Carlisle Barracks, PA: U.S. Army War College Strategic Studies Institute.

Gertz, B. 2000. "The North Korean Missile Threat." *Air Force Magazine* 83 (1): 38–43.

Glaser, B. S. and B. M. Garrett. 1986. "Chinese Perspectives on the Strategic Defense Initiative." *Problems of Communism* 34 (March-April): 28–44.

Gleason, M. P. 2006. "European Union Space Initiatives: The Political Will for Increasing European Space Power." *Astropolitics: The International Journal of Space Power and Policy* 4 (1): 7–41.

Gorin, P. 1998. "Zenit: The Soviet Response to Corona." In *Eye in the Sky: The Story of the Corona Spy Satellites,* edited by D. A. Day, J. M. Logsdon, and B. Latell, 157–170. Washington, D.C.: Smithsonian Institution Press.

Harford, J. J. 1997. *Korolev: How One Man Masterminded the Soviet Drive to Beat America to the Moon.* New York: Wiley.

Hyodo, S. 2005. "First Ever Sino-Russian Joint Military Exercises-Russia Rapidly Moving Closer to China. Tokyo: National Institute for Defense Studies. [Online article or information; retrieved 6/20/06.] www.nids.go.jp/english/dissemination/briefing/2006/pdf/092.pdf.

Johnson-Freese, J. 2003. "Houston, We Have a Problem: China and the Race to Space." *Current History* 102 (September): 259–265.

Killian, J. R. 1977. *Sputnik, Scientists, and Eisenhower: A Memoir of the First Special Assistant to the President for Science and Technology.* Cambridge, MA: MIT Press.

Kornukov, A.M. 2001. "Apropos of the Grown Role of Confrontation in the Aerospace Sphere and Air Force Tasks in 21st-Century Military Operations." *Military Thought* 10 (5): 6–12.

Krige, J. 1994. *Reflections on Europe in Space.* Noordwijk, the Netherlands: ESA Publications Division.

Krige, J. and A. Russo. 2000. *A History of the European Space Agency 1958–1987: Volume I: The Story of ESRO and ELDO.* Paris: European Space Agency. [Online article or information; retrieved 6/15/06.] www.esa.int/esapub/sp/sp1235/sp1235v1web.pdf.

Krige, J., A. Russo, and L. Sebasta. 2000. *A History of the European Space Agency 1958–1987: Volume II: The Story of ESA, 1973 to 1987.* Paris: European Space Agency. [Online article or information; retrieved 6/15/06.] www.esa.int.esapub/sp/sp1235/sp1235v2web.pdf.

Launius, R. D., J. M. Logsdon, and R. W. Smith, eds. 2000. *Reconsidering Sputnik: Forty Years Since the Soviet Satellite.* Amsterdam: Harwood Academic.

Lee, C.M. 2001. "North Korean Missiles: Strategic Implications and Policy Responses." *The Pacific Review* 14 (1): 85–120.

Lele, A. 2005. "China: A Growing Military Space Power." *Astropolitics: The International Journal of Space Power and Policy* 31 (1): 67–75.

Lim, T. W. 2004. "Implications of the People's Liberation Army's Technocratization for U.S. Power in East Asia." *Asian Affairs* 31 (1): 30–39.

Lindstrom, G. and G. Gasparini. 2003. *The Galileo Satellite System and Its Security Implications.* Paris: European Union Institute for Security Studies. [Online article or information; retrieved 6/16/06.] www.iss-eu.org/occasion/occ44.pdf.

Logsdon, J. M. 2002. "A Security Space Capability for Europe?: Implications for U.S. Policy." *Space Policy* 18 (4): 271–280.

MacInnis, P. 2003. *Rockets: Sulfur, Sputnik, and Scramjets.* Crows Nest, Australia: Allen & Unwin.

Madders, K. 1997. *A New Force at a New Frontier: Europe's Development in the Space Field in the Light of its Main Actors, Policies, Law and Activities From its Beginnings up to the Present.* Cambridge, UK: Cambridge University Press.

Mathers, J. G. 1998. "A Fly in Outer Space: Soviet Ballistic Missile Defence During the Khrushchev Period." *The Journal of Strategic Studies* 21(2): 38–40.

McCabe, T.R. "The Chinese Air Force and Air and Space Power. 2003. " *Air and Space Power Journal,* 17 (3)(Fall): 73-83.

McDougall, W. A. 1997. *The Heavens and the Earth: A Political History of the Space Age.* Baltimore: Johns Hopkins University Press.

McLean, A. 1995. "Integrating European Security Through Space." *Space Policy* 11 (4): 239–248.

McLean, A. 1999. "European Exploitation of Space: When Rather Than If." *RUSI Journal* 144 (5): 47.

Menshikov, V.A. 2000. "Russia's Military-Space Policy in the 21st Century." *Military Thought* 9 (5): 36–39.

Mowthorpe, M. 2002. "The Soviet/Russian Approach to Military Space." *The Journal of Slavic Military Studies* 15(3): 25.

Mulvenon, J., Tanner, M. S., Chase, M. S., Frelinger, D. R., Gompert, D. C., Libicki, M. L., and Pollpeter, K. R. 2006. *Chinese Responses to U.S. Military Transformation and Implications for the Department of Defense.* Santa Monica, CA: Rand Corporation. [Online article or information; retrieved 6/12/06.] www.rand.org/pubs/monographs/2006/RAND_MG340 .pdf.

Murray III, W. S. and R. Antonellis. 2003. "China's Space Program: The Dragon Eyes the Moon (and Us)." *Orbis* 47 (4): 645–652.

NASA History Office. 2007. *Sputnik and the Dawn of the Space Age..* [Online article or information; retrieved 10/24/2007] www.hq.nasa.gov/office/pao/History/sputnik/.

Neufeld, M. J. 1996. *The Rocket and the Reich: Peenemunde and the Coming of the Ballistic Missile Era.* Cambridge, MA: Harvard University Press, 1996.

Nguyen, H. P. 1993. "Russia's Continuing Work on Space Forces." *Orbis* 37(3): 413–23.

Oberg, J. 2002. *Star-Crossed Orbits: Inside the U.S.-Russian Space Alliance.* New York: McGraw-Hill.

Patterson, J. B. 1995. *China's Space Program and Its Implications for the United States.* Maxwell Air Force Base, AL: Air War College Air University.

Peter, N. 2005. "Space and Security: The Emerging Role of Europe." *Astropolitics: The International Journal of Space Power and Policy* 3 (3): 265–296.

Pillsbury, M. 2000. *China Debates the Future Security Environment.* Washington, D.C.: National Defense University Press. [Online article or information; retrieved 6/12/06.] http://purl .access.gpo.gov/GPO/LPS4402.

Portree, D. S. F. 1998. *NASA's Origins and the Dawn of the Space Age.* Washington, D.C.: National Aeronautics and Space Administration, History Office. [Online article or information; retrieved 6/12/2006.] www.hq.nasa.gov/office/pao/History/monograph10/spaceage.html.

Roberts, B. 2003. *China and Ballistic Missile Defense: 1955 to 2002 and Beyond.* Alexandria, VA: Institute for Defense Analyses.

Russian Space Web. 2006(a). "Soviet Intelligence on the German Rocketry." [Online article or information; retrieved 5/26/06.] www.russianspaceweb.com/a4_poland.html.

Russian Space Web. 2006(b). "Searching for a Boss: Origin of the Soviet Rocket Industry." [Online article or information; retrieved 5/26/06.] www.russianspaceweb.com/centers_industry _origin.html.

Russian Space Web. 2006(c). "Tests in Kapustin Yar." [Online article or information; retrieved 5/26/06.] www.russianspaceweb.com/kapyar_a4.html.

Russian Space Web. 2006(d). "Rockets R-1 Family." [Online article or information; retrieved 5/26/06.] www.russianspaceweb.com/r1.html.

Russian Space Web. 2006(e). "Rockets R-2 Family." [Online article or information; retrieved 5/26/06.] www.russianspaceweb.com/r2.html.

Russian Space Web. 2006(f). "Chronology: Missile Race." [Online article or information; retrieved 5/26/06.] www.russianspaceweb.com/chronology_missiles.html.

Russian Space Web. 2006(g). "Rockets: R-5 Family." [Online article or information; retrieved 5/31/06.] www.russianspaceweb.com/r5.html.

Russian Space Web. 2006(h). "Centers: Baikonur: Origins." [Online article or information; retrieved 5/30/06.] www.russianspaceweb.com/baikonur_origin.html.

Russian Space Web. 2006(i). "Rockets: R-7 Family." [Online article or information; retrieved 5/31/06.] www.russianspaceweb.com/r7.html.

Russian Space Web. 2006(j). "Plesetsk." [Online article or information; retrieved 6/2/06.] www .russianspaceweb.com/plesetsk.html.

Russian Space Web. 2006(k). "Title: Chronology: Missile Race." [Online article or information; retrieved 6/2/06.] www.russianspaceweb.com/chronology_missiles.html.

Russian Space Web. 2007. "The Kliper (Clipper) Project in 2006." [Online article or information; retrieved 6/13/07.] www.russianspaceweb.com/kliper_lunar.html.

Saunders, P. C. 2005. "China's Future in Space: Implications for U.S. Security." *AdAstra: The Magazine of the National Space Society* 17 (Spring): 21–23.

Scheffran, J. 1999. "Space Policy and Missile Control in Europe." In *Space Power Interests,* edited by P. Hayes, 92–93, 96–97. Boulder, CO: Westview Press.

Schmidt, A. and F. Verschuur. 1997. *The European Theater Missile Defense Program-A Field for International Cooperation.* Maxwell Air Force Base, AL: Air War College/Air University. [Online article or information; retrieved 6/16/06.] www.au.af.mil/au/awc/awcgate/awc/ 97-166.pdf.

Scobell, A. 2003. *China's Use of Military Force: Beyond the Great Wall and the Long March.* New York: Cambridge University Press.

Siddiqi, A. A. 2003(a). *Sputnik and the Soviet Space Challenge.* Gainesville, FL: University Press of Florida.

Siddiqi, A. A. 2003(b). "The Rockets Red Glare: Technology, Conflict, and Terror in the Soviet Union." *Technology and Culture* 44 (3): 470–501.

Silvestri, S., Blecher, K, Darnis, J. P.,Gasparini, G, Keohane, D, Liegeois, M., Nones, M., Pasco, X., Reinke, N., Riecke, H., Schmitt, B., Sourbes-Verger, I., and Vielhaber, J. 2003. *Space and Security Policy in Europe: Executive Summary.* Paris: European Union Institute for Security Studies. [Online article or information; retrieved 6/14/06.] www.iss-eu.org/occasion/occ48.pdf.

Simon, J., ed. 1990. *Security Implications of SDI: Will We Be More Secure in 2010?* Washington, D.C.: National Defense University Press.

Smith, M. S. 1991. *Space Activities of the United States, Soviet Union and Other Launching Countries/Organizations: 1957–1990.* Washington, D.C.: U.S. Government Printing Office.

Smith, M. S. 2001. *Space Launch Vehicles: Government Activities, Commercial Competition, and Satellite Exports.* Washington, D.C.: Library of Congress, Congressional Research Service.

Smith, M. S. 2005. *China's Space Program: An Overview.* Washington, D.C.: Library of Congress, Congressional Research Service.

Stokes, M. A. 1999. *China's Strategic Modernization: Implications for the United States.* Carlisle Barracks, PA: United States Army War College Strategic Studies Institute.

Szporluk, R. 2000. *Russia, Ukraine, and the Breakup of the Soviet Union.* Stanford, CA: Hoover Institution Press.

Thompson, D. J. and W. R. Morris. 2001. *China in Space: Civilian and Military Developments.* Maxwell Air Force Base, AL: Air University/Air War College. http://purl.access.gpo.gov/ GPO/LPS40021. [Online article or information; retrieved 4/24/00.]June 9, 2006.

Twigg, J. L. 1999. "Russia's Space Program: Continued Turmoil." *Space Policy* 15 (1): 70.

U.S. Central Intelligence Agency. 1954. *Soviet Capabilities and Probable Programs in the Guided Missile Field (NIE 11–6).* Washington, D.C.: Central Intelligence Agency.

U.S. Central Intelligence Agency. 1958. *National Intelligence Estimate 11–5–58: Soviet Capabilities in Guided Missiles and Space Vehicles.* Washington, D.C.: Central Intelligence Agency.

U.S. Central Intelligence Agency. 1962. *National Intelligence Estimate 11–3–62: Soviet Bloc Air and Missile Defense Capabilities Through Mid-1967.* Washington, D.C.: Central Intelligence Agency.

U.S. Central Intelligence Agency. 1967. *NIE 13–8–67 Communist China's Strategic Weapons Program.* Washington, D.C.: Central Intelligence Agency.

U.S. Central Intelligence Agency. 1974. *NIE 13–8–74 China's Strategic Attack Program.* Washington, D.C.: Central Intelligence Agency.

U.S. Central Intelligence Agency. 1983. *Possible Soviet Responses to the U.S. Strategic Defense Initiative.* Washington, D.C.: Central Intelligence Agency.

U.S. Central Intelligence Agency. 1985. *National Intelligence Estimate 11–1–85W: The Soviet Space Program, Key Judgments.* Washington, D.C.: Central Intelligence Agency.

U.S. Central Intelligence Agency. Directorate of Intelligence. 1992. *The Russian Space Launch Vehicle Industry: Looking to Foreign Sales for Survival.* Washington, D.C.: Central Intelligence Agency.

U.S. Congress. House Committee on Science. 1998. *U.S.-Russian Cooperation in Human Spaceflight, Parts I-V.* Washington, D.C.: U.S. Government Printing Office.

U.S. Congress. House Select Committee on U.S. National Security and Military/Commercial Concerns With the People's Republic of China. 1999. *Report.* Washington, D.C.: U.S. Government Printing Office.

U.S. Defense Intelligence Agency. 1984. *Soviet Military Space Doctrine.* Washington, D.C.: Defense Intelligence Agency.

U.S. Department of Defense. 1983. *Soviet Military Power.* Washington, D.C.: U.S. Government Printing Office.

U.S. Department of Defense. 1986. *Soviet Military Power.* Washington, D.C.: U.S. Government Printing Office.

U.S. Department of Defense. 1988. *Soviet Military Power: An Assessment of the Threat.* Washington, D.C.: U.S. Government Printing Office.

U.S. Department of Defense. 1989. *Soviet Military Power: Prospects for Change.* Washington, D.C.: U.S. Government Printing Office.

U.S. Department of Defense. 1990. *Soviet Strategic and Space Programs.* Washington, D.C.: U.S. Department of Defense.

U.S. Department of Defense. 1991. *Military Forces in Transition.* Washington, D.C.: U.S. Government Printing Office.

U.S. Department of Defense. 2000. *Annual Report on the Military Power of the People's Republic of China 2000.* [Online article or information; retrieved 6/12/06.] www.dod.mil/news/Jun2000/china06222000.htm.

U.S. Department of Defense. 2002. *Annual Report on the Military Power of the People's Republic of China 2002.* [Online article or information; retrieved 6/12/06.] http://purl.access.gpo.gov/GPO/LPS24358.

U.S. Department of Defense. 2003. *Annual Report on the Military Power of the People's Republic of China 2003.* [Online article or information; retrieved 6/12/06.] http://purl.access.gpo.gov/GPO/LPS24358.

U.S. Department of Defense. 2004. *Annual Report on the Military Power of the People's Republic of China 2004.* [Online article or information; retrieved 6/12/06.] http://purl.access.gpo.gov/GPO/LPS24358.

U.S. Department of Defense. 2006. *Annual Report on the Military Power of the People's Republic of China 2006.* [Online article or information; retrieved 6/12/06.] http://purl.access.gpo.gov/ GPO/LPS24358.

U.S. National Academies. 2005. "The International Geophysical Year." [Online article or information; retrieved 5/31/06.] www.nas.edu/history/igy/.

United States Mission to the European Union. 2004. "U.S., EU Working on Global Positioning System Agreement." [Online article or information; retrieved 6/16/06.] http://useu.usmission .gov/Article.asp?ID=E255A7F0-B78E-4b02-BA5F-1BE913DE8630.

United States Mission to the European Union. 2006. "Galileo & GPS." [Online article or information; retrieved 6/16/06.] http://useu.usmission.gov/Dossiers/Galileo_GPS/default.asp.

Western European Union. 2002. "Homepage." [Online article or information; retrieved 6/15/06.] www.weu.int/.

Zabusky, S. E. 1995. *Launching Europe: An Ethnography of European Cooperation in Space Science.* Princeton, NJ: Princeton University Press.

Zak, A. 2002. "Konstantin Tsiolkovsky Slept Here." *Air and Space Smithsonian* 17 (3): 62–69.

Zelikow, P. and C. Rice. 1995. *Germany Unified and Europe Transformed: A Study in Statecraft.* Cambridge, MA: Harvard University Press.

Zhang, H. 2005. "Action/Reaction: U.S. Space Weaponization and China." *Arms Control Today* 35 (December): 6–11.

Zhuk, E.I. 2003. "Astronautics: The Military-Political Aspect." *Military Thought* 12 (2): 209–216.

5

Selected U.S. Laws and International Agreements on Military Uses of Space

S INCE THE BEGINNING of space exploration, national governments and international government organizations have sought to prevent space from becoming an arena of human conflict. They have sought to codify this desire into national and international law through a series of legal agreements that have attempted to prevent space from becoming a forum for national or international military confrontation. Most of these agreements have been done under United Nations (UN) auspices, and the UN's Office for Outer Space Affairs (UNOOSA) serves as a clearinghouse and monitoring mechanism for keeping track of these agreements. Some of these pacts have been bilateral agreements between militarily prominent nations like the United States and the former Soviet Union.

The quality, reliability, and viability of these and similar arms control agreements is controversial with different assesments of these agreeements appearing in scholarly literature and political debate (Wallop, 1987). This chapter presents background information on these agreements and the contextual content when they were ratified. One of these agreements, the 1972 Antiballistic Missile (ABM) Treaty between the United States and the former Soviet Union is no longer in effect having been terminated by the United States in 2001. The other agreements remain in force.

These agreements are the Communications Satellite Act (1962), Limited Test Ban Treaty (1963), International Agreement on Peaceful Uses of Outer Space (1967), International Agreement on the Rescue of Astronauts, the Return of Astronauts, and the Return of Objects Launched into Outer Space (1968), Antiballistic Missile Treaty (1972), Liability Convention (1972), Registration Convention (1976), Moon Agreement (1984), and Ballistic Missile Launch Notification Agreement (1988).

Communications Satellite Act

The modern U.S. communication satellite industry began with congressional passage of the Communications Satellite Act (COMSAT) in 1962. This statute sought to establish

NASA astronauts repair an International Telecommunications Satellite in 1992. *(NASA)*

a framework for providing a commercial satellite system to serve international economic needs and it enabled the United States to join with other countries in forming the International Telecommunications Satellite Organization (INTELSAT) to provide basic telecommunications services. These services including satellite television, wireless phone service, and broadband Internet access have revolutionized personal, commercial, governmental, and international economic and political activity.

This legislation remains applicable nearly four and half decades after its initial enactment. The United States remains heavily involved in international satellite organizations such as INTELSAT and International Maritime Satellite Organization (INMARSAT). The continuing and growing importance of satellite technologies in areas such as wireless communications, computer networking, space electronics, and other applications signify that COMSAT's impact will be felt by U.S. and international users of satellite communications services for the foreseeable future (U.S. Congress, Senate Committee on Commerce, Science, and Transportation, Subcommittee on Communications 1999; Lee 1977; Musolf 1983; Schnapf 1985; Galloway 1992).

Selected provisions from this important legislation include giving new telecommunication services maximum availability and global coverage as soon as possible with particular emphasis on providing these services to less developed countries; U.S. participation in this agreement occurring through a governmentally regulated private corporation; State Department assistance to U.S. businesses desirous of entering this emerging global marketplace; and the president being responsible for ensuring that U.S. relationships with applicable foreign and international commercial and governmental organizations are in U.S. national interest (Communications Satellite Act of 1962, 87–624).

Limited Test Ban Treaty

The Limited Test Ban Treaty, officially called "Treaty Banning Nuclear Weapon Tests in the Atmosphere, in Outer Space, and Under Water," was signed by the United States, Great Britain, and the Soviet Union in Moscow on August 5, 1963, and entered into force on October 10. The Test Ban Treaty prohibits nuclear weapons tests or other nuclear explosions in the atmosphere, outer space, and under water. Efforts to sign such a treaty began in May 1955 when the Subcommittee of Five (the United States, United Kingdom, Canada, France, and the Soviet Union) of the UN Disarmament Commission began discussions on this possibility (U.S. Department of State, Bureau of Verification, Compliance, and Implementation(a), n.d., 1).

Negotiations continued off and on for eight years until agreement was finally reached by the Americans, British, and Soviets on July 25, 1963, with the formal signing occurring in Moscow on August 5 by Secretary of State Dean Rusk (1909–1994), Soviet foreign minister Andrei Gromyko (1909–1989), and British foreign minister Lord Alexander Douglas-Home (1903–1995). The U.S. Senate ratified the treaty on September 24 by an 80–19 vote, President John F. Kennedy ratified it on October 7, and the treaty entered into force on October 10 when the three original signatories deposited their instruments of ratification (United States Department of State, Bureau of Verification, Compliance, and Implementation(a), n.d., 1–5).

The Limited Test Ban Treaty has lasted for over four decades and has been signed by 108 countries although France and North Korea are prominent nonsignatories. The treaty is an important pact because it represents the first international attempt to prevent the presence and testing of nuclear weapons in space and there are a number of different perspectives on the treaty's significance and value (United States Department of State, Bureau of Verification, Compliance, and Implementation (a), n.d., 7–10; Broomfield 1965; U.S. Congress, Office of Technology Assessment, 1985; Oliver 1998; Wenger and Gerber 1999; Burr and Montford 2003; Schrafstetter and Twigge 2004).

Selected provisions of this treaty include prohibiting nuclear weapons tests in outer space or under water; the ability of participants to propose treaty amendments; and individual participants having the ability to withdraw from the treaty if they believe events have occurred that jeopardize their supreme national interests (U.S. Department of State, Bureau of Verification, Compliance, and Arms Control(a), n.d., 5–7).

This treaty has endured and become an important international arms control agreement. Like most international arms control agreements, though, it lacks enforcement and compliance mechanisms, and it is uncertain whether nations such as Iran, North Korea, or other nations or terrorist groups will adhere to it in the future.

Outer Space Treaty

This agreement is officially called the "Treaty on Principles Governing the Activities of States in the Exploration and Use of Outer Space, Including the Moon and Other Celestial

Bodies," and is commonly called the Outer Space Treaty (OST). OST was signed in Washington, London, and Moscow on January 27, 1967, and entered into force on October 10 of that year. The overall purpose of OST was that treaty signatories would not place nuclear weapons or other weapons of mass destruction in orbit around the earth or install such weapons on the moon, celestial bodies, or artificial satellites; that human use of the moon and other celestial bodies would be restricted to peaceful purposes and that they could not be used to establish military bases, installations, or fortifications; test weapons; or conduct military exercises; and that installations, equipment, and vehicles on the moon and other celestial bodies be open to representatives from treaty participants (U.S. Department of State, Bureau of Verification, Compliance, and Arms Control(b), n.d. 1–2).

Background for the OST began in August 1957 when Western countries such as the United States proposed developing an international inspection system for verifying the testing of space objects as part of international disarmament proposals. These proposals were rejected by the Soviet Union, which was testing its Intercontinental Ballistic Missile and about to orbit the Sputnik satellite. Such proposals continued in subsequent years and President Dwight Eisenhower, in a September 22, 1960 address to the UN General Assembly, proposed applying the principles of the Antarctic Treaty to outer space and celestial bodies.

Soviet disarmament objectives during the early 1960s included provisions for ensuring outer space was demilitarized. However, the Soviets would not separate space militarization from other disarmament uses and refused to agree to restrict military uses of outer space unless the United States eliminated short-range and medium-range missiles at its foreign military bases.

The Soviet position changed after signing the 1963 Limited Test Ban Treaty and on September 19, 1963, Gromyko told the UN General Assembly that the Soviet Union desired to conclude an agreement prohibiting the orbiting of nuclear weapons-carrying platforms. This policy change, and subsequent U.S. and Soviet negotiations in the mid 1960s, eventually resulted in the OST as we know it. Ninety-one countries have signed OST as of April 2006 (U.S. Department of State, Bureau of Verification, Compliance, and Arms Control(b), n.d. 1–2; U.S. Congress, Senate Committee on Aeronautics and Space Sciences 1967; U.S. Congress, Senate Committee on Foreign Relations 1967; United Nations 1984; Menon 1988; Martinez 1998; Berry 2001; Sparling 2003; Riviera 2004).

OST has become a fixture of international arms control agreements over the last four decades. However, it has never been subject to a crisis testing its durability, its enforcement provisions are nonexistent, and it may require modification as countries and international government organizations such as the United States, Russia, China, and the European Community achieve more permanent and long-term presences in space during the upcoming century (United States Department of State, Bureau of Verification, Compliance, and Implementation(b), n.d., 2–6).

International Agreement on the Rescue of Astronauts, the Return of Astronauts, and the Return of Objects Launched into Outer Space

This agreement, known as the Rescue Agreement, was negotiated from 1962–1967 by the UN Committee on the Peaceful Uses of Outer Space's Legal Subcommittee. A consensus agreement was reached by the UN General Assembly in 1967 through Resolution 2345 of the 22nd General Assembly, and the agreement entered into force in December 1968. The Rescue Agreement serves as a supplement to articles 5 and 8 of the OST. This agreement seeks to ensure that countries take all possible steps to rescue and assist astronauts in distress and promptly return them to their country of origin and that nations shall, if requested, assist countries seeking to recover space objects that have returned to Earth outside the territory of the launching state. A total of 88 countries have ratified and 25 have signed the Rescue Agreement as of January 1, 2006, and two international governmental organizations (European Space Agency and European Organization for the Exploitation of Meteorological Satellites) have stated they accept the Rescue Agreement's rights and obligations (United Nations Office of Outer Space Affairs 2006(a), 1; U.S. Congress, Senate Committee on Aeronautical and Space Sciences 1968; United Nations 2002, 9–12).

The Rescue Agreement can be viewed as an international first responders' agreement applied to outer space. Its provisions are eminently sensible and consistent with international law agreements on land, maritime, and aerial rescue and humanitarian assistance.

Antiballistic Missile Treaty

The Antiballistic Missile (ABM) Treaty was signed by the United States and the Soviet Union in 1972. Background for this pact began with the first round of the Strategic Arms Limitation Talks between these two countries in November 1969 and negotiations occurred until the treaty was signed on May 26, 1972. The ABM Treaty was ratified by the U.S. Senate on August 3, 1972, and entered into force on October 3 of that year (U.S. Arms Control and Disarmament Agency 1996, 110–114).

The ABM Treaty sought to limit Soviet and U.S. ballistic missile defense sites. Initially each side was limited to two missile defense sites, each having no more than one hundred interceptors. A 1974 protocol to the treaty reduced to one the number of missile defense sites each county could deploy, and theoretically, neither country could build a new missile defense site even if it closed the original site. The Soviets established a missile defense site at Moscow and the United States established its site at Grand Forks, North Dakota but closed the Safeguard ABM system there in February 1976 a few months after this system became operational (U.S. Missile Defense Agency n.d., 1).

The ABM Treaty experienced a contentious reception during its nearly three-decade life. Democratic U.S. administrations and the Soviet Union and its Russian Federation

Leonid Brezhnev of the Soviet Union (left) and President Richard Nixon (right) shake hands in Moscow during talks regarding the Anti-Ballistic Missile Treaty of 1972. The treaty was based on the desire of both nations to avoid nuclear war and was the first significant arms limitation treaty between the United States and the Soviet Union. *(National Archives)*

successor tended to support the treaty as being what they viewed as a cornerstone of strategic stability. In contrast, Republican U.S. administrations tended to be more critical of the ABM Treaty believing that it restricted the United States' ability to defend itself and its allies from emerging ballistic missile defense threats from countries such as the former Soviet Union and North Korea. Contentiousness over this treaty was often reflected in written assessments (U.S. Congress, Senate Committee on Foreign Relations 1987; Stutzle, Bhupendra, and Cowen 1987; Bunn 1992; Glynn 1992; Gray 1993; U.S. Congress, Senate Committee on Governmental Affairs, Subcommittee on International Security, Proliferation, and Federal Services 2000; Lee 2000; Wilkening 2000; Burr 2003; U.S. Congress, Senate Committee on Foreign Relations 2001; Ruse 2002; Sirak 2002).

This controversy reached its end on December 13, 2001 when the George W. Bush administration announced its withdrawal from the treaty, which took effect in July 2002. In making its withdrawal announcement, the Bush administration cited the emerging security threats noted above as its primary rationale but also pledged to continue working with Russia and other countries to combat weapons of mass destruction and their delivery mechanisms (U.S. Department of State 2001, 1–2).

The ABM Treaty was doomed from the start because it sought to restrict the ability of countries to defend themselves against nuclear missile attacks and codified the ethically dubious strategy of mutually assured destruction (MAD) into international security, strategic planning, and law. Further, it is remarkable that the ABM Treaty lasted as long as it did because of its grievous structural flaws. The Soviet Union's blatant violations of the ABM Treaty ensured that this pact was merely a scrap of paper, and the growing use of ballistic missiles by countries such as Iraq, North Korea, and others during the 1990s ultimately would result in the United States making the decision to abrogate this treaty. This abrogation received a muted reaction from Russia.

Liability Convention

The Convention on International Liability for Damage Caused by Space Objects, or the Liability Convention, was negotiated by the Legal Subcommittee of the UN's International Committee on the Peaceful Uses of Outer Space between 1963 and 1972. Overall agreement on this pact was reached in 1971 through Resolution 2777 of the 26th General Assembly and the convention entered into force in September 1972 (United Nations Office on Outer Space Affairs 2006(b), 1).

The primary intent of this convention was making the country launching a spacecraft legally liable for paying compensation caused by its space objects on the earth's surface, to aircraft, or for damage caused to other space objects. The convention also establishes procedures for settling damage claims. A total of 82 countries have ratified the convention, and 25 have signed the Liability Convention as of January 1, 2006; the European Space Agency, European Organization for the Exploitation of Meteorological Satellites, and European Telecommunications Satellite Organization have also announced their acceptance of Liability Convention obligations (United Nations Office on Outer Space Affairs 2006(b); Christol 1980; Forkosch 1982; U.S. Congress, Senate Committee on Commerce Science and Transportation, Subcommittee on Science, Technology, and Space 1988; Hurwitz 1992; Bender 1995; Hwan 1995; Kayser 2001).

The Liability Convention performs a useful function in that it sets up provisions for providing legal redress and compensation for any individual, organization, or nation who incurs personal or financial injury from wayward space objects. With any legal issue, there is the possibility of frivolous lawsuits being filed or excessive awards given by an overzealous court. Nevertheless, this convention helps provide a legal framework for such issues to be resolved in a reasonably effective and just manner.

Registration Convention

The Convention on Registration of Objects Launched Into Outer Space, or the Registration Convention, has its beginnings in 1962 when the UN began keeping records of objects launched into outer space as a result of Resolution 1721B from the 16th General Assembly. The Registration Convention has been force since 1976, and 45 states have ratified the Convention, and 4 had signed it as of January 1, 2006.

The purposes of this pact require that launching states provide the UN with information on each space object they launch including the name of the launching state, a pertinent designator of the object such as its registration number, its basic orbital parameters, and general function (United Nations Office on Outer Space Affairs 2006(c), 1–2; Sundahl

2000; United Nations General Assembly, Committee on the Peaceful Uses of Outer Space, Legal Subcommittee 2005(a); United Nations General Assembly, Committee on the Peaceful Uses of Outer Space 2005(b).

A searchable database of this register is accessible at www.unoosa.org/oosa/osoindex .html. The Registration Convention is one of the most practical international space law agreements. It serves as an inventory of objects currently launched into space and in orbit and provides detailed and updated information on the location of these spacecraft. With such a database, it is possible that there may be omissions, and it is also possible that countries or organizations may consciously not list objects or craft they have launched into space. Despite these caveats, this searchable database is very helpful for determining which objects are in space and their countries of origin.

Moon Agreement

The Agreement Governing the Activities of States on the Moon and Other Celestial Bodies, commonly called the Moon Agreement, was prepared from 1972–1979 by the Legal Committee of the UN Office on Outer Space Affairs. It was adopted in 1979 by General Assembly Resolution 34/68, but it did not enter into force until Austria became the fifth country to ratify the Agreement in July 1984. The purpose of the Moon Agreement is to ensure that the moon and other celestial bodies are used exclusively for peaceful purposes, that their physical environments should not be disrupted, that the UN should be informed of any facilities established on these bodies, that the moon's natural resources are humankind's common heritage, and that international rules should be established to regulate the exploitation of these resources when such exploitation becomes feasible. Twelve states have ratified and an additional four have signed the Moon Agreement as of January 1, 2006 (United Nations Office on Outer Space Affairs 2006(d), 1; U.S. Congress, Senate Committee on Commerce, Science, and Transportation, Subcommittee on Science Space and Transportation 1980; U.S. Congress, Senate Committee on Commerce, Science, and Transportation 1980; Bogaert 1981; U.S. Congress, Office of Technology Assessment 1991; Hoffstadt 1994; Reynolds 1995).

Key Moon Agreement provisions include this agreement applying to other celestial bodies in the solar system besides the earth; that human activities on the moon must follow international law including the UN Charter; that using the threat of force on the moon is prohibited; that countries shall inform the UN, the public, and international scientific community of their moon exploration and use; that the moon's existing environmental balance should not be disrupted; and that individual countries should try to resolve moon-related disputes bilaterally or by other peaceful means (United Nations 2002, 27–35).

The Moon Agreement remains in force nearly a quarter century after its ratification. However, the absence of human moon activity since the U.S. Apollo missions of the late 1960s–early 1970s gives this pact limited value. This could change in the years to come if

U.S. plans to return to the moon in 2018 are realized and if China, Russia, or the European Union decide to pursue manned lunar missions in the years to come. The interaction of these powers on the moon would test the Moon Agreement's efficacy and viability.

Ballistic Missile Launch Notification Agreement

The Ballistic Missile Launch Notification Agreement is an agreement between the United States and the former Soviet Union that was signed at the Moscow Summit by Secretary of State George Shultz (1920–) and Soviet foreign minister Edward Shevardnadze (1928–) on May 31, 1988. The principal purpose of the agreement is reducing the risk of nuclear war through misinterpretation, miscalculation, or accident. The United States proposed that both sides give each other advance notification of planned launches of ICBMs and SLBMs. The Soviets agreed to this, and the agreement calls for both sides to give each other at least 24 hours notification of the planned date, launch, area, and impact area for any ICBM and SLBM. In addition, the agreement also calls for these launch notifications to be provided through Nuclear Risk Reduction Centers, which are communications links responsible for exchanging information with foreign governments to support arms control treaties and security enhancing arrangements (U.S. Arms Control and Disarmament Agency 1996; U.S. Department of State, Bureau of Verification, Compliance, and Implementation(c), n.d., 1).

Specific agreement provisions call for each side giving at least 24 hours advanced notice of the planned date, launch area, and area of impact for any strategic ballistic missile

A Trident intercontinental ballistic missile is launched from a submarine, the USS *Nevada,* on September 30, 1986. The launch was a demonstration. *(U.S. Department of Defense)*

launch; the quadrant of an ocean or body of water where a launch is supposed to occur; the geographic coordinates of the planned impact area or areas of reentry vehicles; and the size of the impact area (U.S. Arms Control and Disarmament Agency 1996, 348–349).

The Missile Launch Notification Agreement was strengthened in 2000 by a Memorandum of Agreement between the United States and the Russian Federation on June 4, 2000 on establishing a joint center for early warning systems data exchange and missile launch notifications. Provisions of this agreement signed by President Bill Clinton and Russian president Vladimir Putin include exchanging information on ballistic missile and space vehicle launches by each party; creating conditions for preparing and maintaining a unified database to exchange notifications on launches of these vehicles; exchanging information on ballistic missile launches from other countries that could threaten the United States or Russia or create strategic uncertainty and lead to misinterpretations of U.S. or Russian intentions; providing information on other launches or experiments that could disrupt each party's missile early warning systems; and delivering the necessary infrastructure to facilitate the operations of this agreement (*Weekly Compilation of Presidential Documents* 2000, 1280–1283).

The Missile Launch Notification Agreement remains in force, although it is unknown how current U.S.–Russian controversy over the proposed U.S. ballistic missile defense system will affect this agreement. This agreement does not apply to any other country including current and potential future possessors of ballistic missile arsenals such as China, India, Iran, North Korea, and Pakistan. Consequently, it is difficult to assess how useful this bilateral U.S.–Russian agreement will be as a template for future bilateral or multilateral missile launch notification agreements between the U.S. and other countries.

References and Further Reading

Bender, R. 1995. *Space Transport Liability: National and International Aspects.* Boston: M. Nijhoff.
Berry, N. 2001. "Existing Legal Constraints on Space Weaponry." *Defense Frontier* 30 (2): 5–6.
Bogaert, E. 1981. "The Moon Treaty: Achievement and Future Problems." *Studia Diplomatica* 34 (6): 655–672.
Broomfield, L. P. 1965. "Outer Space and International Cooperation." *International Organization* 19 (3): 603–621.
Bunn, G. 1992. *Arms Control by Committee: Managing Negotiations With the Russians.* Stanford, CA: Stanford University Press.
Burr, W. and H. L. Montford, eds. 2003. *The Making of the Limited Test Ban Treaty, 1958–1963.* Washington, D.C.: National Security Archive. [Online article or information; retrieved 4/19/06.] www.gwu.edu/~nsarchiv/NSAEBB/NSAEBB94/.
Christol, C. Q. 1980. "International Liability for Damage Caused by Space Objects Under the 1967 Outer Space Treaty and the 1972 Convention on International Liability for Damage Caused by Space Objects." *American Journal of International Law* 74 (April): 346–371.
Communications Satellite Act of 1962, Public Law 87–624, U.S. Statutes at Large 76 (1962), 419–427.

Forkosch, M. D. 1982. *Outer Space and Legal Liability.* Boston: M. Nijhoff.

Galloway, J. F. 1992. "Commercializing Outer Space." *National Forum* 72 (3): 34–36.

Glynn, P. 1992. *Closing Pandora's Box: Arms Races, Arms Control, and the History of the Cold War.* New York: New Republic Books/Basic Books.

Gray, C. S. 1993. "Space Power Survivability." *Airpower Journal* 7 (4): 27–42.

Hoffstadt, B. 1994. "Moving the Heavens: Lunar Mining and the 'Common Heritage of Mankind' in the Moon Treaty." *UCLA Law Review* 42 (December): 575–621.

Hurwitz, B. A. 1992. *State Liability for Outer Space Activities: In Accordance With the 1972 Convention on International Liability for Damage Caused by Space Objects.* Boston: M. Nijhoff.

Hwan, K. D. 1995. "Some Considerations on the Liability of the Compensation for Damages Caused by Space Debris." *Law Technology* 28 (4): 1–28.

Kayser, V. 2001. *Launching Space Objects: Issues of Liability and Future Prospects.* Boston: Kluwer Academic Publishers.

Lee, W. E. 1977. *The Communications Satellite Act of 1962: The Creation of a New Communications Policy.* Ph.D. diss. University of Wisconsin-Madison, Madison, WI.

Lee, W. T. 2000. "The ABM Treaty Was Dead on Arrival." *Comparative Strategy* 19 (2): 145–165.

Martinez, L. F. 1998. "Satellite Communications and the Internet: Implications for the Outer Space Treaty." *Space Policy* 14 (May): 83–88.

Menon, P.K. 1988. *The United Nations Efforts to Outlaw the Arms Race in Outer Space: A Brief History With Key Documents.* Lewiston, NY: Mellen Press.

Musolf, L. D. 1983. *Uncle Sam's Private Profitseeking Corporations: Comsat, Fannie Mae, Amtrak, and Conrail.* Lexington, MA: Lexington Books.

Oliver, K. 1998. *Kennedy, Macmillan, and the Nuclear Test-Ban Debate, 1961–1963.* New York: St. Martin's Press.

Reynolds, G. H. 1995. "The Moon Treaty: Prospects for the Future." *Space Policy* 11 (May): 115–120.

Riviera, T. 2004. *Redefining Military Activities in Space: A Viable Compromise Over the Military Uses of Space.* LL.M. thesis, George Washington University, Washington, D.C. [Online article or information; retrieved 4/20/06.] http://handle.dtic.mil/100.2/ADA426438.

Ruse, M. A. 2002. "Reflections on the 1972 Antiballistic Missile Treaty and National Missile Defense." *Aerospace Power Journal* 16 (1): 69–76.

Schnapf, L. 1985. "Explorations in Space Law: An Examination of the Legal Issues Raised by Geostationary, Remote Sensing, and Direct Broadcast Satellites." *New York Law School Review* 29 (4): 687–748.

Schrafstetter, S. and S. Twigge. 2004. *Avoiding Armageddon: Europe, the United States, and the Struggle for Nuclear Nonproliferation, 1945–1970.* Westport, CT: Praeger.

Sirak, M. 2002. "Life After the ABM (Anti-Ballistic Missile) Treaty." *Jane's Defence Weekly* 37 (June 19): 50.

Sparling, W. P. 2003. "Cries of the Hunchback: Is Space a Theatre of War or a Sanctuary?" *Marine Corps Gazette* 87 (5): 63–65.

Stutzle, W., Bhupendra J., and R. Cowen, eds. 1987. *The ABM Treaty: To Defend or Not to Defend?* New York: Oxford University Press.

Sundahl, M. J. 2000. "Unidentified Orbital Debris: The Case for a Market-Share Liability Regime." *Hastings International and Comparative Law Review* 24 (Fall): 125–154.

U.S. Arms Control and Disarmament Agency. 1996. *Arms Control and Disarmament Agreements: Texts and Histories of Negotiations.* Washington, D.C.: U.S. Government Printing Office.

U.S. Congress. Office of Technology Assessment. 1985. *Anti-Satellite Weapons, Countermeasures and Arms Control.* Washington, D.C.: U.S. Government Printing Office.

U.S. Congress. Office of Technology Assessment. 1991. *Exploring the Moon and Mars: Choices for the Nation.* Washington, D.C.: U.S. Government Printing Office.

U.S. Congress. Senate Committee on Aeronautical and Space Sciences. 1968. *Agreement on the Rescue of Astronauts, and the Return of Objects Launched Into Outer Space: Analysis and Background Data.* Washington, D.C.: U.S. Government Printing Office.

U.S. Congress. Senate Committee on Aeronautics and Space Sciences. 1967. *Treaty on Principles Governing the Activities of States in the Exploration and Use of Outer Space, Including the Moon and Other Celestial Bodies.* Washington, D.C.: U.S. Government Printing Office.

U.S. Congress. Senate Committee on Commerce, Science, and Transportation. 1980. *Agreement Governing the Activities of States on the Moon and Other Celestial Bodies.* Washington, D.C.: U.S. Government Printing Office.

U.S. Congress. Senate Committee on Commerce, Science, and Transportation. Subcommittee on Communications. 1999. *S. 276, Open-Market Reorganization for the Betterment of International Telecommunications Act.* Washington, D.C.: U.S. Government Printing Office.

U.S. Congress. Senate Committee on Commerce, Science, and Transportation. Subcommittee on Science, Technology, and Space. 1980. *The Moon Treaty.* Washington, D.C.: U.S. Government Printing Office.

U.S. Congress. Senate Committee on Commerce, Science, and Transportation. Subcommittee on Science, Technology, and Space. 1988. *Commercial Expendable Launch Viability.* Washington, D.C.: U.S. Government Printing Office.

U.S. Congress. Senate Committee on Foreign Relations. 1967. *Treaty on Outer Space.* Washington, D.C.: U.S. Government Printing Office.

U.S. Congress. Senate Committee on Foreign Relations. 1987. *The ABM Treaty and the Constitution.* Washington, D.C.: U.S. Government Printing Office.

U.S. Congress. Senate Committee on Foreign Relations. 2001. *The Administration's Missile Defense Program and the ABM Treaty.* Washington, D.C.: U.S. Government Printing Office.

U.S. Congress. Senate Committee on Governmental Affairs. Subcommittee on International Security, Proliferation, and Federal Services. 2000. *The Future of the ABM Treaty.* Washington, D.C.: U.S. Government Printing Office.

U.S. Department of State. 2001. *ABM Treaty Fact Sheet: Announcement of Withdrawal from the ABM Treaty,* 1–2. [Online article or information; retrieved 4/25/06.] www.state.gov/t/ac/rls/fs/2001/6848.htm.

U.S. Department of State, Bureau of Verification, Compliance, and Implementation(a). n.d. *Treaty Banning Nuclear Weapons Tests in the Atmosphere, in Outer Space and Under Water,* 1–10. [Online article or information; retrieved 4/19/06.] www.state.gov/t/ac/trt/4797.htm.

U.S. Department of State. Bureau of Verification, Compliance, and Implementation(b). n.d. *Treaty on Principles Governing the Activities of States in the Exploration and Use of Outer Space, Including the Moon and Other Celestial Bodies,* 1–6. [Online article or information; retrieved 4/20/06.] www.state.gov/t/ac/trt/5181.htm.

U.S. Department of State. Bureau of Verification, Compliance, and Implementation(c). n.d. *Nuclear Risk Reduction Center,* 1. [Online article or information; retrieved 4/28/06.] www.state .gov/t/vci/nrrc/.

U.S. Missile Defense Agency. n.d. *Fact Sheet: History of the Missile Defense Organization,* 1. [Online article or information; retrieved 4/25/06.] http://www.defenselink.mil/specials/missile defense/history4.html.

United Nations. 1984. *United Nations Treaties on Outer Space.* New York: United Nations.

United Nations. 2002. *United Nations Treaties and Principles on Outer Space.* New York: United Nations.

United Nations General Assembly. Committee on the Peaceful Uses of Outer Space, Legal Subcommittee. 2005(a). *Practice of States and International Organizations on Registering Space Objects: Background Paper by the Secretariat.* New York: United Nations General Assembly.

United Nations General Assembly. Committee on the Peaceful Uses of Outer Space. 2005(b). *Questionnaire on Possible Legal Issues With Regard to Aerospace Objects: Replies Received From Member States.* New York: United Nations General Assembly.

United Nations Institute for Disarmament Research. 1987. *Problems Related to Outer Space.* New York: United Nations Institute for Disarmament Research.

United Nations Office on Outer Space Affairs. 2006(a). *Agreement on the Rescue of Astronauts, the Return of Astronauts, and the Return of Objects Launched into Outer Space,* 1. [Online article or information; retrieved 4/21/06.] www.unoosa.org/oosa/en/SpaceLaw/rescue.html.

United Nations Office on Outer Space Affairs. 2006(b). *Convention on International Liability for Damage Caused by Space Objects.* 1. [Online article or information; retrieved 4/26/06.] www.unoosa.org/oosa/en/SpaceLaw/liability.html.

United Nations Office on Outer Space Affairs. 2006(c). *Convention on Registration of Objects Launched into Outer Space.* 1–2. [Online article or information; retrieved 4/27/06.] www .unoosa.org/oosa/en/SORegister/regist.html.

United Nations Office on Outer Space Affairs. 2006(d). *Agreement Governing the Activities of States on the Moon and Other Celestial Bodies.* 1. [Online article or information; retrieved 4/28/06.] www.unoosa.org/oosa/en/SpaceLaw/moon.html.

Wallop, M. and A. Codevilla. 1987. *The Arms Control Delusion: How Twenty-Five Years of Arms Control Has Made the World Less Safe.* San Francisco: Institute for Contemporary Studies Press.

Weekly Compilation of Presidential Documents. 2000. "Russia-United States Memorandum of Agreement on Establishment of a Joint Center for Early Warning Systems Data Exchange and Missile Launch Notifications." 36 (23)(June 12): 1280–1283.

Wenger, A. and M. Gerber. 1999. "John F. Kennedy and the Limited Test Ban Treaty: A Case Study of Presidential Leadership." *Presidential Studies Quarterly* 29 (2): 460–487.

Wilkening, D. A. 2000. "Amending the ABM." *Survival,* 42 (1): 29–45.

PART 2

6

U.S. Defense
Department Resources

T HE U.S. DEPARTMENT OF DEFENSE (DOD) and individual U.S. armed services produce numerous resources on space warfare and defense. These materials can include reports of weapons systems' test results, congressionally mandated policy program updates, military doctrinal statements from individual armed services, scientific and technical reports, theoretical speculations on what warfare in space may look like, and other topics.

This chapter examines the multifaceted information resources on space warfare and defense produced by DOD and the individual armed services with particular emphasis on resources produced by the U.S. Air Force and its component entities. These resources reflect a wide range of viewpoints depending on the political, military, and budgetary priorities of the presidential administration or armed service branch they were written for.

U.S. Department of Defense

The current institutional incarnation of the DOD dates from 1949 National Security Act amendments establishing it as an executive department headed by the secretary of Defense. DOD's primary responsibility is providing the military forces necessary to defend the United States and its national interests.

A global access point to DOD and military resources is the Web site www.defense link.mil/. A useful overall resource for U.S. military policy and space warfare policy is the secretary of Defense's *Annual Report* to the president and Congress. Published by DOD's Office of the Executive Secretary, this publication is accessible from 1996–present at www .defenselink.mil/execsec/adr_intro.html and also features reports from the Secretaries of the Air Force, Army, and Navy, which may contain information about the space strategies and policies of those armed services.

Defense Advanced Research Projects Agency

The Defense Advanced Research Projects Agency (DARPA) was established in 1958. Its original mission was preventing the United States from being surprised by technological events such as the Soviet launch of Sputnik. This basic objective remains today,

The Pentagon in Arlington, Virginia houses the Department of Defense. It is the world's largest office building and approximately 25,000 people work there. *(Library of Congress)*

although DARPA also seeks to create technological surprise for U.S. enemies. DARPA engages in advanced and applied research and development programs for DOD and conducts prototype projects that may be included in future DOD or military projects. A key DARPA mission is placing particular emphasis on capabilities future military commanders might want and expediting those capabilities into existence through technology demonstrations.

The highly specialized nature of DARPA's work is executed by technical and support offices such as the Advanced Technology Office, Defense Sciences Office, Information Processing Technology Office, Information Exploitation Office, Microsystems Technology Office, Special Projects Office, and Tactical Technology Office. Programmatic work carried out by these offices occurs in space control applications, information assurance, biological warfare defense, advanced mathematics, national security warning and decision making, space systems development, next-generation computational and information systems, mobile distributed command and control, sensors and sensor exploitation, precision kill capabilities, defenses against low-technology air vehicles and missiles, and defenses against GPS jamming.

Further information about DARPA activities is available at www.darpa.mil/. These include news releases (1997–present), detailed descriptions on the activities of DARPA organizational components, agency budget information, and details on how to do business with DARPA. Detailed descriptions are also provided for ongoing or historical DARPA programs with relevant space warfare and defense programs including Geospatial Representation and Analysis, Global Positioning Experiments, High Precision Laser Designator, Innovative Space-Based Radar Antenna Technology, Integrated Battle Command, Multifunction Electro-Optics for Defense of U.S. Aircraft, Novel Satellite Communication, Persistent Ocean Surveillance, Space Surveillance Telescope, and Synthetic Aperture Radar for Tactical Imaging. The video Web cast *DARPA's Space Legacy* (2002) provides additional institutional historical background.

Defense Information Systems Agency

The Defense Information Systems Agency (DISA) was established by the secretary of Defense as the Defense Communications Agency in 1960 and received its current name in 1991. DISA plays a crucial role in ensuring the security of U.S. military command, control, communications, and information systems and the communication needs of U.S. political and military leaders under peace and wartime conditions. It provides various kinds of technical support to the secretary of Defense and military agencies, ensures the interoperability of the Worldwide Military Command and Control System, the Defense Communications System, theater and tactical command and control systems, related NATO and allied communication systems, and national security emergency preparedness telecommunications functions of the National Communications System prescribed by Executive Order 12472.

DISA's Web site (www.disa.mil) provides additional information about the agency's functions and activities though it contains many resources restricted to users in the .gov or .mil Internet domains. Examples of publicly accessible resources include an organizational chart, press releases, business contracting information, and links to the Web sites of DISA military combatant command offices such as Strategic Command.

Defense Science Board

The Defense Science Board (DSB) is part of the Office of the Undersecretary of Defense for Acquisition, Technology, and Logistics. It was established in 1956, and its responsibilities include reporting to the Assistant Secretary of Defense for Research and Development on science and technology developments of interest to DOD.

Historical and contemporary information on DSB activities can be found on its Web site, www.acq.osd.mil/dsb/. These resources include historical information and the board's charter, links to other armed service science advisory organizations, descriptions of current task forces and their activities (covering topics such as improvised explosive devices and 21st century strategic technology vectors), and newsletter (June 1998–present).

A particularly important feature of this Web site is the text of DSB reports from 1993–present. Noteworthy examples of these reports covering aspects of space warfare and defense include *Report of the Defense Science Board Task Force on Simulation, Readiness, and Prototyping* (1993), *Tactics and Technology for 21st Century Military Superiority* (1996), *Space and Missile Tracking System* (1996), *Theater Missile Defense* (1996), *Satellite Reconnaissance* (1998), *High Energy Laser Weapons Systems Applications* (2001), *Acquisition of National Security Space Programs* (2003), *Missile Defense Phase III Modeling and Simulation* (2004), *Contributions of Space-Based Radar to Missile Defense* (2004), *The Future of the Global Positioning System* (2005), and *US/UK Task Force Report-Defense Critical Technologies* (2006).

Defense Support Program Satellites

Defense Support Program (DSP) satellites are operated by the U.S. Air Force Space Command. The purpose of these satellites is protecting the United States and its allies by detecting missile launches, space launches, and nuclear detonations. DSP has existed since the early 1970s, and its satellites use an infrared sensor to detect heat from missile and booster plumes against the earth's background while being in geosynchronous orbit

The Air Force Space Command-operated Defense Support Program (DSP) satellites are a key part of North America's early warning systems. In their 22,300-mile geosynchronous orbits, DSP satellites help protect the United States and its allies by detecting missile launches, space launches, and nuclear detonations. *(Northrop Grumman)*

22,300 miles above the earth. Data from DSP satellites is relayed to various locations including the North American Aerospace and Defense Command and U.S. Space Command early warning centers in Cheyenne Mountain near Colorado Springs, Colorado.

Defense Technical Information Center and Scientific and Technical Information Network

The Defense Technical Information Center (DTIC) was started just after World War II to translate captured German and Japanese military scientific and technical information. Initially established as the Central Documents Office on October 13, 1948 by the secretaries of the Navy and Air Force, it became DTIC in October 1979. Overall information on DTIC is accessible at www.dtic.mil/, and its Scientific and Technical Information Network (STINET) provides access to a phenomenal number of full text reports on various defense subjects from defense contractors and military agencies.

Public access to DTIC-STINET resources is provided at http://stinet.dtic.mil/. Examples of these resources include a search thesaurus and descriptions of various component parts such as access to military journal articles and the space science collection. The highlight of this Web site, which makes it an essential resource for those studying space warfare and defense, is its repository of technical reports on assorted aspects of space warfare and defense. A representative sampling of these reports includes:

- *Reengineering the Doctrinal Latticework of Military Space* (1998) http://handle.dtic .mil/100.2/ADA357705
- *Determining if "Space Weather" Conditions Should Be Considered in the Intelligence Preparation of the Battlefield Process* (1998) http://handle.dtic.mil/100.2/ADA350126
- *Ballistic Missile Defense Technology Overview for the 7th Annual AIAA Technology Readiness Conference* (1998) http://handle.dtic.mil/100.2/ADA355980
- *Space as an Area of Responsibility (AOR), Is it the Right Solution?* (1998) http://handle .dtic.mil/100.2/ADA363149
- *Use of Commercial Space Assets by the Joint Force Commander* (1999) http://handle .dtic.mil/100.2/ADA363150
- *Component Based Simulation of the Space Operations Vehicle and the Common Aero Vehicle* (1999) http://handle.dtic.mil/100.2/ADA363022
- *Space Control for the Theater Commander: Naval Blockade as Precedent* (1999) http:// handle.dtic.mil/100.2/ADA370673
- *Evaluation of the Space and Naval Warfare Systems Command (SPAWAR) Cost and Performance Measurement* (1999) http://handle.dtic.mil/100.2/ADA373342
- *Back to the Future: Space Power Theory and A.T. Mahan* (2000) http://handle.dtic.mil/ 100.2/ADA432172
- *The Viability of U.S. Anti-Satellite (ASAT) Policy: Moving Toward Space Control* (2000) http://handle.dtic.mil/100.2/ADA435085

- *Medium Brigade 2003: Can Space-Based Communications Ensure Information Dominance?* (2000) http://handle.dtic.mil/100.2/ADA388156;
- *Some Principles of Space Strategy (or "Corbett in Orbit")* (2000) http://handle.dtic.mil/100.2/ADA430980;
- *Navy Space Operations in the 21st Century: Sailing Among the Stars* (2000) http://handle.dtic.mil/100.2/ADA378506
- *Space Forces Support for the Joint Forces Commander: Who's In Charge?* (2000) http://handle.dtic.mil/100.2/ADA378593;
- *Space Weaponization* (2000) http://handle.dtic.mil/100.2/ADA433750
- *The "Space" of Aerospace Power: Why and How* (2000) http://handle.dtic.mil/100.2/ADA394062
- *Putting Space Control on the Front Burner in Operational Planning* (2000) http://handle.dtic.mil/100.2/ADA381751;
- *The Warfighters' Counterspace Threat Analysis (WCTA): A Framework for Evaluating Counterspace Threats* (2000) http://handle.dtic.mil/100.2/ADA384609
- *Improving Satellite Surveillance Through Optimal Assignment of Assets* (2003) http://handle.dtic.mil/100.2/ADA419447;
- *Redefining Military Activities in Space: A Viable Compromise Over the Military Uses of Space* (2004) http://handle.dtic.mil/100.2/ADA426438; and
- *United States National Security Policy and the Strategic Issues for DOD Space Control* (2005) http://handle.dtic.mil/100.2/ADA431824.

Defense Threat Reduction Agency

The Defense Threat Reduction Agency (DTRA) was created on October 1, 1998 from the preexisting Defense Special Weapons Agency. DTRA's institutional mandate involves protecting the United States and its allies by reducing the threat from weapons of mass destruction including chemical, biological, radiological, nuclear weapons, and high explosives. These defensive activities are carried out by DTRA personnel and resources emphasizing areas such as cooperative threat reduction, on-site inspection, technology security, combat security, and threat control and reduction on a global scale.

DTRA's Web site (www.dtra.mil) provides further information about agency activities and operations. Accessible materials include a Web cast video describing DTRA's work, resources on DTRA activities for enforcing various international arms control and security agreements such as the Nuclear Nonproliferation Treaty and the Strategic Arms Reduction Treaty with Russia, and links to various U.S. Government and international government organization reports on reducing the proliferation of weapons of mass destruction.

Numerous historical books describing DTRA activities are also accessible including *On-Site Inspections under the CFE Treaty: A History of the On-Site Inspections Agency and CFE Treaty Implementation, 1990–1996* (1996), *Treaty on Open Skies* (1999), and *Creating the Defense Threat Reduction Agency* (2002).

Department of Defense Directives

DOD issues numerous documents in its execution of U.S. national security policy. These publications include directives, issuances, instructions, administrative instructions, and other publications to carry out departmental activities and implement policies. DOD's Communications and Directives directorate is responsible for providing a single uniform system for executing departmental policies and procedures.

These directives and issuances are accessible at www.dtic.mil/whs/directives/. Understanding these documents requires presenting a more detailed description of their nature. DOD directives are broad policy documents containing what is required by the president, legislation, or the secretary of Defense to start, govern, or regulate actions conducted by DOD components. Directives also establish or describe programs or organizations, define missions, grant authority, and assign responsibilities.

Memorandums are issued by the secretary of Defense, deputy secretary of Defense, and their designated assistants. They are not published in the DOD directives system and implement policy documents such as DOD directives, federal laws, and executive orders. DOD instructions implement the policy and describe plans or actions for carrying out policies, operating programs and activities, and assigning responsibilities within these programs or activities. An Administrative Instruction is the medium implementing or supplementing DOD Directives or Instructions impacting the activities of the Office of the Secretary of Defense and DOD field agencies. There are several examples of DOD directives relating to space warfare and defense policy issues. Examples of these documents include *Directive 3200.11-D: Major Range and Test Facility Base Summary of Capabilities* (1983); *Directive 3230.3: DOD Support for Commercial Space Launch Activities* (1986); *Directive 3100.10: Department of Defense Space Policy* (1999); *Directive 3222.2: DOD Electromagnetic Environmental Effects (E3) Program* (2004); *Directive 4120.15: Designating and Naming Military Aerospace Vehicles* (2004); and *Directive 5134.9: Missile Defense Agency* (2004).

Joint Chiefs of Staff and the Joint Electronic Library

The Joint Electronic Library (JEL) is produced by the military's Joint Chiefs of Staff under DTIC auspices. JEL features information on the military doctrine of individual U.S. armed services along with theoretical and operational aspects involving the joint collaboration of all military forces. Information in JEL is intended to promote joint doctrine awareness and management among U.S. armed forces to enhance joint, interagency, and multinational interoperability along with enhancing military war-fighting capabilities. JEL is accessible at www.dtic.mil/doctrine/. These resources including the journal *Joint Force Quarterly* (Summer 1993–present) and a variety of doctrinal documents emphasizing how two or more armed services can work together to integrate missions and objectives in military operations. Examples of such publications include *Joint Pub 2–03 Joint Tactics, Techniques, and Procedures for Geospatial Information and Services Support to Joint Operations* (1999); *Joint Pub 3–01 Joint Doctrine for Countering Air and*

Missile Threats (1999); *Joint Pub 3–14 Joint Doctrine for Space Operations* (2002); and *Pamphlet for Future Joint Operations: Bridging the Gap Between Concepts and Doctrine* (2002).

Missile Defense Agency

The Missile Defense Agency (MDA) was established in January 2002 updating the Ballistic Missile Defense Organization created during the Clinton administration to replace the Strategic Defense Initiative Organization established during the Reagan administration.

MDA serves as the primary agency directing U.S. missile defense programs. In MDA's organic document, Secretary of Defense Donald Rumsfeld emphasized what he saw as DOD's primary missile defense priorities.

A. First, to defend the U.S., deployed forces, allies, and friends.

B. Second, to employ a Ballistic Missile Defense System (BMDS) that layers defense to intercept missiles in all phases of their flight (e.g., boost, midcourse, and terminal) against all ranges of threats.

C. Third, to enable the Services to field elements of the overall BMDS as soon as practicable. To that end, we have started to deploy the Patriot Advanced

A Standard Missile-3 (SM-3) is launched from the Aegis destroyer USS *Decatur* (DDG 73), during a Missile Defense Agency ballistic missile flight test on June 22, 2007. Two minutes later, the SM-3 intercepted a separating ballistic missile threat target, launched from the Pacific Missile Range Facility, Barking Sands, Kauai, Hawaii. The test was the ninth intercept, in eleven program flight tests, by the Aegis Ballistic Missile Defense, the maritime component of the "Hit-to-Kill" Ballistic Missile Defense System, being developed by the Missile Defense Agency. *(U.S. Navy)*

Capability–3 system [in 2002], after successful testing, as the first line of defense against short-range missiles.

D. Fourth, to develop and test new technologies, use prototype and test assets to provide early capability, if necessary, and improve the effectiveness of deployed capability by inserting new technologies as they become available or when the threat warrants an accelerated capability.

MDA's Web site (www.mda.mil) provides a profusion of information resources about agency activities and U.S. missile defense programs. Accessible resources include biographies of key agency officials, an organizational chart, ballistic missile frequently asked questions (FAQs) such as "How Fast is the Kill Vehicle Going When it Hits the Hostile Reentry Vehicle?," resources for prospective business contractors, news releases (1994–present), and Quicktime video webcasts of selected missile defense system tests.

Fact sheets are provided on various topics including *Aegis Ballistic Missile Defense* (2005); *Airborne Laser* (2005); *Command, Control, Battle Management, and Communications* (2005); *Ground-Based Midcourse Defense* (2005); *Sea-Based X-Band Radar* (2006); *Space Tracking and Surveillance System* (2005); *Targets and Countermeasures* (2005); and *Theater High Altitude Area Defense* (2005). A variety of reports are also provided on MDA's Web site including agency budget information from 1985–present; *MDA Glossary* (n.d.); *Report of the Panel on Reducing Risk in Ballistic Missile Defense Flight Test Programs* (1998); *Record of Decision to Establish a Ground-Based Midcourse Defense Extended Test Range* (2003); *Ballistic Missile Defense System Draft Programmatic Environmental Impact Statement* (2004); *A Day in the Life of the Ballistic Missile Defense System (BMDS)* (2005); *Ground-Based Midcourse Defense (GMD); Sea-Based X-Band Radar (SBX) Placement and Operation;* and *Adak, Alaska Environmental Assessment and Draft Finding of No Significant Impact* (2005).

Joint National Integration Center

The Joint National Integration Center (JNIC) serves as MDA's research, testing, modeling, and simulation forum. Located near Colorado Springs, Colorado, JNIC's mission involves providing missile defense related analysis, system-level engineering, integration, and evaluation support for acquiring, developing, and deploying missile defense systems and architectures; supporting the development of joint and combined missile defense doctrine, research, and operational concepts; and supporting military combatant commands by integrating missile defense concepts, space exploitation, battle management command, control, communications, computers, and intelligence, and by conducting joint and combined simulations, war games, and participating in missile defense exercises as directed.

JNIC's Web site (www.mda.mil/jnic) provides additional information about center activities. These resources include descriptions of the activities of tenant organizations such as the Center for Research Support, which is responsible for supplying satellite command and control support including satellite data processing, display, and distribution; the Cheyenne Mountain Training System whose activities include training operations crew members and some maintenance crew members assigned to Cheyenne Mountain Air Station along with replicating this base's training at the Missile Training Center and Space Training Center; and the Space Warfare Center whose institutional purpose is advancing U.S. space capabilities and employment concepts through tactics, developing, testing, analysis, and training programs.

Additional accessible resources provided through JNIC's Web site include employment opportunities, links to other MDA program components, and succinct descriptions of JNIC program areas such as interoperability testing, analysis, modeling and simulation, and war games and exercises.

National Geospatial Intelligence Agency

The National Geospatial Intelligence Agency (NGA) was created on November 24, 2003 when the 2004 Defense Authorization Act was signed into law. NGA replaced predecessor agencies such as the National Imagery and Mapping Agency (NIMA) established in 1996 and the Defense Mapping Agency established in 1972, which had additional predecessor agencies within the military. NGA's institutional mandate is providing timely imagery, imagery intelligence, and geospatial information supporting national security objectives to relevant policymakers.

NGA's Web site (www.nga.mil) provides information about agency activities, the text of a 2000 commission report on its NIMA predecessor agency, press releases (1996–present), information on careers and business opportunities within NGA, and assorted fact sheets and publications including *Terrain Visualization* (n.d.); *DOD Evasion Chart* (1996); *NGA's High-Resolution Terrain Information Test Range: Final Report* (2001); and *Geospatial Intelligence Basic Doctrine* (2004).

National Reconnaissance Office

The National Reconnaissance Office (NRO) is responsible for conducting satellite surveillance for U.S. intelligence agency and military operations, which it has done since 1961. Official acknowledgement of NRO's existence did not occur until it was declassified by the deputy secretary of Defense as recommended by the Director of Central Intelligence on September 18, 1992.

NRO's Web site (www.nro.gov) features assorted resources describing the office's activities. These include information on doing business with NRO; news releases (1995–present); selected speeches by NRO officials, such as the March 16, 2006 NRO budget request statement made by NRO director Dr. Donald M. Kerr before the House Armed Services Committee; imagery from the historic Corona intelligence reconnaissance satellite program that NRO was involved with and Web casts describing Corona; biographical information about current and former NRO Directors; and an organizational chart featuring the names of NRO component entities, such as the Signals Intelligence Systems Acquisitions and Operations Directorate and Office of Space Launch.

National Security Space Office

The National Security Space Office (NSSO) is part of the Office of the Undersecretary of Defense for Acquisition, Technology, and Logistics. NSSO was established in May 2004 by merging the National Security Space Architect and National Security Space Integration offices. NSSO's purpose is integrating and coordinating defense and intelligence space activities to achieve unified effort. Its Web site is www.acq.osd.mil/nsso/.

Strategic Command

Strategic Command, also called United States Strategic Command (STRATCOM) is located at Offut AFB, Nebraska. STRATCOM is one of the military's nine unified combatant commands, and it is charged with providing the U.S. global deterrence capabilities and synchronizing DOD efforts to combat adversary weapons of mass destruction on a global scale. STRATCOM seeks to achieve such capabilities through advocating and applying integrated intelligence, surveillance, and reconnaissance (ISR); space and global strike operations; information operations; integrated missile defense; and assertive command and control.

Command origins date back to the March 1946 creation of the U.S. Air Force's Strategic Air Command (SAC) at Offut where SAC bombers served as the genesis of the U.S. emerging nuclear deterrent against the Soviet Union's nuclear arsenal. STRATCOM replaced SAC on June 1, 1992 following the Soviet Union's collapse. This new organization brought the planning, targeting, and wartime employment of U.S. strategic forces under a single commander while daily force training, maintenance, and equipment responsibilities stayed with the Air Force and Navy. A separate Space Command force existing at this time was merged into STRATCOM on October 1, 2002.

STRATCOM's Web site (www.stratcom.mil) features information about organizational entities including Joint Functional Component Commands (JFCC) for Integrated Missile Defense, Intelligence, Surveillance, and Reconnaissance, Network Warfare, Space and Global Strike, and the Joint Information Operations Center. Additional resources include biographies of key STRATCOM personnel, a succinct command history, recent news releases, and speeches and congressional testimony from STRATCOM leaders.

Fact sheets on organizational activities are also provided with representative samples including *Manned Space Flight Support* (2004); *Military Space Forces* (2004); *Space Control* (2004); *Joint Functional Component Command for Integrated Missile Defense* (2005); *Theater Ballistic Missile Warning* (2005); and *Global Operations Center* (2006).

Joint Functional Component for Space and Global Strike

The Joint Functional Component for Space and Global Strike (JFCCSGS) is part of Strategic Command and was established in January 2005. It is responsible for optimizing operational planning, execution, and force management for STRATCOM's mission of deterring attacks against the United States. JFCCSGS collaborates with other government and military agencies to support or execute global space or strike operations. This can involve providing integrated analysis of STRATCOM's global mission capabilities, developing and providing space and global strike execution recommendations, providing continual space situational awareness of assigned space forces, and coordinating and maintaining tactical level intelligence supporting operational needs for space and global strike component commands. The JFCCSGS Web site (www.stratcom.mil/SGS) provides information such as biographies of leaders, how JFCCSGS relates to other STRATCOM entities, and access to the Offutt AFB newsletter *Air Pulse*. The major source of information on this Web site is detailed descriptions of JFCCSGS organizational entities and their responsibilities. These component parts include J0 (Office of the Commander and the Staff Support Agencies), which is responsible for the command's goals, mission, vision, and leadership; J1 (Manpower and Personnel) whose responsibilities include administrative and personnel support to those assigned to JFCCSGS staff; J2 (Intelligence), which is responsible for presenting clear, accurate, predictive, and timely analysis of military situations to assist commanders and staff in their planning and decision making; J3 (Operations), which manages the Global Operations Center by providing global mission area situational awareness to STRATCOM senior leadership while also conducting mission analysis, leading course of action development, and performing contingency and crisis action planning; and J4 (Logistics), which monitors daily logistics capability to support forces and provides expertise as required.

Additional JFCCSGS organizations and their responsibilities include J5 (Plans and Policy), which is responsible for providing planning products and planning support to STRATCOM deliberative/adaptive planning efforts and other military planning efforts for national and theater level objectives; J6 (C4 Systems), which provides functional, maintenance, and sustainment support for operational command and control systems to ensure their reliability across the combat spectrum; J7 (Exercises), which serves as the primary integrating organization supporting JFCCSGS exercises, war gaming, readiness, and training requirements in support of command space, global strike, and information operations objectives; and J8 (Capability and Resource Integration), which is responsible for planning, programming, and executing the command's annual budget.

Joint and Individual U.S. Armed Service Resources

Various resources on space warfare and defense are produced by joint military entities (supporting the operations of two or more armed services) and individual branches of the U.S. armed forces. These consist of professional military education institutions such as National Defense University and Air University and units and facilities of individual armed services such as the Air and Space Expeditionary Force Center and Army Space and Missile Defense Command. These organizations and their information resources are profiled below.

National Defense University

National Defense University (NDU) and its component organizations train military and civilian leaders from the United States and other countries for national security policy-making positions. NDU also seeks to provide augmented understanding of U.S. and international security issues as part of its research mission.

Further information about NDU and its multifaceted component parts is accessible at www.ndu.edu/. Examples of NDU entities with numerous freely accessible Web-based resources dealing with space warfare and defense include the NDU Library, Institute for National Strategic Studies, Center for Technology and National Security Policy, and Center for the Study of Chinese Military Affairs.

NDU educational institutions such as the Industrial College of the Armed Forces and National War College also produce pertinent information resources that are profiled below.

Industrial College of the Armed Forces

The Industrial College of the Armed Forces (ICAF) was established in 1924 as the Army Industrial College. It acquired its current name in 1946 and became part of NDU in 1976. ICAF's institutional mandate is to prepare selected military officers and civilians for senior leadership and staff positions by engaging in postgraduate and affiliated research on national security strategy and industrial resources, placing particular emphasis on how acquisition and joint logistics are integrated into national security strategy. The ICAF Web site (www.ndu.edu/icaf) provides additional information about college curricular and research missions. A particularly noteworthy resource is the detailed studies and analyses of individual defense and related industries prepared by ICAF students, which are accessible from 2000–present. Examples of relevant industry analyses prepared for 2004 include Aircraft, Electronics, Information Technology, Manufacturing, Space, and Weapons.

National War College

The National War College (NWC) was established in 1946 as an upgraded replacement for the combined Army–Navy staff college, which existed from 1943–1946. NWC has produced more than 8,000 graduates who have assumed positions in the U.S. military or government and foreign militaries and governments. The college's mission is to prepare

Eagle adorns loggia of the National War College at Fort Lesley J. McNair in Washington, D.C. The National War College is one of the U.S. major professional military educational institutions. *(Library of Congress)*

future armed forces leaders, State Department officials, and leaders for other civilian governmental agencies for high-level policy, command, and staff responsibilities through senior-level curriculum and research in national security policy and strategy.

Information about NWC and its curricular and research activities is accessible at www.ndu.edu/nwc/. These resources include clip art of foreign weapons systems, the current *Student Handbook,* faculty biographical information and descriptions of their areas of expertise, and descriptions of the college's writing programs.

A National War College highlight is the presence of student research papers on various national security policy topics. Representative samples of these works include "The Evolution of the National Reconnaissance Office: Out From Deep Black Space and into the Defense Bureaucracy" (1995); "The 1972 Anti-Ballistic Missile Treaty: A Need for Change" (1996); "Deploying an Operational Anti-Satellite Capability: A Need for Change" (1996); "National Missile Defense: High Technology in a Strategic Vacuum" (2000); "Back to the Future: Space Power Theory and A.T. Mahan" (2000); "The Rise and Fall of the 1972 Anti-Ballistic Missile Treaty: A Study of U.S. Decisionmaking" (2003); and "The High Ground" (2004).

U.S. Air Force

The United States Air Force (USAF) was established by the 1947 National Security Act and is a military department within DOD. USAF is headed by the secretary of the Air Force and operates under the secretary of Defense's authority, direction, and control. The secretary of the Air Force is concerned with the organization, training, logistical assistance, administration, research and development, and other USAF activities as directed by the president and secretary of Defense. USAF's overall mission is defending the United States by controlling and exploiting air and space. Although USAF is considered the preeminent U.S. armed service dealing with military space policy its activities in this area are also partially duplicated by the Army and Navy.

General information about USAF activities, operations, and policies is accessible at www.af.mil/. The next group of entries examines the multifaceted resources on space warfare and defense produced by USAF component organizations.

Air Force Doctrine Center

The Air Force Doctrine Center (AFDC) is located at Maxwell AFB, Alabama and is responsible for researching, developing, producing, and storing USAF statements on various military operations covering strategic and tactical aspects of service missions (U.S. Air Force 2005, 1). AFDC is accessible at www.e-publishing.af.mil/. Representative samples of AFDC publications covering space warfare include *Spacelift Operations* (1998); *Space Warning Operations* (1998); *Satellite Command and Control Operations* (1999); *Operational Test and Evaluation for Space and Intercontinental Ballistic Missile (ICBM) Systems* (2001); *Air Force Space Command Unit Intelligence Support* (2003); *Space Control/Surveillance Operations* (2004); and *Launch and Range Roles and Responsibilities* (2005).

Air Force Office of Scientific Research

The Air Force Office of Scientific Research (AFOSR) is located in Washington, D.C. and has various domestic and international locations. AFOSR was established in 1951 in the headquarters of the Air Force Research and Development Command. Its creation derives from the realization that there is an intimate relationship between science, technology, and air force operations. Consequently, AFOSR has been responsible for sponsoring cutting-edge scientific research to assist the Air Force in its operational planning. AFOSR's Web site (www.afosr.af.mil) describes and details the activities of research program areas such as Aerospace and Materials Sciences and Physics and Electronics, along with descriptions of programs within these areas such as space power and propulsion, unsteady aerodynamics and hypersonics, remote sensing and imaging, sensors in the space environment, space electronics/university nanosatellites, and space sciences. The Web site also includes the newsletter *Research Highlights* (1995–present) and technical articles on space operations and satellites from the magazine *Technology Horizons.*

The Scientific Advisory Board (SAB) is affiliated with AFOSR and promotes the exchange of scientific and technical information between USAF and the scientific community that can strengthen Air Force service missions (U.S. Air Force Scientific Advisory Board n.d., 1). SAB's Web site (https://www.sab.hq.af.mil) provides information about board activities including listings and biographies of board members and descriptions of reports, which are accessible through the DTIC STINET Web site (http://stinet.dtic.mil). Examples of SAB reports accessible through this site include *New World Vistas: Air and Space Power for the 21st* Century (multiple volumes) (1996) and *Space Surveillance, Asteroids, Comets, and Space Debris: Volume 1 Space Surveillance* (1997). SAB's Web site also provides summaries of recent and ongoing research projects such as *Operationalizing Space Launch* (2004), *Persistence at Near Space Altitudes* (2005), and *Space Survivability* (2006).

Air University

Air University (AU) is located at Maxwell AFB, Alabama. Since its 1946 establishment, AU's mission has been to conduct professional military, graduate, and continuing education for officers, enlisted personnel, and civilians to prepare them for leadership, command, staff, and management responsibilities. These leadership missions are augmented by research in aerospace education, leadership, and management while also playing an integral role in developing and testing air force doctrine, concepts, and strategy. These instructional and research missions are carried out by AU component organizations such as Air War College; Air Command and Staff College; College of Aerospace, Doctrine, Research, and Education; School of Advanced Air and Space Studies; and Air University Press.

General information about AU operations and entities can be found at www.au.af .mil/. The crucial importance of AU information resources in conducting space warfare and defense research, and the depth and extent of these resources, are demonstrated in the next several entries of this chapter.

Air University Center for Strategy and Technology

The Air University Center for Strategy and Technology (CSAT) was established at AU's Air War College in 1996. CSAT's mission is engaging in long-term strategic thinking about technological implications of U.S. national security. The Center emphasizes education, research, and publishing supporting the integration of technology into national strategy and policy. CSAT is supported by strategic, scientific, and technological institutions, and it seeks to engage with Air Force and other DOD organizations to identify potential research project topics with the results of these findings being disseminated to senior military and political leaders, think tanks, educational institutions, and other interested parties (Air University, Center for Strategy and Technology 2005, 1).

Further information about CSAT is available at http://csat.au.af.mil/. Resources provided here include links to the Web sites of military and civilian government research laboratories, links to selected think tank Web sites, and various scientific and technology publications. Accessible CSAT publications include the following examples from CSAT's Occasional Paper series *Lasers in Space: Technological Options for Enhancing U.S. Military Capabilities* (1997); *Lasers and Missile Defense: New Concepts for Space-Based and Ground-Based Laser Weapons* (1998); *Weaponization of Space: Understanding Strategic and Technological Inevitabilities* (1999); *Airborne and Space-Based Lasers: An Analysis of Technological and Operational Compatibility* (1999); *Reusable Launch Vehicles: Rethinking Access to Space* (2000); *Using Lasers in Space: Laser Orbital Debris Removal and Asteroid Deflection* (2000); *Space-Based Global Strike: Understanding Strategic and Military Implications* (2001); *Sustained Space Superiority: A National Strategy for United States* (2002); and *The Decision Maker's Guide to Robust, Reliable, and Inexpensive Access to Space* (2004).

CSAT's Web site also provides links to recent historical Air Force studies speculating on the roles space will play in future military operations with these studies including *Spacecast 2020* (1993–1994), *Air Force 2025* (1996), and the multivolume *New World Vistas: Air and Space Power in the 21st Century* (1996).

Air University Library

The Air University Library (AUL) provides a variety of information resources for Air University faculty and students and some resources for users not affiliated with the university. General access to AUL is provided at http://aulibrary.maxwell.af.mil/. From here it is possible to search the library's Online Public Access Catalog (OPAC), which may include links to full text reports, the Air University Library Index to Military Periodicals (AULIMP) http://purl.access.gpo.gov/GPO/LPS3260, which provides bibliographic citations to articles from military science journals from 1988–present, links to other AU research center Web sites and publications, and Web-based bibliographies on various military and international political topics with representative samples including *Asymmetric Warfare* (2005); *Ballistic Missile Defense* (2005); *Counterspace* (2003); *Intelligence, Surveillance, and Reconnaissance (ISR) Programs* (2005); *Precision Guided Munitions* (2005); *Separate Space Force* (2005); and *Space: Military Aspects* (2005).

Air University Press

Air University Press (AUP) was established September 28, 1953 by General Order No. 54 from AU's Deputy Commander General John DeForrest Baker. This document stressed that AUP was to publish significant research and scholarly contributions consistent with the university's mission, which will enhance institutional recognition and scholarly cachet in the academic community.

Fairchild Library located at the Air University at Maxwell Air Force Base in Alabama. *(U.S. Department of Defense)*

General information about AUP is accessible at www.au.af.mil/au/aul/aupress/. Accessible resources include information about press operations, how prospective authors can submit manuscripts, how to order books, and the full text of many press publications on various military topics including space warfare and defense. Examples of accessible books include *Battlefield of the Future: 21st Century Warfare Issues* (1998); *The Air Force Role in Developing International Outer Space Law* (1999); *Beyond the Paths of Heaven: The Emergence of Space Power Thought* (1999); *Into the Unknown Together: The DOD, NASA, and Early Spaceflight* (2005); and *Space Power Integration: Perspectives from Space Weapons Officers* (2006).

AUP also published distinct series of reports on various aspects of aerospace power doctrine, which are profiled below.

CADRE Papers

CADRE Papers are reports produced under the auspices of AU's College of Aerospace, Doctrine, Research, and Education (CADRE), which seeks to deliver a multidimensional education, research, and war-gaming pedagogical experience to develop leaders capable of applying air, space, and cyberspace power into military operations.

CADRE is responsible for producing *Air and Space Power Journal,* available at http://purl.access.gpo.gov/GPO/LPS951 (1967–present), which is USAF's professional military journal. CADRE Papers are accessible at www.au.af.mil/au/aul/aupress/Indexes/title_ndx _cadre.htm. Examples of space warfare and defense titles in this series include *Does the United States Need Space-Based Weapons?* (1999) and *Flying Reactors: The Political Feasibility of Nuclear Power in Space* (2005).

Fairchild Papers

Fairchild Papers are another AU Press monographic series accessible at www.au.af.mil/ au/aul/aupress/Indexes/fairchild_papers_titles.htm. Pertinent space warfare and defense titles in this series include *Ten Propositions Regarding Space Power* (2002) and *Whither Space Power: Forging a Strategy for a New Century* (2002).

Maxwell Papers

The Maxwell Papers is another AU Press monographic series whose emphasis covers current and future issues of interest to the Air Force and DOD. Access to these analyses is available at www.au.af.mil/au/aul/aupress/Indexes/maxwell_papers_online.htm. Pertinent space war and defense titles in this series include *China as a Peer Competitor?: Trends in Nuclear Weapons, Space, and Information Warfare* (1999); *Growing the Space Industrial Base: Policy Pitfalls and Prospects* (2000); *U.S.-Led Cooperative Theater Missile Defense in Northeast Asia: Challenges and Issues* (2000); *A Separate Space Force: An 80-Year Old Argument* (2000); *China in Space: Civilian and Military Developments* (2001); and *Enabling Intelligence, Surveillance, and Reconnaissance Effects for Effects-Based Operations Conditions* (2005).

Wright Flyers

Wright Flyers is a series of occasional papers sponsored by AU's Air Command and Staff College. These papers are accessible at www.au.af.mil/au/aul/aupress/Indexes/wright _flyers_online.htm with *Rapid Dominance: Integrating Space into Today's Air Operations Center* (2000) and *Microsoft, Al-Jazeera, and the Predator: The Challenge of Effects-Based Operations in the Global War on Terrorism* (2005) serving as representative samples of pertinent analysis from this series.

Air University Student Research Studies

As a graduate educational institution, AU faculty and students produce a variety of information resources. Some of those produced by AU faculty and affiliated scholars have already been profiled; here the focus is on student research papers dealing with space warfare and defense that are produced by students at AU's five major educational institutional programs: Air Command and Staff College, Air Force Fellows, Air Force Institute of Technology, Air War College, and School of Advanced Air and Space Studies. These

research papers and theses are all accessible at https://research.au.af.mil/showstudent
.aspx?type=student, and chronological access to these resources dates back to 1992.

Air Command and Staff College

The Air Command and Staff College (ACSC) serves as the Air Force's professional
military education school. ACSC responsibilities include preparing field grade officers,
international military officers, and U.S. citizens to assume positions of increasing responsibility in military and other governmental areas. It emphasizes teaching the skills required for aerospace operations supporting joint commands as well as leadership and
command. Examples of ACSC student papers on space warfare and defense include *Planetary Asteroid Defense Study: Assessing and Responding to the Natural Space Debris Threat*
(1995); *The Military Utility of German Rocketry During World War II* (1997); *The Airborne
Laser—A Revolution in Military Affairs* (1997); *Space Applications in the Logistics Arena:
An Analysis of Project Combat Track* (1997); *Achieving Affordable Operational Requirements
on the Space Based Infrared System (SBIRS): A Model for Warfighter and Acquisition Success*
(1997); *Future Roles of Air and Space Power in Combatting Terrorism* (1997); *Distinguishing Space Power from Air Power: Implications for the Space Force Debate* (1998); *Space
Power Theory: A Rising Star* (1998); *Clausewitz on Space: Developing Military Space Theory
Through a Comparative Analysis* (1999); *How is U.S. Space Power Jeopardized by an Adversary's Exploitation, Technological Developments, Employment and Engagement of Laser
Antisatellite Weapons* (2000); *Defending the Final Frontier: Commercial Space System Vulnerabilities to Directed Energy Weapon Threats* (2000); *Solar Power Constellations: Implications for the United States Air Force* (2000); *DOD Use of Commercial Wideband Satellite
Communication Systems: How Much is Needed and How Do We Get It?* (2001); *The National Missile Defense Debate in the Post 9–11 Context* (2002); *Building a Cadre of Space
Professionals With Responsible Lift* (2003); and *Spacepower Theory: Lessons from the Mas-
ters* (2005).

Air Force Fellows

The Air Force Fellows (AFF) program allows a small number of carefully chosen and
experienced officers to serve one-year tours studying national security policy and strategy
at civilian universities or think tanks. These AFF fellows provide advice on national security policy and explain USAF and DOD programs and policies to nationally recognized
scholars, foreign dignitaries, and prominent policy analysts while gaining enhanced insights and understanding through their interactions with civilian leaders.

Samples of AFF space warfare and defense research analyses include *Making the Expeditionary Aerospace Force Work—Now!* (2000); *National Missile Defense: Laying the Ground-
work for Future U.S. Security Policy* (2001); *Through a Glass, Darkly: Innovation and Transformation in the Twenty-First Century Air Force* (2001); *The International Development of*

Space and Its Impact on U.S. National Space Policy (2003); *Air and Space Expeditionary Force Crisis Action Leadership for Commanders* (2004); and *Flying Reactors: The Political Feasibility of Nuclear Power in Space* (2004).

Air Force Institute of Technology

The Air Force Institute of Technology (AFIT) is part of AU although it is located at Wright-Patterson AFB in Dayton, Ohio. AFIT serves as USAF's graduate engineering and management school and its technical professional continuing education institution.

General information about AFIT is accessible through its Web site, www.afit.edu/. Examples of AFIT student papers emphasizing scientific and technological aspects of space warfare and defense include *Whole Spacecraft Vibration Isolation* (1999); *Space Launch Operations and the Lean Aerospace Initiative* (1999); *Space Range Scheduling and the Lean Aerospace Initiative* (2000); *Navigation of Satellite Cluster* (2000); *Using GPS as a Reference System to Hit a Moving Target* (2001); *Parameter Study for Optimizing the Mass of a Space Nuclear Power System Radiation Shield* (2002); *Issues in Modeling Military Space* (2002); *Modeling Aerospace Ground Equipment Usage in Military Environments* (2002); *Space Time Adaptive Processing and Clutter Classification Integration and Evaluation* (2002); *The Air Warrior's Value of National Security Space* (2003); *Development, Fabrication, and Ground Test of an Inflatable Structure Space-Flight Experiment* (2003); *Characterization and Ground Test of an Inflatable Rigidizable Space Experiment* (2004); *Reusable Space Vehicle Ground Operations Baseline Conceptual Model* (2004); and *Design of a Space-Borne Autonomous Infrared Tracking System* (2004).

Air War College

Air War College (AWC) is the Air Force's senior professional school. AWC instruction and research emphasizes joint operations and using aerospace power to support national security while serving as a resource promoting education and dialogue on national and international aerospace issues.

Representative AWC student papers include *China's Space Program and Its Implications for the United States* (1995); *The New DOD Space Management Process: A Critical Analysis* (1996); *What the Warfighter Should Know About Space: A Report on U.S. Space Command Joint Space Support Teams* (1997); *Command and Employment of Space Power: Doctrine for the Asymmetric Technology of the 21st Century* (1997); *Increasing the Weaponization of Space: A Prescription for Further Progress* (1998); *Who Will Command the High Ground?: The Case for a Separate Area of Responsibility for Space* (1998); *Can the U.S. Air Force Weaponize Space?* (1998); *Planetary Defense: Legacy for a Certain Future* (1998); *Increased Military Reliance on Commercial Communications Satellites: Implications for the War Planner* (1998); *Military Dependence on Commercial Satellite Communication Systems—Strength or Vulnerability?* (1999); *Prompt Global Strikes Through Space: What*

Military Value? (2000); *The Command of Space: A National Vision for American Prosperity and Security* (2001); *How to Institutionalize Space Superiority in the United States Air Force* (2002); and *Spacepower as a Coercive Force* (2003).

School of Advanced Air & Space Studies

The School of Advanced Air and Space Studies (SAASS) seeks to educate strategists in the art and science of aerospace warfare. SAASS's faculty teach a graduate-level curriculum emphasizing the theories, history, applications, design, and effective expression of aerospace strategies, operational concepts, and related policies in the context of conflict, deterrence, and war. Students participating in this program have an average weekly reading demand of 1,200–1,500 pages, and they are required to prepare a thesis based on original source documents.

Pertinent SAASS student theses include *Concepts of Operations for a Renewable Space Launch Vehicle* (1996); *Safe Heavens: Military Strategy and Space Sanctuary Thought* (1997); *Does the United States Need Space-Based Weapons?* (1998); *Do We Need Separate Space Theory: The Lessons of History* (2001); *Defense or Deterrence?: The Future of Missile Defense* (2002); *Space Weapons and Space Power* (2003); *Globalness: Toward a Space Power Theory* (2003); *The Best Defense: Charting the Future of US Space Strategy and Policy* (2005); and *Theater Space Warfare: Rewriting the Joint Playbook* (2005).

National Space Studies Center

AU's National Space Studies Center (NSSC) is responsible for promoting and sponsoring research and education on employing space power by creating and maintaining a depository and clearinghouse for space information and expertise.

The NSSC Web site (http://space.au.af.mil) provides access to a variety of materials describing center activities. These include links to instructional materials such as AU course syllabi, space-related course material from NASA and civilian universities, links to DOD and military services space policy doctrinal documents, news about various civilian and military space developments, and links to space fact sheets from other Air Force organizations.

Accessible publications include the *Air University Space Primer* (2003) and links to other publications on military space produced by civilian, military, and governmental organizations.

U.S. Air Force Academy

The United States Air Force Academy (USAFA) is located in Colorado Springs, Colorado and is responsible for providing undergraduate education to facilitate the development of aerospace officers with the knowledge, discipline, and motivation to lead the USAF. The academy was established in 1954 and has an enrollment of approximately 4,000 cadets.

Cadets of the Air Force Academy Class of 2003 celebrate at graduation ceremonies as the Air Force Thunderbirds fly overhead. *(U.S. Air Force)*

General information about USAFA curriculum, programs, and research is accessible at the academy Web site, www.usafa.af.mil/.

Air Force Academy Institute for National Security Studies

The Air Force Academy's Institute for National Security Studies (INSS) was created in 1992 as a collaborative effort between the USAFA dean of faculty and the Policy Division of the Division of the Nuclear and Counterproliferation Directorate of USAF headquarters and became an independent research center in 2004. INSS's mission is promoting national security research for DOD within the military academic community while supporting the Air Force national security education program. During its first 12 years of existence, INSS has sponsored over $2.5 million in research at military and civilian universities (U.S. Air Force Academy Institute for National Security Studies n.d., 1–2).

The INSS Web site (www.usafa.af.mil/df/inss) provides information about institute activities and reports produced under institute sponsorship as well as information on how to submit report proposals for possible INSS sponsorship. Access is provided to various publications including the institute's Occasional Papers series with relevant examples including *The Viability of U.S. Anti-Satellite Policy: Moving Toward Space Control* (2000); *United States Military Space: Into the 21st Century* (2002); *"All Our Tomorrows": A Long-*

Range Forecast of Global Trends Affecting Arms Control Technology (2002); *India's Emerging Security Strategy, Missile Defense, and Arms Control* (2004); and *The Art of Peace: Dissuading China From Developing Counter-Space Weapons* (2005).

Air Force Research Laboratory Directed Energy Directorate

The Air Force Research Laboratory Directed Energy Directorate (AFRLDED) is located at Kirtland AFB near Albuquerque, New Mexico. AFRLDED serves as DOD's leading center for lasers, high-power microwaves, and other directed energy technologies. Its multiple missions include supporting user needs for directed energy weapons applications and addressing mission area deficiencies; exploiting directed energy technology for USAF and DOD applications; enabling the Air Force to avoid technological surprise; fostering awareness of directed energy's potential for Air Force and DOD applications; and exploring directed energy technology offering high payoff for directed energy capabilities and applications.

AFRLDED's Web site (www.de.afrl.af.mil) contains additional information describing laboratory missions and activities. These resources include descriptions of AFRLDED program areas such as counter electronics, force protection, long-range strike, precision engagement, and space control, news releases (2004–present), descriptions of awards received by directorate personnel, and an image gallery describing specific directorate programs. A particularly useful feature of the AFRLDED Web site is the presence of numerous program fact sheets with examples including *YAL-1A Attack Laser: The World's First Laser-Armed Combat Aircraft* (2002); *High-Power Microwaves* (2002); *Airborne Laser* (2003); *Airborne Laser: A Brief History* (2003); *Testing: Paving the Way to Missile Shootdown* (2003); *Directed Energy Directorate: Developing Speed-of-Light Weaponry* (2004); and *Relay Mirror Technology* (2006).

Air Force Research Laboratory Sensors Directorate

The Air Force Research Laboratory Sensors Directorate (AFRLSD) is located at Wright-Patterson AFB in Dayton, Ohio. AFRLSD's mission is leading the discovery, development, and integration of affordable sensor and countermeasure technologies for U.S. war fighters, which enables complete air and space freedom for U.S. forces while denying sanctuary to hostile forces.

The AFRLSD Web site (www.afrl.af.mil/sn) features descriptive information about directorate programs in automatic target recognition and sensor fusion, electro-optical sensors and countermeasures technology, radio-frequency sensors and countermeasures technology, and descriptions about directorate research accomplishments in areas such as the new phase shifter electronically scanned antenna for space-based and unmanned combat air vehicle sensors, evaluating the joint air-to-surface stand-off missile's antijam global positioning satellite system technology, software accelerating automated target recognition development, and other research and technological advances.

Air Force Research Laboratory Space Vehicles Directorate

The Air Force Research Laboratory Space Vehicles Directorate (AFRLSVD) is also located at Kirtland AFB with an adjunct branch at Hansom AFB, Massachusetts. AFRLSVD is responsible for developing and transitioning high-payoff space technologies supporting U.S. war fighters while also utilizing commercial, civil, and other governmental capabilities for national advantage.

The AFRLSVD Web site (www.vs.afrl.af.mil/Directorate) provides additional descriptions of directorate activities. These include information about directorate product lines involving battle-space environment, spacecraft technology, and integrated experiments and evaluation. These product lines conduct research and development in areas such as the solar mass ejection imager all-sky camera, detecting ionospheric atmospheric impacts on radio-frequency war-fighting systems, active sensors such as those used by space-based radars, and spacecraft instrumentation.

Additional information resources include news releases (2004–present), information on directorate interactions with the broader scientific community such as the Space Scholars Program, an image gallery of research areas, and fact sheets on various programs. Examples of these fact sheets include *XSS-11 Microsatellite* (2005); *Space Countermeasures Hands On Program* (2006); *Cryocoolers Infrared Sensors to Enable Space Intelligence, Surveillance, Reconnaissance, and Situational Awareness* (2006); and *The Communication/ Navigation Outage Forecasting System* (2006).

U.S. Air Force Space Command

U.S. Air Force Space Command (AFSPACOM) is located at Peterson AFB in Colorado Springs, Colorado. AFSPACOM was activated on October 1, 1982 from several preexisting Air Force space operational entities. The command was initially organized to manage missile warning and space-tracking systems, and it would expand its sphere of influence by acquiring the Air Force's space launch mission and gaining control of the United States' intercontinental ballistic missile force in 1993. An important recent development in AFSPACOM's institutional evolution was DOD merging U.S. Space Command with STRATCOM in an effort to improve combat effectiveness and expedite information collection and assessment.

AFSPACOM's mission is defending the United States by controlling and exploiting space. It does this by providing routine and reliable space-based support for war fighters and continuously improving command abilities to support combat forces. AFSPACOM uses four mission areas to implement its operations: counterspace, space force enhancement, space force application, and mission support. Counterspace refers to operations intended to attain and maintain a desired degree of space superiority by allowing friendly forces to maximize space capabilities while preventing adversaries from using these capabilities. Space force enhancement emphasizes providing capabilities to facilitate or support air, land, sea, and space military operations. Space force application consists of conducting global operations by directly and promptly applying force from and through space against terrestrial targets. Space support is responsible for managing launch and satellite operations; operating, servicing, recovery, and repositioning satellites once they are in orbit, and commanding, controlling, tracking, and receiving satellite telemetry. Mission support involves supporting logistics, communications, information management, and other personnel infrastructure and sustainment matters so that AFSPACOM personnel can execute their missions.

The AFSPACOM Web site (www.peterson.af.mil/hqafspc) has additional resources describing command operations. These includes the *Crosshairs* column produced by AFSPACOM's commander; news releases (January 2004–present); information on launch operations at Cape Canaveral, Florida, and Vandenberg AFB, California; a photo gallery featuring ICBM launches and satellites; the text of current and archived AFSPACOM base newspapers such as the 21st Space Wing's *Space Observer, Space and Missile Times, The Missileer, Satellite Flyer,* and *Astro News;* along with information about command component organizations such as the 45th Space Wing at Patrick AFB, Florida, the 30th Space Wing AFB, and the 91st Space Wing at Minot AFB, North Dakota. Additional resources include the current *Almanac, Air Force Space Command: Strategic Master Plan FY 06 and Beyond* (2003); *High Frontier: The Journal for Space and Missile Professionals* (2004–present); and numerous fact sheets including *Pave Paws Radar System* (n.d.); *Atlas II Launch Vehicle* (2005); *Defense Satellite Communications System* (2005); *Milstar Satellite Communications System* (2005); and *Ground-Based Electro-Optical Deep Space Surveillance* (2006).

National Security Space Institute

The National Security Space Institute (NSSI) is also located at Peterson AFB and was activated on October 18, 2004. NSSI is responsible for providing space education training programs for space staff members and providing instruction on military space systems, space warfare concepts, and space tactical employment. The institute's three schools carrying out this curriculum are the space operations school, space professional school, and space tactics school. Information on NSSI can be accessed at https://www.peterson.af.mil/nssi/. Materials available here include listings of institute administrators, a local map showing NSSI's location, admissions information, and course descriptions and schedules. Examples of courses offered include Advanced Course Missile Warning, Counterspace Planning and Integration, Director of Space Forces, Space Fundamentals, Space in the Air and Space Operations Center, Space Operations Course, and Weapons School Preparation Course.

Space and Missile Systems Center

The Air Force Space and Missile Systems Center (SMC) is located in Los Angeles and serves as a technical center responsible for researching, developing, and acquiring military space systems. SMC's work covers space force enhancement, space support, counterspace, force application, and transformation and covers various programs and weapons systems including GPS satellites, the MILSTAR joint-service communications satellite system, the Defense Meteorological Satellite Program, the Space-Based Infrared System (SBIRS), and the Space Tracking and Surveillance System (STSS).

The SMC Web site (www.losangeles.af.mil) provides descriptions of organizational components including the Historian's Office, news releases (1999–present), the newsletter *Astro News* (2001–present), and various resources from the Historian's Office on topics such as the Air Force Satellite Control Network, launch vehicles, satellite systems, and space systems in combat. Numerous fact sheets are also provided including *Most Commonly Asked Questions and Answers on GPS* (n.d.); *Atmospheric Interceptor Technology Program* (1996–1998); *Satellite and Launch Control Systems* (2000); *Space-Based Radar* (2001); *Milstar Satellite Communications System* (2003); *Wide-Band Gap Filler Satellite* (2004); and *Defense Support Program* (2005).

The Schriever Space Complex in Los Angeles is home to the Air Force's Space and Missile Systems Center. *(U.S. Air Force)*

Air Force Space Battlelab

The Air Force Space Battlelab (AFSB) is located at Schriever AFB near Colorado Springs, Colorado. Established on June 30, 1997, AFSB is responsible for identifying space operations and logistics concepts and rapidly assessing their potential for advancing joint war fighting and Air Force concepts of operations (CONOPS). Key Air Force CONOPS examined by the Battlelab include global strike task force, global response task force, global mobility task force, nuclear response task force, homeland security task force, space command and control, intelligence, surveillance, and reconnaissance task force, and expeditionary air and space force.

AFSB is organized into two team units carrying out its evaluative work. These are the Concept Development Team, which seeks promising ideas or concepts from the Air Force and space communities, along with industry and academia, to review for viability and contributing to Air Force requirements. The Initiative Demonstration Team uses various techniques including prototype demonstrations, modeling and simulation, war gaming, and exercise evaluations to evaluate the military worthiness of promising concepts. The AFSB Web site (www.schriever.af.mil/battlelab) includes a list of frequently asked questions and information about historical and ongoing Battlelab initiatives such as Hyperspectral Imagery collection upon Pike's Peak, Space Environment Network Display, Space Object Identification in Living Color, Space Tracking of RV Convoys, Infrared Cloud Monitor, Jungle Eyes, which seeks to demonstrate the ability to image targets through canopied jungle foliage using a laser-based imaging sensor mounted on an airborne platform, and Near Earth Object Tracking, which seeks to provide accurate detection and tracking of small objects in low earth orbit.

Air and Space Expeditionary Force Center

The Air and Space Expeditionary Force Center (ASEFC) is a direct reporting unit to the Air Combat Command at Langley AFB, Virginia. ASEFC is responsible for executing Air Force battle rhythm and strives to plan and deliver air and space power to the right place and time to support Air Force mission requirements. It consists of three divisions: Air and Space Expeditionary Operations (AEO), Air and Space Expeditionary Combat Support (AES), and Air and Space Expeditionary Plans (AEP). AEO seeks to integrate all air and space assets for contingency operations in global support of combatant commander requirements by flying units and their direct support personnel with the resources required for deploying in operations ranging from humanitarian assistance to major regional conflicts. AES services all aviation and combat support functional areas dedicated to contingency operations in global support of combatant commander requirements. AEP responsibilities encompass strategic planning, construction, and implementation and oversight of ASEFC cyclical and rotation timelines.

ASEFC does not have its own Web site, but a detailed fact sheet describing its activities can be found on the USAF Web site at www.af.mil/factsheets/.

National Air and Space Intelligence Center

The National Air and Space Intelligence Center (NASIC) is located at Wright-Patterson AFB in Dayton, Ohio. It serves as the national center for integrated intelligence on aerospace systems, forces, and threats. NASIC seeks to produce integrated and predictive air and space intelligence operations to facilitate military operations and the policy-making process and to force modernization. Its ultimate objectives are seeing that U.S. air and space forces are prepared to engage in information operations, defeat future threats, are prepared for global engagement, and are never surprised by foreign air and space capabilities. NASIC's Web site (www.aia.af.mil/units/nasic.asp) features information about center activities, historical information about operations such as acquiring a Mig–29 jet fighter from the Moldovan Air Force, listings of current and historical center commanders, and information on center positions and how to apply for these positions.

North American Aerospace Defense Command

The North American Aerospace Defense Command (NORAD) is a joint U.S.–Canadian organization located in Cheyenne Mountain near Colorado Springs, Colorado. NORAD's mission is providing aerospace warning and control for North America. Aerospace warning is defined as monitoring man-made objects in space and detecting, validating, and warning of attack against North America by aircraft, missiles, or space vehicles utilizing military support arrangements with other military commands. Aerospace control involves ensuring air sovereignty and air defense of U.S. and Canadian airspace.

NORAD's commander is appointed by and responsible to the president of the United States and Canadian prime minister. The commander's headquarters are at nearby Peterson AFB. Cheyenne Mountain maintains a central collection and coordination facility for a worldwide sensor system to provide NORAD's commander and U.S. and Canadian leadership with an accurate picture of any aerospace threat. Subordinate region headquarters at Elmendorf AFB, Alaska; Canadian Forces Base Winnipeg, MB; and Tyndall AFB, Florida receive direction from the commander and control operations in their individual areas of responsibility.

NORAD's Web site (www.norad.mil) provides biographical information about command leaders, news releases (2001–present), a historical overview of U.S. homeland security, instructional material on homeland security including a course syllabus, information on potential employment opportunities, information on potential business contracting opportunities, descriptions of regional NORAD commands such as the Canadian Region, and a brief organizational history synopsis.

30th Space WingB

The 30th Space Wing is located at Vandenberg AFB, California. This unit is responsible for managing DOD space and missile testing, placing satellites into polar orbit from the West Coast, and using expendable rocket boosters such as the Delta II and Titan IV to carry out its missions. Additional 30th Space Wing activities include West Coast launch activities for the Air Force, NASA, and various private sector contractors. These responsibilities are carried out by the space wing's Operations Group, Mission Support Group, Medical Group, and Launch Group. The 30th Space Wing Web site is located at www .vandenberg.af.mil/. It features wing leader biographies, descriptions of organizational activities, news releases (2003–present), listings and descriptions of unclassified launch missions (April 2002–present), and the current issue of *Space and Missile Times* newspaper.

U.S. Army

The Continental Congress established the American Continental Army on June 14, 1775; the first U.S. Congress established the Department of War on August 7, 1789; and the 1947 National Security Act established the Department of the Army headed by the secretary of the Army. The U.S. Army's mission is organizing, training, and supplying active and reserve land forces to defend the United States. Information about overall army activities can be found at www.army.mil/. The U.S. Army also has an extensive involvement in space warfare and defense activities, which began in the aftermath of World War II to the present. Early Army historical accomplishments in this area include the 1957 creation of the first program office for ballistic missile defense and successfully intercepting an intercontinental ballistic missile on July 19, 1962. Army agencies involved in these activities are profiled below.

Assistant Secretary of the Army–Acquisitions, Logistics, and Technology)

The assistant secretary of the Army (Acquisitions, Logistics, and Technology), ASA (ALT) is responsible for executing the Army's acquisition functions and management systems, overseeing army logistics management functions and operations, executing army research and development functions, directing the Army Science Board, ensuring weapons system production readiness, overseeing the army's industrial base and preparedness programs, and supporting Department of the Army space and strategic acquisition programs. The ASA (ALT) Web site (https://webportal.saalt.army.mil) provides information on component organizational entities dealing with acquisition and systems management, policy and procurement, and research and technology along with information on Army Science Board activities. Procurement and contracting information is also provided along with access to the Army Digital Library, which features numerous publications and handbooks dealing with military acquisitions and logistics matters. Examples of relevant Army Science Board studies accessible through DTIC STINET include *Prioritizing Army Space Needs* (1998), *Technical and Tactical Opportunities for Revolutionary Advances* (2000), and *Directed Energy* (2004).

Army Command and General Staff College

The Army Command and General Staff College (CGSC) is located at Fort Leavenworth, Kansas. CGSC was initially established as the School of Application for Cavalry and Infantry on January 6, 1882, was renamed CGSC in 1947, and received congressional authorization in 1974 to award the master's of military science degree to its graduates. CGSC seeks to educate leaders in professional military values and practices, serve as the key agent for the U.S. Army's Leadership Development Program, develop army doctrinal guidance, and promote and support the growth of military art and science.

General information about CGSC activities and programs can be found at www.cgsc .army.mil/. These resources include information about the college and its educational philosophy, the online catalog for its Combined Arms Research Library, and resources about component organizations such as the Combat Studies Institute, School for Advanced Military Studies, School for Command Preparation, and Schools of Combined Arms and Staff Services.

Relevant publicly accessible publications that can address space warfare and defense issues include articles from the journal *Military Review* (1922–present), and various reports and student theses including *Envisioning Future Warfare* (1995); *Arming the Skies: The Right Time Has Not Arrived* (2000); *A Fork in the Path to the Heavens: The Emergence of an Independent Space Force* (2002); *Determining if Space is an Applicable Component to Intelligence Preparation of the Battlefield for Ranger Operations When Facing Non-Nation-State Adversaries* (2002); *Examination of Intercontinental Ballistic Missile Defense Development Within the United States from 1952 to 1965* (2003); *Space Support: Enabler of the Unit of Employment* (2003); *Service Ownership of the Patriot Missile System: Army or Air Force* (2003); *For Want of an Nail: An Assessment of Global Positioning Satellite Replacement* (2004); *Directed Energy Weapons: Do We Have a Game Plan?* (2004); *Space Control: Is Army Investment Necessary?* (2004); and *Joint Theater Missile Defense in Taiwan: Protecting United States Interests and Friends* (2004).

Army Doctrine Center–Reimer Library

The General Dennis J. Reimer Training and Doctrine Digital Library provides one-stop access to approved army training and doctrinal materials at www.adtdl.army.mil/

and access through the Army Publishing Directorate at www.usapa.army.mil/. However, access to these resources is restricted to .mil domain users. Freely accessible Army training and doctrinal publications are accessible through the Global Security.org Web site at www.globalsecurity.org/military/library/policy/army/fm/ with Army field manuals receiving prominent coverage here. Examples of relevant space warfare and defense field manuals include *FM 100–18: Space Support to Army Operations* (1995); *FM 90–43: Multiservice Procedures for Joint Theater Missile Target Development* (1999); *FM 44–100: U.S. Army Air and Missile Defense Operations* (2000); *FM 100–12: Army Theater Missile Defense Operations* (2000); *FM 3.01–16: Multiservice Tactics, Techniques, and Procedures for Theater Missile Defense Intelligence Preparation of the Battlespace* (2002); and *FM 3.01–85: Patriot Battalion and Battery Operations* (2002).

Army Space and Missile Defense Command

Army Space and Missile Defense Command (SMDC) was created by the Department of the Army on October 1, 1997. SMDC is headquartered in Arlington, Virginia and has satellite operations in locales such as Colorado Springs, Colorado, and Huntsville, Alabama, and serves as the Army's preeminent space and national missile defense organization. Its mission is ensuring that Army war fighters have access to space assets and products to achieve decisive victory with minimum casualties and providing effective missile defense to protect the United States, its deployed military forces, and the forces of U.S. allies. Further information on SMDC activities is available at www.smdc.army.mil/. Accessible resources include descriptions of organizational components such as the Future Warfare Center and the Space and Missile Defense Technical Center, press releases (December 1995–present), a space and missile defense acronyms glossary, *The Eagle* newspaper (February 1998–present), and *Army Space Journal* (Spring 2002–present).

Additional SMDC resources include a series of fact sheets on command research programs and activities with representative examples including *Advanced Measurements Optical Range* (n.d.); *Distributed Imaging Radar Technology* (n.d.); *Future Warfare Center* (n.d.); *High Energy Laser Systems Test Facility* (n.d.); *Joint Awareness Warfighter-Space* (n.d.); *Kill Assessment Program* (n.d.); *Multiple Kill Vehicles* (n.d.); *Space and Missile Technical Center* (n.d.); *Space and Missile Defense Command Test and Evaluation Directorate* (n.d.); *Studies and Analysis Division* (n.d.); and *TRADOC System Manager: Ground-Based Midcourse Defense* (n.d.).

Aviation and Missile Command

The Army's Aviation and Missile Command (AMCOM) is headquartered at Redstone Arsenal, Alabama and is part of the Army's Material Command. AMCOM was formed on October 1, 1997 and its responsibilities include developing, acquiring, fielding, and sustaining aviation, vehicle, and unmanned missile systems while ensuring the readiness of these systems with seamless transition to combat operations.

Additional details on AMCOM are provided on its Web site, www.amcom.redstone .army.mil/. Relevant resources include command leader biographies; links to AMCOM organizational component Web sites such as the Command Analysis Directorate, Intelligence and Security Directorate, History Office, and Inspector General Office; business contracting information; employment opportunities; photos of weapons systems such as Theater High-Altitude Air Defense; and news releases (January 1998–present).

Accessible publications include the weekly newspaper *Redstone Rocket* (August 21, 2002–present) and numerous historical publications including *Army Ordnance Satellite Program* (1958); *Development, Production, and Deployment of the Nike Ajax Guided Missile System, 1945–1959* (1962); *History of the Field Army Ballistic Missile Defense System Project, 1959–1962* (1963); *History of the Basic Honest John Rocket System, 1950–1964* (1964); *History of the Redstone Missile System* (1965); *History of the Chaparal/FAAR Air Defense System* (1977); and *History of the Jupiter Missile System* (Declassified 1978) along with additional resources on the historical development and evolution of Army missile defense programs including video Web casts.

Fort Greely–Alaska

This facility, located in Fort Greely, Alaska is an Army facility operating a ground-based midcourse ballistic missile defense system with the 1st Space Brigade and the 100th Missile Brigade being the SMDC units assigned to this location. This facility was formally activated on January 22, 2004, and it is responsible for defending the United States against intermediate and long-range ballistic missile attacks while also providing security and operational control for ground-based interceptors based in Alaska.

An embryonic Web site, www.usarak.army.mil/greely, provides some information on this facility, which will, hopefully, include more detail in the future.

Ronald Reagan Ballistic Missile Defense Test Site

The Ronald Reagan Ballistic Missile Defense Test Site (RTS) is located on Kwajalein Atoll and Wake Island in the Republic of the Marshall Islands in the Pacific Ocean. The test site's mission is supporting ballistic missile testing and space operations, which it has done for nearly 40 years. RTS sensors allow the testing of ballistic missiles and ballistic missile interceptor capabilities. The RTS Web site at www.smdc.army.mil/RTS.html provides additional information on range activities. These include the weekly *Kwajalein Hourglass* (June 4, 1999–present), information on local meteorological conditions, descriptions of space operations activities emphasizing the tracking and surveillance of deep space and synchronous satellites, an overview of RTS meteorological support systems, an overview of the RTS mission control center, and a description and map of RTS missile launch facilities.

White Sands Missile Range

The White Sands Missile Range (WSMR) is located in south central New Mexico near Las Cruces and just north of El Paso, Texas. WSMR's mission involves offering various testing, evaluation, research, and assessment of various military systems and commercial products. Examples of these services include offering the largest open-air/overland missile-testing range in the hemisphere along with conducting environmental testing and computer modeling of various missile systems.

The WSMR Web site (www.wsmr.army.mil) provides information about the activities of range component organizations such as the Aerial Cable Facility, Electromagnetic Test Facility, High Energy Laser Systems Test Facility, Launch Facilities, and Warhead Testing. Numerous fact sheets are also provided including *Rockets: History and Theory* (n.d.); *High Energy Laser Systems Test Facility* (n.d.); *The Corporal Missile Program* (n.d.); and *White Sands Statistics* (Fiscal Years 1994–present).

A Pershing II battlefield support missile is fired from an erector/launcher vehicle on McGregor Range at White Sands. *(U.S. Department of Defense)*

A team of Vanguard I scientists mount the satellite in the rocket. Conducted by the Naval Research Laboratory, Vanguard was the first American satellite program. *(Naval Research Laboratory)*

U.S. Navy

U.S. Navy institutional origins begin with the October 13, 1775 establishment of the Continental Navy of the American Revolution by the Continental Congress. A Department of the Navy and Office of the Secretary of the Navy were established by statute on April 30, 1798, and the National Security Act Amendments of 1949 established the contemporary Department of the Navy in DOD. The U.S. Navy's mission is protecting the United States by effectively prosecuting sea war including seizing or defending naval bases, supporting all U.S. military forces, and maintaining freedom of the seas.

The Navy's historical involvement with space dates back to World War II's aftermath when the Naval Research Laboratory began probing the upper atmosphere using captured German V-2 rockets. This involvement has continued in the ensuing six decades and is performed in multiple naval facilities described below.

Naval Network Warfare Command

The Naval Network Warfare Command (NETWARCOM) is headquartered in Norfolk, Virginia. It was initially established established on July 12, 2002 as Naval Network and Space Operations Command (NNSOC) through the merger of the Naval Space Command and Naval Network Operations Command whose historical provenance dates from 1983 for Naval Space Command and 1953 for the Naval Network Operations Command's parent agency. NNSOC was disestablished in 2006 and its functions transferred to NETWARCOM.

NETWARCOM is responsible for operating and maintaining the Navy's global telecommunications, information and space systems, and services to directly support operations, training and education, and providing innovative solutions to war fighters. Its domestic and international facilities and personnel also handle responsibilities in areas such as voice and IP connectivity, ground and space segments for naval satellite communications systems, providing space-related operational intelligence to Navy and Marine Corps forces through tactical communication channels, satellite telemetry and tracking, directly down-linking space tactical data, supporting various theater missile defense requirements, and institutionalizing naval space education through curriculum sponsorship at institutions such as the Naval Postgraduate School and Naval War College. Additional information on NETWARCOM is provided through its Web site, www.netwarcom.navy .mil/. These resources include command leader biographies, news releases, a fact sheet featuring budget information, issues of *Info Domain* magazine (July 2006-present), and publications such as *Naval Network Warfare Command Strategy 2006-2010* (2007), and descriptions of NNSOC training activities.

Naval Postgraduate School

The Naval Postgraduate School (NPS) dates from a 1945 statute making it a fully accredited graduate institution, and it moved to its present location in Monterrey, California in 1951. NPS consists of nearly 1,500 students representing officers from U.S. military services and nearly thirty countries and selected U.S. Government employees. These students study and conduct research in areas of interest to the Navy and other DOD entities. Examples of master's and doctoral degrees offered by NPS include national security affairs, aeronautical engineering, astronautical engineering, computer science, meteorology, operations research, and systems management.

The NPS Web site (www.nps.navy.mil) contains recent press releases, information about NPS faculty and their research interests, and links to NPS pedagogical and research centers including the Spacecraft Research and Design Center, Systems Technology Battle Laboratory, Center for Civil-Military Relations, Center for Information Systems Security Studies and Research, The Cebrowski Institute for Innovation and Information Superiority, the NPS Library, Center for Contemporary Conflict, and Center for Joint Services Electronic Warfare.

Additional instructional materials include descriptions for courses such as Space Systems Engineering, Space Systems Operations, Military Applications of Space, Orbital Mechanics and Launch Systems, Air/Ocean Remote Sensing for Interdisciplinary Curricula, Military Satellite Communications, and Launch Vehicle Performance and Selection. Numerous research reports produced by NPS faculty, and in some cases students, are also accessible on the NPS Web site. Examples include *Computer Aided Thermal Analysis of a Technology Demonstration Satellite (NPSAT1)* (2003); *Unmanned Vehicle Distributed Sensor Management and Information Exchange Demonstration* (2004); *Formal Specification and Run-Time Monitoring within the Ballistic Missile Defense Project* (2005); *Analysis of the Performance Characteristics of the Naval Postgraduate School MWR-O5XP Mobile Weather Radar* (2005); *Trident Warrior Experimentation Process* (2005); and *Measuring Customer and Employee Loyalty at Space and Naval Warfare Systems Center Charleston* (2005).

Naval Research Laboratory

The Naval Research Laboratory (NRL) began operations in 1923 and is headquartered in Washington, D.C. with additional locations nationwide. NRL conducts multidisciplinary research on scientific and technological developments in fields such as physical, engineering, environmental, and space sciences, providing multidisciplinary support to Naval Warfare Centers, and space and space systems technology development and support. NRL also cooperates with its parent organization the Office of Naval Research in coordinating, executing, and promoting Navy and Marine Corps scientific and technology programs through universities, government laboratories, commercial, and nonprofit organizations. Further information about NRL activities can be found at www.nrl.navy .mil/. These resources document NRL accomplishments and include news releases (1996– present), descriptions of organizational entities and their work such as the Naval Center for Space Technology and the Ocean and Atmospheric Science Directorate and that directorate's Space Science Division, and the Office of Naval Research's Future Naval Capabilities program. Business contracting information is also provided. Accessible publications include NRL's *Fact Book* (2004), *Naval Research Laboratory's Major Facilities* (2005), and *Annual Report* (2005).

Naval War College

The Naval War College (NWC) is located in Newport, Rhode Island and provides graduate education for naval officers. Since its 1884 establishment, NWC's mission has been enhancing the professional capabilities of its students to make sound decisions in combat, staff, and management positions in naval, joint, and combined environments; provide solid understanding of military strategy and operational art; instill joint attitudes and perspectives; and serve as a research and gaming center to develop advanced strategic, war-fighting, and campaign concepts for future deployment of maritime, joint, and combined forces.

Information about NWC's multifaceted operations can be found at www.nwc.navy .mil/. These resources include biographies of faculty and descriptions of their research interests, information on college departments such as the Strategy and Policy Department,

National Security Decision Making Department, and Center for Naval Warfare Studies, along with information on library resources, the Naval War College Press, and recent news releases.

Relevant publications accessible on NWC's Web site include articles from the scholarly journal *Naval War College Review* (Autumn 1996–present) and various reports including *Theater Ballistic Missile Defense From the Sea: Issues for the Maritime Component Commander* (1998); *The Limits of Transformation: Officer Attitudes Toward the Revolution in Military Affairs* (2003); *Military Transformation and the Defense Industry After Next: The Defense Industry Implications of Network-Centric Warfare* (2003); *China's Nuclear Force Modernization* (2005); and *Naval Power in the 21st Century: A Naval War College Review Reader* (2005).

Navy Doctrine

The U.S. Navy has a number of doctrinal documents stressing the factors it emphasizes in conducting various naval operations. Naval Department Directives from the secretary of the Navy can be found at http://doni.daps.dla.mil/ with relevant examples being *SecNav Instruction 5400.39C: Department of the Navy Space Policy* (2004) and *SecNav Instruction 5400.43: Navy Space Policy Implementation* (2005). Additional naval doctrinal publications are produced by the Naval Warfare Development Command (NWDC). Accessible NWDC doctrinal publications are available at www.nwdc.navy.mil with representative samples including *Naval Doctrinal Publication 1: Naval Warfare* (1994), *Naval Doctrinal Publication 6: Naval Command and Control* (1995), and *Navy Warfare Library NTTP 1–01* (2005).

Pacific Missile Range Facility

The Navy's Pacific Missile Range Facility (PMRF) is located at Kekaha, Hawaii on Kauai Island. Its mission is providing integrated range service in a contemporary multi-threat and multidimensional environment, which produces the safe conduct and evaluation of training missions and delivering quality products to improve stakeholder abilities to achieve readiness and other national security objectives. Space, air, and surface tracking of missile launches are provided by PMRF radar sites and underwater communications transducers, and PMRF is linked to additional range and data-processing facilities and is capable of transmitting real-time test and exercise data and video anywhere in the United States due to microwave, fiber-optic, and satellite communication resources.

PMRF's Web site at www.pmrf.navy.mil/ provides information on the range's mission and physical environment, listings of local support systems and services provided by other federal agencies such as the Naval Undersea Warfare Center, recently implemented range systems upgrades, and information on employment opportunities.

Space and Naval Warfare Systems Command

Space and Naval Warfare Systems Command (SPAWAR) is responsible for supporting U.S. Navy and Marine Corps electronic systems, equipment, C4I, surveillance, and reconnaissance and space systems capabilities.

SPAWAR's Web site (www.spawar.navy.mil) features an organizational chart, command leader biographies, descriptions of organizational components such as the Program Executive Office for C4I and Space, and information on recently awarded business contracts.

Examples of accessible publications include *SPAWAR Instruction 2450.1: Electromagnetic Environmental Effects (E3) Control Within the Space and Naval Warfare Systems Command and Warfare Systems of the Battle Force* (1991); *SPAWAR Instruction 5430.35A: Designation of NAVSTAR Global Positioning System (GPS) Program Office* (1991); *SPAWAR Instruction 3090.1: C4ISR System Criteria for Shipboard Topside Integration* (2003); *Naval Space at the Forefront of Transformation: Bringing New Capabilities to the Joint, National, Naval Warfighter* (2004); *Integrating Interests/Finding Common Ground* (2005); *Kill Chains and Weapons on the Tactical Edge* (2005); and *Program Executive Office C4I Integrated Network Centric Warfare Roadmap* (2005).

7

Non–Defense Department U.S. Government Resources: Congress, Independent Agencies, and Commissions

Although the U.S. Defense Department and military are the primary participants in U.S. space warfare and defense policymaking and producers of pertinent documentation, there are several additional federal agencies engaged in various forms of space science research and policymaking. Understanding these agencies' activities and their information resources is also important for those wishing to have a more complete understanding of the U.S. Government's widespread interest in space science and how civilian and military space science and technology research and policy-making applications and interests can intersect in multiple areas.

The agencies that are profiled in this chapter include departmental components of executive branch agencies such as the Commerce Department and the Executive Office of the President, independent agencies such as NASA and quasi-governmental agencies such as the National Academies, congressional committees responsible for funding and over-seeing the performance of federal agency programs, congressional support organizations, and presidential and congressional commissions consisting of luminaries from various professional spheres who are appointed to issue reports and make recommendations on assorted public policy issues.

U.S. Department of Commerce

The U.S. Department of Commerce was initially created on February 14, 1903 as the Department of Commerce and Labor, and its current institutional incarnation dates from a March 4, 1913 law creating a separate Department of Labor. The Commerce Department's multifaceted responsibilities include promoting U.S. international trade, economic growth, and technological enhancement, and subsequent entries describe Commerce Department agencies engaged in various space science research activities that can have military applications and implications.

Aerial view of the Herbert Hoover Building that houses the Department of Commerce in Washington, D.C., which includes the National Oceanic and Atmospheric Administration that conducts major research programs involving satellite technology. *(iStockPhoto)*

Defense Meteorological Satellite Program

The Defense Meteorological Satellite Program (DMSP) is a DOD program adminis-tered by the Air Force Space and Missile Systems Center and is also part of the National Oceanic and Atmospheric Administration's (NOAA) Geophysical Data Center. DMSP has been in existence since 1958, and its purpose is tracking existing weather systems for military operational planning from an orbit altitude of approximately 528 miles. Program satellites also measure local charged particles and electromagnetic fields to determine how the ionosphere may impact ballistic missile early warning radar systems and long-range communications while also predicting how the space environment may impact satellite operations.

Important recent developments in DMSP's history include President Clinton's May 1994 decision to have DOD and the Commerce Department merge their previously sepa-rate polar-orbiting weather satellite programs and DMSP operations being transferred to Suitland, Maryland, in June 1998. Additional noteworthy DMSP facilities include track-ing stations at New Boston Air Force Station, New Hampshire; Thule Air Base, Greenland; Fairbanks, Alaska; and Kaena Point, Hawaii who all receive DMSP data then electroni-cally transfer that data to the Air Force Weather Agency at Offut Air Force Base, Nebraska.

Information about various DMSP programs and activities can be found through its Web site at www.ngdc.noaa.gov/dmsp/. Accessible resources include selected satellite launch data, information on program data services and pricing, and descriptions of DMSP sensors such as the operational line-scan system monitoring global cloud distribution and cloud top temperatures and the SSM/I microwave image sensor measuring atmospheric, ocean, and terrain microwave brightness temperatures. Additional resources include bibliographic citations to publications by DMSP personnel and the text of presentations including "Low-Light Imaging of the Earth at Night" (2001) and "Developmental Sprawl Impacts on the Terrestrial Carbon Dynamics of the United States" (2002).

Earth Resources Observation and Science (EROS) Data Center

The Earth Resources Observation and Science (EROS) Data Center is part of the U.S. Geological Survey (USGS) and located about 15 miles north of Sioux Falls, South Dakota. EROS serves as the data management, systems development, and research field center for USGS National Mapping Division. It opened in the early 1970s and has approximately 600 government and contractor employees in South Dakota, at a field office in Anchorage, Alaska, and at the NASA Ames Research Center in Moffett Field, California.

The EROS Data Center Web site (http://edc.usgs.gov) provides several resources about center activities. These include a virtual tour of the South Dakota facility; news releases

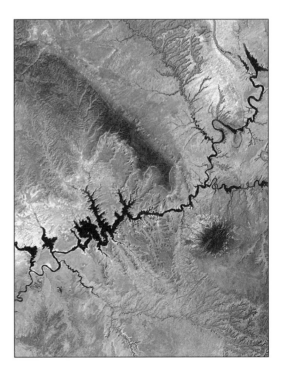

Lake Powell in southern Utah stretches hundreds of miles from Lees Ferry in Arizona to the Orange Cliffs of southern Utah, LANDSAT image. *(USGS)*

from October 2000–present; historical data about the LANDSAT satellite program along with technical data about these satellites; LANDSAT imagery from domestic and international locations featuring photos of Bolivian deforestation, Basra, Iraq, and southern Nevada wildfires during the summer of 2005; and information about U.S. international Earth satellite monitoring activities and participation in the UN Environment Program.

Additional EROS information resources include information about satellite programs besides LANDSAT; links to relevant NASA satellite program resources; information and imagery produced by the National Satellite Land Remote Sensing Data Archive; and publications including the *EROS Quarterly Report* (2004-present) and the *EROS Annual Report* (2004).

National Environmental Satellite, Data, and Information Service (NESDIS)

The National Environmental Satellite, Data, and Information Service (NESDIS) is part of NOAA created October 3, 1970 by Federal Reorganization Plan No. 4. NESDIS's responsibilities include operating the United States' civilian geostationary and polar-orbiting environmental satellites. These sources enable NESDIS to provide environmental data for forecasts, national security, and weather warnings in order to protect life and property. Additional uses of this data include assisting in energy distribution, developing global food supplies, managing natural resources, and recovering mariners and pilots in distress.

NESDIS's Web site at www.nesdis.noaa.gov/ features detailed descriptions of its institutional missions, current program budget information, news releases (November 2000–present), descriptions of organizational components and links to their Web sites, and information about NESDIS interactions with other federal agencies and foreign counterpart governmental agencies.

Accessible publications include NESDIS's *Annual Report* (2004), *NESDIS Strategic Plan FY 2005–2010* (2005), and *FY 2007 Budget Blue Book* (2006).

National Oceanic and Atmospheric Administration (NOAA) Satellites

NOAA satellite activities and operations are extensive enough to require a separate entry. The gateway to NOAA's multifaceted satellite operations is www.nesdis.noaa.gov/satellites.html. NESDIS's organizational components with satellite activities include the Geospatial Data and Climate Services Group, Geostationary Environmental Operational Satellite Series-R, International Affairs Office, National Climatic Data Center, National Coastal Data Development Center, National Geophysical Data Center, National Oceanographic Data Center, National Polar-Orbiting Operational Environmental Satellite System, Office of Research and Applications, Office of Satellite Data Processing and Distribution,

Office of Satellite Operations, Office of Space Commercialization, and the Office of Systems Development.

The Geospatial Data and Climate Services (GDCS) Group seeks to provide cross-cutting service throughout NOAA to support data management and information services within NESDIS, other NOAA entities and federal organizations, and international organizations on assorted data and information management issues. GDCS administers the Environmental Services Data and Information Management Program, NOAA's central repository of more than 14,000 metadata descriptions on the NOAA server, Federal Geographic Data Committee activities within NOAA, and U.S. contributions to the International Global Climate Observing System programs.

The Geostationary Environmental Operational Satellite Series-R (GOES-R) Program Office is responsible for improving spacecraft and instrument technologies for enhancing the timeliness and accuracy of weather forecasts and improving the detection and observation of meteorological developments directly affecting public safety and economic health; with the first launch of this series of satellites scheduled for 2012. Information on GOES-R activities is accessible at https://osd.goes.noaa.gov/.

The Office of International and Interagency Affairs (OIA) is responsible for coordinating NOAA interactions with relevant foreign counterpart agencies and international government organizations and developing U.S. policies on international issues affecting NOAA. Information about OIA is accessible at www.international.noaa.gov/.

The National Climatic Data Center (NCDC) serves as the world's largest weather data archive. It operates the World Data Center for Meteorology in Asheville, North Carolina, and the World Data Center for Paleoclimatology in Boulder, Colorado and also supports several regional climate centers in the United States and the state climatologists' program. Access to NCDC's multiple information resources and data sets is provided at www.ncdc.noaa.gov/.

The National Coastal Data Development Center (NCDDC) strives to assist ecosystem management by providing access to national coastal data resources. NCDDC attempts to reach this objective by integrating diverse coastal data from multiple repositories and providing users with Internet access to this data using existing and emerging technologies. Further information on and access to these resources is provided at www.ncddc.noaa.gov/.

The National Geophysical Data Center (NGDC) is headquartered in Boulder, Colorado. Its institutional mandate includes providing stewardship, products, and services for geophysical data describing the solid earth, marine and solar terrestrial environments, and earth observations from space. NGDC's Web site (www.ngdc.noaa.gov) features a variety of information resources, data, and imagery describing its activities and research.

The National Oceanographic Data Center (NODC) is headquartered in Silver Spring, Maryland with regional offices at other U.S. locations. NODC is responsible for managing the acquisition, ingest processing, quality control, and long-term oceanographic data preservation. Additional information about NODC data and access to its resources such as ocean water temperatures is provided through its Web site, www.nodc.noaa.gov/.

Artist's concept of a National Polar-Orbiting Environmental Satellite System satellite. *(National Oceanic and Atmospheric Administration)*

The National Polar-Orbiting Operational Environmental Satellite System (NPOESS) is a satellite system responsible for monitoring global environmental conditions and collecting and disseminating weather, atmospheric, oceanic, land, and near-space environmental data. This mission has been carried out since 1994 when previously separate Commerce and Defense Department programs were merged. Imagery and information on NPOESS are provided on its Web site, www.ipo.noaa.gov/.

NESDIS's Office of Research and Applications (ORA), which is slated to become the Center for Satellite Applications and Research, is responsible for conducting research on using satellite data for monitoring specific meteorological, climatological, oceanographic, and environmental characteristics. Information about ORA organizational components including the Satellite Meteorology and Climatology Division and Satellite Oceanography Division, along with imagery and assorted information resources, are accessible at www.orbit.nesdis.noaa.gov/star/.

Office of Satellite Data Processing and Distribution (OSDPD) activities include directing the operation of central ground facilities responsible for ingesting, processing, and distributing environmental satellite data and relevant derivative products to domestic and foreign users. Information on OSDPD organizational components such as the Satellite Services Division, Information Processing Division, and Direct Services Division, along with relevant imagery and information resources, are accessible at www.osdpd.noaa.gov/.

Office of Satellite Operations (OSO) is responsible for managing and directing NOAA satellite operations and acquiring remotely sensed data. These activities include operational responsibility for the Satellite Operations Control Center in Suitland, Maryland, and Command and Data Acquisition centers in Wallops, Virginia and Fairbanks, Alaska, which command, control, and track satellites while also acquiring the data they generate. Additional OSO responsibilities include launching, activating, and evaluating new satellites; performing detailed evaluations of satellite and ground system anomalies; preparing procedures for responding to these anomalies; setting and coordinating satellite operation and data acquisition schedules to meet user needs; and evaluating satellite and operational facility technical performance and procedures. Information and news about and imagery from OSO operations is accessible at www.oso.noaa.gov/.

The Office of Space Commercialization (OSC) is the Commerce Department unit responsible for encouraging an economic and public policy environment that enhances the U.S. commercial space industry's growth and international competitiveness. OSC activities occur in the areas of policy development, market analysis, and outreach and education. Office activities emphasize selected commercial space industry areas including satellite navigation, satellite imaging, space transportation, and entrepreneurial space business.

A variety of information resources are accessible on OSC's Web site, www.nesdis.noaa .gov/space/. Examples of these resources include PowerPoint presentations such as "GPS-Galileo Negotiations: Commercial Issues at Stake" (2002); "Promoting Commercial Interests in GPS" (2002); "The Global Positioning System: A Worldwide Information Utility" (2003); descriptions of satellite systems such as GPS; listings and information resources from OSC-sponsored conferences; and reports including *Trends in Space Commerce* (2001); *Suborbital Reusable Launch Vehicles and Applicable Markets* (2002); and *Space Economic Data* (2002).

NESDIS's Office of Systems Development (OSD) responsibilities include managing NOAA operational geostationary and polar-orbiting environmental satellite programs. OSD attempts to provide the requisite spacecraft, launch services, and ground systems to ensure the uninterrupted flow of remotely sensed environmental data to protect life, property, the environment, and economic development. This office also cooperates closely with other NOAA offices, federal agencies, foreign technical agencies, international scientific and technical organizations, and its constituencies to fulfill these responsibilities. Information on OSD operations is available at www.osd.noaa.gov/.

Executive Office of the President—Office of Science and Technology Policy

The Office of Science and Technology Policy (OSTP) is part of the Executive Office of the President. OSTP was established by Congress in 1976 and given an institutional mandate to advise the president and Executive Office of the President personnel on the impact of science and technology on domestic and international affairs. Institutional responsibilities of OSTP include leading federal interagency efforts to develop and implement scientifically and technologically sound policies and budgets; working with the private sector to make sure federal science and technology spending enhances economic prosperity, environmental quality, and national security; building strong partnerships between federal, state, and local governments, foreign countries, and the scientific community; and evaluating the size, quality, and effectiveness of federal science and technology programs.

OSTP's Web site (www.ostp.gov) provides access to additional materials describing the office's mission and activities. These include links to OSTP component organization Web sites such as the National Science and Technology Council, National Nanotechnology Initiative, and the National Coordination Office for Networking and Information Technology Research and Development. Additional resources provided include federal scientific program budget information from fiscal year 2004–present featuring breakdowns by agencies such as the Defense Department and functional areas such as Space Science and Exploration, reports such as *The Science and Technology of Combating Terrorism* (2003), *U.S. Space Transportation Policy* (2005), and the text of meeting agendas and presentations.

Federal Aviation Administration

The Federal Aviation Administration (FAA) was formally established through the 1958 Federal Aviation Act and became part of the Department of Transportation in 1967. FAA's multifaceted missions include maintaining and enhancing safety and security in air travel, encouraging and developing civil aeronautics including new aviation technologies, creating and operating common air traffic control systems for civil and military aircraft, and regulating U.S. commercial space transportation.

The FAA's Associate Administrator for Commercial Space Transportation (AACST) is responsible for regulating and promoting the U.S. commercial space transportation industry. AACST activities include licensing private sector launching of space payloads on expendable launch vehicles and commercial space launch facilities, setting insurance requirements to protect individuals and property, and ensuring that these space transportation activities are compliant with U.S. domestic and foreign policy.

Further information on AACST activities can be found at http://ast.faa.gov/. Accessible materials include listings of recent commercial space launches by company, site launched, and with cargo descriptions; listings of current position openings; the text of relevant international space law such as *The Convention for International Liability for Damage Caused by Space Objects* (1972); and relevant U.S. national laws including the *Commercial Space Act of 1998* (1998), *Commercial Space Transportation Competitiveness Act of 2000* (2000), and the *Commercial Space Launch Amendments Act of 2004* (2004).

Overall federal policy reports such as *U.S. Space Transportation Policy* (2005) are featured as are reports on space transportation in categories such as forecasts, special reports, *Quarterly Launch Reports* (1996–present), the annual *Commercial Space Transportation: Year in Review* (1997–present), licensing and safety reports, the annual *Development and Concepts: Vehicles, Technologies, and Spaceports* (1998–present), and various working group reports. Sample titles for reports within these categories include *Guidelines for Experimental Permits for Reusable Suborbital Rockets* (2005) and *Guidelines for Reusable Launch and Reentry Vehicle Reliability Analysis* (2005).

SpaceShipOne glides down for approach to the Mojave airport. The ship was the first commercial vehicle to travel in space. The Federal Aviation Administration awarded the ship's pilot its first commercial astronaut wings. *(Courtesy of Scaled Composites, LLC)*

Federal Communications Commission

The Federal Communications Commission (FCC) was established by the 1934 Communications Act. Its responsibilities include regulating interstate and foreign communications by radio, television, wire, satellite, and cable; ensuring the orderly development and operation of broadcast services; providing rapid and efficient national and international telephone and telegraph services at reasonable rates; and using communications for promoting life and property safety along with national defense.

General and specific information about overall FCC activities are accessible on the agency's Web site, www.fcc.gov. FCC activities pertinent to space policy and defense policy are carried out by its Media, International, and Wireless Telecommunications Bureaus. Media Bureau responsibilities include developing, recommending, and administering policy and licensing programs for media regulation including broadcast television and radio and satellite services in the United States and its territories.

The Media Bureau's Web site (www.fcc.gov/mb) features information about the bureau's various divisions including its Industry Analysis Division and Office of Communication and Industry Information. Examples of accessible Media Bureau reports on industries it regulates include *Annual Assessment of the Status of Competition in the Market for Delivery of Video Programming* (1997–present) and *Competition Between Cable Television and Direct Broadcast Satellite-It's More Complicated Than You Think* (2005).

International Bureau responsibilities include developing, recommending, and administering policies, standards, procedures, and programs for regulating international telecommunications facilities and services and licensing satellite facilities under its jurisdiction. The International Bureau also is the FCC's principal representative in international organizations and assists U.S. trade policymakers in negotiating and implementing international telecommunications trade agreements.

Further information on International Bureau activities is accessible at www.fcc.gov/ib/. Resources available here include descriptions of the activities of bureau component entities such as the Satellite Division, announcements on upcoming public meetings, announcements of regulatory actions, and the text of presentations by Bureau personnel such as *A Perspective on the Commercial Satellite Industry* (2003). Sample International Reports include *FCC Report to Congress As Required by the Orbit Act* (dealing with U.S. satellite industry global competitiveness) (2001–present), *International Bureau Annual Report* (2003–present), *International Telecommunications Data* (2003), and *Optimizing Opportunities: A Satellite Report* (2004).

The Wireless Telecommunications Bureau's mandate involves administering domestic commercial and private wireless telecommunications programs and rules. Commercial wireless encompasses cellular, paging, personal communications, specialized mobile radio, air-ground, and simple exchange telecommunications services. Private wireless services meet the customized internal communication demands of selected users and include public safety, microwave, aviation, and marine services.

Further details on this bureau's activities are provided at http://wireless.fcc.gov/. Resources available here include descriptions of bureau activities and services, information on electromagnetic spectrum auctions and various wireless services, announcements about regulatory actions, and information on emerging technologies such as Third Generation Wireless. Other available materials include press releases (1994–present) and reports such as *Annual Report and Analysis of Competitive Market Conditions With Respect to Commercial Mobile Services* (1995–present).

National Aeronautics and Space Administration (NASA)

The National Aeronautics and Space Administration (NASA) was established in 1958 by the National Aeronautics and Space Act and it was an institutional extension of the National Advisory Committee on Aeronautics, which had been researching flight technology for over 40 years.

NASA serves as the U.S. civilian space research agency and cooperates with the U.S. military as well. NASA headquarters are in Washington, D.C., and it possesses various field facilities in locations across the United States and internationally. Institutional

The shuttle Endeavour is maneuvered into place inside of the Orbiter Processing Facility at Kennedy Space Center in 2007. *(NASA)*

NASA research areas encompass aeronautics by researching and developing new flight technologies; creating new capabilities for human and robotic exploration; enhancing space science knowledge by exploring the earth, moon, Mars, and beyond to produce various societal benefits; and space operations that develop technological capabilities for enhancing space exploration and the development of programs such as the international space station.

There are five NASA component organizations that provide informative information resources relevant to space warfare and defense. They are NASA Earth Observing System, History Office, National Space Science Data Center, Office of Space Operations, and Technical Reports Center.

NASA Earth Observing System

The Earth Observing System (EOS) is administered from NASA's Goddard Space Flight Center in Greenbelt, Maryland. EOS consists of series of satellites and a data system supporting polar-orbiting and low inclination satellites for long-term observations of the global land surface, biosphere, solid Earth, atmosphere, and oceans with the goal of producing enhanced understanding of the earth.

EOS's Web site (http://eospso.gsfc.nasa.gov) provides additional program information. These materials include a calendar listing upcoming events that EOS personnel will participate in; descriptions and imagery from EOS projects such as the Sample Project Sea-Viewing Wide Field-of-View Sensor, which provides quantitative data on global oceanic bio-optic properties; information on the location of EOS satellites; a calculator that enables users to predict when an EOS satellite will pass over designated geographic locales; news releases (March 1999–present); contact information for NASA and academic participants in specific EOS programs; and descriptions of individual EOS data-gathering programs.

NASA History Office

NASA's History Office was established in 1959 to document and preserve the agency's history. Its mission involves disseminating aerospace information as widely as possible and enabling NASA managers and policymakers to understand and benefit from past institutional accomplishments and failures. The History Office seeks to produce scholarly and popular work that is accessible to NASA constituents and to a variety of external audiences interested in aerospace trends and developments.

The History Office Web site (http://history.nasa.gov) serves as a gateway to a universe of informative resources on NASA's historical development and evolution and the history of numerous individual space programs. Accessible resources include a What's New site; an online guide for conducting NASA history research; a topical index containing links to NASA resources on topics such as aeronautics, human spaceflight, satellites, and space policy; and documentary Web sites such as *Key Documents in the History of Space Policy* (www.hq.nasa.gov/office/pao/History/spdocs.html), which includes the text of important documents in NASA's institutional development.

A particularly important highlight of this Web site is the links to numerous full-text historical reports. Representative samples include *History of Research in Space Biology and Biodynamics at the U.S. Air Force Missile Development Center, Holloman Air Force Base, New Mexico, 1946–1958* (1958); *NASA Office of Defense Affairs: The First Five Years* (1970); *Aeronautics and Space Report of the President* (1995–present); *Beyond the Ionosphere: Fifty Years of Satellite Communication* (1997); *Together In Orbit: The Origins of International Participation in the Space Station* (1998); *Transiting from Air to Space: The North American X-15* (1998); *Power to Explore: A History of the Marshall Space Flight Center, 1960–1990* (1999); *Toward Mach 2: The Douglas D-558 Program* (1999); *Communications Satellite History* (2000); and *Looking Backward, Looking Forward: Forty Years of U.S. Human Spaceflight Symposium* (2002).

NASA National Space Science Data Center

The National Space Science Data Center (NSSDC) is the principal archive for NASA's space science data. NSSDC defines space science as encompassing astronomy, astrophysics, solar and space plasma physics, and lunar and planetary science. This center was established at the Goddard Space Flight Center in 1966, provides online information resources for NASA and non-NASA data, and for spacecraft and experiments generating NASA space science data.

Information resources on NSSDC's Web site (http://nssdc.gsfc.nasa.gov) include information about its disciplinary services of universe exploration, earth–sun exploration, solar system exploration, and related imagery resources from these areas. Accessible publications include the monthly *SpaceWarn Bulletin* produced in collaboration with the World Data Center for Satellite Information (1991–present) and *Annual Report* (1997–present).

NASA Office of Space Operations

The Office of Space Operations (OSO) has facilities at the Johnson Space Center in Texas, the Kennedy Space Center in Florida, the Marshall Space Flight Center in Alabama, and the Stennis Space Center in Mississippi. OSO's mission is providing NASA with the leadership and management for human space exploration in and beyond low-earth orbit. This office currently emphasizes NASA activities dealing with the space shuttle and international space station while also participating in NASA launch services, space transportation, and space communications supporting human and robotic exploration.

Astronauts work in the Mission Control Center during a space shuttle mission to the International Space Station at the Johnson Space Center in Houston. *(U.S. Air Force)*

OSO's Web site (www.hq.nasa.gov/osf) features detailed information about the International Space Station including *Station Status Reports* (March 19, 2004–present), space shuttle program developments, the text of NASA space transportation policy documents such as *NPD 8610.24B Launch Services Program (LSP) Pre-Launch Readiness Reviews* (2005), information about NASA space communication program capabilities including reports such as *NASA 4.0 Communication and Navigation Capability Roadmap: Executive Summary* (2005), and information about the space launch activities of private sector contractors such as Boeing and Lockheed Martin along with the space launch activities of foreign counterpart agencies such as the European Space Agency and Japanese Aerospace Exploration Agency.

NASA Technical Reports

NASA and private sector contractors have produced tens of thousands of reports on various aspects of aeronautics and space science. Many of these reports and related documents such as journal articles, conference and meeting papers, technical videos, mission-related operational documents, and preliminary data are searchable and available through the NASA Technical Reports Server (NTRS).

NTRS is accessible at http://ntrs.nasa.gov/. A variety of search and browsing options are provided to assist searching this multifaceted database. Examples of NTRS's reports covering space warfare and defense applications include *Converting the Minuteman Missile into a Small Satellite Launch System* (1993); *Declassified Intelligence Satellite Photography (DISP) Coverage of the Antarctic* (1998); *Adaptive Routing in Wireless Communication Networks Using Swarm Intelligence* (2001); *Mobile Aerial Tracking and Imaging System (MATRIS) for Aeronautical Research* (2004); *STARSAT: A Project to Evaluate Ground Tracking of Small Objects in Space* (2004); and *Oceanic Situational Awareness Over the Gulf of Mexico* (2005).

National Space-Based Positioning, Navigation, and Timing Executive Committee

The National Space-Based Positioning, Navigation, and Timing Executive Committee (PNT) was established by presidential directive in December 2004. PNT is an interagency organization consisting of representatives from the Commerce, Defense, Homeland Security, State, and Transportation Departments, the military, Executive Office of the President agencies such as the Office of Management and Budget and National Security Council, and independent government agencies such as NASA. Committee responsibilities cover decision making about the policies, architectures, requirements, and resource allocations for maintaining and upgrading the United States' space-based PNT infrastructure. PNT advice and recommendations ensure that this infrastructure's services, such as the Global Positioning System (GPS), are consistent in supporting U.S. national security, homeland security, foreign policy, economic, public safety, and scientific interests.

The PNT Web site (http://pnt.gov) features the committee's charter; biographical information on committee members who are often deputy secretaries from Cabinet departments; listings of committee meetings; and fact sheets and presentations such as *U.S. Space-Based Positioning, Navigation, and Timing Policy* (2004), *U.S. International Efforts to Promote Compatibility and Interoperability with the Global Positioning System* (2005), *Global Navigation Satellite Systems for Aviation* (2005), *The Growing Impact of Satellite Navigation Services* (2006), and *Space-Based PNT Modernization Update* (2006) along with links to information resources compiled by PNT's predecessor agency, the Interagency GPS Executive Board (1997–2004).

State Department

The U.S. Department of State, or State Department, serves as the president's advisor in formulating and executing U.S. foreign policy and promoting the nation's long-range security and well-being and has executed these responsibilities since 1789. The State Department's Web site (www.state.gov) serves as a gateway to its rich variety of information resources.

Four State Department bureaus engage in policy responsibilities covering space foreign policy and space warfare and defense issues. They are the Bureau of International

U.S. president George W. Bush delivers remarks from the South Lawn of the White House in Washington, D.C. following a trip to Iraq by U.S. secretary of defense Donald Rumsfeld and U.S. secretary of state Condoleezza Rice in 2006. *(Brooks Kraft/Corbis)*

Security and Nonproliferation; Bureau of Political-Military Affairs; Bureau of Verification, Compliance, and Implementation; and the Historian's Office. Their work and information resources are covered below.

Bureau of International Security and Nonproliferation (ISN) responsibilities include coordinating efforts to facilitate international consensus on weapons of mass destruction (WMD) proliferation; dealing with proliferation threats by nonstate entities and terrorist groups by improving physical security, using interdiction and sanctions; participating in international security arrangements such as the Proliferation Security Initiative; coordinating the implementation of relevant international treaties and arrangements to deal with contemporary security problems; working with the United Nations and other international organizations to reduce and eliminate WMD threats; and supporting foreign partners attempting to prevent and protect against potential terrorist use of WMD.

ISN's Web site (www.state.gov/t/isn) provides information about this office's multifaceted responsibilities. Available resources include descriptions of the activities of Bureau offices such as the Office of Cooperative Threat Reduction, Office of Missile Threat Reduction, and Office of Nonproliferation and Disarmament Fund; information on international nonproliferation regimes the United States participates in such as the Missile Technology Control Regime; materials describing U.S. technology export control activities; the text of relevant treaties the United States participates in such as the Ballistic Missile Launch Notification Treaty and Outer Space Treaty; and fact sheets regarding various U.S. nonproliferation programs and policy announcements.

Bureau of Political-Military Affairs (PM) responsibilities include providing policy direction for the State Department in international security, military operations, defense strategy and policy, military use of space, and defense trade.

Resources on PM's Web site (www.state.gov/t/pm) include links to the Web sites of bureau entities such as the Office of Plans, Policy, and Analysis; Office of International Security Operations; and Directorate of Defense Trade Controls and descriptions of their responsibilities; as well as press releases and speeches by PM officials (2001–present); annual reports such as *Foreign Military Training and DOD Engagement Activities of Interest* (2000–present); and links to bureau reports from 1997–2000.

The Bureau of Verification, Compliance, and Implementation (VCI) provides oversight of policy and resources in all subjects concerning verifying compliance with international arms control, nonproliferation, and disarmament agreements and commitments. VCI uses U.S. intelligence assets to verify whether other countries are in compliance with relevant bilateral or multilateral arms control agreements, and it advises the State Department on funding and assignment priorities for intelligence collection resources and analysis supporting arms control and nonproliferation objectives. VCI also works closely with other federal agencies to create and maintain relevant databases and information management systems for arms control activities, while also conducting verifiability appraisals of all international arms control and nonproliferation agreements and commitments the United States may participate in.

More information on Bureau activities can be derived at www.state.gov/t/vci/. These activities and resources include information on organizational components such as the Nuclear Risk Reduction Center; the text of relevant arms control agreements; information about the William C. Foster Fellows Visiting Scholar Program enabling scholars to participate in State Department arms control, disarmament, and nonproliferation programs; and publications such as press releases (2002–present) and the report *Adherence to and Compliance With Arms Control and Nonproliferation Agreements and Commitments* (2001 and 2005).

The Office of the Historian is responsible for preparing and publishing *Foreign Relations of the United States* (*FRUS*) and other historical analyses of U.S. foreign policy. General information on this office and its work are accessible at www.state.gov/r/pa/ho/. Online access to *FRUS* is available at http://purl.access.gpo.gov/GPO/LPS1155. *FRUS* volumes are arranged by presidential administration and then by countries, regions, or topics within these administrations. Selected volumes are provided through this Web site from the Truman administration to the Nixon administration. U.S. foreign and national security policy dealing with space warfare and defense can be found in *FRUS*'s arms control and disarmament and national security policy volumes.

Congressional Resources

The U.S. Congress and congressional support agencies also produce numerous information resources dealing with space warfare and defense along with scientific and other issues affecting U.S. space policy. The U.S. Constitution grants Congress significant powers in the areas of national security policy formulation such as creating military forces, funding these forces and affiliated government agencies, providing oversight of these agencies, and the power to raise money to fund these forces and agencies.

The next section of this chapter examines congressional committees having policy jurisdiction over military or civilian space programs and the information resources they produce. A later section of this chapter examines the information resources produced by current congressional support agencies such as the Congressional Budget Office, Congressional Research Service, and Government Accountability Office while also examining the valuable materials produced by the Office of Technology Assessment, which served as a congressional support agency from 1972–1995.

House Armed Services Committee

The House Armed Services Committee was established on January 2, 1947, when preexisting committees on military and naval affairs were merged. The committee's overall jurisdiction covers topics ranging from and including ammunition depots, forts, overall defense policy, Department of Defense and military service operations, defense and military intelligence related activities, scientific research and development supporting the armed

U.S. Navy officials appear before the House Armed Services Committee to give testimony and answer questions concerning the 2007 fiscal year National Defense Authorization budget request. Pictured foreground left-to-right: Chief of Naval Operations USN Admiral Michael G. Mullen; Secretary of the Navy, the Honorable Donald C. Winter; and Commandant of the Marine Corps, U.S. Marine Corps General Michael W. Hagee. *(U.S. Department of Defense)*

services, and other issues. The Committee's subcommittee on Strategic Forces is charged with overseeing military space programs and ballistic missile defense.

In presenting its oversight plan for the 109th Congress (2005–2006), the Armed Services Committee uses the following language to describe its military space policy program assessment:

> Particular attention will be given to the policies and programs associated with the protection of national security space assets and the development of space-based effects in military operations. The Committee will assess Department of Defense efforts to leverage industry and academia for the purposes of increasing the quality of space-qualified personnel involved in space programs.
>
> Further, the committee will engage the space community to develop a clearly articulated and coherent space control policy as well as explore opportunities to further integrate space assets with the nation's warfighting capabilities.

Missile defense is another area of military activity attracting the House Armed Services Committee's scrutiny. The Committee's missile defense oversight objectives incorporate the following:

The Committee will continue to monitor the Department of Defense's plans to accelerate fielding of an initial capability for several missile defense programs. The Committee will focus on three areas: tracking of key milestones for the development and testing of missile defense elements and the effect on future program viability, tracking the Ronald Reagan National Defense Authorization Act for Fiscal Year 2005 (Public Law 108–375) requirement for establishing system baselines and operational test and evaluation criteria, and transitioning of missile defense elements to the individual military services for eventual acquisition and operation.

The Committee's Web site (www.house.gov/hasc) features a variety of information resources including press releases (1996–present), relevant congressional bills and committee reports (1995–present), listings of committee and subcommittee members, the opening statements of witnesses testifying at committee hearings (1997–present), and audio Web casts of many committee hearings. Examples of relevant committee space policy related hearings include *Status of Military Space Activities* (2004) and *Space Cadre/Space Professionals* (2005).

House Permanent Select Intelligence Committee

The House Permanent Select Intelligence Committee was created in 1977 to "oversee and make continuing studies of the intelligence and intelligence-related activities and programs of the United States Government and to submit to the House appropriate proposals for legislation and report to the House concerning such intelligence and intelligence-related activities and programs."

Committee oversight responsibilities encompass governmental intelligence programs from agencies such as Central Intelligence Agency, Defense Intelligence Agency, Department of Homeland Security, National Geospatial Intelligence Agency, National Reconnaissance Office, National Security Agency, and U.S. Air Force Intelligence, Surveillance, and Reconnaissance. During the 109th Congress, the committee consists of four subcommittees dealing with terrorism/human intelligence, analysis, and counterintelligence, technical and tactical intelligence, intelligence policy, and oversight.

The Committee's Web site (http://intelligence.house.gov) provides information about committee activities including committee reports on legislation, transcripts of some public hearings, and news releases (2003–present).

House Science Committee

The House Science Committee officially began on January 3, 1959 as a successor to the Science and Astronautics Committee created in 1946. The Science Committee has devoted particular attention to astronautics, including agencies such as NASA, but its overall oversight emphasis has been on federal science and technology policy.

The Science Committee Web site at www.house.gov/science/ features information resources describing committee activities; descriptions of its subcommittees dealing with the environment, energy, research, and space; video Web casts of selected hearings; legislative history information for bills being reviewed by the committee; and transcripts and witness opening statements from committee hearings 2001–present. Examples of accessible hearings dealing with various aspects of space policy include *The Future of Human Space Flight* (2003), *NASA-Department of Defense Cooperation in Space Transportation* (2004), *Ongoing Problems and Future Plans for NOAA Weather Satellites* (2005), and *Future Markets for Commercial Space* (2005).

Senate Armed Services Committee

The Senate Armed Services Committee was created as part of the 1946 Legislative Reorganization Act. Its multifaceted responsibilities, like those of its House counterpart, include oversight of the Defense Department, individual armed services, overall defense policy, and aeronautical and space activities dealing with weapons systems development and military operations.

From left, Chairman of the Joint Chiefs of Staff Marine Gen. Peter Pace, Secretary of Defense Robert M. Gates, and Under Secretary of Defense (Comptroller) and Chief Financial Officer Tina W. Jonas testify at the House Armed Services Committee hearing about the 2008 Defense Department budget at the Rayburn House Office Building in Washington, D.C., Feb. 7, 2007. *(U.S. Department of Defense)*

The committee's six subcommittees during the 109th Congress focus on the following areas: air-land forces, emerging threats and capabilities, personnel, readiness and management support, seapower, and strategic forces. Additional information on committee activities and committee publications is accessible at http://armed-services.senate.gov/. Available resources include listings of committee and subcommittee members, press releases (1999–present), witness opening statements from committee hearings (1998–present), and the text of bills reviewed by the committee and legislative reports filed by the committee (1997–present).

Examples of relevant committee hearings include *Report of the National Commission for the Review of the National Reconnaissance Office and the Report of the Independent Commission on the Review of the National Imagery and Mapping Agency* (2002), *Report of the Commission to Assess United States National Security Space Management and Organization* (2002), *Space Acquisition Policies and Processes* (2004), and *Department of Defense Authorization for Appropriations For Fiscal Year 2005* (2005).

Senate Commerce, Science, and Transportation Committee

The Senate Commerce, Science, and Transportation Committee history dates back to 1816 when the Senate created a Committee on Commerce and Manufactures. This committee went through several nomenclature changes until it acquired its present name in 1977. Its current oversight responsibilities national science, engineering, and technology policy and civilian aeronautical and space science policy.

Detailed information on committee activities is provided on its Web site, http://commerce.senate.gov/. Materials available here include listings of committee and subcommittee members; information on its nine subcommittees including those dealing with aviation, science and space, technology, innovation, and competitiveness; news releases (2003–present), Web casts of selected hearings, and witness opening statements at committee hearings (2001–present).

Examples of committee hearings dealing with various aspects of space policy include *International Space Station Research* (2005), *Human Spaceflight: The Space Shuttle and Beyond* (2005), *Weather Modification* (2005), and *National Polar-Orbiting Operational Environmental Satellite System Oversight* (2006).

Senate Intelligence Committee

The Senate Select Committee on Intelligence was established in 1976 to facilitate enhanced congressional oversight of U.S. intelligence agency programs and activities. In its 2003 activities report the committee described its mission as follows: . . . "to ensure that the Intelligence Community provides the accurate and timely intelligence necessary to identify and monitor threats to the national security; to support the executive and legislative branches in their decisions on national security matters; to ensure that U.S. military commanders have the intelligence support to allow them to prevail swiftly and decisively on the battlefield, and to ensure that all intelligence activities and programs conform with the Constitution and laws of the United States."

The Senate Intelligence Committee Web site (http://intelligence.senate.gov) provides further information about committee activities. Resources available here include a roster of committee members; the text of committee procedural rules; information about its jurisdiction including conducting the nomination and confirmation of presidential intelligence policymaker nominations; the text of laws such as the 1978 Foreign Intelligence Surveillance Act and 2001 USA Patriot Act; press releases (1999–present); the text of relevant legislation and committee reports such as the annual intelligence authorization acts; and witness statements from selected committee hearings such as the annual *Current and Projected National Security Threats to the United States* (2003–present) and *Nomination of Ambassador John D. Negroponte to be Director of National Intelligence* (2005).

Congressional Support Agencies

Congressional support agencies provide additional assistance to Congress in conducting oversight of various public policy issues beyond that provided by the professional staffs of representatives, senators, and committees. The work of the Congressional Budget Office, Congressional Research Service, Government Accountability Office, and the Office of Technology Assessment are reviewed below.

Congressional Budget Office

The Congressional Budget Office (CBO) was established in 1974 by the Congressional Budget and Impoundment Control Act, which gave Congress effective control over the federal budgetary process. CBO began operations in February 1975, and its institutional mandate is providing economic and budget information to Congress to support the budget and legislative processes.

CBO's Web site (www.cbo.gov) provides access to information resources including job openings, descriptions of its operations, how it conducts its analyses of the federal budget and the budgets for specific federal agency programs, letters to members of Congress on budget issues, CBO director testimony before congressional committees, and the text of a variety of statistics and reports.

Examples of relevant CBO reports include *Budgetary and Technical Implications of the Administration's Plan for National Missile Defense* (2000); *Estimated Costs and Technical Characteristics of Selected National Missile Defense Systems* (2002); *The Long-Term Implications of Current Defense Plans* (2003–present); *The Army's Bandwidth Bottleneck* (2003); *Alternatives for Boost-Phase Missile Defense* (2004); *Alternatives for Future U.S. Space-Launch Capabilities* (2006); and *Alternatives for Military Space Radar* (2007).

Congressional Research Service

The Congressional Research Service (CRS) is part of the Library of Congress and serves as Congress's research arm. CRS historical origins date back to 1914 when it was created as the Legislative Research Service and its institutional evolution has seen it develop from a legislative statute compiler to an objective issue analysis provider for members of Congress, their staff, and congressional committees. CRS received its current name as a result of the 1970 Legislative Reorganization Act.

Its institutional orientation has seen CRS focus on prioritizing service to meet congressional needs, which has had the practical effect of restricting access to these reports to congressional members and their staffs even though such reports are financed with tax dollars. Some members of Congress have introduced legislation to make these reports publicly accessible on the Internet although such proposals have not passed as of early 2007.

Despite this congressional sluggishness in making CRS reports accessible, they can be found on the Web sites of numerous enterprising governmental, nonprofit, and academic organizations. Examples of organizations featuring significant collections of CRS reports include the U.S. State Department's Foreign Press (http://fpc.state.gov/c18183.htm), the Federation of American Scientists (www.fas.org/man/crs/), and the University of North Texas Library (http://digital.library.unt.edu/govdocs/crs/), which has the most exhaustive coverage of CRS reports, dating back to 1990.

Representative samples of CRS reports dealing with space warfare and defense, some of which are published and updated regularly, include *Military Transformation: Intelligence, Surveillance, and Reconnaissance* (2003); *Iran's Ballistic Missile Capabilities* (2004); *Military Role in Space Control: A Primer* (2004); *High Altitude Electromagnetic Pulse (HEMP) and High Power Microwave (HPM) Devices: Threat Assessments* (2004); *Airborne Laser (ABL): Issues for Congress* (2005); *Military Space Programs: Issues Concerning DOD's SBIRS and STSS Programs* (2005); *Intelligence Surveillance, and Reconnaissance (ISR) Programs: Issues for Congress* (2005); *Ballistic Missile Defense: Historical Overview* (2005); and *Missile Defense: The Current Debate* (2005).

Government Accountability Office

The Government Accountability Office (GAO) was established in 1921 as the General Accounting Office and is responsible for auditing how federal agencies handle government funds and evaluating the performance of government programs for Congress. GAO changed its name to the Government Accountability Office on July 7, 2004 to try to better reflect the professional analytical and evaluative services it provides instead of being stereotyped as an accounting agency.

GAO's Web site (www.gao.gov) features an extensive archival repository and variety of current and historical information resources such as office correspondence with governmental officials, the opening statements of GAO witnesses testifying before congressional committees, and reports documenting governmental program performance. Examples of relevant congressional testimony include *Implications of SDIO's Changing Ballistic Missile Defense Architecture* (1991); *Ballistic Missile Defense: Information on Theater High Altitude Area Defense (THAAD) and Other Theater Missile Defense Systems* (1994); *Military Space Programs: Opportunities to Reduce Missile Warning and Communication Satellites Cost* (1994); *Missile Defense: Knowledge-Based Process Would Benefit Airborne Laser Decision-Making* (2002); and *Polar-Orbiting Operational Environmental Satellites: Technical Problems, Cost Increases, and Schedule Delays Trigger Need for Difficult Trade-Off Decisions* (2005).

GAO reports covering space warfare and defense program issues include *Ballistic Missile Defense: Information on Directed Energy Programs For Fiscal Years 1985 Through 1993* (1993); *National Space Issues: Observations on Defense Space Programs and Activities* (1994); *Space Acquisitions: DOD Needs a Departmentwide Strategy for Pursuing Low-Cost Responsive Tactical Space Capabilities* (2000); *Missile Defense: Review of Results and Limitations of an Early National Missile Defense Flight Test* (2002); *Navy Working Capital Fund: Backlog of Funded Work at the Space and Naval Warfare Systems Command Consistently Understated* (2003); *Missile Defense: Alternative Approaches to Space Tracking and Surveillance System Need to be Considered* (2003); *Military Space Operations: Common Problems and Their Effects on Satellite and Related Acquisitions* (2003); and *Defense Acquisitions: Missile Defense Agency Fields Initial Capability but Falls Short of Original Goals* (2003).

Office of Technology Assessment

The Office of Technology Assessment (OTA) was a congressional support agency that existed from 1972–1995. OTA was created to provide Congress with timely analysis of scientific issues and its functions, as stated in its authorizing statute, including identifying existing or probable technological impacts, identifying alternative technologies for implementing specific programs, identifying alternative programs for achieving compulsory goals, and presenting analytical findings to congressional policymakers.

OTA reports are available in many federal depository libraries. An electronic archive of OTA reports is available in the *OTA Legacy* CD-ROM published by the U.S. Government Printing Office and through a Web site at Princeton University's Woodrow Wilson School of Advanced International Affairs (www.princeton.edu/~ota/). Examples of pertinent OTA space policy reports include *Anti-Satellite Weapons, Countermeasures, and Arms Control* (1985); *Ballistic Missile Defense Technologies* (1985); *Space Stations and the Law: Selected Legal Issues* (1986); *Access to Space: The Future of U.S. Space Transportation Systems* (1990); *Affordable Spacecraft: Design and Launch Alternatives* (1990); *Monitoring Limits on Sea-Launched Cruise Missiles* (1991); and *U.S.-Russian Cooperation in Space* (1995).

U.S. Government Commissions and Advisory Organizations

U.S. Government commissions and advisory organizations can provide valuable information on space war and defense issues. Such organizations can be appointed by the president or Congress to research public policy issues and issue reports containing additional technical details on this issue and while also recommending solutions to problems facing these issues. These organizations generally have a limited life span of one to two years although the National Academies have been in existence since the Civil War. Members of these commissions are experts from federal, state, and local governments along with recognized authorities from academia, business, the military, and nonprofit organizations.

Most commission and advisory organization reports are available in many federal depository libraries and, in recent years, on the Internet. Works on space warfare and defense produced by the National Academies and a number of recent U.S. Government commissions are presented below.

National Academies

The National Academies, commonly known as the National Academy of Sciences (NAS), was established by Congress in 1863 to "investigate, examine, and report on any subject of science or art," when requested by a government agency. NAS advises the U.S.

Scientists pose with Explorer I, the first successful U.S. satellite, at the National Academy of Sciences in 1958. The satellite was launched shortly after President Dwight D. Eisenhower's establishment of the National Aeronautics and Space Administration (NASA) in 1958. *(NASA)*

Government on scientific and technological matters and includes a variety of component entities including the National Research Council, National Academy of Engineering, and Institute of Medicine. NAS is a private organization and does not receive direct federal appropriations but financial support for academies research projects comes from individual federal agency contracts and grants.

Overall information on NAS operations and research activities can be found on its Web site, www.nas.edu/. The work of three NAS entities, which can encompass space warfare and defense, is examined below: the Air Force Studies Board, Army Research Laboratory Technical Assessment Board, and Naval Studies Board.

Air Force Studies Board

The Air Force Studies Board (AFSB) is responsible for discussing science and technology issues pertinent to the Air Force and helps develop studies conducted by independent ad hoc National Academies committees. The Board conducts periodic meetings to discuss assignments to pursue and seeks to ensure the distribution of scientific and engineering knowledge through published peer-reviewed reports on studies conducted for the Air Force and other governmental entities.

AFSB's Web site (www7.nationalacademies.org/afstb) provides a diverse array of resources describing the board's mission. These materials include biographical information on board members and their institutional affiliation, information on current program activities and projects such as the Standing Committee on Technology Insight-Gauge, Evaluate, and Review, Future Department of Defense Propulsion Needs, and Future Air Force Needs for Survivability with some of these program Web sites featuring meeting agendas.

A number of reports are accessible through the AFSB Web site including *Hypersonic Technology for Military Application* (1990); *Review and Evaluation of the Air Force Hypersonic Technology Program* (1998); *Review of the Future of the U.S. Aerospace Infrastructure and Aerospace Engineering Disciplines to Meet the Needs of the Air Force and the Department of Defense* (2001); *Review of the Department of Defense Air, Space, and Supporting Information Systems Science and Technology Program* (2001); *Evaluation of the National Aerospace Initiative* (2004); *Assessment of Department of Defense Basic Research* (2005); *Avoiding Surprises in an Era of Global Technology Advances* (2005); and *A Review of United States Air Force and Department of Defense Aerospace Propulsion Needs* (2006).

Army Research Laboratory Technical Assessment Board

The Army Research Laboratory Technical Assessment Board (ARLTAB) was established in 1995 and is responsible for assessing the scientific and technical quality of Army Research Laboratory (ARL) research and development efforts. ARLTAB carries out its mandate through six panels reviewing ARL activities in air and ground vehicle technology;

armor/armaments; digitization/communications science; sensors and electron devices; soldier systems; and survivability/lethality analysis.

Further information about ARLTAB is accessible at www7.nationalacademies.org/arltab/. Accessible materials include biographical information on board members, meeting agendas, and descriptive information on the project areas listed in the previous paragraph. No relevant ARLTAB space warfare and defense reports are accessible on this Web site, although there is a link for contacting the National Academies Public Access Records Project Office to review publicly available project materials.

Naval Studies Board

The Naval Studies Board (NSB) was established in 1946 at the initiative of the Office of Naval Research to advise the Navy on submarine design and systems technology issues. Over the next six decades NSB has conducted research and analysis affecting most scientific and engineering subjects requested by the Department of the Navy or Chief of Naval Operations. Examples of topics reviewed by NSB include theater missile defense, defending naval forces against biological and chemical threats, using autonomous vehicles to support naval operations, and other subjects.

The NSB Web site (www7.nationalacademies.org/nsb) features board staff contact information, biographies of current NSB members, and information about current projects including Command, Control, Computers, Communications, Intelligence, Surveillance, and Reconnaissance (C4ISR) for Future Naval Strike Groups, Distributed Remote Sensing for Naval Undersea Warfare, and the Role of Naval Forces in the Global War on Terror.

A remarkable variety of reports are also accessible through this Web site with these including *Technology for the United States Navy and Marine Corps, 2000–2035: Becoming a 21st-Century Force* (1997); *Network-Centric Naval Forces: A Transition Strategy for Enhancing Operational Capabilities* (2000); *Naval Forces Capability for Theater Missile Defense* (2001); *An Assessment of Precision Time and Time Interval Science and Technology* (2002); *The Role of Experimentation in Building Future Naval Forces* (2004); *The Navy's Needs in Space for Providing Future Capabilities* (2005); *FORCENet Implementation Strategy* (2005); and *Identification of Promising Naval Aviation Science and Technology Opportunities* (2006).

Aerospace Industry Commission

This commission, officially known as the Commission on the Future of the U.S. Aerospace Industry, was established in 2000 by the Defense Authorization Act for fiscal year 2001. Chaired by former representative Robert Walker (Republican from Pennsylvania, 1977–1997), this commission was directed to study the sufficiency of the federal government's aerospace research, development, and procurement budget; determine whether the then existing aerospace export control system maintained a proper balance between protecting national security and facilitating unrestricted market access; evaluate the quality of U.S. international trade laws and policies for ensuring the U.S. aerospace industry's competitive posture; review the status of U.S. space launch infrastructure; and evaluate the quality of higher education programs in aerospace science and engineering.

The Commission released its *Final Report* in 2002, and that report is accessible at http://purl.access.gpo.gov/GPO/LPS43534. Report recommendations include advocating NASA and DOD develop and support future launch capability requirements; developing a U.S. military industrial base policy; removing barriers to defense purchases of commercial aerospace products and services; creating a government-wide management structure to establish national aerospace policy; creating a federal interagency task force to develop a national aerospace workforce strategy to enhance public awareness of this industry's importance; and substantially increasing federal spending on aerospace research.

Commission on U.S. National Security Space Management and Organization

The Commission on U.S. National Security Space Management and Organization was created in 1999 by the Defense Authorization Act for fiscal year 2000. The Commission's charter directed it to examine which military space assets could be used to support U.S. military operations, existing interagency coordination processes concerning national security space asset operations, relationships between intelligence and nonintelligence aspects of national security space, how military space issues are discussed in professional military education, and the potential advantages and disadvantages of establishing a military branch dedicated to national security space missions or similar entities or officials within DOD.

Report of the Commission to Assess United States National Security Space Management and Organization was released in 2001 and is accessible at www.defenselink.mil/pubs/space20010111.html. Its recommendations included establishing space activity as a fundamental U.S. national interest; encouraging DOD to develop and deploy space systems to deter attack and defend U.S. earth and space interests; recognizing the crucial roles played by commercial and civilian space sectors in domestic and international economic affairs and national security; and developing a cadre of military and space professionals within DOD, the intelligence community, and other governmental branches.

Commission to Assess the Ballistic Missile Threat to the United States

The Commission to Assess the Ballistic Missile Threat, also known as the Rumsfeld Commission because it was chaired by Donald Rumsfeld prior to his becoming secretary of Defense in 2001, was established in 1996 by the fiscal year 1997 Defense Authorization Act to review the nature and extent of existing and emerging ballistic missile threats to the United States.

Donald Rumsfeld served in a number of positions under most Republican presidents since Dwight D. Eisenhower. In 2001, he became secretary of defense in the George W. Bush administration serving from 2001–2006. *(U.S. Department of Defense)*

The Rumsfeld Commission released an unclassified version of its report in 1998 and an executive summary and working papers are accessible through the Federation of American Scientists Web site, www.fas.org/irp/threat/missile/rumsfeld/.

The Commission report reviewed and analyzed the overall international security environment with emphasis on countries that have shown interest in developing ballistic missiles including China, India, Iran, Iraq, North Korea, Pakistan, and Russia. Report conclusions stress that there are concerted efforts by numerous nations to acquire ballistic missiles with biological or nuclear payloads that may pose a growing threat to the United States and its allies; threats to the United States from these emerging capabilities are deeper, more substantive, and evolving faster than documented in U.S. intelligence community reports and estimates; the ability of the intelligence community to provide timely and accurate estimates of ballistic missile threats is eroding and U.S. abilities in such detection requires augmented resources and methodology; and the warning times the United States can expect for new threatening missile deployments are declining and the United States may have little or no warning before such deployments become operational.

Electromagnetic Pulse Commission

The Electromagnetic Pulse (EMP) Commission was established in 2000 by the National Defense Authorization Act in fiscal year 2001. In establishing this organization, Congress directed it to assess the nature and extent of potential high-altitude EMP threats to the United States from state or nonstate entities that have or could obtain nuclear weapons and ballistic missiles permitting them to conduct a high-altitude attack against the United States in the next 15 years, the vulnerability of U.S. military and civilian systems to such attack with particular emphasis on civilian infrastructure and emergency preparedness vulnerabilities, the United States' ability to repair and recover from damage inflicted on civilian and military assets from EMP attack, and the feasibility and cost of hardening selected military and civilian systems against such attack.

An unclassified executive summary of the commission report was released in 2004, was accessible on the House Armed Services Committee Web site until 2007, and is accessible on the Global Security.org Web site at http://www.globalsecurity.org/wmd/library/congress/2004_r/04–07–22emp.pdf. Report findings stress the United States' heavy dependence on electronics, energy, financial and transportation systems, heavy industry, information networks, and telecommunications leveraging contemporary technology and how the vulnerability of these infrastructures invites and rewards attacks. EMP attacks, involving the detonation of nuclear warheads 40–400 kilometers above the earth's surface, can disrupt or damage electronic and electric systems throughout most of the United States almost simultaneously as determined by an adversary.

Commission report recommendations include pursuing intelligence, interdiction and deterrence to discourage EMP attacks against the United States and its interests; recognizing EMP attacks and distinguishing between them and normal electric power outages; clearly defining the federal government's responsibilities in an EMP attack and giving the Department of Homeland Security (DHS) the appropriate authority to respond; improving the ability of telecommunications systems to withstand sustained loss of utility-supplied electric power; DHS, the Federal Reserve Board, Treasury Department, and other agencies developing contingency plans to recover key financial systems promptly following EMP attack; federal, state, and local governments establishing plans to ensure food availability to the general population if there is major disruption to the food infrastructure; DHS and DOD jointly conducting a systematic assessment on the significance of space systems supporting governmental continuity, strategic military force protection, and critical tactical force support functions so these responsibilities can be executed in view of possible EMP threats; national leadership keeping the public reliably informed; and protecting critical military capabilities such as satellite navigation systems, satellite and airborne intelligence and targeting systems, adequate communications infrastructure, and missile defense to ensure effectual tactical U.S. military responses to EMP attacks.

National Imagery and Mapping Agency Commission

A classified appendix to the fiscal year 2000 Defense Department appropriations bill called for the creation of the Independent Commission on the National Imagery and Mapping Agency (NIMA). The NIMA Commission was charged with looking at this agency, which is responsible for providing timely and accurate geospatial intelligence to the president and military.

Cape Town and the Cape of Good Hope, South Africa, appear in the foreground of this perspective view generated from a LANDSAT satellite image and elevation data from the Shuttle Radar Topography Mission (SRTM), a cooperative project between the National Aeronautics and Space Administration (NASA), the National Geospatial Intelligence Agency (NGA), and the German and Italian space agencies. *(SRTM Team NASA/JPL/NIMA)*

The commission's congressional creators charged it with reviewing the best course for NIMA's strategic technology development and acquisition programs, whether it is desirable for NIMA to make greater use of commercial imagery collection and exploitation, geospatial information, and information and data storage and retrieval, and the adequacy of then current NIMA budget resources.

The text of the NIMA Commission report, released in 2001, can be found on the Federation of American Scientists Web site at http://fas.org/irp/agency/nima/commission/. Commission recommendations included having the chairman of the Joint Chiefs of Staff commission a study on the demands and constraints military doctrine places on imagery intelligence and geospatial information; NIMA should inform customers of the true cost of national technical means imagery to promote conservation of this scarce resource and support rational economic decisions about using commercial imagery; relevant Defense Department policymakers should work with NIMA leadership to ensure the agency has sufficient personnel and financial resources; NIMA should look to commercial technology developers and producers for decisions to its acquisition problems; NIMA should establish a Technological Advisory Board whose members have governmental and private sector experience; and that the secretary of Defense, director of Central Intelligence, and Congress should mandate that NIMA's director serve for five years.

NIMA became the National Geospatial Intelligence Agency on November 24, 2003 when President George W. Bush signed the fiscal year 2004 Defense Authorization Bill.

National Reconnaissance Office (NRO) Commission

The National Reconnaissance Office (NRO) Commission was established in 1999 and charged with reviewing the NRO's roles and mission, organizational structure, technical skills, commercial imagery use, launch vehicles acquisition, and relationships with other federal agencies.

The NRO Commission issued its report in November 2000, and this report is accessible at http://fas.org/irp/nro/commission/. Report recommendations include requiring the secretary of Defense and Director of Central Intelligence to determine proper roles for NRO, the National Security Agency, and NIMA in tasking processing, exploitation, and dissemination activities; ensuring that the aforementioned policymakers have a common understanding of NRO's current and future capabilities and application of its technology to meet the needs of mission partners and customers; establishing an Office of Space Reconnaissance under the NRO director's leadership to increase NRO's ability to use the best space technology to resolve intelligence problems; and having this office work closely with NRO to achieve proper balance between NRO systems strategic and technical requirements.

U.S.–China Economic and Security Review Commission

The U.S.–China Economic and Security Review Commission was established in the fiscal year 2001 Defense Authorization Act. The Commission's responsibilities include monitoring, investigating, and reporting to Congress on the national security implications of the United States and China's bilateral economic and trade ties. Congress also directed this commission to prepare annual reports whose contents were to include the portion of Sino–U.S. goods and service trade that China dedicates to military systems or systems with military applications, whether Chinese acquisition of military or dual-use technologies contributes to proliferating weapons of mass destruction, analysis of writings or statements by Chinese officials concerning military competition with the United States or its Asian allies, potential effects of Chinese financial transactions on U.S. national security interests, whether China's trade surplus with the United States enhances China's military budget, and an overall assessment of whether Chinese national security challenges to the United States are increasing or decreasing.

The Commission released its initial report *The National Security Implications of the Economic Relationship Between the United States and China* in July 2002. Recommendations in this document included having the U.S. Government expand its collection, analysis, and translation of open-source Chinese language materials and making them widely available through increased funding; having the president designate an executive branch agency to coordinate compiling a database of all official government-to-government and federal government funded programs with China; creating a federally mandated corporate reporting system to gather data for providing expanded understanding of Sino–U.S. trade and investment relationships; prohibiting satellite launch cooperation with China until it implements a commitment to restrict proliferation of weapons of mass destruction and technologies to other countries and organizations; continuing DOD dialogue with Taiwan on security related issues; having DOD and the FBI jointly review Chinese targeting of sensitive U.S. defense technologies and taking steps to deny Chinese access to and purchase of these resources.

Numerous resources about commission activities can be found at www.uscc.gov/. These include press releases (2001–present), listings of commission members and professional staff, and Web cast videos of selected hearings. *Annual Reports* for 2002 and 2004–2006 are also provided and each of these reports includes commissioner policy recommendations.

Commission hearing transcripts from 2001–present are also included with examples of topics dealing with space national security issues including *Export Controls to China* (2002), *China's Proliferation Practices and the Challenge of North Korea* (2003), *Field Investigation on China's Impact on the U.S. Manufacturing Base* (2004), *China's Proliferation Practices and Role in the North Korean Crisis* (2005), *China's High Technology Development* (2005), and *China's Military Modernization and U.S. Export Controls* (2006).

Additional accessible resources on this Web site include reports commissioned by the Commission to facilitate its work. Examples of these materials include *The Impact of Foreign Weapons and Technology on the Modernization of China's People's Liberation Army* (2004), *The Impact of U.S.-China Trade and Investment on Key Manufacturing Sectors* (2005), *U.S.-China Advanced Technology Trade: An Analysis for the U.S.-China Economic and Security Review Commission* (2005), and *An Assessment of China's Anti-Satellite and Space Warfare Programs, Policies and Doctrines* (2007).

This commission's Web site is an extremely valuable resource for tracking trends and developments in the multifaceted political, economic, and military relationships between the United States and China, including areas of space warfare, defense, and technology.

8

U.S. Research Institutions

L ITERATURE AND DEBATE over space warfare and defense is conducted in many U.S. research institutions or think tanks. These organizations may be funded by academic institutions, corporations, the military, or government agencies. Work produced by these organizations is published and available in many U.S. and foreign academic libraries, and many of these organizations freely publish and distribute their material through their Web sites. Individuals employed by these organizations are often scholars and former governmental or military policymakers. These individuals may present their research findings and opinions to government and military policymakers or they may testify before congressional oversight committees; they are often interviewed in newspapers, on television and radio news, and may also present their views through Internet blogs or other Web-based communication modes. This chapter describes the work of various U.S. research institutions that produce freely available Internet resources dealing with space warfare and defense. These organizations include industry groups, think tanks, commercial groups, and advocacy organizations.

American Institute of Aeronautics and Astronautics

The American Institute of Aeronautics and Astronautics (AIAA) was established in 1963, has 41,000 members, and its headquarters are in Reston, Virginia. Its membership includes scientists and engineers in aeronautics and astronautics, and its mission includes exchanging technological information through publications and conferences to promote technical progress in these arenas and to enhance members' professional expertise. AIAA also runs a public policy program striving to provide federal policymakers with essential technical information and policy guidance on aerospace issues. It carries out its policy program activities through congressional testimony, position papers, and workshops.

AIAA's Web site (www.aiaa.org) contains significant information resources describing organizational activities. These include information on upcoming conferences such as the 4th Annual U.S. Missile Defense Conference in Washington, D.C., information on professional training and instructional courses, news on aerospace industry trends and developments, descriptions of organizational committees and sections, and details on public policy program activities.

Several AIAA publications are available through its Web site, though some of these may only be accessible through computers in libraries subscribing to AIAA publications.

Examples of these information resources, which cover U.S. and international aerospace developments, include the periodical *Aerospace America* (September 2000–present) and the scholarly journals *AIAA Journal* (January 1963–present), *Journal of Propulsion and Power* (January/February 1985–present), and *Journal of Spacecraft and Rockets* (January/February 1964–present).

Additional accessible information resources include the opening statements of AIAA expert witnesses before congressional oversight committees, the archives of AIAA's policy-watch news containing news of governmental aerospace policy developments from May 2004–present with information on the president's proposed defense and NASA budgets being highlights of the February 10, 2006 edition of this resource, and various aerospace information and policy papers prepared by AIAA personnel. Examples of these publications include *Ballistic Missile Defense: A Challenge to Space Technology* (1984), *Export Control Policy and the U.S. Satellite Industry* (1999), *Recommended Government Actions to Address Critical U.S. Space Logistics Needs* (2004), and *The Versatile Affordable Advanced Turbine Engines (VAATE) Initiative* (2006).

Arms Control Association

The Arms Control Association (ACA) is a Washington, D.C.-based organization founded in 1971 seeking to enhance public understanding and support for what the organization considers effective arms control policies for journalists and scholars.

ACA's Web site (www.armscontrol.org) contains descriptions of association sponsored events (1999–present); press releases (2001–present); the text of various international arms control agreements including those dealing with weapons in space; resources on countries of arms control concern such as Iran; and subject resources dealing with space, missile defense, and other arms control issues such as the Comprehensive Test Ban Treaty.

Accessible publications include articles from the periodical *Arms Control Today* (January/February 1997–present), fact sheets such as *The Anti-Ballistic Missile (ABM) Treaty at a Glance* (2003) and *U.S. Missile Defense Programs at a Glance* (2004), and articles such as "Weapons in the Heavens: A Reckless and Radical Option" (October 2004).

Brookings Institution

The Brookings Institution (BI) is one of the United States' major public policy research organizations. Founded in 1916, it has a staff of 250, a $31-million annual budget, and its research interests encompass a variety of domestic and international public policy issues.

Features of BI's Web site (www.brookings.edu) include information on its multifaceted research areas, descriptions of its scholars, their areas of expertise, links to some of their publications, information about past and upcoming institute-sponsored events, and the complete text or excerpts from publications dealing with space warfare and defense such

Brookings Institution. *(Shepard Sherbell/Corbis)*

as *Beyond Missile Defense: Countering Terrorism and Weapons of Mass Destruction* (2001), *Neither Star Wars Nor Sanctuary: Constraining the Military Uses of Space* (2004), and *Preserving U.S. Dominance While Slowing the Weaponization of Space* (2005).

Center for Nonproliferation Studies

The Center for Nonproliferation Studies (CNS) is located in Monterrey, California and is part of the Monterey Institute of International Studies. Established in 1989, CNS's staff includes over 40 specialists and 50 graduate students located in Monterey, Washington, D.C., and Almaty, Kazakhstan. CNS's institutional purpose is preventing the spread of weapons of mass destruction by training nonproliferation specialists and distributing timely information and analysis. Further information about CNS's multifaceted programs and research activities are provided on its Web site, http://cns.miis.edu/. These information resources include descriptions of organizational program areas including the Weapons of Mass Destruction Terrorism Research Program, East Asian Nonproliferation Program, and International Organizations and Nonproliferation Program. Publications discussing space warfare and other nonproliferation topics include the scholarly journal *Nonproliferation Review* (1993–present), the newsletter *International Export Control Observer* (October 2005–present), and numerous reports including *A History of Ballistic Missile Development in the DPRK* (2000), *Missile Proliferation and Defenses: Problems and Prospects* (2001), *Ballistic Missile Defense and Northeast Asian Security: Views from Washington, Beijing, and*

Tokyo (2001), *New Challenges in Missile Proliferation, Missile Defense, and Space Security* (2003), and *Future Security in Space: Commercial, Military, and Arms Control Trade-Offs* (2003).

Center for Security Policy

The Center for Security Policy (CSP) is a conservative-oriented institution founded in 1988; it has a staff of four and an annual budget of approximately $850,000. Its mission involves serving as a foreign and national security policy information resource for government officials, press, industry, and the public, and developing strategies to facilitate the work of policymakers engaged in these issues.

CSP's Web site, www.centerforsecuritypolicy.org/, features a variety of information resources organized into geographical and functional areas. Its military space materials include articles and journalistic op-eds supporting missile defense and related subjects including *The Blackout Next Time* (an op-ed dealing with electromagnetic pulse) (2003); *Restructure, Don't Cut the Missile Defense Program: Focus Should Be on Deployment of Near-Term Anti-Missile Systems* (2004); *Anti-Anti-Missile Defense* (2004); *The High Ground: The Next Missile Defense Battle Heats Up in Space* (2004); and *The Rods from God: Are Kinetic-Energy Weapons the Future of Space Warfare?* (2005).

Center for Strategic and Budgetary Assessments

The Center for Strategic and Budgetary Assessments (CSBA), located in Washington, D.C., was founded in 1983, has a staff of seven, and its annual operating budget is $500,000. CSBA is a nonpartisan research organization seeking to provide timely analyses of military spending and national security policy issues for policy makers, the media, and interest groups.

A variety of information resources are provided through CSBA's Web site, www .csbaonline.org/. Besides containing information on organizational activities and a staff directory, several publications dealing with space warfare or defense are posted including *Future Warfare 20XX Wargame Series: Lessons Learned Report* (2001), *The Military Use of Space: A Diagnostic Assessment* (2001), and *Classified Funding in the 2006 Defense Budget Request* (2005).

Center for Strategic and International Studies

The Center for Strategic and International Studies (CSIS) is located in Washington, D.C. and is a nonpartisan research institute founded in 1962 specializing in providing practical insights to policymakers on international security issues.

CSIS's Web site (www.csis.org) features a stellar array of information resources. These include biographical information on institutional scholars, press releases (1997–present), listings of CSIS-sponsored events (1999–present), and descriptions of institute programs including the Human Space Exploration Initiative, Technology and Public Policy Project, and the Transnational Threats Project. Its Web site also features publications on a variety of international strategic issues with representative samples of resources dealing with space warfare and defense including articles from the scholarly journal *Washington Quarterly* (1999–present) and reports such as *A Sober Second Look: Reassessing the Logic of Missile Defense* (2000), *China and the U.S: National Missile Defenses and Chinese Nuclear Modernization* (2001), *Remote Sensing Satellites and Presidential Decision Directive 23* (2003), *U.S.-Russian Missile Defense Cooperation: Limits of the Possible* (2003), *Responding to Asymmetric Threats in Space* (2005), *A Flight From Responsibility: Canada and Missile Defense of North America* (2005), and *The Still Untrodden Heights: Global Imperatives for Space Exploration in the 21st Century* (2005).

Chinese Military Power (Aerospace Section)

Chinese Military Power (CMP) is part of the Project on Defense Alternatives (PDA) sponsored by its parent institution the Commonwealth Institute. This institute is based in Cambridge, Massachusetts and conducts a variety of public policy research. Founded in 1991, PDA institutional objectives include promoting what it sees as reliable and cost-effective defenses against aggression; using military structures that it contends will not

China's first manned spacecraft, the Shenzhou-5, blasts off from the Jiuquan Satellite Launch Center in the northwestern province of Gansu in 2003. *(Xinhua/Xinhua Photo/Corbis)*

contribute to international tensions or crisis instability; allowing significant reductions in military spending and armed force sizes; enhancing progress in arms control; gradually demilitarizing international relations; and facilitating increasing reliance on collective and global peace-keeping entities and nonmilitary methods of conflict prevention, containment, and resolution.

PDA's Web site covering its overall array of information resources is accessible at www.comw.org/pda/, while its Chinese Military Power Web site emphasizing Chinese security trends and development is www.comw.org/cmp/. A variety of materials describing Chinese military aerospace developments are featured on this Web site including documents such as *The Chinese Threat to American Leadership in Space* (2001); *New Questions About U.S. Intelligence on China: An Analysis of the March 2005 Report by the U.S. National Air and Space Intelligence Center* (2005); *China's Future in Space: Implications for U.S. Security* (2005); *Action/Reaction: U.S. Space Weaponization and China* (2005); and *China's Space Program: A Strategic and Political Analysis* (2005).

Federation of American Scientists

The Federation of American Scientists (FAS), located in Washington, D.C., was founded in 1945 and has 2,500 members and a professional office staff of 18. Its annual budget is $3 million. FAS membership includes scientists, engineers, and other individuals concerned with societal impacts of science and seeks to provide what it believes are science-based perspectives on public policy issues.

The FAS Web site (www.fas.org) includes information about federation activities in a variety of national security related program areas such as intelligence, terrorism, U.S. weapons systems, and weapons in space. Publicly accessible federation periodicals include *Public Interest Report* newsletter (1946–present) and *Secrecy News* (September 2000–present).

In addition, the text of many reports produced by FAS or by government agencies on space war and defense issues are also provided. Examples of these resources include documents by FAS personnel such as *Not So Fast: Comments on "Estimates of Performance and Cost for Boost Phase Intercept" Presented to the Marshall Institute's Washington Roundtable on Science and Public Policy by Greg Canavan on 24 September 2004* (2005?) and *Ensuring America's Space Security* (2005), links to government and military reports on space defense maintained by FAS from agencies such as Air University, the Army Science Board, and Defense Science Board, and FAS maintained Web sites on military space programs involving satellite tracking, geodesy and mapping, imagery intelligence, wide-area ocean surveillance, antisatellite weapons, and a listing of military satellites in orbit.

GeoEye

GeoEye (formerly Space Imaging) is a for-profit company located in Thornton, Colorado with various branch offices in the United States and other countries. It was founded in 1994 and seeks to provide space imagery and aerial photography to document continually changing features of the earth's environment, natural resources, and human development. GeoEye applications are used to provide solutions and analytical tools for various business, economic, environmental, and security situations internationally.

GeoEye's Web site (www.geoeye.com) features press releases (1995–present); descriptions of company product lines and some technical specifications for these products in imagery such as Ikonos satellites; radar products such as Radarsat; digital terrain models such as IM-1; and software products such as Carterra Analyst, which allows for the viewing, manipulation, and integration of imagery with other data to expedite decision-making.

White papers such as *Homeland Security* (2002) and *What is Imaging Radar?* (2005) are also noteworthy features of www.geoeye.com, along with descriptions of ongoing corporate activities in homeland security, regional and government support, and ensuring secure electronic data delivery. However, satellite photography is the hallmark characteristic of this Web site with representative samples including a photograph of the Kandahar, Afghanistan airfield on April 23, 2001 and a later photograph of this site on October 10, 2001 after its bombing by U.S. forces during Operation Enduring Freedom; photographs of the Pentagon between September 7, 2001 and September 7, 2002; before and after photographs of communities and regions affected by Hurricane Katrina in 2005; regions affected by the 2005 Pakistani Kashmir earthquake; and photographs of 2006 Winter Olympic venues in and near Torino, Italy.

George Washington University Space Policy Institute

The Space Policy Institute (SPI) is part of George Washington University's Elliott School of International Affairs in Washington, D.C. SPI was established in 1987 and conducts research on space policy issues relating to U.S. space policy and cooperative and competitive space policy contacts the United States has with other countries. Institute activities include research and conferences on these topics. SPI receives funding from George Washington University, individuals, corporations, foundations, and government sources.

SPI's Web site (www.gwu.edu/~spi) features a descriptive institutional overview, biographical information about institute faculty and listings of their publications, information about courses including the syllabus for the Fall 2005 "U.S. Space Policy" course, and information about current and recent institute research projects such as the U.S.–European gap in defense technologies and dual-purpose space technologies having both commercial and military applications.

Accessible publications include *Just Say Wait to Space Power* (2001), *High Resolution Earth Observations From Space: What Are Today's Issues?* (2001), *Space and Military Power in East Asia: The Challenge and Opportunity of Dual-Purpose Space Technologies* (2002?), *Europe's Ambitions in Space* (2002), *Space Economic Data* (2002), and *Reflections on Space as a Vital National Interest* (2003).

Elliott School of International Affairs at George Washington University, home of the Space Policy Institute. *(Claire Duggan, The George Washington University)*

Global Security

Global Security is located in Alexandria, Virginia. It was founded in 2000 and provides exhaustive online coverage of emerging news in defense, space, intelligence, weapons of mass destruction, and homeland security. Global Security sees its institutional mandate as providing innovative approaches to emerging security problems by reducing reliance on nuclear weapons and their possible use, transforming conventional U.S. military forces to meet post–Cold War security environment threats, supporting space technology initiatives to strengthen international peace and security, and improving the capabilities of the U.S. intelligence community respond to existing and emerging threats.

Numerous pertinent information resources are accessible through Global Security's Web site, www.globalsecurity.org/. These include materials broken into topical areas such as military, weapons of mass destruction, intelligence, homeland security, space, policy, and a weekly "public eye" feature presenting a satellite photograph of an international security area of interest, with a January 2006 photo highlighting the Iranian nuclear uranium enrichment site at Natanz and a June 2006 photo covering the North Korean Musudan-ri Missile Test Facility.

A "hot topics" section on the homepage features links to information resources on the European Union's Galileo navigation satellite, the National Security Agency and domestic surveillance, North Korea's nuclear weapons program, and news reports on military topics from a variety of U.S. and international sources from 1997–present. Global Security's Web site also features links to the text of various U.S. Government agency space policy documents from 1988–present and analyses presented by Global Security personnel and other analysts such as *The Military Capabilities and Implications of China's Indigenous Satellite-Based Navigation System* (2004), *China and Russia Challenging the Space Leadership of the United States* (2005), and *The Case for Missile Defense in the Arabian Gulf* (2005). These multifaceted information resources combine to make Global Security an essential resource for those studying contemporary and recent historical space war and defense issues.

Heritage Foundation

The Heritage Foundation is located in Washington, D.C. and has become a major conservative public policy research institution. Founded in 1973, it sees its mission as developing and advocating conservative public policies based on free enterprise, limited government, traditional values, and strong national defense.

Detailed information about the Heritage Foundation and its work are provided through its Web site at www.heritage.org/. Available resources include listings of Heritage policy analysts broken down by subject expertise with links to their writings, links to foundation Web sites delineated by various areas of domestic policy and international affairs, and news releases from 2000–present.

Examples of accessible Heritage Foundation resources dealing with space warfare and defense include *America Needs a New Space Launch Vehicle* (2001); *Strategic Synchronization: The Relationship Between Strategic Offense and Defense* (2002); *China and the Battlefield in Space* (2003); *The Operational Missile Defense Capability: A Historic Advance for the Defense of the American People* (2004); *When Government Regulations Hinder Security: Shoulder-Fired Missile Defenses* (2005); *The 2005 Quadrennial Defense Review: China and Space—The Unmentionable Issues* (2005); and *Slipping the Surly Bonds of the Real World: The Unworkable Effort to Prevent the Weaponization of Space* (2005).

Institute for Defense Analyses

The Institute for Defense Analyses (IDA) is located in Alexandria, Virginia. Its institutional origins date back to 1947 when Secretary of Defense James Forrestal established a Weapons System Evaluations Group to produce technical analyses of weapons systems and programs. Its subsequent history has seen IDA evolve into a federally funded research and development center advising the Defense Department and military on national security issues requiring scientific and technical expertise. To preserve its institutional autonomy, IDA does not work for individual military departments, private industry, or foreign governments.

IDA's Web site (www.ida.org) lists members of its board of trustees and corporate officers, links to project Web sites including "Command Post of the Future," "Defense Science Study Group," and "Military Critical Technologies List," and descriptions of ongoing research areas such as C3, ISR and Space Systems, National Security Strategy Issues, Sensors, Surveillance and Target Acquisition, and Space, Air, Missile, and Weapons Technology.

Access to some IDA research reports is provided through the National Technical Information Service Web site (www.ntis.gov) or through the Federally Funded Research and Development Centers Web site of the Defense Technical Information Center (http://stinet .dtic.mil/special/ffrdc.html). Examples of some IDA reports accessible here include *Duel Between an ASAT With Multiple Kill Vehicles and a Space-Based Weapons Platform With Kinetic Energy Weapons* (1986), *Schedule-Assessment Methods for Surface-Launched Interceptors* (1995), *FY96 Analysis of the Ballistic Missile Defense Interoperability Standards* (1996), *China and Ballistic Missile Defense: 1955 to 2002 and Beyond* (2003).

International Assessment and Strategy Center

The International Assessment and Strategy Center (IASC) is located in Alexandria, Virginia. Established in 2004, IASC is independent and nonpartisan and seeks to provide governmental and military policymakers with research and analyses of international affairs and national security issues looking 10–20 years into the future. IASC organizational assessments make multidisciplinary examinations of current and future trends and scenarios while also looking at ways U.S. policy responses to these developments can utilize diplomatic, economic, information, military, and political assets.

IASC's Web site (www.strategycenter.net) includes research project descriptions such as the Asian Security and Democracy Project, the Eurasian Sand Table, Military Balance Databases, and Trends in International Islam; biographical information on affiliated scholars; and listings of center publications. Examples of relevant IASC publications on space warfare and defense issues include *North Korea's New Missiles* (2004); *Pakistan's Long-Range Ballistic Missiles: A View From International Defense Exhibition and Seminar (IDEAS)*(2004); *Top Ten Chinese Military Modernization Developments* (2005); *China's New Strategic Cruise Missiles: From the Land, Sea, and Air* (2005); *China's Manned Military Space Ambitions* (2005); and *Will North Korea Midwife a New Historical Era?* (2006).

MissileThreat.com

MissileThreat.com is affiliated with the Claremont Institute in Claremont, California. It seeks to promote the importance of ballistic missile defense believing that the United States remains threatened by ballistic missiles armed with nuclear weapons or other weapons of mass destruction.

Further information about MissileThreat.com is provided by its Web site, www .missilethreat.com, which began in 2003. Accessible resources include news stories on bal-

Shock-absorbing pads fall away from the surface of an MGM-118A Peacekeeper intercontinental ballistic missile as it emerges from its launch canister. This is the first test launch of the Peacekeeper. *(U.S. Department of Defense)*

listic missile threats and defenses from January 2000–present, an extremely useful database called "Ballistic Missiles of the World," and threat scenario presentations demonstrating the consequences of a ballistic missile attack on critical U.S. infrastructures such as an ICBM attack on Alaska's Prudhoe Bay oil reserves, a missile strike on Hoover Dam and how such a strike would affect Las Vegas, and a Quicktime video simulation of a Chinese missile attack on Los Angeles. Publications provided include *Our Founding Principles and Ballistic Missile Defense* (2004), *Policy Statement on Ballistic Missile Defense* (2004), and *Independent Working Group Report: Missile Defense, the Space Relationship and the Twenty-First Century* (2006).

National Institute for Public Policy

The National Institute for Public Policy (NIPP), located in Fairfax, Virginia, was founded in 1981, and has a staff of twenty. Its organizational mission encompasses examining rapidly evolving international foreign policy and security issues such as the effectiveness of post–Cold War nuclear deterrence, the ability of the United States and its allies to counter weapons of mass production proliferation and missile delivery systems, and the future of NATO and other U.S. and allied military compacts. NIPP's Web site (www .nipp.org) features biographies of professional members, listings of advisory board members, and descriptions of institute programs such as The Future of Ballistic Missiles, Strategic Offensive Forces and the Nuclear Posture Reviews "New Triad," European Perspectives on U.S. Ballistic Missile Defense, and Rationale and Requirements for U.S. Nuclear Forces and Arms Control.

Representative publications on space warfare and defense by NIPP personnel include *European Perspectives on U.S. Ballistic Missile Defense* (2002), *Understanding "Asymmetric" Threats to the United States* (2002), and *Wars of the Future: Implications for the Reform of Russian Armed Forces* (2004).

National Remote Sensing and Space Law Center

The National Remote Sensing and Space Law Center (NRSSLC) is located at the University of Mississippi in Oxford, Mississippi. Established in 2000 as part of that university's law school, NRSSLC seeks to create and disseminate objective and timely research on remote-sensing and space and aviation research. The center defines remote sensing as including satellite, airborne, and ground-based observation and imaging of the earth's surface, interior, oceans, and atmosphere. NRSSLC also examines related legal issues affecting remote sensing in areas such as intellectual property, international law, using imagery as legal evidence, and environmental licensing issues.

The NRSSLC Web site (www.spacelaw.olemiss.edu) features information about the center's mission, listings of staff members, information on Mississippi organizations engaged in remote-sensing activities such as the University of Mississippi Geoinformatics Center, descriptions of NRSSLC publications such as *Proceedings: The First International Conference on the State of Remote Sensing Law* (2002) and *Landsat 7: Past, Present, and Future* (n.d), and information about the *Journal of Space Law*. Staff presentations are also included with examples of these including *U.S. Domestic Space Law Regime* (2001), *Legal Implications of National Security Operations in Space: Space Warfare and Law Enforcement* (2002), *A Brief Survey of Remote Sensing Law Around the World* (2003), *Licensing and the Landsat Story: Law and Policy 1972–2003* (2003), *Legal Issues Using Satellite, Aerial, and UAV Platforms* (2003), and *Beginner's Guide to U.S. Satellite System Data Policy* (2003).

National Security Archive

The National Security Archive (NSA) is a nonprofit research institution affiliated with The George Washington University. It was founded in 1985 by journalists and scholars and receives nearly $2.3 million in annual revenue from publication sales and annual support from private organizations such as the Carnegie Foundation, Ford Foundation, and John and Catherine T. MacArthur Foundation. NSA's mission is serving as an international affairs research institution and maintaining an archive of declassified U.S. government documents obtained through Freedom of Information Act (FOIA) requests.

The archive's Web site (www.gwu.edu/~nsarchiv) contains information about NSA's documentary collections, news releases (May 1997–present), information about subscrip-

Yongbyon, the center of North Korean nuclear research activities, as photographed on March 17, 1970, by a KH-4B Corona satellite. *(National Security Archive (www.nsarchive.org))*

tion services it offers such as the Digital National Security Archive, and descriptions and sample documents from microfiche collections available for purchase including *Military Uses of Space, 1945–1991* (1991), *U.S. Nuclear History: Nuclear Arms and Politics in the Missile Age, 1955–1968* (1997), and *China and the U.S.: From Hostility to Engagement, 1960–1998* (1999).

An especially welcome feature provided by the NSA is its Electronic Briefing Books series available at www.gwu.edu/~nsarchiv/NSAEBB/.

This resource features over 100 freely accessible documentary compilations on various aspects of U.S. foreign and national security policy as of February 2006. Representative samples for those studying U.S. space warfare and defense issues include *U.S. Satellite Imagery, 1960–1999* (1999), *Missile Defenses Thirty Years Ago: Deja Vu All Over Again?* (2000), *The Secret History of the ABM Treaty, 1969–1972* (2001), *Eyes on Saddam: U.S. Overhead Imagery of Iraq* (2003), and *The Spy Satellite So Stealthy That the Senate Couldn't Kill It* (2004).

Nautilus Institute

The Nautilus Institute (NI) was founded in 1992, is located in San Francisco with an international office in Melbourne, Australia, and conducts research on topics such as environmental insecurity, international security policy, and global governance issues.

NI's Web site (www.nautilus.org) features listings of institute board members, biographies of affiliated scholars, and links to the Web sites of current and former institute programs. Examples of relevant publications relating to space warfare and defense include

The Political and Strategic Imperatives of National Missile Defense (2000), *British Approaches to Nuclear Disarmament and National Missile Defense* (2000), *Assessment of the North Korean Missile Threat* (2003), *Theater Missile Defense in Asia* (n.d.), and *U.S. BMD Program Under Bush Administration: Its Influence on Arms Race and Proliferation in East Asia* (n.d.).

Praeger Security International

Praeger Security International (PSI) is an online subscription database being offered by Greenwood Publishing Group beginning in 2006. This resource will provide online access to over 500 titles in international security, defense and foreign policy, military history, and terrorism from a variety of disciplinary and political perspectives.

General information about PSI is available at www.greenwood.com/psi/ and with representative titles in this database including *Sky State: The Space Debris Crisis* (2003); *Ballistic Missile Defense: Still Trying After All These Years* (2004); *Satellites: Communication, Observation, Navigation and Detecting* (2004); and *Thunder Over the Horizon: From V-2 Rockets to Ballistic Missiles* (2006).

Rand Corporation

The Rand Corporation is one of the most influential public policy think tanks in the United States and internationally. Its origins date back to December 1945 as Project Rand, a venture involving the Army Air Force and Douglas Aircraft Company. In May 1946 it issued *Preliminary Design of an Experimental World-Circling Spaceship*, which sought to describe how man-made satellites might be designed and perform. On May 14, 1948, Rand was incorporated as a nonprofit corporation in California and listed its institutional mandate as being: "To further and promote scientific, educational, and charitable purposes, all the public welfare and security of the United States of America."

Rand is headquartered in Santa Monica, California and has offices in Washington, D.C. and other locales. It provides nonpartisan public policy research in a variety of social science disciplines with an acute emphasis on national security issues. Rand has benefited from close relationships with and support from numerous U.S. Government agencies including the U.S. Air Force. Rand's Web site (www.rand.org) is a treasure trove of information resources including press releases (1995–present); listings of governmental, corporate, academic, and other supporters of Rand work; descriptions and Web site links for organizational component organizations including the Arroyo Center, which conducts research for the U.S. Army, and the National Security Research Division and its functional and regional geographic subdivisions. Additional Web site features include congressional testimony by Rand personnel (1993–present) and listings of Rand scholars arranged by name and area of expertise.

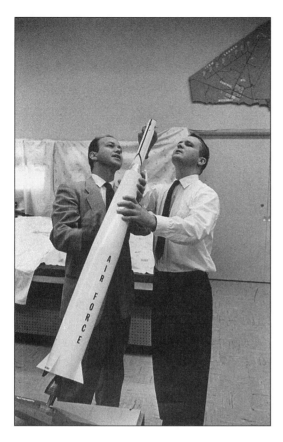

Charles Heffern (L) with space-rocket expert Robert Buchheim (R) at Rand Corporation Research Institution with model of Thor-Able rocket, 1958. *(Leonard Mccombe/Time Life Pictures/Getty Images)*

Numerous publications are provided through Rand's Web site including the journal *Rand Review* and its predecessor *Rand Research Review* (1993–present) and reference publications such as *Selected Rand Abstracts: A Guide to Rand Publications* (1998–present). The highlight of Rand's Web site is the full text access it provides to innumerable research reports on various public policy topics. Reports regarding space warfare and defense are featured prominently with examples including *Life Cycle Cost Assessments for Military Transatmospheric Vehicles* (1997); *Space: Emerging Options for National Power* (1998); *Trends in Space Control Capabilities and Ballistic Missile Threats: Implications for ASAT Arms Control* (1998); *The Changing Role of the U.S. Military in Space* (1999); *Commercial Observation Satellites: At the Leading Edge of Global Transparency* (2001); *Ballistic Missile Defense: A German-American Analysis* (2001); *Army Air and Missile Defense: Future Challenges* (2002); *Space Weapons, Earth Wars* (2002); *Mastering the Ultimate High Ground: Next Steps in the Military Uses of Space* (2003); *Toward Fusion of Air and Space: Surveying Developments and Assessing Choices for Small and Middle Powers* (2003); *Communications Networks to Support Integrated Intelligence, Surveillance, Reconnaissance, and Strike Operations* (2004); *Supporting Air and Space Expeditionary Forces: A Methodology for Determining*

Air Force Deployment Requirements (2004); *Building a Multinational Global Navigation Satellite System: An Initial Look* (2005); *High Altitude Airships for the Future Army* (2005); *Improving the Development and Utilization of Air Force Space and Missile Officers* (2005); and *Supporting Air and Space Expeditionary Forces: Capabilities and Sustainability of Air and Space Expeditionary Forces* (2006).

Stimson Center–Space Security Project

The Henry Stimson Center in Washington, D.C. was founded in 1989 and named for the U.S. Secretary of State from 1929–1933. It is a nonprofit and nonpartisan institution seeking to enhance international peace and security through analytical research and public outreach.

The Stimson Center's Web site, www.stimson.org/, contains press releases (October 1998–present), listings of affiliated scholars and their areas of expertise, descriptions of past center-sponsored events, and descriptions of historical and current center-sponsored projects including ones dealing with chemical and biological weapons nonproliferation, regional security in South Asia, global health security, and space security.

Space Security Project objectives include increasing public awareness of what the Stimson Center sees as the dangerous consequences of flight testing and deploying space weapons, giving policymakers, legislators, negotiators, and nongovernmental organizations information to making what Project participants consider prudent space security choices, and offering pragmatic alternatives to space weapons.

Resources provided on the Space Security Project Web site (www.stimson.org/wos) include statistics on the amount of satellites and orbital debris in space and publications such as *Space Assurance or Space Dominance?: The Case Against Weaponizing Space* (2003); *Model Code of Conduct for the Prevention of Incidents and Dangerous Military Practices in Outer Space* (2004); *Weapons in the Heavens: A Radical and Reckless Option* (2004); *Outer Space Threats* (2005); *Code of Conduct for Outer Space* (2005); and *Space Security or Space Weapons: A Citizen's Guide to the Issues* (2005).

Stratfor

Stratfor is an Austin, Texas-based commercial global intelligence organization founded in 1996. It specializes in providing its clientele with geopolitical and commercial intelligence, forecasting, and strategic policy analysis and provides a variety of fee-based information products and services to its customers. Stratfor's Web site (www.stratfor.com) features descriptions of its research and data gathering methodology, organizational leaders biographies, references to organizational analysis in print and electronic media, and information about subscribing to company products and services.

9

Foreign and International Government Organizations and Research Centers

ORGANIZATIONS DEALING WITH SPACE WARFARE and defense are located in numerous countries. These include national and international government organizations with policy-making responsibilities encompassing space science and national security. They can also include research institutions or think tanks taking public-policy positions engaging in civilian or military space science research, which can take advocacy positions on military activities in space and related national or international security issues. This chapter includes a representative sampling of these governmental and research organizations. It describes these organizations, features information about where they are located, lists their Web sites, and describes English-language information resources they produce regarding space warfare and defense. Entries are listed in alphabetical order by the organization's name.

Australia's Commonwealth Scientific and Industrial Research Organization

Australia's Commonwealth Scientific and Industrial Research Organization (CSIRO) was established in 1926 and is located in Clayton South, Victoria, Australia. Its primary missions as the Australian national science agency include executing scientific research, assisting Australian industry and furthering Australian national interests, and encouraging and facilitating the application and use of its research results or other scientific research.

Information on CSIRO activities can be found on its Web site, www.csiro.au/. Information resources accessible here include descriptions of CSIRO's space science research emphases in astronomy, space facilities, astrophysics, radio astronomy, and space engineering.

Freely available sample publications include the issues of *Ecos Online* magazine from 1984–present and CSIRO's most recent *Annual Report* to the Australian Parliament.

Australian Air Force–Air Power Development Centre

The Royal Australian Air Force's (RAAF) Air Power Development Centre was established in 1989 at RAAF Air Base in New South Wales. Its multifaceted institutional missions include promoting RAAF strategic air power doctrine, educating military and other communities about aerospace power, encouraging and facilitating the professional development of air force personnel in aerospace power, applying historical experience to existing and emerging aerospace challenges, contributing to the development of present and future aerospace doctrinal concepts, and enhancing the ability of future Australian aerospace contributions to coalition military operations. The Air Power Development Centre's Web site (www.raaf.gov.au/airpower) contains a number of information resources on space warfare and defense including *Space Operations: An Australian Perspective* (2001), *AAP 1000 Fundamentals of Australian Aerospace Power (2002), Aerospace Issues from the Iraq War: Imponderables and Pointers* (2003), and *Putting Space Into RAAF Aerospace Power Doctrine* (2004).

Australian Defence College

The Australian Defence College (ADC) is part of the Australian Defence Department in Canberra. Its institutional mission is promoting the learning and growth of military and civilian leaders from Australia and overseas who have professional interests in national and international defense and security issues. ADC offered its first classes in January 1970, received a major reorganization in 1997, and consists of three component organizations: the Australian Defence Force Academy, Australian Command and Staff College, and Centre for Defence and Strategic Studies.

A variety of information resources are accessible through ADC's Web site (www.defence .gov.au/adc) including the college handbook, issues of *Australian Defence Force Journal* (1997–present), and reports such as *AEGIS TMD: Implications for Australia* (2002).

Canadian Space Agency

The Canadian Space Agency (CSA) was established in 1989 by the Canadian Space Act and its headquarters are in Longeuil, Quebec and locations in the Ottawa area. CSA is responsible for promoting the development and application of space knowledge for Canadians and humanity, and its leadership reports to Industry Canada, which is a Cabinet-level department within the Canadian Government.

CSA's Web site (www.space.gc.ca) features information about the agency's mission and activities. Information resources include descriptions of CSA earth observation and satellite technology programs, annual parliamentary budget estimates (2001/2002–present), *Annual Performance Report* (2002–present), *Canadian Space Strategy* (2003), and various other resources documenting its multifaceted research activities.

Canadian Astronaut Team, 2002. Back row, from left to right: Canadian astronauts Chris Hadfield, Dave Williams and Bjarni Tryggvason. Front row, from left to right: Bob Thirsk, Julie Payette and Steve MacLean. *(Canadian Space Agency 2002)*

China National Space Administration

The China National Space Administration (CNSA) is the civilian space agency within China responsible for national space policy and China's space program. It was created in 1993 when the Ministry of Aerospace Industry was split into CNSA and the China Aerospace Agency (CASC), and further organizational restructuring occurred in 1998 when CASC was split into several small state-owned enterprises to facilitate a system that would be more economically competitive. CNSA is now part of the Commission of Science, Technology, and Industry for National Defense. CNSA departmental components include general planning, system, engineering, science, technology, and quality control, and foreign affairs. CNSA's Web site (www.cnsa.gov.cn) provides access to some English language information about agency activities including news releases and the text of *China's Space Activities White Paper* (2000), which is China's official governmental space policy document.

Defence R&D Canada

Defence R&D Canada (DRDC) is part of the Canadian Department of National Defence and has been in operation since 1947. Its institutional purpose is ensuring that Canadian forces are scientifically and operationally relevant to their mission responsibilities. DRDC headquarters are in Ottawa with six research centers scattered across Canada. It employs 1,500 people, its annual budget is $306,000,000, and it engages in active and ongoing collaboration with industry, international allies, academe, other government departments, and the national security community.

Information on DRDC can be found at its Web site, www.drdc.gc.ca/. Examples of relevant technical reports produced under DRDC auspices include *Space-Based Radar Simulation Laboratory (SBRSL); Software Design Document-Volume II SBR ISIRS Model Library* (1993); *Design and Testing Considerations for Hardening a Frigate Against EMP Threat* (1994); *Debris From Ballistic Missile Defence: An Analysis Tools for Policy/Planning Studies* (1995); *Naval Force Missile Defence Calculator: A Rapid Prototype* (2002); *A Foray into Laser Projection and the Visual Perception of Aircraft Aspect* (2002); and *Integration of Space-Based Radar in the Coalition Assets Surveillance Architecture-Interoperability* (2003).

European Defence Agency

The European Defence Agency (EDA) was created on July 12, 2004 by a joint action of the European Union's Council of Ministers. Its institutional mission is "to support the Member States and the Council in their effort to improve European defence capabilities in the field of crisis management and to sustain the European Security and Defence Policy as it stands now and develops in the future." EDA asserts that it will reach its goals by encouraging European Union governments to dedicate defense expenditures to meeting emerging challenges instead of historical threats and identifying common security needs and promoting collaboration to achieve mutually beneficial solutions among member countries. Such activities, according to EDA, will produce better European military capabilities, stronger European defense industries, and enhanced value for European taxpayers. Further information about EDA activities can be derived from its Web site, www.eda.europa.eu/. Examples of information resources available here include descriptions of the activities of its directorates of capabilities development, armaments cooperation, industry and market, and research and technology; agency budget information; organizational charts; and publications such as EDA's semiannual reports to the European Union Council.

European Space Agency

The European Space Agency (ESA) is headquartered in Paris and is the European Union agency responsible for developing European space capabilities. Consisting of 17 member countries, ESA staff numbered 1,907 as of February 2005, its estimated 2006 budget is approximately 2,904,000,000 Euros, and the agency has been in existence since the late 1950s and received its present name in 1975. ESA's Web site (www.esa.int) features numerous resources describing its programs and services in areas such as earth observation, human spaceflight, launchers, spacecraft engineering, spacecraft operations, and telecommunications. Information resources on ESA's Web site include press releases, selected Web casts, issues of *ESA Bulletin* (1994–present), ESA's *Annual Report* (1994–present), selected scientific proceedings, ESA's official two-volume *A History of the European Space Agency, 1958–1987* (2000), and historical studies of space activities by ESA

European Space Agency astronaut Thomas Reiter during a space walk at the International Space Station, August 3, 2006. Reiter and National Aeronautics and Space Administration (NASA) astronaut Jeff Williams installed and replaced equipment and set up scientific experiments on the exterior of the space station during the five-hour, 54-minute walk. *(European Space Agency/NASA)*

member countries including *Finland and the Space Era* (2003) and *Austria's History in Space* (2004).

European Space Policy

The European Union's European Space Policy Web site, http://ec.europa.eu/enterprise/space/, launched in April 2001 to provide news and information about the European Union's space policy programs and policies. Examples of particularly important European space developments include Galileo satellite navigation, the Global Monitoring for the Environment and Security (GMES) initiative, and other pertinent projects and programs concerning space-based telecommunications, international cooperation, and European space programs.

Accessible information resources include news releases and a variety of reports and documents including *STAR 21: Strategic Aerospace Review for the 21st Century* (2002); *The Security Dimensions of GMES* (2003); *Global Monitoring for Environment and Security (GMES): Establishing a GMES Capacity by 2008 (Action Plan 2004–2008)*(2004); *Report of the Panel of Experts on Space and Security* (2005); *European Space Policy: Preliminary Elements* (2005); and *GMES E-news* (June 2005–present).

European Telecommunications Satellite Organization

The European Telecommunications Satellite Organization (EUTELSAT) is based in Paris and was created in 1977 as an international government organization before being privatized in 2001. It serves as Europe's leading satellite operator for video and data services along with fixed satellite services. Its fleet of 22 satellites enables vendors to supply customers with radio and television broadcasting services, broadband Internet access, and professional data network solutions providing coverage for Europe, the Middle East, Africa, and significant portions of Asia and North and South America. Its Web site (www.eutelsat.com) provides further information about organizational activities including the newsletter *Via Eutelsat News* (February 2005–present), press releases (January 2003–present), a listing of Board of Directors members, and various financial reports and statistical data.

European Union Institute for Security Studies

The European Union Institute for Security Studies (EUISS) was established in its current institutional form by the European Council on July 20, 2001 and is part of the European Union's Common Foreign and Security Policy organizational architecture. Its organizational mission is seeking to create what it regards as a European security culture, enhancing strategic debate, promoting European Union interests, and engaging in transatlantic security dialog with European countries, Canada, and the United States.

Numerous resources are accessible through the EUISS Web site, www.iss-eu.org/. These include descriptions and transcripts from institute sponsored seminars; the text of the newsletter *Bulletin* (2002–present); institute sponsored books; and the text of the *Chaillot Papers and Occasional Papers* monographic series with *National Missile Defence and the Future of Nuclear Policy* (2000), *The Galileo Satellite System and Its Security Implications* (2003), and *Space and Security Policy in Europe* (2003) being representative samples of EUISS publications on space warfare and defense policy.

European Union Satellite Centre

The European Union Satellite Centre (EUSC) is located in Torrejon, Spain, near Madrid. EUSC was established by the European Council on July 20, 2001 and became operational on January 1, 2002. Its institutional mandate involves seeking to exploit and produce information obtained from analyzing space observation imagery to support the European Union's Common Foreign and Security Policy and carrying out expert personnel training in digital geographic information systems and imagery analysis. Additional missions covered by EUSC incorporate general security surveillance, treaty verification, arms and proliferation control, maritime surveillance, and environmental monitoring.

EUSC's Web site (www.eusc.org) provides information on the organization's mission, job openings, descriptions of training courses such as "Interpreting Nuclear Installations Using Commercial Satellite Imagery," and the text of selected documents including *Council Joint Action of July 20, 2001: On the Establishment of a European Union Satellite Centre* (2001) and *Staff Regulations of the European Union Satellite Centre* (2005).

French National Aerospace Research Establishment

The French National Aerospace Research Establishment (ONERA), headquartered in Chatillon, was established in 1946 and has satellite facilities in other French communities. Reporting to the French Ministry of Defense its multifaceted missions include assisting government agencies responsible for coordinating civil and military aerospace policy; directing and executing aerospace research; designing, producing, and operating the resources necessary for manufacturers research and testing; making available and commercializing research results and enhancing industry application of this research; and supporting French training policy for scientists and engineers.

ONERA's Web site, www.onera.fr/, contains descriptions of its research branch activities in areas such as fluid mechanics and energetics, materials and structures, physics, information processing and systems, information about its interactions with other European and international aerospace research and governmental organizations, information on training symposiums, and post-doctoral employment opportunities. Numerous general publications are also accessible including the current *Annual Report* along with multifaceted technical publications from 1990–present with representative titles including *Experimental Investigation of a Supersonic Rocket Engine Plume Using OH-Emission, OH-PLIF, and CARS Thermometry* (2003), *Flying Wing Aerodynamic Studies: ONERA and ONR* (2005), and *Progress in Solving Aerodynamic Issues Faced by Space Vehicles* (2005).

German Aerospace Centre

The German Aerospace Centre (DLR), headquartered in Cologne, was established in 1969 and serves as Germany's national space agency providing support for German space activities and representing Germany in international space science forums. DLR has nearly 5,000 employees, consists of 30 institutes, and administers an overall budget of nearly 760,000,000 Euros. DLR's Web site (www.dlr.de) contains some English language descriptions of organizational activities including coverage of ongoing research and programs in earth observation, navigation, communication, space transportation, the International Space Station, and manned space flight. An accessible English-language DLR document is *German Space Program* (2001).

Control room of the German Aerospace Center. *(German Aerospace Center (DLR))*

Global Network Against Weapons & Nuclear Power in Space

The Global Network Against Weapons & Nuclear Power in Space is an international leftist political activist organization formed in 1992 at various U.S. locations and consisting of an international board of directors. Group objectives include applying space technology to social and environmental needs on Earth, preventing confrontation and improving international cooperation in space, banning space weapons and military installations by national and international law, and banning nuclear power in space. Information resources on this organization's Web site, www.space4peace.org/, include information on conferences they have sponsored from 1998–present; links to U.S. military policy statements on space war and defense; documents from the United Nations Office for Outer Space Affairs; the text of a hypothetical World Space Preservation Treaty; and the text of congressional bill H.R. 2420—the Space Preservation Act of 2005 sponsored by Representative Dennis Kucinich (Democrat from Ohio), which would seek to keep space demilitarized.

Indian Space Research Organization

The Indian Space Research Organization (ISRO) is located in Bangalore and other locales. Its initial establishment dates back to the Indian Government's June 1972 creation of the Space Commission and Department of Space. ISRO is responsible for developing Indian space programs with an emphasis on satellites, launch vehicles, sounding rockets, and related ground systems.

ISRO's Web site (www.isro.org) includes press releases from 1999–present, program budget information, issues of the newsletter *Space India* (2002–present), and the 2006–2007 *Annual Report.*

Institute for Cooperation in Space

The Institute for Cooperation in Space (ICIS) is located in Vancouver, Canada and Loja, Ecuador. It is an advocacy organization founded in 1983 seeking to promote efforts to ban weapons in space and promote greater international cooperation, with the goal of demilitarizing space exploration and industry and using it for civilian purposes.

ICIS's Web site (www.peaceinspace.com) features descriptions of institute educational initiatives, selected press releases, sample resolutions supporting ICIS objectives from various governmental entities, selected statements of support for space demilitarization from international leaders, an April 2002 *Toronto Star* article calling on Canada to prevent space weaponization, and the text of a proposed *International Space Preservation Treaty* (2005).

International Institute of Strategic Studies

The International Institute of Strategic Studies (IISS) is a London-based organization founded in 1958 consisting of over 2,500 members representing over 100 countries. IISS's mission is providing authoritative and objective information on international security issues for governmental, business, and academic audiences.

IISS's Web site (www.iiss.org) provides a variety of multifaceted information resources describing its activities and research on international security issues. Site contents include information on sponsored conferences, article abstracts from the scholarly journal *Survival,* information on the institute's annual *Strategic Survey* and its armed conflict database, a listing of IISS experts by subject, and information on IISS's Adelphi Papers monographic series found in many university libraries internationally. Titles from this series of interest to those studying space war and defense issues are *Ballistic Missile Defense and Strategic Stability* (2000) and *Protecting Critical Infrastructures Against Cyber-Attack* (2003).

International Maritime Satellite Organization (INMARSAT)

The International Maritime Satellite Organization (INMARSAT) was created in 1979 as an international governmental organization to utilize emerging satellite mobile communications technology to enhance maritime communications and the safety of lives at sea. INMARSAT communications services began in February 1982, and on April 15, 1999 it became the first international government organization to privatize, although it still maintains crucial maritime safety public service commitments.

INMARSAT's Web site (www.inmarsat.com) features information about the services it provides for aeronautical, governmental, and maritime customers; descriptions of its satellite and data services; descriptions of how it has helped the American and British militaries fulfill their telecommunication requirements; and its homeland security activities in areas as diverse as airborne surveillance, customs and border protection, maritime domain awareness, and mobile command centers.

International Telecommunications Satellite Organization (INTELSAT)

The International Telecommunications Satellite Organization (INTELSAT) was established in 1964 as the first global communications satellite network and has been responsible for broadcasting video signals of Neil Armstrong's first moon walk, the U.S.– Soviet "hot line" facilitating Cold War communication between the White House and Kremlin, and distributing broadcasts of every Olympics since 1968. INTELSAT was privatized on July 18, 2001 and is formally called Intelsat, Ltd.

INTELSAT's Web site (www.intelsat.com) provides information about its historical development and evolution, corporate networks, and relationships with governmental agencies. It also features the text of press releases from 2003–present, photos of satellites, earth stations, and corporate leadership personnel, a promotional video Web cast, fact sheets on individual satellite systems such as IS-901 and IS-905, a glossary of international satellite terms, maps of regional satellite coverage areas, and documents such as its 2002 and 2003 *Annual Report* along with other financial documents filed with the U.S. Securities and Exchange Commission.

Jane's Information Group

Jane's Information Group is located in Coulson, Surrey, England, and has affiliate offices in numerous international locales. Founded in 1898, it is a major compiler and provider of intelligence and analysis on international security issues garnering a reputation for accuracy, authoritativeness, and impartiality. Its products provide defense news and analysis, information on military systems and equipment, international geopolitical intelligence and news analysis, terrorism intelligence and assessment, and risk assessments for businesses and industries exploring prospective markets and nations.

Jane's Web site (www.janes.com) provides additional information about company products and services. Relevant space war and defense resources described here include *Jane's Defence Weekly, Jane's International Defence Review, Jane's World Air Forces, Jane's Space Directory,* and *Jane's International ABC Aerospace Directory.*

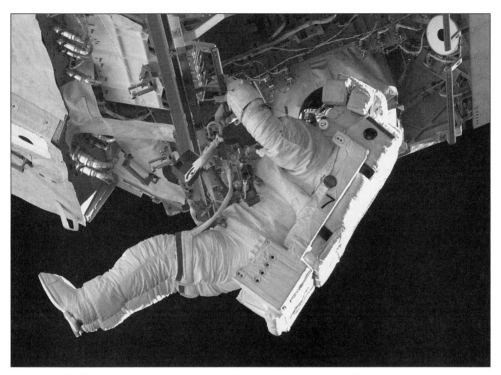

Astronaut Soichi Noguchi, STS-114 mission specialist representing Japan Aerospace Exploration Agency (JAXA), participates in the mission's third session of extravehicular activity. *(NASA)*

Japan Aerospace Exploration Agency

The Japan Aerospace Exploration Agency (JAXA) was established on October 1, 2003 to centralize Japanese space science efforts and is located in Tokyo and other locations in Japan along with having various international liaison offices. JAXA is a consolidation of three preexisting agencies: The Institute of Space and Astronautical Science (ISAS), the National Aerospace Laboratory of Japan (NAL), and the National Space Development Agency of Japan (NASDA). ISAS's institutional mandate had been space and planetary research, NAL emphasized next-generation aviation research and development, and NASDA was responsible for developing large launch vehicles such as satellites and Japanese components of the International Space Station.

JAXA's Web site (www.jaxa.jp) features descriptions of individual agency site facilities, information about its programs involving launch vehicles, space transportation systems, satellites, and space science research, photo archives, and news releases. The agency's Digital Archives section includes issues of the periodical *NASDA Report* (May 1998–September 2003), a space law database, and detailed brochures describing JAXA programs and projects.

Lancaster University–Centre for Defence and International Security Studies

Lancaster University's Centre for Defence and International Security Studies (CDISS) was established in 1990 in Lancaster University's Department of Politics and International Relations and served as an independent institution since January 2004 at Henley-on-Thames, Oxfordshire. Its institutional objectives are conducting international defense and security research and fostering cooperation between academic, government, and industry on these issues.

The center's Web site (www.cdiss.org) features press comments on international security issues by CDISS personnel, information on forthcoming CDISS-sponsored events, and descriptions of center research activities in areas such as space security, missile threats and responses, and emerging international security threats. Resources of particular relevance to those studying space war and defense include publications such as *Britain's BMD/WMD Priorities* (1998), *Missile Defence: From Cold War to Hot Peace* (2004), *Consistency and Change in British Approaches to Missile Defence* (2004), and *Future Conditional: War & Conflict After Next* (2005).

Royal United Services Institute

The Royal United Services Institute (RUSI) is located in London. Founded in 1831 by the Duke of Wellington, RUSI strives to report, debate, and provide information on defense and international security issues to government, military, political, academic, commercial, and media organizations.

RUSI's Web site (www.rusi.org) features information about organizational programs and activities. Descriptions are provide of RUSI organizational components focusing on military sciences, international studies, homeland security and resilience, and command, control, communications, computers, information/intelligence, surveillance, and targeting acquisition and reconnaissance (C4ISTAR). Examples of space war and defense information publications from RUSI include *Acquisition of Networked Enabled Capability* (2004) and listings of relevant papers in RUSI's Whitehall Papers monographic series such as *International Missile Defence?: Opportunities, Challenges and Implications for Europe* (2002) and *Missile Defence in a New Strategic Environment* (2003).

Russian Space Science Internet

The Russian Space Science Internet (RSSI) is a consortium of Russian commercial and academic institutions engaging in space science–related research. RSSI was established in April 1993 as a result of a joint decision between Russian and U.S. space agencies to increase cooperation on space science issues between these two countries.

RSSI's Web site (www.rssi.ru) features information about organizational activities and links to the Web sites of participating institutions including the Russian World Geophysical Data Center, the Russian Academy of Sciences Institute of Astronomy, and the Space Research Institute.

The Russian Federation and the former Soviet Union have played a significant role in space exploration and in military astronautics. Additional Web sites providing information about Russian civilian and military space activities include the Russian Space Agency, www.federalspace.ru/, which has some English language content; Ministry of Defense, www.mil.ru/, whose contents are primarily in Russian; Russian Space Web, www.russian spaceweb.com/, which features current and historical information on Russian space activities; NASA's Marshall Space Flight Center's archivally maintained Russian Space Agency site, http://liftoff.msfc.nasa.gov/rsa/rsa.html; and the Federation of American Scientists Russia and Military Space Projects site, www.fas.org/spp/guide/russia/military/, which features information on Russian imagery intelligence, antisatellite weaponry, signals intelligence, early warning systems, and national security support systems providing additional information on Russian military and civilian space activities.

Swedish National Space Board

The Swedish National Space Board (SNSB) is located in Solna, Sweden. Its institutional missions include distributing government grants for space research, technology

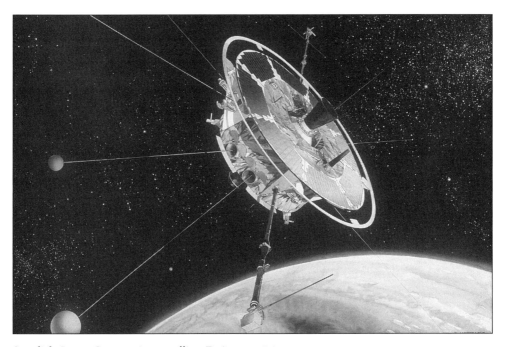

Swedish Space Corporation satellite, Freja. *(Swedish Space Corporation)*

development and remote-sensing activities, initiating space and remote-sensing development and research, and acting as Sweden's contact for international cooperation in space science activities.

SNSB's Web site (www.snsb.se) features organizational and staff information; links to Swedish space industry companies and their Web sites; links to the Swedish Defence Research Agency Web site, www.foi.se/; information on Swedish earth observation satellite activities; and descriptions of board research in astronomy, human space flight, material sciences in microgravity, and space sciences. Additional resources include information about historical and ongoing Swedish satellite programs and publications such as *Space Research in Sweden 2000–2001* (2002), *Space Research in Sweden 2002–2003* (2004), and *The ODIN Satellite's Sharp Eyes in Space* (n.d.).

United Kingdom–British National Space Centre

The British National Space Centre (BNSC), headquartered in London, was established in 1985 and is a collaborative venture of 11 British government departments and research councils to coordinate British civil space activity on national and international levels.

BNSC's Web site, www.bnsc.gov.uk/, features information about its partnering organizations such as the Ministry of Defence (www.mod.uk/) and Office of Science and Technology (www.osti.gov.uk/) and links to their Web sites; descriptions of center activities in areas such as earth observation, exploiting space, industry collaboration, space exploration; and the educational benefits of space science. Accessible publications include *UK Space Strategy 2003–2006 and Beyond* (2003), *BNSC Export Assistance Strategy* (2005), and links to other British Government documents on space policy from organizations such as the National Audit Office and the House of Commons Committee on Public Accounts.

United Kingdom–Ministry of Defence–Defence Equipment & Support

Defence Equipment & Support (DE&S) is a British Ministry of Defence entity responsible for delivering ministry information and communication services to meet ministry and military requirements. It was created on April 1, 2007 consolidating preexisting agencies. Its workforce of 29,000 military and civilian employees provides services ranging from fixed and mobile telephones to satellite communication links while also encompassing computer networks and infrastructures.

DE&S's Web site (www.mod.uk/DefenceInternet/MicroSite/DES) provides a variety of information resources describing agency activities. These include descriptions of its satellite communications team and the responsibilities of its Directorate Chief Technology Officer. Accessible organizational publications include *DES in Brief* (2007) and *DE&S News* (April 2007–present).

United Kingdom–Ministry of Defence–Defence Science and Technology Laboratory

The Defence Science and Technology Laboratory (DSTL) was established on July 2, 2001 and serves as the Ministry of Defence's key advisor and laboratory for scientific and technology issues facing the British military. Its workforce consists of approximately 3,000 personnel.

DSTL's Web site, www.dstl.gov.uk/, provides overviews of laboratory capabilities in areas such as policy and capability studies, air systems, missiles and countermeasures, electronics, sensors, and weapons detection. Additional information resources include details on career opportunities with DSTL, the text of press releases (2001–present), information on DSTL support for British military forces in Iraq, and descriptions of publications such as *Defence Reports Abstracts* and *Defence Technology Alerts.*

United Nations Conference on Disarmament

The United Nations Conference on Disarmament (CD) is located in Geneva, and its current institutional incarnation dates from 1979 succeeding its predecessor the United Nations disarmament forum. Consisting of 66 members, CD seeks to address most multilateral arms control and disarmament problems. Its areas of interest include preventing what it sees as an arms race in outer space, nuclear war prevention, promoting nuclear disarmament, preventing the use of weapons of mass destruction, and promoting comprehensive global disarmament programs and transparency in armaments.

CD's Web site, http://disarmament2.un.org/cd/, features annual committee work agendas, press releases (2002–present), the conference's *Annual Report* (1993–present), conference documents (2000–present), listing of member countries, meeting minutes (2000–present), and links to other UN disarmament information resources and Web sites.

United Nations General Assembly Committee on Peaceful Uses of Outer Space

The United Nations General Assembly Committee on Peaceful Uses of Outer Space (COPUOS) was established in 1959 by General Assembly resolution 1472 XIV for reviewing international cooperation in peaceful uses of space, planning programs in this area to be carried out under UN sponsorship, encouraging research and information dissemination on space issues, and studying legal problems stemming from space exploration. COPUOS consists of 67 member countries, Scientific and Technical and Legal Subcommittees, and meets annually to answer questions submitted by the General Assembly and discuss issues raised and reports submitted by member states. COPUOS's Web site, www.oosa.unvienna.org/COPUOS/copuos.html, is hosted by the UN Office for Outer Space Affairs. Accessible materials on this Web site include listings of member countries and

General view of the United Nations (UN) Conference on Disarmament as Iranian foreign minister Manouchehr Mottaki gives a speech, March 30, 2006, in Geneva amid an international standoff over Tehran's nuclear program. *(AFP/Getty Images)*

when they joined, a historical overview of COPUOS, and a collection of committee proceedings and reports in the UN's six official languages: Arabic, Chinese, English, French, Russian, and Spanish. Examples of these documents include *Report of the Committee on the Peaceful Uses of Outer Space General Assembly Official Records* (1993–present), unedited transcripts of 2003 COPUOS meeting minutes, *Report of The Scientific and Technical Subcommittee* (1998–present), *Report of the Legal Subcommittee* (1993–present), and transcripts of Legal Subcommittee meetings (2000–present).

United Nations Office for Outer Space Affairs

The United Nations Office for Outer Space Affairs (UNOOSA) is located in Vienna, and its original establishment was 1958. It is responsible for facilitating international cooperation in the peaceful uses of space and serves as a secretariat for COPUOS. UNOOSA is responsible for administering the UN Programme on Space Applications, which seeks to improve space science and technology for international economic and social development with particular emphasis on developing countries. This program also sees UNOOSA conduct training courses and other activities in areas such as remote sensing, communications, satellite meteorology, search and rescue, introductory space science, satellite navigation, and space law.

Additional UNOOSA activities include preparing and maintaining the *Register of Objects Launched Into Outer Space* for the UN Secretary General and preparing reports and studies on various aspects of space science, technology, and international space law.

An impressive array of information resources is provided on the UNOOSA Web site, www.oosa.unvienna.org/. These include listings of and links to new Web site content, detailed descriptions of the Programme on Space Applications, the online *Register of Objects Launched Into Outer Space* featuring annual entries from 1976–present, links to national space agency Web sites, links to international space law Web sites, and a compilation of various space law resources compiled by UNOOSA.

Numerous publications are also accessible through this Web site. These include the full text of various bilateral and multilateral international space cooperation agreements produced by the UN and other international government organizations, the full text of General Assembly resolutions on outer space (1958–present), and an index of national research on space debris and nuclear power in space.

Examples of specific publications provided by UNOOSA include *National Research on Space Debris, Safety of Space Objects With Nuclear Power Sources on Board and Problems Relating to Their Collision With Space Debris* (1995–present); *The Space Millenium: Vienna Declaration on Space and Human Development* (1999); *International Cooperation in the Peaceful Uses of Outer Space: Activities of Member States* (1999–present); *United Nations Treaties and Principles on Outer Space* (2002); *Status of International Agreements Relating to Activities in Outer Space as of . . .* (2004–present); the newsletter *Space Law Update* (2004–present); *Proceedings United Nations/Brazil Workshop on Space Law: Disseminating and Developing International Space Law: The Latin America and Caribbean Perspective* (2005); and the Web site *National Space Law Database* www.unoosa.org/oosa/en/SpaceLaw/national/index.html.

10

Research Assistance: Periodical Indexes, Scholarly and Trade Journals, Scholarly Books, Documentary Collections, and Library of Congress Subject Headings

Periodical Indexes

Numerous trade and scholarly journals produce articles covering space warfare and defense. Information on these publications is provided later in this chapter. Truly effective scholarly, research, however, requires the use of indexes to retrieve citations to individual articles. Numerous print and electronic periodical indexes can be used to find articles on space warfare and defense in such journals and do so in a more efficacious manner than conducting an Internet search.

Some of these indexes are freely available on the Internet, and their Web site URLs are listed below. Other indexes are produced by commercial companies and may be available in selected academic or public libraries. An example of one of these periodical indexes is the Air University Library Index to Military Periodicals produced by Air University Library at Maxwell Air Force Base in Alabama, which is a long-standing index of military science literature. It covers from 1988–present and is freely accessible to the public at http://purl.access.gpo.gov/GPO/LPS3260 and features detailed citations and links to subject headings for additional research. Users should check local libraries to determine if they have paper or electronic copies of the articles cited in this resource.

America: History and Life

This ABC-CLIO–produced resource indexes articles, book chapters, dissertations, and books on American and Canadian history from 1450 to the present. A standard feature in medium and large academic research libraries, it is particularly valuable for those conducting historical research on space warfare and defense.

EBSCO's Military and Government Collections

Produced by a prominent serials vendor to libraries, this resource provides full text access to articles from nearly 300 journals and periodicals as well as to numerous pamphlet resources with retrospective coverage dating back to the mid-1980s. General information is accessible on the vendor's Web site, www.ebsco.com/.

Historical Abstracts

This ABC-CLIO–produced resource indexes articles, dissertations, book chapters, and books on national and international history outside North America from 1450 to the present. It is available in many medium and large academic libraries.

LexisNexis Government Periodicals Index

Published by LexisNexis Inc., this resource provides access to 170 U.S. Government agency periodicals from 1988 to the present. Availability is primarily in medium or large academic libraries. General information is accessible at www.lexisnexis.com/academic/1univ/govper/.

Public Affairs Information Service International (PAIS)

This resource is produced by the Online Computer Library Consortium (OCLC) in Dublin, Ohio. It provides access to scholarly public policy literature from journal articles, books, book chapters, and selected U.S. Government documents. Information on PAIS can be found at www.pais.org/, and many academic libraries subscribe to its print or online services.

Staff College Automated Periodicals Index (SCAMPI)

SCAMPI is produced collaboratively by the Joint Forces Staff College Library, National Defense University Library, and Defense Technical Information Center. It provides bibliographic access to a variety of popular and scholarly military publications and selected public policy research institution reports from 1997–present. SCAMPI is freely accessible at http://www.dtic.mil/dtic/scampi/.

Worldwide Political Science Abstracts

Worldwide Political Science Abstracts (WPSA) is published by Cambridge Scientific Abstracts. It indexes articles from political science journals from 1975–present and also provides some retrospective coverage from 1960–1974. General information on this database is accessible at www.csa.com/factsheets/polsci-set-c.php.

Scholarly and Trade Journals

A number of scholarly and trade journals produce articles and information on space warfare and defense. Scholarly journals publish articles that have gone through the peer review process in which the journal's editorial board, consisting of experts and scholars in that field, reviews proposed articles to determine their suitability for publication. Trade journals focus on trends and developments in particular industries or services, with aerospace and defense trade journals being publications that produce significant publications on space warfare and defense. Scholarly journals are distributed in print and electronic formats and have varying degrees of availability at U.S. and foreign academic libraries.

A small number of these journals published by government agencies and nonprofit organizations may be freely available on the Internet. However, most of these journals and trade publications are published by commercial for-profit publishers and are not freely available in print or electronic format. College and university libraries that have print and electronic access to these journals have paid for this access by negotiating contractual agreements with the publishers of these periodicals. Such agreements may restrict electronic access to these journals to users who are part of a university community such as faculty and students with university identification numbers. These agreements also may stipulate that only computers in the university library or the university's IP range may be used to access electronic journal contents.

A useful directory of scholarly and trade periodicals is *Ulrich's International Periodicals Directory*. This annual multivolume set, published by R.R. Bowker, is a key source in many academic library reference collections for locating periodical information.

Two subscription based projects provide subscribing academic libraries with access to numerous electronic journals on various subjects: JSTOR and TDNet. JSTOR provides access to recent and historical issues of scholarly journals in several social science disciplines. Information about JSTOR is accessible at www.jstor.org/. TDNet is an Israeli-based company providing access to electronic journal articles in multiple subjects at many academic and research institutions. Information on this service is accessible at www.tdnet.com/.

An additional aspect of scholarly journal publishing to be highlighted is the growth of the Open Access Movement, which seeks to provide a counterpoint to the occasionally restrictive access policies commercial publishers place on gaining access to their works. This movement advocates that scholars publish their research in journals that do not have restrictive public access policies or that do not charge high and continually rising institutional subscription prices for their journals. Information on this increasingly influential movement in scholarly publishing can be found at www.publicknowledge.org/issues/openaccess/.

The following is a representative sampling of important scholarly and trade journals producing articles on space warfare and defense. Information provided will include the journal's name, publisher, paper and electronic International Standard Serial Numbers (ISSN), publication frequency and history, and general information about its accessibility including a URL if it is available freely to the general public.

Aerospace America

Aerospace America has been published monthly by the American Institute of Aeronautics and Astronautics since 1932. Its ISSN is 0740–722X and general information about the journal is accessible at www.aiaa.org/aerospace/. Samples of recent articles published in *Aerospace America* include "Military Satellite Market: Assessing the U.S. Share" (November 2004) and "Examining the U.S. Aerospace Workforce" (August 2005).

Aerospace and Defense Industry Profile

Aerospace and Defense Industry Profile is produced by Datamonitor in London and available annually. This resource is also distributed through the library periodicals vendor EbscoHost and provides information on aerospace and defense industries in various international regions. Information on Datamonitor and its industry analyses is available at www.datamonitor.com/. Sample reports produced by *Aerospace and Defense Industry Profile* for 2005 include profiles for Asia–Pacific, Europe, Germany, Japan, the United Kingdom, and United States.

Aerospace Science and Technology

Aerospace Science and Technology is published by Elsevier Science and appears in eight issues annually. Its ISSNs are 1270–9638 and 1626-3219, its current version dates from 1997, and general information on it can be found at www.elsevier.com/locate/aescte. Representative articles in recent issues include "Tightly Controlled GPS/INS Integration for Missile Applications" (October 2004) and "A New Approach to On-Board Station Keeping of GEO Satellites" (November 2005).

Air & Space Power Journal

Air & Space Power Journal or *Aerospace Power Journal* is the U.S. Air Force's premier professional military journal and is produced quarterly by Air University at Maxwell Air Force Base, Alabama. Its ISSNs are 0897–0823 and 1555-385X and current and many historical issues are freely accessible to the general public at http://purl.access.gpo.gov/GPO/LPS25494. Sample articles from recent issues include "Space War in Joint Operations: Evolving Concepts" (Summer 2004); "The Space Campaign: Space-Power Theory Applied to Counterspace Operations" (Summer 2004); "Mahan on Space Education: A Historical Rebuke of a Modern Error" (Winter 2005); and "Space Power: An Ill-Suited Space Strategy" (Fall 2006). This journal is essential reading for those studying cutting-edge space war and defense thought.

Air Power History

Air Power History is published quarterly by the Air Force Historical Foundation. It has been published since 1954, its ISSN is 1044–016X, and general information on it can be found at www.afhistoricalfoundation.com/. Sample articles include "Hypersonic Technology and Aerospace Doctrine" (Fall 1999), "General Bernard A. Schriever: A Technological Visionary" (Spring 2004), "Open Skies Policy and the Origin of the U.S. Space Program" (Summer 2004), and "Eisenhower and Ballistic Missile Defense: The Formative Years, 1944–1961" (Winter 2004).

Annals of Air and Space Law

Annals of Air and Space Law is published annually by the McGill University Institute of Air and Space Law. Its ISSN is 0701–158X, it has been published since 1976, and general information is accessible at www.mcgill.ca/iasl/. Sample articles include "Legal Regime for Keeping Outer Space Free of Armaments: Prospects?" (2002); "Space Law, the U.S. National Missile Defense Initiative and the Common Concern for Global Security" (2002); and "Policy and Legal Options Regarding Possible Deployment of Further Military Capabilities in Outer Space" (2005).

Astropolitics: The International Journal of Space Power and Policy

Astropolitics: The International Journal of Space Power and Policy is published by the British-based Frank Cass publishers. It began production in 2003 and is published three times a year, its ISSNs are 1477–7622 and 1557-2943, and general information on it is available at www.astropolitics.org/. Sample articles include "China: A Growing Military Space Power" (Spring 2005); "Was It Really 'Space Junk'?: U.S. Intelligence Interest in Space Debris That Returns to Earth" (Spring 2005); "An Assessment of Anti-Satellite Capabilities and Their Strategic Limitations" (Summer 2005); and "U.S.-India Space Partnership: The Jewel in the Crown" (August 2006). This journal is essential reading for those interested in geopolitical and strategic aspects of space.

Aviation Week and Space Technology

Aviation Week and Space Technology is arguably the single most influential trade periodical profiling space warfare and defense trends and developments. It has been published weekly since 1916 by McGraw-Hill, and its ISSN is 0005–2175. General information about this periodical is accessible at www.aviationnow.com/avnow/. Sample articles include "Indispensable Intel" (October 24, 2005); "Satellite Tradeoffs" (November 21, 2005); and "The National Security Nexus" (March 19, 2007), along with the weekly "Washington Week" and "Industry Outlook" columns.

Aviation Week Homeland Security and Defense

Aviation Week Homeland Security and Defense is a subset of *Aviation Week and Space Technology* that has been published weekly since February 2002. Its ISSN is 1545–486X and general information can be found at www.aviationnow.com/avnow/spSec/hs.jsp. Sample articles include "Government, Industry Tighten Security at 'Vulnerable' Satellite Ground Stations" (May 8, 2002) and "ASI Offers Abundant Opportunities for Sensor Technologies 'Report Finds'" (November 2, 2005).

CQ Weekly Report

CQ Weekly Report, called *Congressional Quarterly Weekly Report* until April 1998, is published by Congressional Quarterly, Inc. It has been published since 1945, its ISSNs are 0010–5910 and 1521-5997, and it specializes in chronicling congressional legislative activities. Examples of recent articles dealing with space warfare and defense include "Missile Defense: A Multilayered Program" (October 26, 2002) and "Red Moon Rising: The New Space Race" (October 17, 1999).

Defense Daily

Defense Daily is a trade newsletter published by Access Intelligence, LLC and has been published daily since 1959. Its ISSNs are 0889–0404 and 1930-644X, and general information on it can be found at www.pbimedia.com/cgi/catalog/info?DD. Recent representative sample articles include "AFRL Moves Aerospace Relay Mirror System Demonstration to 2006" (October 20, 2005) and "Raytheon to Produce Global Hawk Ground Control Segments" (December 1, 2005).

Defense Daily International

Defense Daily International is a supplement to *Defense Daily* covering international defense developments and has been published since 2000. Representative articles include "BMDO Plans for First GBI Capability, Space Weapon Test By 2005" (July 20, 2001), "Myers Pushes for Space Based Radar Demonstration" (February 8, 2002), and "Innovative Concepts to Enable Australian MRH90 Network Centric Capabilities" (November 18, 2005).

Defense Monitor

Defense Monitor is published 10 times a year by the Washington, D.C. think tank the Center for Defense Information. It has been published since 1972, its ISSN is 0195–6450, and it is freely available from 1997–present at www.cdi.org/. Its articles, reflecting a leftist ideological perspective, include "Highlighting Missile Weaknesses and Unacceptable U.S. Policy on Space" (November/December 2004), "China-U.S. Dialog on Space" (March/April 2005), and "Bush Policy Would Start Arms Race in Space" (May/June 2005).

Defense News

Defense News is a weekly newsletter covering defense industry developments. It is published by Defense News Media Group since 1986, its ISSN is 0884–139X, and general information and some articles can be found at www.defensenews.com/. Examples of recent articles include "Israel Successfully Tests Anti-Missile System" (December 2, 2005) and "Russia Defends Iran Missile Sale" (December 5, 2005).

International Security

International Security is produced quarterly by the Belfer Center for Science and International Affairs at Harvard University's John F. Kennedy School of Government and published by Massachusetts Institute of Technology Press. It has been published since 1976, its

Despite its youth as a nation, Israel has boasted a strong military since its inception in 1948. Israel's technical superiority over its opponents has been aided by a close relationship with America. Here a joint test between Israel and the United States launches an Arrow-2 anti-ballistic missile into the skies above California in 2004. The missile is specifically designed to defend against potential threats to Israel. *(U.S. Department of Defense)*

ISSNs are 0162–2889 and 1531-4804, and general information on this journal can be accessed through the Belfer Center Web site http://bcsia.ksg.harvard.edu/ and the publisher's Web site http://mitpress.mit.edu/. Recent *International Security* articles dealing with space warfare and defense include "Nuclear Deterrence, Nuclear Proliferation, and National Missile Defense" (March 2003) and "Space Weapons: Crossing the U.S. Rubicon" (Fall 2004).

Journal of Electronic Defense

Journal of Electronic Defense is published monthly by the Association of Old Crows, an international aerospace and electronic warfare professional association. It has been published since 1978, its ISSN is 0192–429X, and it is oriented to covering electronic technology and applications affecting the military and defense industry. General information about this organization is accessible at www.crows.org/. Sample articles include "Lost in Space: Could Space-Based Weapons Help Protect Military Capability?" (January 2005); "U.S. Congress Questions Skyrocketing Space Costs" (September 2005); "Testing Continues on USAF Airborne Laser" (November 2005); and "NATO to Launch BMD Program" (May 2006).

Journal of Space Law

Journal of Space Law is published by the National Remote Sensing Center at the University of Mississippi. This journal is published semiannually, its ISSN is 0095–7577, and it has been published since 1977. General information on it is available at www.spacelaw.olemiss .edu/journal/. Sample articles include "Liability for Global Navigation Satellite Services: A Comparative Analysis of GPS and Galileo" (Spring 2004) and "No Space Colonies: Creating a Space Civilization and a Need for a Defining Constitution" (Spring 2004).

Military and Aerospace Electronics

Military and Aerospace Electronics has been published monthly by PennWell Corporation in Tulsa, Oklahoma since 1990. Its ISSN is 1046–9079, and general information and articles from the newest issue are accessible at http://mae.pennnet.com/. Sample articles include "ViaSat Demonstrates Mobile Broadband Technology for Command and Control" (March 2005); "Silicon-Based Shielding May Protect Military Electronics from EMP" (May 2005); and "Air Force Eyes Data-Security Architecture for Satellite Telemetry" (September 2005).

Military Technology

Military Technology is published monthly by the German publisher Monch Publishing Group in Bonn. Its ISSN is 0722–3226, it has been published been published monthly since 1977, and general information is accessible at www.monch.com/html/magazines/ miltech.htm. Recent sample articles include "Expeditionary Communications: What It Takes" (May 2005), "Taiwan ABM System Takes Shape" (July 2005), and "Russia's Military Aerospace Industry: An Assessment" (August 2005).

National Journal

National Journal is published weekly by the National Journal Group and covers federal government policy and political developments. It has been published since 1969, its ISSNs are 0360–4217 and 0898-6916, and general information is accessible at www.nationaljournal .com/. Pertinent sample articles include "The Future is Here" (May 11, 2002) and "Weapons in the High Heavens" (September 17, 2005).

Quest: The History of Spaceflight Quarterly

Quest: The History of Spaceflight Quarterly is published by the University of North Dakota's Space Studies Department and provides historical perspectives on international achievements in manned and unmanned spaceflight. *Quest* has been published since 1992, its ISSN is 1065–7738, and general information on it can be found at www.spacebusiness .com/quest/. Representative articles include "The NRO in the 21st Century: Ensuring Global Information Superiority" 11 (3)(2004); "A History of the United States Anti-Satellite Program and the Evolution to Space Control and Offensive and Defensive Counterspace" 11 (3)(2004); "Safeguard: North Dakota's Front Line in the Cold War" 12 (1)(2005); and "Secret Boost Glider Projects of the Cold War: America's Winged Space Plane Studies of the 1950's" 13 (2)(2006).

Space Fax Daily

Space Fax Daily has been published daily since 1984 by Space Age Publishing and reports on space industry technology developments. Its ISSN is 1048–2652 and general information is accessible at www.spaceagepub.com/. Representative articles from recent issues include "BAE Systems 70mm Laser-Guided Rocket Achieves Two Direct Hits" (October 4, 2005), "Giant China Space-Tracking Ship Makes Rare Visit" (October 27, 2005), and "ISRO to Launch Israel's Spy Satellite" (November 15, 2005).

Space Policy

Space Policy is a quarterly scholarly journal published by Elsevier since 1985. Its ISSN is 0265–9646, and general information on it is accessible at www.elsevier.com/locate/spacepol. Recent articles include "Keeping the Peace in Outer Space: A Legal Framework for the

Prohibition of the Use of Force" (November 2004), "Leadership for New U.S. Strategic Directions" (February 2005), and "Will China Become a Military Space Superpower?" (August 2005).

Scholarly Books

A significant and growing array of scholarly literature on space warfare and defense, along with relevant international political issues, has been produced since the earliest years of the space age. Works produced on these topics by government agencies and think tanks have been covered elsewhere; presented below are works produced by university professors and other interested scholars in the United States and worldwide. This section examines primarily works that have been produced from the 1980s to the present. The works covered here represent a diverse spectrum of viewpoints and are of varying quality. Nevertheless, it is hoped that this listing provides readers the opportunity to explore the variety of work that has been produced to date examining the importance and implications of space warfare and defense in U.S. and international political, diplomatic, and military discussion and analysis.

Many of these works are available in U.S. and foreign academic libraries and some public libraries. It is also possible to purchase these books through their publishers' Web sites or through major new and used book retail Web sites such as amazon.com or abebooks.com. Book International Standard Bibliographic Numbers (ISBNs) are included to facilitate ordering and access, and information in parentheses indicates if the book is part of a monographic series produced by its publisher. Readers should be aware that cloth and paperback editions of the same book have different ISBNs.

David Christopher Arnold. 2005. *Spying From Space: Constructing America's Satellite Command and Control Systems.* (Centennial of Flight Series). College Station, TX: Texas A&M University Press. ISBN 1–585–44385–9.

This work covers developments in American satellite reconnaissance beginning with an Air Force plane capturing film dropped from a satellite on August 14, 1960. It details the development of command and control systems that made intelligence gathered from rockets and satellites useful.

Aspen Strategy Group. 1986. *Anti-Satellite Weapons and U.S. Military Space Policy.* Lanham, MD: Aspen Institute for Humanistic Studies and University Press of America, Inc. ISBN 0–8191–5477–6.

This panel report examined the increasingly contentious nature of antisatellite weapons (ASATs) in U.S. policy debates of the mid-1980s. Report contents cover evolving and expanding military uses of space, ASAT and U.S. security interests, the need for U.S. protection of its space systems, the role of strategic defenses in space security, and panel recommendations such as preventing "quick kill" threats to high altitude satellites.

Donald R. Baucom. 1992. *The Origins of SDI, 1944–1983.* (Modern War Studies) Lawrence: University Press of Kansas. ISBN 0–7006–0531–2.

Provides detailed coverage of U.S. efforts to develop defenses against ballistic missiles from World War I until 1992. It demonstrates how the Reagan administration's Strategic Defense Initiative evolved from the technological and military legacies of strategic nuclear weapons programs and the declining popularity of offensive nuclear deterrence policies.

Doug Beason. 2005. *The E-Bomb: How America's New Directed Energy Weapons Will Change the Way Future Wars Will Be Fought.* Cambridge, MA: Da Capo Press. ISBN 0–3068–1402–1.

Beason discusses how directed energy weapons such as lasers, high-powered microwaves, and particle beams are increasingly becoming the focal point of U.S. military operations, and how these weapons will grow in importance during the 21st century. *E-Bomb* describes the factors constituting these weapons and gives examples of how they have been effective in battle and of problems directed energy can cause in military environments. Subsequent sections of this work examine differences between lasers and high-power microwaves, the individuals behind the development of high-energy lasers and microwaves, how the Defense Department has come to place increased reliance on these weapons, the origins and development of the airborne laser program, how high-energy lasers have become global weapons, and possible future trends and developments in directed energy weapons technology.

Matt Bille and Erika Lashock. 2004. *The First Space Race: Launching the World's First Satellites.* (Centennial of Flight Series). College Station, TX: Texas A&M University Press. ISBN 1–585–44356–5.

Portrays efforts by the United States and Soviet Union to launch the world's first space satellites between 1955–1958. Topics addressed include the efforts of the U.S. Army and Navy, Soviet programs, and the perceived military, political propaganda, scientific, and technological advantages of being the first nation in space.

Neville Brown. 1990. *New Strategy Through Space.* Leicester, UK: Leicester University Press. ISBN 0–7185–1279–0.

This quirky philosophical review of military space policy begins by examining how the Strategic Defense Initiative sought to render obsolete existing U.S.–Soviet strategies of nuclear deterrence. Later chapters examine how lasers, particle beam weapons, and kinetic energy weapons can influence military space policymaking. Additional subjects analyzed include geopolitical dimensions of military space, possible Soviet and Chinese military space responses, and the potential value of international arms control regimes in outer space.

William E. Burrows. 1986. *Deep Black: Space Espionage and National Security.* New York: Random House. ISBN 0–394–54124–3.

Examines the variety of U.S. air and space intelligence gathering capabilities from World War II to the time of publication. Covers various satellites and aircraft such as the RC-135, U-2, and SR-71.

Ivo H. Daalder. 1987. *The SDI Challenge to Europe.* Cambridge, MA: Ballinger. ISBN 0–8873–0197–5.

An air-to-air front close-up of an SR-71A strategic reconnaissance aircraft. The SR-71 is unofficially known as the "Blackbird." *(U.S. Department of Defense)*

Written in the aftermath of the failure of the 1986 Reagan–Gorbachev Reykjavik summit to reach an arms control agreement due to differences over the Strategic Defense Initiative (SDI), Daalder assesses how different European countries view SDI's political, technological, and military implications. British, French, and German perspectives are reviewed, and the text of a March 27, 1986 U.S.–West German SDI participation agreement is also included.

Dwayne A. Day, John M. Logsdon, and Brian Latell, eds. 1998. *Eye in the Sky: The Story of the Corona Spy Satellites.* (Smithsonian History of Aviation Series). Washington, D.C.: Smithsonian Institution Press, 1998. ISBN 1–56098–830–4.

This book examines the significance of recently declassified Project Corona satellite photographs taken between 1960–1972 by 145 spy satellite missions. The over 800,000 reconnaissance photographs provided the United States valuable intelligence on military installations and force movements in the former Soviet Union, China, and Middle East. Chapters in this book provide background on the technological and political factors creating Corona, the origins of the National Reconnaissance Office, and Soviet response to Corona through its Zenit program.

David H. DeVorkin. 1992. *Science With a Vengeance: How the Military Created the US Space Sciences after World War II.* New York: Springer-Verlag. ISBN 0–387–94137–1 (paperback).

Provides detailed historical coverage of how military research and development has sculpted U.S. space science research. DeVorkin begins by describing the early rocketry experiments of Robert Goddard and proceeds to analyze how German's V-2 program and scientists influenced early U.S. military astronautics. The work goes on to describe the roles played in U.S. military astronautic research by facilities such as the White Sands Proving Ground and by organizations such as the Naval Research Laboratory. Coverage is provided of various research accomplishments made by these military space programs including the development of ballistic missiles.

Everett C. Dolman. 2001. *Astropolitik: Classical Geopolitics in the Space Age.* (Cass Series: Strategy and History). London and Portland, OR: Frank Cass. ISBN 0–7146–8197–0 (paperback).

A treatise that uses geopolitics and applies it to current and future military space strategy. Chapter topics address issues such as space's geopolitical and military strategic relevance to national and international security, contending political visions of space between advocates of international control of space or individual nations controlling space, and the need for the United States to incorporate space into its national security policymaking.

Craig R. Eisendrath, Melvin A. Goodman, and Gerald E. Marsh. 2001. *The Phantom Defense: America's Pursuit of the Star Wars Illusion.* Westport, CT: Praeger. ISBN 0–275–97183-X.

This is a highly critical assessment of what the authors see as misguided and wasteful efforts by the United States to develop ballistic missile defenses. The authors contend that system-testing results offer little hope that effective deployment is possible, that such defenses will alienate key allies and heighten security threats from China and Russia, and claim that threats from rogue regimes such as Iran and North Korea are overstated.

Frances Fitzgerald. 2000. *Way Out There in the Blue: Reagan, Star Wars, and the End of the Cold War.* New York: Simon & Schuster. ISBN 0–6848–4416–8.

Fitzgerald presents an ideologically polemical account of the Reagan administration's Strategic Defense Initiative and goes beyond that administration to criticize what she sees as misguided U.S. attempts to construct ballistic missile defense systems.

George Friedman and Meredith Friedman. 1996. *The Future of War: Power, Technology, and American World Dominance in the Twenty-First Century.* New York: Crown Publishers. ISBN 0–5177–0403-X.

The authors believe that the United States will retain global military dominance because of the growth of precision-guided weapons and its technological leadership in producing such weapons. They describe why they believe many historical and contemporary military technologies such as gunboats and manned aircraft are of decreasing relevance and why they believe that controlling space is an integral factor if the United States is to retain global military supremacy.

Crockett L. Grabbe. 1991. *Space Weapons and the Strategic Defense Initiative.* Ames, IA: Iowa State University Press. ISBN 0–8138–1277–1.

This work describes various military, political, and technical issues involved with developing and deploying space weapons. Grabbe begins with an introduction to missile defense systems describing the roles played by boost-phase intercept and midcourse and terminal intercept missile defense systems. Subsequent chapters address possible counter-measures to ballistic missile defense systems such as attacks on these systems, what the author sees as the impact on strategic defense and arms control treaties of the Strategic Defense Initiative, and his contention that the United States should invest its resources in stabilizing and reducing the nuclear threat. Appendices feature descriptions and graphs for technical matters such as how x-ray and free-electron lasers work.

Brian Harvey. 2000. *The Japanese and Indian Space Programmes: Two Roads into Space.* (Springer-Praxis Books in Astronomy and Space Sciences). London and New York and Chichester, UK: Springer in association with Praxis Publishing. ISBN 1–85233–199–2.

This work examines the space policies of these two emerging economic and military countries. It stresses that Japan will place increasing security emphasis on satellites fol-lowing the 1998 North Korean ballistic missile launch signaling that country's intent to incorporate these weapons into its military arsenal. Historical coverage is provided of the institutional development and evolution of India and Japan's space programs. In the au-thor's view, Indian military astronautics are focused on monitoring security concerns ema-nating from Pakistan and China.

Brian Harvey. 2001. *Russia in Space: The Failed Frontier?* (Springer-Praxis Books in Astronomy and Space Sciences). London and New York and Chichester, UK: Springer in association with Praxis Publishing. ISBN 1–85233–203–4 (paperback).

This book provides a historical account of the rise and decline of Russian civilian and military astronautics. Chapter titles cover developments in space science, rocket engine development, and commercial applications. A chapter on military space policy examines Russian military space programs from 1992 until the book's publication covering military photo-reconnaissance, electronic intelligence, communications, and early warning systems.

Brian Harvey. 2004. *China's Space Program: From Conception to Manned Spaceflight.* (Springer-Praxis Books in Astronomy and Space Sciences). London and New York and Chichester, UK: Springer in association with Praxis Publishing. ISBN 1–85233–566–1 (paperback).

Provides coverage of the historical and ongoing evolution of China's national space program. Detailed information is provided on Chinese rocket and satellite programs along with potential ways the Chinese may seek to establish military assets in space. China's emergence as a significant player in international space policy was confirmed by the successful October 2003 launching, orbiting, and return of astronaut Yang Liwei on a Chinese-built Shenzou 5 rocket.

Peter Hayes, ed. 1996. *Space Power Interests.* Boulder, CO: Westview Press. ISBN 0–8133–8879–1.

This collection of essays seeks to ask whether international security policymaking can avoid long-range missile proliferation in the near and intermediate future. Issues addressed in individual chapters include the challenges presented by space launch and missile proliferation; U.S., Russian, and Chinese space power and interests; European

UNSCOM expert checking a Chinese-made Silkworm missile in Iraq following the Persian Gulf War. *(UNSCOM/Corbis Sygma)*

space policy and missile control; prospects for international space cooperation and a nonproliferation regime; future trends in arms control and verification; and the experiences of the former United Nations Special Commission (UNSCOM) in trying to verify land-based ballistic missiles in Iraq.

Peter L. Hays, James M. Smith, Alan R. Van Tassel, and Kenneth J. Reynolds,. eds. 2000. *Spacepower for a New Millenium: Space and U.S. National Security.* New York: Mc-Graw-Hill. ISBN 0–0724–0170–2.

This work examines how military space activities might enhance U.S. security by looking at current and future issues including missile defense and the most efficacious ways of organizing military space. Examples of essay topics include integrating national space policy and national defense, charting new directions for missile defense, organizing for space-based intelligence collection, future military space technologies, and the need for a "space navy" to defend the commercial basis of America's wealth.

Bhupendra Jasani, ed. 1987. *Space Weapons and International Security.* New York and Stockholm: Oxford University Press and Stockholm International Peace Research Institute (SIPRI). ISBN 0–19–829102–7.

This work is based on the proceedings of a July 1985 Stockholm conference on technical and political issues concerning space weapons sponsored by the Stockholm International Peace Research Institute (SIPRI). An international array of contributors produced essays on various topics including technical characteristics of space weapons, whether such weapons can be controlled by international agreement, means of counteracting space strike weapons, the implications of U.S. and Soviet ballistic missile defense programs for the ABM Treaty, Soviet attitudes toward strategic defense systems, and how nonaligned nations viewed the Strategic Defense Initiative.

Thomas Karas. 1983. *The New High Ground: Systems and Weapons of Space Age War.* New York: Simon and Schuster. ISBN 0–671–47025–6.

This early 1980s work describes then present and possible future roles of U.S. military space technology and policy. Individual chapters examine the Air Force's organizational operations in space, the space shuttle's role in facilitating space transportation, infrastructure provided by the space industry including communications, reconnaissance, weather forecasting, and geodetics, the role of ASATs in space, and strengths and weaknesses of space-based weapons systems.

Stephen Lambakis. 2001. *On the Edge of Earth: The Future of American Space Power.* Lexington, KY: University Press of Kentucky. ISBN 0–8131–2198–1.

This work promotes an assertive U.S. military policy stance and presence in space. Contents examine how space impacts the U.S. and international relations, possible implications of space for U.S. military strategy, how space may be used to militarily attack the United States and how technologically inferior adversaries can use space to gain military advantage against the United States, the evolution of national defense space policy since the Eisenhower Administration, and why the United States is unprepared for a future military presence in space. It is essential reading for exponents of an expanded U.S. military presence in space.

David T. Lindgren. 2000. *Trust But Verify: Imagery Analysis in the Cold War.* Annapolis, MD: Naval Institute Press. ISBN 1–5575–051807.

Study of how the United States and the former Soviet Union used aerial imagery analysis during the Cold War to promote their respective national security objectives and interests. Topics examined included the role played by imagery analysis during the Cuban Missile Crisis, the importance of Project Corona, and how imagery analysis was used to verify compliance with arms control agreements.

Kevin Madders. 1997. *A New Force at a New Frontier: Europe's Development in the Space Field in the Light of its Main Actors, Policies, Law and Activities From its Beginnings up to the Present.* Cambridge, UK: Cambridge University Press. ISBN 0–521–57096–4.

This work covers the efforts of Western European countries and the European Union to develop national and continental space programs and policies through the mid-1990s. Topics addressed include the Cold War and Sputnik's civilian legacy, the beginning of European international satellite communications, increasing European cooperation in civilian and military space research and development, the rise, development, and evolution of the European Space Agency as a forum for European space policy programming, European–U.S. space cooperation, and possible future trends and developments characterizing European space policymaking.

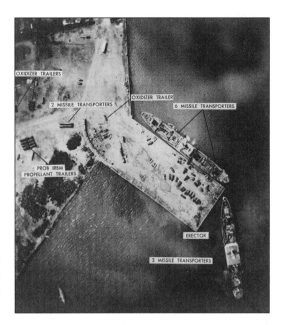

View from U.S. reconnaissance aircraft of Mariel Bay, Cuba. In October 1962 Soviet missile equipment and transport ships were photographed by U.S. U-2 spy planes, leading to the Cuban Missile Crisis. *(Library of Congress)*

William C. Martel, ed. 2001. *The Technological Arsenal: Emerging Defense Capabilities.* Washington, D.C.: Smithsonian Institution Press. ISBN 1–56098–961–0.

Compilation of essays addressing how late twentieth-century technological trends are revolutionizing warfare. Examples of chapters with particular relevance to space warfare and defense cover the military technology options provided by space lasers, how lasers impact missile defense, commercial and military applications of space operations vehicles, and how airborne and space lasers may impact battlefield operations.

Walter A. McDougall. 1997. *". . . The Heavens and the Earth: A Political History of the Space Age.* Baltimore: Johns Hopkins University Press. First published in 1985. ISBN 0–8018–5748–1.

This Pulitzer Prize–winning history provides exhaustive coverage and analysis of the political, diplomatic, and military policymaking prompting the development of the U.S. and Soviet space programs. Chapters cover topics such as the roles of nuclear deterrence and satellite surveillance in prompting U.S. and Soviet military interest in space; political and strategic factors prompting the U.S. decision to land on the moon; the growth of scientific and computer science research generated by the space programs in both countries; and the human and political foibles of the individuals, institutions, and government policymakers in the development and evolution of these national space programs—essential historical reading.

Alistair W.M. McLean and Fraser Lovie. 1997. *Europe's Final Frontier: The Search for Security Through Space.* Commack, NY: Nova Science Publishers. ISBN 1–5607–2462–5.

This work describes and analyzes the growth of space as a forum for military activity emphasizing the evolution of the Western European Union as a European security entity and the increasing importance of space for overall European military security.

Matthew Mowthorpe. 2003. *The Militarization and Weaponization of Space.* Lanham, MD: Lexington Books. ISBN 0–07391–0713–5.

This work is an analysis of space militarization and weaponization emphasizing the efforts of countries such as the United States, the Soviet Union/Russian Federation, and China. Chapter topics address the U.S. approach to military space during the Cold War, how the United States and Soviet Union addressed ballistic missile defense in the ABM Treaty, Soviet and Russian approaches to military space during and after the Cold War, China's military space program, how the United States dealt with Soviet ASAT programs, implications of the space-based laser for ballistic missile defense, how the revolution in military affairs affects space militarization, and the United States' post–Cold War military space policy.

Michael J. Neufeld. 1995. *The Rocket and the Reich: Peenemunde and the Coming of the Ballistic Missile Era.* Cambridge, MA: Harvard University Press. ISBN 0–674–77650-X.

Presents historical analysis of Nazi Germany's program to develop rocket weapons at Peenemunde in an effort to inflict last-ditch military vengeance on the soon to be victorious allied forces. Nazi rocket/missile programs can be seen as the beginning of the nuclear and space ages in modern warfare. Neufeld provides detailed coverage of the accomplishments and setbacks experienced by German efforts in this area as well as emphasizing the high human costs of these efforts. Following the war German scientists involved in this program such as Wernher von Braun were used by the United States and the former Soviet Union to launch their own military and civilian space programs.

Joseph S. Nye, Jr., and James A. Schear, eds. 1987. *Seeking Stability in Space: Anti-Satellite Weapons and the Evolving Space Regime.* Lanham, MD: Aspen Strategy Group and University Press of America. ISBN 0–8191–6422–4 (paperback).

This compilation of essays seeks to present a framework for assessing security consequences of ASAT weapons and military uses of space. Topics reviewed include U.S. military policy and ASAT weapons, protecting military space assets, the impact of potential negotiating restraints on ASAT weapons, and verifying limits on these weapons systems.

Keith B. Payne, ed. 1983. *Laser Weapons in Space: Policy and Doctrine.* Boulder, CO: Westview Press. ISBN 0–86531–937–5.

This compilation of essays examines policy issues associated with using space-based lasers for ballistic missile defense. Subjects examined and analyzed within these treatises include the role of the Antiballistic Missile (ABM) Treaty and other arms control agreements in developing missile defense systems, technical issues of space-based missile defense such as what type of program the United States should use, implications of then existing arms control agreements for space-based missile defense lasers, Soviet policy options for dealing with possible U.S. deployment of these lasers, how space-based lasers may impact U.S. military strategic doctrine, and how these lasers may be relevant to the Reagan administration's strategic nuclear weapons policy.

Uri Raanan and Robert L. Pfaltzgraf, Jr., eds. 1984. *International Security Dimensions of Space.* Hamden, CT: Archon Books. ISBN 0–208–02023–3.

This compilation of essays analyzes international security aspects of space from the political and technological perspectives of the early 1980s. Issues addressed in these essays include Soviet military space doctrine, U.S. and Soviet ballistic missile defense programs, whether space will become a sanctuary or military theater, possible defenses against offensive military satellites, and Soviet views of U.S. and Soviet space-based intelligence collecting tactics. Additional chapters address the strengths and weaknesses of U.S. space infrastructure, space activities of European countries and Japan, how current and future military technologies and space law may affect the 1967 Outer Space Treaty, and how arms control may have an impact on national and international military space policy.

Jeffrey T. Richelson. 1990. *America's Secret Eyes in Space: The U.S. Keyhole Spy Satellite Program.* New York: Harper & Row. ISBN 0–88730–285–8.

This book covers how the U.S. Keyhole satellite program supplied targeting information to U.S. military planners on potential military targets within the Soviet Union and how it also played a role in monitoring arms control agreements between these two countries and provided information on the deployment of Soviet nuclear forces. Richelson highlights information on this once secret program's development and evolution from the 1950s through the 1980s. It features analysis of Soviet attempts to steal the satellite's manual through the auspices of disgruntled CIA employee William Kampiles and descriptions of how these satellites were used to gather intelligence on the Soviet Union and other international areas of concern to U.S. intelligence policymakers.

Jeffrey T. Richelson. 1999. *America's Space Sentinels: DSP Satellites and National Security.* (Modern War Studies). Lawrence, KS: University Press of Kansas. ISBN 0–7006–1096–0 (paperback).

Richelson provides a historic overview and analysis of the U.S. military's defense support program (DSP) satellites whose primary responsibility has been providing the first warning of nuclear missile attacks against the United States. Contents describe diplomatic, political, scientific, and technical issues involved in creating and sustaining this program, including the need for satellite monitoring stations to be established at domestic and international locations such as Alamogordo, NM and Nurrungar, Australia, interrelationships between the Defense Department and system contractors such as Lockheed and McDonnell-Douglas, and possible future roles DSP satellites might play in developing U.S. ballistic missile defense systems.

Jeffrey T. Richelson. 2001. *The Wizards of Langley: Inside the CIA's Directorate of Science and Technology.* Boulder, CO: Westview Press. ISBN 0–8133–6699–2.

This book provides historical coverage of the multiple roles played by the CIA's Directorate of Science and Technology in promoting U.S. intelligence gathering and analysis while striving to enhance U.S. national security. A chapter on space reconnaissance describes the CIA's relationship with the National Reconnaissance Office (NRO) in satellite intelligence programs such as Project Corona, the bureaucratic contentiousness that could occur between the CIA, NRO, and Defense Department over satellite intelligence, and technological evolutions in U.S. satellite and aeronautic intelligence collection capabilities.

Michael Russell Rip and James M. Hasik. 2002. *The Precision Revolution: GPS and the Future of Aerial Warfare.* Annapolis, MD: Naval Institute Press. ISBN 1-5575-0973-5.

The authors stress how GPS technology is part of a revolution in military affairs that has placed greater emphasis on the role of highly sophisticated technologies such as precision-guided munitions in conducting military operations. Contents provide historical background on military air and space navigation, the United States' NAVSTAR GPS, and the Russian GLONASS global navigation satellite system. Subsequent sections of this work stress military requirements of GPS systems, how these systems influence electronic warfare, and how GPS influences and limits intelligence gathering and analysis, the role played by GPS in the 1999 war over Kosovo, and how the 9/11 terrorist attacks are an example of military operations using precision guided munitions.

William H. Schauer. 1976. *The Politics of Space: A Comparison of the Soviet and American Space Programs.* New York: Holmes & Meier, Publishers. ISBN 0–8419–0185–6.

This work is a comparative analysis of U.S. and Soviet space programs from Sputnik's launch in 1957 until this work's 1976 publication. Chapter contents include the pre-Sputnik provenance of Soviet rocketry and Soviet space program organization; early Soviet and American views of space military operations; international cooperation in outer space exploration and use; international law's outer space applications; and domestic and international aspects of space exploration such as communication, meteorological, navigational, and earth resource satellites.

Asif A. Siddiqi. 2003. *Sputnik and the Soviet Space Challenge.* Gainesville, FL: University Press of Florida. ISBN 0–8130–2626-X (paperback).

This first-volume history of the Soviet space program describes the historical development and evolution of the Soviet space program from just after World War II until the mid-1960s. Particular emphasis is placed on the role played by German scientists in this program's early years and how Stalin and other Soviet leaders viewed the program's progress and setbacks. Exhaustive coverage and documentation are provided of the individuals, institutions, and events shaping Soviet efforts in this area, and acute attention is paid to military issues and factors.

Asif A. Siddiqi. 2003. *The Soviet Space Race With Apollo.* Gainesville, FL: University Press of Florida. ISBN 0–8130–2628–8 (paperback).

The second and concluding volume of this history covers from roughly the mid-1960s until recent times the personalities, events, and institutions shaping Soviet civilian and military space policy from its zenith as a serious competitor to the United States to the decline Soviet space programs have experienced in recent years. Both of Siddiqi's works are essential reading for those desirous of understanding the historical development and evolution of the Soviet space program.

Robert M. Soofer. 1988. *Missile Defenses and Western European Security: NATO Strategy, Arms Control, and Deterrence.* (Contributions in Military Studies). Westport, CT: Greenwood Press. ISBN 0–313–26351–5.

This work sought to refute European skepticism about the Reagan administration's Strategic Defense Initiative. Soofer argues that missile defense will not have a negative impact on international arms control and asserts that theater and strategic missile defense can enhance nuclear deterrence by protecting the United States and its allies from Soviet attacks.

Paul B. Stares. 1985. *The Militarization of Space: U.S. Policy, 1945–1984.* (Cornell Studies in Security Affairs). Ithaca, NY: Cornell University Press. ISBN 0–8014–9471–0.

This work provides an analytical overview and appraisal of U.S. military space policy, beginning with coverage of U.S. military space programs from 1945–1957 with subsequent chapters examining the military space policies of the Eisenhower, Kennedy, Johnson, Nixon, Ford, and Carter administrations and the first term of the Reagan presidency. The concluding chapter stresses the author's concern with what he sees as Reagan administration attempts to militarize space. Appendices enumerate U.S. space program expenditures and U.S.–Soviet antisatellite tests and space launches.

Paul B. Stares. 1987. *Space and National Security.* Washington, D.C.: The Brookings Institution. ISBN 0–8157–8110–5.

This work examines whether the United States should develop antisatellite (ASAT) weapons as part of its national security strategy. Issues addressed in *Space and National Security* include overviews of how U.S. and Soviet military space programs use satellites, the military value of these satellites, existing threats to space systems, the usefulness of ASAT weapons, and relevant space arms control issues. Stares concludes that there is no need for the United States to develop ASAT weapons and that U.S. space defense policy should focus on enhancing satellite survivability and relying on international agreements to enhance satellite security.

Gerald M. Steinberg, ed. 1988. *Lost in Space: The Domestic Politics of the Strategic Defense Initiative.* Lexington, MA: Lexington Books. ISBN 0–669–14011–2.

Compilation of essays seeking to examine what the authors see as the domestic U.S. political implications of the Strategic Defense Initiative (SDI). Topics addressed in these essays include the roles of presidential and congressional activity in space policy initiation and oversight, the role of scientists in SDI policy and technological feasibility debates, bureaucracy's influence on research and development within the Strategic Defense Initiative Organization, the influence of defense contracting in SDI programs, and a concluding thematic chapter stressing the editor's assertion that SDI support was predicated on a faith-based belief in the ability of science and technology to solve national security dilemmas.

Matthew J. Von Bencke. 1997. *The Politics of Space: A History of U.S.-Soviet/Russian Competition and Cooperation in Space.* Boulder, CO: Westview Press. ISBN 0–8133–3192–7.

This work provides a historical overview of how space policy rivalry between the United States and the former Soviet Union evolved into a degree of relative cooperation between the United States and the Russian Federation by the middle 1990s. This cooperation has been most pronounced in commercial space ventures such as space stations Freedom and Mir. An appended space age historical chronology is particularly useful for coverage of key space policy events involving both countries.

Documentary Collections

There are commercially produced documentary collections on various aspects of military space policy that may be available in academic research libraries in the United States and globally. One collection worth examining is *U.S. Military Uses of Space, 1945–1991*. Produced by the National Security Archive of Washington, D.C.'s George Washington University, this resource contains over 700 documents and nearly 15,000 pages of documents on U.S. military space organizations, operations, and policies. The collection features reports, memoranda, and cables on U.S. military space policy from organizations such as the National Security Council, the Defense Department's Advanced Research Projects Agency, and United States Space Command. Further information on this collection is accessible at www.gwu.edu/~nsarchiv/nsa/publications/mus/militaryus.html.

Library of Congress Subject Headings

Keyword searching is commonly used to look for books and articles in library online catalogs and databases. A more precise way of searching these catalogs is using Library of Congress Subject Headings (LCSH). Examples of LCSH searches to retrieve books on space warfare and defense include:

Artificial Satellites Astronautics and State
Astronautics, Military
Astronautics, Military United States Space Warfare
Space Warfare Periodicals
Space Surveillance
Space Weapons

Although it takes a little time to learn the geographic and disciplinary subdivisions of LCSH, the patience involved in learning this system helps produce more precise search results than doing vague keyword searches such as "space and war" and "space and weapons." Library Online Public Access Catalogs (OPACs) contain links to other LCSHs used to catalog a book once a book record has been retrieved from the OPAC search. By clicking on these LCSH links in a book's OPAC record, users can see other books on that subject in their libraries' OPAC that may not be locatable by a simple keyword search.

SPACE WARFARE AND DEFENSE DICTIONARY AND GLOSSARY

This is a compilation of historical and current acronyms and terms often used in discussions and analysis of space warfare and defense.

ABL (Airborne Laser)   This weapons system is mounted on a modified Boeing 747–400 series of freighter aircraft and uses a laser to destroy missiles soon after they are launched.

Ablative Shield   Spacecraft shield that chars, melts, and evaporates when exposed to intense heat during atmospheric reentry or laser attack. Helps insulate space vehicle subsurfaces.

ABM (Antiballistic Missile)   A weapons system that seeks to destroy or disable incoming ballistic missiles fired by hostile nations or organizations toward a country's population, military assets, or critical civilian infrastructures.

ACDA (Arms Control and Disarmament Agency)   This U.S. Government agency, which was established in 1961, was responsible for negotiating international arms control agreements with other countries and with international government organizations and verifying other countries' compliance with these agreements. Its areas of focus included nuclear, chemical, and biological weapons. ACDA's functions were taken over by the State Department's Bureau of Verification and Compliance in 2000.

Achieving Orbit   When satellites are propelled beyond the atmosphere at speeds exceeding 17,000 miles per hour, which counteracts the earth's gravitational pull.

Active Defense   Employing weapons systems to deter, deflect, defeat, or deal with enemy attacks.

Active Sensor   Device that transmits a signal then records reflections to detect, locate, identify, and/or track targets.

Adaptive Optics   Techniques compensating for atmospheric distortion that degrade laser beams and light-sensitive sensors such as telescopes and cameras.

Aerospace Plane   Spacecraft capable of operating effectively in the atmosphere and space.

AFBMD (Air Force Ballistic Missile Division)   Created in 1954 as the Western Development Division, the AFBMD received this designation in 1957 and was headquartered in Los Angeles and responsible for developing the Air Force's ballistic missile programs. Air Force reorganization in 1961 would result in another name change for this entity.

AFSATCOM (Air Force Satellite Communications System)   is the organizational structure responsible for developing and maintaining the U.S. Air Force's satellite communication system.

AFSPACOM (Air Force Space Command)   Located at Peterson AFB, Colorado, this Air Force component organization is responsible for defending North America through space and intercontinental ballistic missile operations. AFSPACOM has been carrying out these responsibilities since its September 1, 1982 creation.

AIT (Advanced Interceptor Technology)   Missile Defense Agency program permitting this agency to purchase increased numbers of other interceptors and ballistic missile defense system components within budgetary limits because of technological enhancements in this technology and savings in other missile defense acquisition programs.

Altitude   The height above sea level influences the performance of satellites. A minimum altitude of 60 miles is necessary for satellites to orbit without being pulled into automatic reentry by gravity. Satellites positioned between 60–100 miles altitude require repeated engine activation to avoid reentry within 24 hours. Satellites at 200 miles can orbit for nearly a year without using their engines. Satellites beyond 1,200 miles altitude can stay in orbit permanently, and satellites at 22,300 miles altitude can remain over the same point on the earth's surface.

Apogee   Maximum altitude obtained by a spacecraft orbiting the earth.

ARPA (Advanced Research Projects Agency)   This agency was created in 1958 to serve as the Defense Department's program for supporting cutting-edge scientific and technological research with military applications. It became the Defense Advanced Research Projects Agency (DARPA) in 1972.

ASAT (Antisatellite Weapon)   A system capable of disrupting, damaging, or destroying spacecraft in orbit from positions on land, sea, air, or space.

Atmosphere   Envelope of air surrounding the earth. Prompt effects on reentry vehicles begin about 60 miles above the surface. Prompt effects on ascending spacecraft and ballistic missiles end at the same altitude. Delayed effects extend much farther from Earth.

ATP (Advanced Technology Program)   A U.S. Department of Commerce program intended to help U.S. companies make optimal use of emerging technologies. ATP involves federal agencies such as the National Institute of Standards and Technology collaborating with private sector companies to develop and exploit these technologies.

Ballistic Missile   Pilotless projectile propelled into space from land, sea, or air. Velocity, gravity, and aerodynamic drag largely determine missile trajectory after powered flight ends.

Battle Management   Procedures and equipment, including computers and data displays, helping commanders make expeditious and sound decisions during combat.

Blackout   Disruption of radio and radar transmissions for varying lengths of time after one or more nuclear explosions in space ionize the earth's atmosphere. Short-wave, high-frequency propagations are most susceptible.

BMD (Ballistic Missile Defense)   Measures to intercept, destroy, or neutralize hostile ballistic missiles. This is done through weapons, target acquisition, tracking, and guidance sensors and related installations.

BMDO (Ballistic Missile Defense Organization)   Successor organization to the Strategic Defense Initiative Organization (SDIO). Defense Department organization serving as the U.S. Government's agency for engaging in ballistic missile defense research from May 1993–January 2002 when its functions were assumed by the Missile Defense Agency.

BMEWS (Ballistic Missile Early Warning System)   This became the United States' first operational missile detection radar in 1959. It was designed to provide warning about missile attacks against the United States and its allies, and the system included facilities in Greenland, Alaska, and England. BMEWS was replaced by the Solid State Phased Array Radar System (SSPARS) in 2001.

Boost Phase   Powered flight of a ballistic missile from launch until final rocket-stage burnout, taking three to five minutes.

Brilliant Pebbles   Proposed late-1980s and early-1990s ballistic missile defense interceptor system.

BSTS (Boost Surveillance and Tracking System)   A system intended to provide early, accurate, and reliable tactical warning and attack assessment of hostile ballistic missile launches while also monitoring peacetime launches.

Bureau of International Security and Arms Proliferation   U.S. State Department agency responsible for coordinating and directing U.S. arms control and weapons counterproliferation policies.

C4I (Command, Control, Communications, Computers, and Intelligence)   A military term commanders use to describe how headquarters commanders can control subordinate units.

CIA (Central Intelligence Agency)   The primary civilian U.S. intelligence agency responsible for conducting intelligence operations in foreign countries and assessing national security trends and developments in these countries and from transnational sources such as terrorist groups.

CINCAD (Commander in Chief, Aerospace Defense Command)   Military command leader of this U.S. military combatant command.

CINCSPACE (Commander in Chief, U.S. Space Command)   Military commander of the U.S. Space Command.

Circular Orbit   Orbit where the perigee and apogee are roughly equal.

Circumterrestrial Space   Region adjacent to the earth's atmosphere from an altitude of about 60 miles to 50,000 miles. Most military space activities occur here.

CMO (Central Measurement and Signals Intelligence (MASINT) Office) Defense Intelligence Agency   This office is responsible for directing MASINT activities within the Defense Intelligence Agency (DIA). Examples of MASINT include acoustic intelligence, infrared intelligence, laser intelligence, nuclear intelligence, optical intelligence, and unintentional radiation intelligence.

COMINT (Communications Intelligence)   Messages or voice information acquired from intercepting foreign communications.

Command Guidance   Precomputed and/or event driven instructions, transmitted in real time, steering and controlling spacecraft from remote locations. Reliable communication links required.

Concealment   Actions and conditions preventing enemy observation but providing no protection against weapon effects. Clouds, camouflage, and stealth technology are representative samples.

CONUS (Continental United States)   Military acronym referring to the 48 contiguous states of the United States and excluding Alaska, Hawaii, and U.S. territorial possessions such as Guam.

Coorbital ASAT   Antisatellite interceptor duplicating the flight path of its intended space target then attacking without delay.

COPUOS (Committee on the Peaceful Uses of Outer Space)   United Nations General Assembly committee established in 1959 whose responsibilities include reviewing the status of peaceful international cooperation in space, developing relevant programs for United Nations sponsorship, promoting and disseminating continuing space research, and studying legal problems developing from space exploration.

Cover   Physiographic conditions protecting targets against enemy weapons and adverse environments while also preventing observation. Representative samples include terrain masks and subterranean installations on the earth, the moon, or another planet.

CSTC (Consolidated Satellite Test Center)   This Sunnyvale, California facility serves as the center of an international network for tracking satellites, which includes additional facilities in the United States, United Kingdom, Greenland, and the Indian Ocean.

DARPA (Defense Advanced Research Projects Agency)   U.S. Department of Defense agency seeking to promote cutting edge technological research with highly relevant military applications. Previously ARPA.

Dazzle   Temporary blinding of astronauts or sensors by lasers or nuclear explosions.

Decoy   Object simulating a particular target type (spacecraft or missile warhead) to deceive enemy sensors and divert attacks.

Deep Space   Interplanetary space beyond the earth–moon system or circumterrestrial space.

Defensive Satellite Weapon   System capable of disrupting, damaging, or destroying enemy ASAT weapons from land, sea, air, or space.

DEW (Directed Energy Weapon)   An intense, tightly focused, precisely aimed beam of atomic/subatomic particles or electromagnetic energy designed to attack distant targets at the approximate speed of light.

DIA (Defense Intelligence Agency)   Established in 1961, DIA is responsible for collecting, producing, and analyzing military and military-related intelligence for the Secretary of Defense, Joint Chiefs of Staff, other military entities, and to nondefense sources when appropriate.

Dissimulation   Deceptive measures making targets seem like decoys.

DOD (Department of Defense)   The U.S. Government's principal agency for formulating and implementing national security policy. Includes numerous departmental components as well as departments representing individual armed services such as the Air Force, Army, and Navy.

DMSP (Defense Meteorological Satellite Program)   A cooperative program between the U.S. Defense and Commerce departments responsible for providing weather data for U.S. military operations.

DSB (Defense Science Board)   Organization created in 1956 to advise the Assistant Secretary of Defense for Research and Engineering (now Under Secretary of Defense for Acquisition, Technology, and Logistics) on how scientific knowledge can help in providing information and knowledge on emerging weapons systems. DSB consists of civilian and military members who are appointed based on their scientific and technological prominence.

DSP Satellites (Defense Support Program Satellites)   This satellite network helps protect the United States and its allies by detecting missile launches, space launches, and nuclear detonations from geosynchronous orbit 22,300 miles above the earth's surface.

Earth–Moon System   Space and its contents in a hypothetical sphere extending nearly 480,000 miles in all directions from the earth. Visible and invisible features in this system include the moon, earth-crossing asteroids, the atmosphere, gravity, and Van Allen radiation belts.

Electronic Countermeasures   Form of electronic warfare seeking to prevent or degrade enemy use of the electromagnetic spectrum. Jamming is a typical tactic.

Electro-Optical Imagery   Imagery created from electronic signals, which subsequently convey different light levels in the scene being observed.

ELINT (Electronic Intelligence)   Intelligence gathering by using electronic sensors. The type of electronic transmission and its source are of particular interest to ELINT analysts. This intelligence can be used to determine the locations of command and control centers and weapons systems so they can be attacked during wartime.

Elliptical Orbit   An ellipse-shaped orbit where the apogee and perigee are not equal.

EMP (Electromagnetic Pulse)   Extremely powerful current resulting from a nuclear explosion in space, peaks 100 times faster than lightning, then bolts toward the earth. Unshielded electronics within several hundred miles of the epicenter may be disabled.

Endoatmospheric Weapon   Device designed to intercept spacecraft or missile warheads within the earth's atmosphere.

Exoatmospheric Weapon   Device designed to intercept spacecraft or missile warheads in space.

Fast-Burn Booster   Ballistic missile engine functioning for 100 seconds or less after launch. Employment makes boost-phase defense very difficult.

FOBS (Fractional Orbital Bombardment System)   Weapons system developed by the Soviets during the early 1960s whose purpose was to launch a satellite in space, then have it leave orbit so it could attack U.S. and allied targets from regions such as the South Pole that were not covered by the NORAD warning system. FOBS was discontinued by the Soviets in 1983 according to terms of the never-ratified Strategic Arms Limitation Talks (SALT) II Treaty.

GBL (Ground-Based Laser)   Weapon system fired at aerial or orbiting targets from a ground station.

GCN (Ground Communications Network)   Terrestrial or land-based network for communicating with orbiting satellites.

Geostationary Earth Orbit   Circular orbit at an altitude of 22,300 miles with the orbital plane directly above the equator. A satellite in this orbit travels around the earth at the same speed the earth rotates.

Geosynchronous Earth Orbit   Any elliptical orbit centered over the equator averaging 22,300 miles in altitude and making a single figure eight rotation over the earth each day and flying over the same area of the earth with each rotation.

GPS (Global Positioning System)   Collection of orbiting satellites providing navigation data to military and civilian users internationally.

Ground Track   Territory on Earth that a satellite passes over.

Hardening   Methods used to increase a satellite's ability to endure attack or radiation bombardment.

Hard Kill   Weapon effects forcibly breaking the surface of animate or inanimate targets, damaging or destroying their contents. Violence is evident to distant observers.

HEL (High-Energy Laser)   Any laser weapons system using significant power amounts to destroy or disable hostile satellites or other military assets.

HEO (High-Earth Orbit)   Includes a few satellites operating beyond geosynchronous orbit (greater than 22,300 miles). Satellites in this orbit take 11 days to rotate around the earth.

Homing Device   Embedded and/or on-board instrument vectoring any type weapon toward a target and assist interception.

HRMSI (High-Resolution Multispectral Instrument)   Scientific instrument such as a satellite camera capable of providing high-resolution images of multiple spectrums of the electromagnetic spectrum. Used in remote sensing to acquire land cover data.

ICBM (Intercontinental Ballistic Missile)   Land-based nuclear missile with a range of over 3,500 miles or 5,600 kilometers.

Impulse Kill   Destruction caused by any directed energy weapon delivering a pulse intense enough to vaporize the target surface. Resulting shock wave attacks internal components and may cause structural collapse.

Inclination   Angle made by a satellite's path and the equator and determines which parts of the earth the satellite will pass over. A satellite with a 60° inclination will overfly territory between 60° N and 60° S. Inclinations under 90° correspond to eastward launches while those over 90° refer to westward launches.

Infrared Film   Film sensitive to near-infrared portion of the electromagnetic spectrum. Depends on objects' reflective properties and can be black and white or color.

Infrared Sensor   Devise designed to detect, locate, identify, and/or track targets by recording radiation that those targets emit or reflect on wavelengths longer than visible light (0.72–1,000 microns).

International Telecommunications Satellite Organization (INTELSAT)   International organization owning the communications satellites orbiting the earth. Originally an international government organization, it was privatized in 2001.

ISR (Intelligence, Surveillance, and Reconnaissance)   Intelligence is a military term referring to information and knowledge gained through observation, investigation, analysis, and understanding. Surveillance is systematic observation to collect available data, and reconnaissance is performing a specific mission to obtain specific data. The ultimate result is a system of collection assets and analysis bringing information about potential or real enemies to decision makers such as Washington, D.C. policymakers or local ground soldiers.

IUS (Inertial Upper Stage)   Rocket motor giving the United States the ability to place missile-warning and communications satellites weighing up to 5,300 pounds in geosynchronous orbit and satellites weighing up to 8,000 pounds out of the earth's gravitational field using the Air Force's Titan IVB rocket or NASA's space shuttle.

Jamming   Degrading or drowning out enemy electronic transmissions such as radio and radar signals by electronic warfare devices and tactics.

JCS (Joint Chiefs of Staff)   Military advisory body reporting to the president and secretary of Defense and serving as the principal advisor on national security issues to these officials and to the National Security Council.

JDSCS (Joint Defense Space Communications Station)   Series of satellite tracking and missile launch warning stations in Australia operated jointly by the United States and Australia.

JSTARS (Joint Surveillance Target Attack Radar System)   U.S. Air Force airborne battle management and control platform responsible for conducting ground surveillance to understand enemy activity, supporting attack operations, and targeting against hostile forces.

Keep Out Zone   Negotiated or unilaterally established security area declared off-limits to unauthorized spacecraft. Primarily intended to reduce danger of surprise attack, a restriction potentially useful for arms control purposes.

Keyhole Satellite (KH)   This National Reconnaissance Office (NRO) series of satellites are digital imaging satellites capable of delivering extremely high-resolution pictures in visible light and infrared. They can see at night and use thermal infrared to detect heat sources such as camouflaged and buried structures.

Kinetic Energy Weapon   Device launching, firing, or propelling nonexplosive projectiles to damage or destroy targets. The Brilliant Pebbles program is an example.

LADS (Low Altitude Demonstration Satellite)   Satellites placed in low-earth orbit that are expected to be capable of providing midcourse tracking and object discrimination missile-defense capabilities in theater military conflicts and attacks against North America.

Laser   Light amplification through stimulated emission of radiation.

Laser Weapon   Optical or x-ray device projecting a beam of coherent light intended to attack distant space targets almost instantaneously. Beam deposits energy on target surfaces then penetrates.

Layered Defenses   Protective measures in successive positions along the axis of enemy advance as opposed to a single defensive point. Such defenses are designed to absorb and progressively weaken enemy attacks.

LEO (Low-Earth Orbit)   Space flight between the atmosphere and the bottom of the Van Allen radiation belts ranging in altitude from 60–250 miles.

Liquid Propellant   Any combination of fluid fuel and oxidizer a rocket engine burns. Combustion can be started, stopped, and restarted by controlling propellant flow.

LPAR (Large Phased-Array Radar)   A physically extensive ballistic missile early-warning system.

MASINT (Measurement and Signals Intelligence)   Can include electro-optical, materials, nuclear, radar, radio, and seismic intelligence.

MDA (Missile Defense Agency)   U.S. Defense Department agency currently responsible for conducting U.S. ballistic missile defense research and implementing U.S. ballistic missile defense systems. Predecessor agencies include BMDO and SDIO.

MEL (Mobile Erector Launcher)   The ability to launch missiles from mobile transportation platforms such as railcars or trucks.

MEO (Medium-Earth Orbit)   Any flight path between low-earth orbit (about 250 miles in altitude) and geosynchronous orbits at an average altitude of 22,300 miles.

MGS (Mobile Ground System)   A satellite or missile detection system capable of positioning remotely operated ground sensors at locations of operational interest and sending information obtained from these sensors to the system operator.

MGSU (Mobile Ground Support Unit)   Capability of supporting the MGS at multiple locations.

Midcourse Phase   Ballistic missile trajectory of missile reentry vehicles from the time they separate from the postboost vehicle containing warhead(s) and penetration aids, until the warhead(s) hits the earth's atmosphere. Can occur 20 minutes or less after launch.

MILSTAR (Military Strategic and Tactical Relay)   Series of military communications satellites capable of providing secure and jam-resistant global communications to meet U.S. military users wartime demands.

MIRACL (Midinfrared Advanced Chemical Laser)   The first megawatt-class and continuous wave laser built outside the former Soviet bloc, it is believed to be capable of producing a megawatt output for up to 70 seconds. Originally built to track and destroy antiship cruise missiles, it has evolved to be used in ASAT and ballistic missile defense testing.

MOL (Manned Orbiting Laboratory)   A proposed 1960s era U.S. defense program to launch an orbital laboratory for science and surveillance purposes. Although experiencing some success, the MOL program was plagued by inconsistent funding and cost overruns and was cancelled in 1969.

Molniya Orbits   Very eccentric elliptical orbits with apogees high above the northern hemisphere. Used primarily by Soviet/Russian communications satellites to enhance communications within Russia.

MOS (Multi-Orbit Spacecraft)   Spacecraft capable of orbiting around the earth using divergent orbital paths.

NASA (National Aeronautics and Space Administration)   The U.S. Government's civilian space agency.

NAVSPAWAR (Naval Space and Warfare Systems Command)   Established in 1966, organization is responsible for supporting U.S. Navy and Marine Corps electronic systems; equipment; and command, control, and communications including space assets.

NCMC (NORAD Cheyenne Mountain Complex)   The North American Aerospace Defense Command's Cheyenne Mountain Complex is the joint U.S.–Canadian facility where this organization monitors and responds to real and potential space and airborne threats to continental security. The complex is built to withstand a nuclear explosion.

Neutral Particle Beam   A stream of hydrogen atoms accelerated to almost the speed of light and stripped of an artificially added charge. Such a device works well in space.

NGA (National Geospatial Intelligence Agency)   This agency, created in 2003, is responsible for providing timely, relevant, and accurate geospatial intelligence to support national security to the White House, Congress, military commanders, law enforcement officials, and civil leaders.

NORAD (North American Aerospace Defense Command)   Joint U.S.–Canadian organization responsible for monitoring and responding to air and space threats to continental security.

NPIC (National Photographic and Interpretation Center)   Formed in 1961, NPIC was a CIA organizational component responsible for interpreting aerial and satellite photographic data. Its functions would be taken over in the 1990s by the National Reconnaissance Office, whose existence was officially acknowledged in 1992 despite having existed for three decades.

NRO (National Reconnaissance Office)   Military intelligence agency responsible for ensuring the United States has the technology and space assets required for national security and military operational planning.

NSA (National Security Agency)   Created in 1952, the NSA is responsible for providing U.S. policymakers and war fighters with information obtained from code-breaking and intercept operations while also protecting U.S. signals and information systems from being exploited by national adversaries.

NSC (National Security Council)   Created in 1947, the NSC is the president's principal means for reviewing national security and foreign policy matters with senior national security advisors and cabinet officials. NSC serves as the president's principal arm for coordinating these policies among diverse government agencies.

NTM (National Technical Means)   Intelligence collection by reconnaissance satellites that may involve imagery intelligence, signals intelligence, electronic intelligence and space-based radar. Most commonly used for verifying arms control treaties and monitoring military activities of other nations.

Oblique   Imagery obtained from an angle instead of being directly overhead.

Orbital Period   Time it takes for a satellite to circumnavigate the body it is orbiting. The higher the altitude the longer the orbiting period.

Particle Beam Weapon   An intense, tightly focused, precisely aimed stream of atomic or subatomic particles designed to attack distant targets at nearly the speed of light. This stream deposits energy in depth instead of on target surfaces. Heat and current generation generally produce most damage.

Passive Defense   Measures, other than armed force, to deter, deflect, defeat, or deal with enemy attacks. Can include cover, concealment, hardening mobility, dispersion, and deception.

Passive Sensor   Device designed to detect, locate, identify, and/or track targets without revealing its own position. Target emissions, including infrared radiation and reflected sunlight, are their exclusive information sources.

PATRIOT (Phased Array Tracking to Intercept of Target)   The U.S. Army's most advanced air defense system that is capable of defeating high-performance aircraft and tactical ballistic missiles by shooting them down.

PAVE PAWS (Phased Array Warning System)   Missile warning and space surveillance system operated by Air Force Space Command. Representative facilities are located at Beale AFB, California and Cape Cod Air Force Station, Massachusetts.

Payload   Crew and cargo aboard a spacecraft or missile. Can also include weapons, munitions, guidance/control instruments, sensors, and communications.

Penetration Aid   Any nonlethal device misdirecting enemy defenses or making it easier for spacecraft or ballistic missiles to attack defended targets.

Perigee   Minimum altitude obtained by a spacecraft orbiting the earth.

Period   Time a satellite needs to make one complete revolution around the earth.

Pointing   Aiming with sufficient accuracy so sensors can detect, locate, identify, and/or track targets, and that weapons can engage these targets.

Polar Orbit   An orbit with an orbital plane of 90° inclination. Satellites in such orbits are perpendicular to the equator.

Post-Boost Phase   Ballistic missile's course from the time powered flight ceases until the post-boost vehicle dispenses all warheads and penetration aids.

Post-Boost Vehicle   Part of ballistic missile payload dispensing one or more warheads and penetration aids during post-boost phase.

Post-Strike Assessment   Acquiring and evaluating data indicate the success of an attack and assist subsequent decision-making.

Preferential Defense   Concentrating combat power against selected enemy forces in ways that safeguard critical targets in order of priority and sacrificing, if necessary, less critical assets.

Radar Imagery   Imagery produced bouncing radio waves off an object or area and creating an image using the returning pulse.

Railgun   Electromagnetic weapon designed to launch kinetic energy projectiles against enemy targets.

RAMOS (Russian-American Observation Satellite)   Cooperative U.S.–Russian program to create a satellite for joint global environmental and missile defense monitoring purposes. RAMOS was put on hold by the United States in 2004.

Real-Time Imagery   Imagery transmitted as an event occurs.

Reconnaissance   Intelligence operations collecting information about opponents or territory through visual, aural, or technological observation while patrolling a specified area.

Redout   Blinding or dazzling of infrared sensors by intense infrared radiation in the earth's upper atmosphere following a nuclear explosion.

Reentry Vehicle   Spacecraft, missile warhead, or kinetic energy projectile designed to survive intense and rapid heating when it encounters the earth's atmosphere when returning from space.

Resolution   Minimum size required for at least one dimension of an object to be identifiable by photo analysts.

RLV (Reusable Launch Vehicle)   A space launch vehicle capable of being used for multiple launches into orbit such as the space shuttle.

Rocket Weapon   Any rocket designed to attack enemy targets after launch from the earth, moon, another planet, or an orbiting spacecraft.

SABRS (Space and Atmospheric Burst Reporting System)   Program for detecting real time nuclear events in space by detecting gamma rays, neutrons, protons, and electrons.

SAC (Strategic Air Command)   Located at Offut AFB near Omaha, Nebraska, SAC serves as the command and control center for U.S. strategic forces and oversees military space operations, computer networks, information operations, strategic warning and intelligence assessments, and global strategic planning.

SAINT (Satellite Interceptor)   This 1960s era Air Force program sought to develop a manned spacecraft capable of intercepting, inspecting, and, if necessary destroying hostile satellites.

SALT (Strategic Arms Limitation Treaty)   Series of nuclear arms reduction talks held between the United States and the former Soviet Union during the 1970s.

SAMSO (Space and Missile Systems Organization)   This organization, located at Los Angeles AFB, became responsible for managing Air Force ballistic missile and space systems programs in 1967. Ballistic missile and space system activities were split into separate organizational components in October 1979 and the present Space and Missile Systems Command was activated July 1, 1992.

SATRAN (Satellite Reconnaissance Advance Notice)   A government or military agency giving advance public notice of a satellite launch.

SBEWS (Space-Based Early Warning System)   Ballistic missile attack early warning systems that are based in space.

SBIRS (Space-Based Infrared System)   Program of high-orbiting infrared satellites designed to track and detect ballistic missiles of all sizes. Expected to enter service in 2007.

SBL (Space-Based Laser)   System capable of supporting missile defense efforts. Would consist of satellites containing multimegawatt lasers capable of sending a beam through a large telescope to a target for boost phase intercept and other missions.

SB-LTD (Space-Based Laser Target Designator)   An SBL deciding which section of a missile to target.

SCF (Satellite Control Facility)   A facility, usually ground-based, controlling satellite operations.

SCS (Space Communications Squadron)   Located at Vandenberg AFB's 30th Space Wing, SCS is responsible for delivering voice, visual, and data information services to facilitate Air Force space operations.

SDI (Strategic Defense Initiative)   Ballistic missile defense program developed during the Reagan administration. Referred to as "Star Wars" by program critics.

SDIO (Strategic Defense Initiative Organization)   Defense Department office responsible for implementing the strategic defense initiative during the Reagan and George H.W. Bush administrations. Replaced by the Ballistic Missile Defense Organization in 1993.

SDS (Satellite Data System)   U.S. military communications satellites used from 1976–present. Their purpose is relaying imagery from Keyhole reconnaissance satellites to U.S. ground stations.

Semisynchronous Orbit   Orbit where a satellite makes two daily revolutions around the earth.

Sensor   Instrument designed to measure some physical phenomenon such as electromagnetic radiation. Military space forces use these instruments to detect, locate, identify, and/or track targets; home in on targets; and assist poststrike assessments.

SIGINT (Signals intelligence)   Intelligence information acquired from communications intelligence, electronic intelligence, or telemetry intelligence.

Signature   Distinctive signals, such as electromagnetic radiation, that any object emits or reflects, which sensors use to detect, locate, identify, and/or track targets.

SIR (Shuttle Imaging Radar)   Radar capability sending bursts of energy from an antenna in the NASA space shuttle to the ground and measuring the reflected energy with the same antenna. This capability began in 1981 and continues to the present.

SMTS (Space and Missile Tracking System) Constellation of low altitude satellites supporting theater missile defense by providing global ballistic missile flight tracking capability from launch to reentry.

SMV (Space Maneuver Vehicle) Proposed military space vehicle that is operated on the upper stage of reusable spacecraft and capable of delivering a variety of low-cost payloads to orbiting satellites or spacecraft.

Soft Kill Weapon effects penetrating targets without breaking the surface, which are able to damage or destroy internal components. Violence is not evident to untrained observers.

Solid Propellant Any combination of fuel and oxidizer, besides gases or liquids, energizing a rocket engine.

SOV (Space Operations Vehicle) A projected Air Force military space plane capable of being flexible and reusable and performing a variety of military operations in space such as intelligence, surveillance, and reconnaissance.

Space Command Any headquarters and subordinate elements designed to plan, program, budget for, and operate armed forces that pursue their primary missions away from the earth and its atmosphere.

Space Interceptor Any offensive or defensive spacecraft launched from the earth, the moon, or other planet to rendezvous with an enemy spacecraft to identify, deter, deflect, or destroy.

Space Mine Any offensive space weapon co-orbiting near its intended target, which then attacks that target on command or in accordance with preprogrammed instructions. One of several or many orbital weapons placed to form a protective field in space.

Space Satellite Any unmanned spacecraft with one or more missions including supporting activities on the earth, the moon, or other planets. Representative examples include reconnaissance, surveillance, navigation, and communications.

Spacecraft Propulsion Engines and propellants boosting space vehicles into orbit from the earth, the moon, or another planet.

Spoofing A form of electronic measures or electronic countermeasures deception, which seeks to fool enemy command and control systems by sending false electronic signals.

SPS (Solar Power Satellite) A satellite designed to gather solar energy in space using solar panels.

SSN (Space Surveillance Network) Network of U.S. military space surveillance facilities such as NORAD.

SSPARS (Solid State Phased Array Radar System) Ballistic missile early-warning radar facilities at various facilities in the United States and worldwide.

START (Strategic Arms Reduction Treaty)   Nuclear arms control treaties and proposed treaties between the United States and the Soviet Union/Russian Federation from 1991–present.

Stealth   Technologies and techniques making it difficult for sensors to detect spacecraft in flight. Contributing stealth technologies include structural designs, nonmetallic materials, absorptive coatings, heat shields, emission controls, passive guidance, and electronic countermeasures.

Strategic Warning   Notification that enemy offensive operations may be impending. Such notification may be received minutes, hours, days, or longer before hostilities begin.

Sun-Synchronous Orbit   A near-polar orbit of nearly 82° inclination from the equator. Facilitates satellites orbiting over sunlit areas of the earth allowing reconnaissance satellites to photograph the same portions of the earth at the same time each day. This results in improved imagery analysis since light and shadow will not vary without human activity.

Surveillance   Intelligence operations to collect information through visual, aural, or technological observation (usually clandestine) while following the subject or maintaining close watch.

SWS (Space Warning Squadron)   Air Force Space Command units responsible for monitoring sea-launched or land-based ICBMs launched toward North America. The 10th SWS at Cavalier Air Force Station, North Dakota and the 12th SWS at Thule Air Base, Greenland are representative examples.

Tactical Warning   Notice that enemy offensive operations are in progress. Alerting may occur any time from the attack's initiation until its effect occurs.

Target   Property that a belligerent plans to capture or destroy; area a belligerent plans to control or deny to its opponents; a country, area, agency, installation, person, or group against which intelligence/counterintelligence activities are directed.

Target Acquisition   Detecting, locating, identifying, and tracking any object with sufficient accuracy for military forces to strike it.

TBMDS (Theater Ballistic Missile Defense System)   A ballistic missile defense system designed to identify, track, and defend against ballistic missiles launched at targets within a particular geographic region. A Japanese missile defense system designed to protect against North Korean or Chinese ballistic missile attacks would be an example of a TBMDS.

TDRS (Tracking and Data Relay Satellite)   Satellite capable of linking low-orbiting spacecraft with Earth and transmitting the contents of a 20-volume encyclopedia in one second. TDRS data can be sent to spacecraft such as the space shuttle or to the ground terminal at White Sands, New Mexico.

Terminal Phase   Final trajectory of ballistic missile reentry vehicles from the time they reach the earth's atmosphere until impact, which normally is about a minute.

THAAD (Theater High-Altitude Area Defense)   A U.S. Army program to develop an ABM system against theater or regional threats. THAAD seeks to destroy incoming missiles by firing its own interceptors at the threat, and these interceptors seek to collide with these incoming missiles and carry no explosives.

Thermal Infrared Imagery   Imagery produced by sensing heat emitted by a target that can also be produced under darkness.

Thermal Kill   Destruction of a target by a directed energy weapon that heats structures and internal components until they vaporize, melt, or are deformed.

Tracking   Using sensors to plot the course of targets. Defenders can predict ballistic trajectories if the vehicles being observed cannot maneuver.

TVM (Target Via Missile)   Tracking the path of a missile using another missile and the technology contained within that missile.

Unified Command   A high-level U.S. combatant organization with regional or functional responsibilities including forces from two or more military services. This organization has a broad continuing mission and is established by the president through the secretary of Defense with the Joint Chiefs of Staff's advice and assistance.

USCINCSPACE (U.S. Commander in Chief, Space Command)   The military commander of U.S. Space Command.

USSPACECOM (U.S. Space Command)   Air Force organization responsible for protecting the United States against military attacks in areas ranging from the earth's surface to geosynchronous orbit 22,300 miles above the earth. Headquartered at Peterson AFB, Colorado.

Visible Light Imagery   Imagery produced by sensing light reflecting off a target (i.e., standard photography).

VSS (Visible Light Surveillance System)   A surveillance system capable of viewing and tracking light emitted by a weapons system such as a ballistic missile.

Warhead   An explosive weapon delivered by any ballistic missile or rocket.

X-Ray Laser   A single-shot, self-destructing beam weapon that can engage many distant targets simultaneously at the speed of light. The nuclear explosion furnishing the laser's power also demolishes the target(s).

INDEX

Note: italic page numbers indicate pictures.

ABOUT THE AUTHOR

Bert Chapman is Government Information and Political Science Librarian/Associate Professor of Library Science at Purdue University in West Lafayette, Indiana. He received a B.A. in history and political science at Taylor University-Upland, an M.A. in history at the University of Toledo, an M.S.L.S. at the University of Kentucky, and is the author of *Researching National Security and Intelligence Policy* (2004).